Basic Accounting Practice

M W E Glautier, B Underdown and A C Clark

Third edition

Pitman

PITMAN PUBLISHING
128 Long Acre, London WC2E 9AN

© Guardjust Ltd, B. Underdown, A. C. Clark 1978, 1980, 1985

First published in Great Britain 1978
Second edition 1980
Reprinted 1981, 1982, 1983 (twice)
Third edition 1985
Reprinted 1987, 1988

ISBN 0 273 02426 4

Printed in Great Britain at The Bath Press, Avon

Basic Accounting Practice

Contents

Part 3 Case Problems and Analysis

Foreword

On Financial Control

'Coming home tonight I did go to examine my wife's accounts, and finding things that seemed somewhat doubtful I was angry, though she did make it pretty plain, but confessed that when she do miss a sum she do add something to other things to make it, and upon my being very angry she do protest she will here lay up something for herself to buy a necklace with, which madded me and do still trouble me, for I fear she will forget by degrees the way of living cheap and under sense of want.'

Samuel Pepys (1633–1703) *Diaries*

Titles in the Accounting Theory and Practice Series

Introduction

Basic Accounting Practice focuses attention on the practical aspects of accounting practice with respect to both financial and management accounting. In particular, it is concerned with explaining the basic procedures of financial and management accounting, and in providing a sound understanding at an introductory level of the role of accounting in business.

Understanding accounting requires not only reading the explanation of its procedures, but ensuring that one is able to apply those procedures to an accounting problem. With this in mind, a careful selection of questions and problems has been made to permit the student to reinforce his understanding of the text. Each question is preceded by an explanation of the particular accounting objective to which a procedure is addressed and an illustration is given, where necessary, by way of a more complete exposition of the accounting problem. Care has been taken to ensure a gradual introduction to the complexities involved, and in this sense, *Basic Accounting Practice* has been programmed to begin with the most simple questions and to proceed gradually to more advanced problems.

Moreover, *Basic Accounting Practice* reflects the experience of teaching accounting in the different settings and institutions with which the authors have been associated. A conscious effort has been made to clear away the initial difficulties which students find at the early stages of study by a variety of alternative teaching techniques. Thus, flow-charts, diagrams and illustrations are widely used *in addition to* the conventional accounting format which relies on the manner in which entries are made in the financial records. In some instances, the questions are themselves programmed to contain explanations which may be needed by the student, and which are uncovered by him as he proceeds through these questions. Finally, case problems and a case study are employed with a view to developing further insights into the nature of the accounting problem. Thus, *Basic Accounting Practice* will be found useful in those teaching situations where variety in teaching methods is appreciated by both the teacher and the student.

Basic Accounting Practice is presented in three parts. Part 1 considers financial accounting, which traditionally has been concerned with the control of assets and liabilities by the provision of a system of record keeping. This function is also addressed to the provision of information to investors in the form of profit and loss accounts and balance sheets. Recently, this has been extended to the disclosure of funds flow statements. In effect, financial accounting may be said to be concerned with the process of exchange between the organization and its environment by recording the financial implications of the acquisition of resources and the financial claims which are involved, as well as the disposal of the organization's output in the form of goods and services and the financial rights which are thereby created. Part 2 deals with management accounting, which is concerned with the provision of information for planning and controlling the internal operations of the firm. In effect, management accounting may be said to be concerned with the process of exchange or conversion of resources which have been acquired by the firm into the goods and services which will be dispensed in the course of trade. This exchange may be described as being internal rather than external. Finally, Part 3 provides some exposure to problem situations where accounting plays an influential role in decision making. This is achieved by means of case problems and a case study in which 'accounting numbers' are pitched into the 'business game' where logic and human behaviour interact.

Basic Accounting Practice is directed to the needs of first-year students reading accounting at universities and polytechnics, as well as students taking courses in business and management studies, both at undergraduate and postgraduate level, who require some knowledge of accounting methods. *Basic Accounting Practice* will be found to be particularly relevant for students preparing for the first examinations of the professional institutions and courses which have a practical orientation, such as the Higher National Diploma in Business Studies.

Acknowledgements

We would like to express our gratitude to the Institute of Chartered Accountants in England and Wales for permission to reproduce in full the SSAP 2 (*Disclosure of Accounting Policies*), and the Institute of Cost and Management Accountants for sample questions throughout the book. We would also like to thank Jack Burton of Manchester Polytechnic for supplying some of the drawings.

Except where acknowledged, the names and cases used in this book are totally fictitious and resemblances to any person or factual cases are purely coincidental.

PART 1
Financial Accounting

1 The Financial Accounting Framework

The purpose of this chapter is to outline the financial accounting framework and to analyse its major constituent elements. These are identified as comprising the following:

(1) A conceptual framework which relates the accounting process to an entity defined as the *accounting entity*.
(2) A method for handling financial data which is known as *double entry bookkeeping*
(3) A data classification, processing, storage and retrieval system which is associated with the *ledger*.
(4) A set of procedures for classifying, processing, storing and retrieving data which is known as the *bookkeeping system*.

Accordingly, this chapter is divided into four sections dealing with these respective aspects of the financial accounting framework.

The accounting entity

The accounting entity is a concept which defines the boundaries of data collection, and determines what records are relevant to informed decision making in respect of business activity. The accounting entity may be defined as an individual activity or group of activities which can be recognized clearly as having a separate identity and using economic resources in pursuit of its aims. The recognition of the separation of the economic activity of the accounting entity from the private affairs of its owner or owners is an essential feature of what is known as the *entity concept* irrespective of the legal form which ownership may assume. Thus, the entity concept establishes a distinction between the owner of the business and the business itself, even though it is a one-man business having no separate legal identity. In this respect, L. Jones trading as L. Jones, Greengrocer is seen in accounting as being two separate entities—the former being essentially of a personal and private nature, the latter being the business activity which the entity concept treats as distinct and separate from the former.

Once the accounting entity has been identified, it is possible to view it in two different ways. The proprietary theory or concept views the entity as being merely a vehicle by means of which the owner or proprietor derives income. By contrast, the entity theory or concept views the entity as having its own objectives and interprets the status of the legal owners as similar to that of other external claimants. Owing to its distinct legal status, the joint stock company appears to afford the most realistic example of a form of enterprise which reflects the entity theory. This chapter begins with an examination of the business activities of a sole trader, that is, the typical small business which is usually both owned and managed by a single proprietor. Consequently, the approach adopted initially in this chapter will reflect the proprietary theory of the accounting entity.

Bookkeeping and the dual aspect

The double-entry bookkeeping system has been in existence for some 700 years and its survival has been due to its ability to fulfil certain functions. These functions include keeping an accurate record of indebtedness between the entity and other parties, providing an analysis of expenditure and measuring profit. The first two of these functions are examined in this chapter. In this regard, the purpose of this analysis is to explain the manner in which accounting numbers are derived and aggregated as well as the bookkeeping techniques involved in the manipulation of these numbers.

Double-entry bookkeeping is associated with a standardized set of procedures for recording and explaining basic accounting data. The procedures make use of a specially designed form of stationery. Exhibit 1 below represents an 'account', which is a typical format used to record transactions and to provide at the same time the essential data which explain the circumstances surrounding such transactions.

Exhibit 1 Traditional form of accounting stationery

Dr. (1)   NAME OF ACCOUNT   (2) *Cr.*

Date	Details	Folio	£ p	Date	Details	Folio	£ p
	(3)	(4)					

Notes
(1) *Dr* is notation for *debit*. By convention this indicates the left-hand side of an account.
(2) *Cr* is notation for *credit*. By convention this indicates the right-hand side of an account.

Both these terms are Latin in origin but the abbreviated forms of *Dr* and *Cr* are now merely notation. These terms are used as verbs, nouns and adjectives. Essentially, the term 'debit' indicates an inflow of money value *to* an account and the term 'credit' indicates an outflow of money value *from* an account. The meanings of these terms are different, therefore, from those associated with their use in everyday language.

(3) Each side of an account has space to provide details of the origin and destination of the flow of money value recorded. In the case of a debit entry, the details given would be the name of the account *from which* the flow of money value originated. In the case of a credit entry, the details given would be by the name of the account *to which* the flow of money value has gone. The practice has now been abandoned of prefacing a debit entry by the word *To* and a credit entry by the word *By*.

(4) The reference or 'folio' column is used to indicate the corresponding accounting entry in the ledger.

The double-entry technique of recording financial transactions reflects a fundamental accounting principle which equates the resources held by an enterprise with the claims against an enterprise in respect of these resources. The nature of this basic accounting equation is explained in the following example.

Example 1

Varlberg commits his personal savings of £10,000 to starting his own business as a painter and decorator. He transfers this sum to the business's bank account. In accordance with the accounting entity convention, the financial position of the business may be expressed as follows:

Exhibit 2

Assets	=	Claims against the business
(Bank £10,000)		(Owner's claim £10,000)

The owner's claim against the business is more usually referred to as his *capital* whilst other external claims are referred to as *liabilities*. Exhibit 2 is really a balance sheet or position statement.

Suppose now that Varlberg purchases a van for £4,500 and equipment such as ladders, trestles, brushes, etc., for £750. The basic accounting equation would be redrafted to read:

Exhibit 3

Assets	=	Claims against the business
(Van £4,500 + Equipment £750 + Bank £4,750)		(Capital £10,000)

It may be noted that the distribution of the assets has changed without disturbing the basic equation. The changes which have occurred are as follows:

Van	Equipment	Bank
+ £4,500	+ £750	− £5,250

If Varlberg now purchases from suppliers a quantity of paints and paper costing £500 which he intends to use as his stock-in-trade (inventory) on terms which allow him to make payment for them at the end of the month following that of purchase, the basic equation before payment becomes:

Exhibit 4

Van	+	Equipment	+	Stock	+	Bank	=	Capital	+	Liabilities
£4,500	+	£750	+	£500	+	£4,750	=	£10,000	+	£500

It can be seen that the accounting equation is maintained by an addition to assets (+ stock) and an addition to liabilities (+ creditor) and that the subsequent payment will maintain the equation by a deduction from assets (minus bank) and a deduction from liabilities (minus creditor). The ultimate effects of transactions are summarized below:

Exhibit 5

Summary of changes that maintain the accounting equation

1. Additions and deductions of equal amounts to assets
2. Additions and deductions of equal amounts to capital or liabilities
3. Additions to assets and additions of equal amounts to capital or liabilities
4. Deductions from assets and deductions of equal amounts from capital or liabilities

Question 1
Fill in the missing figures for (a), (b) and (c) below.

Assets £	=	Capital £	+	Liabilities £
4,500	=	(a) ...	+	2,300
(b) ...	=	6,514	+	8,342
24,375	=	16,397	+	(c) ...

Question 2
A series of transactions are listed below from (a) to (l). Place a tick in *one* of the columns 1, 2, 3 or 4 which are based on Exhibit 5 above. Thus, transaction (a) results in an addition of £5,000 to assets (+ bank £5,000) and an addition of £5,000 to capital (+ capital £5,000). A tick should be placed in column 3, and the net increase in the totals of the accounting equation is £5,000.

Note

The transactions are not necessarily connected in any way.

(a) Capital introduced in the form of cash £5,000.

(b) Purchase of vehicle for £2,600 on credit to be paid in full in two months' time.

(c) Paid £2,400 for a lathe for use in the business.

(d) Business obtains a bank loan of £12,000.

(e) Withdrawal of cash £1,000 by the owner for private use.

(f) Payment of bill from creditor for goods £175.

(g) Owner repays business loan out of his private bank account £3,000.

(h) Owner takes trading goods out of business for his own use £120.

(i) Business receives £1,000 from debtor who previously bought some goods on credit.

(j) Business receives £10,000 from insurance company in respect of warehouse burnt down.

(k) Business buys £392 worth of goods intended for resale on credit.

(l) Owner brings his own car valued at £2,300 into business for business use.

Transaction	1	2	3	4	Change in totals of accounting equation
a			✓		Net increase £5,000
b		✓			
c	✓				
d			✓		
e				✓	
f				✓	
g		✓		✓	
h	✓				
i	✓				
j	✓				
k		✓			
l				✓	

The double-entry system of bookkeeping reflects changes in the accounting equation automatically through the procedures on which entries are made in accounts. For example, the data given in Exhibit 4 would be entered as follows

Example 2

Bank account				Capital account		
	£		£			£
(3) Capital	10,000	(1) Van	4,500		(3) Bank	10,000
		(1) Equipment	750			

Van account		
	£	
(1) Bank	4,500	

Equipment account		
	£	
(1) Bank	750	

Purchases account		
	£	
(3) Supplier	500	

Supplier account		
		£
	(3) Goods	500

Notes

(1) The number prefacing each entry categorizes the nature of the changes to the accounting equation associated with each transaction. Thus, the purchase of the van for £4,500 is a class 1 transaction, for this transaction results in an addition of £4,500 to assets (+ Van account) and a deduction of £4,500 from assets (− Bank account).

(2) By convention, the term 'purchases' in bookkeeping is restricted to the purchase of stock. It is not used to describe the acquisition of assets such as plant, equipment, motor vehicles, etc.

(3) The effect of analysing each transaction as consisting of a *debit* entry reflecting a flow of money value *to* an account as well as a *credit* entry reflecting a flow a money value *from* an account is to maintain the accounting equation. Example 2 shows the dual aspect of each transaction which consists of a flow of money value from one account to another account. It will be seen later that the double-entry bookkeeping system can handle more complex entries involving more than two accounts.

The foregoing examples illustrate the application of the accounting equation to such transactions as the introduction of capital and the acquisition of assets. These transactions create claims against the business in respect of the assets acquired. The accounting equation applies equally to the treatment of revenue and expenses.

Example 3

Consider the transactions set out below for S. A. Nary who is just starting business as a fishmonger. All transactions relate to July.

July 1 Opened a business bank account and paid in £6,000.
  1 Paid rent for month of £100 by cheque.
  1 Purchased fittings for £1,200 by cheque.
  1 Paid for refrigerators £700 by cheque.
  2 Purchased motor van £2,000 paid by cheque.
  2 Paid for motor insurance £55 by cheque.

2 Paid for licence for van £40 by cheque.
3 Obtained £800 of fish and canned goods from J. Eulie on credit of seven days.
4 Cash Sales £643.
5 Paid for cleaning—cash £3.
6 Banked £600.

These transactions would be recorded as follows:

Bank account			
	£		£
Capital	6,000	Rent	100
Cash	600	Fittings	1,200
		Refrigerator	700
		Motor	55
		Expenses	40
		Van	2,000
		Bal. c/d	2,505
	6,600		6,600
Bal. b/d	2,505		

Capital account	
	£
Bank	6,000

Fittings account	
	£
Bank	1,200

Refrigerator account	
	£
Bank	700

Rent account	
	£
Bank	100

Motor Van account	
	£
Bank	2,000

Motor Expenses account	
	£
Bank	55
Bank	40

Sales account		
		£
	Cash	643

Purchases account		
		£
	J. Eulie	800

J. Eulie account		
		£
	Purchases	800

Cash account			
	£		£
Sales	643	Cleaning	3
		Bank	600
		Bal. c/d	40
	643		643
Bal. b/d	40		

Cleaning account	
	£
Cash	3

Note

Individual transaction dates have been ignored but in practice these would be recorded as would the references for the opposite account of the double entry.

An important stage in the process of aggregating accounting numbers is to prepare a *trial balance*. This is merely a listing of the balances on *all* the accounts. Nothing is written in the various accounts during the process of extracting a trial balance.

The trial balance is a test of the accuracy of the bookkeeping process. It reflects the accounting equation and the principle that the sum of the debit entries should equal the sum of the credit entries. Accordingly, if the trial balance does not balance, this will be conclusive evidence of error in the bookkeeping process or in the associated arithmetic.

The following trial balance is dated 5 July and summarizes the entries on the accounts of S. A. Nary up to that date.

	Trial balance as at 5 July	
	Debit £	Credit £
Bank account	2,505	
Capital S. A. Nary		6,000
Fittings	1,200	
Refrigerator	700	
Rent	100	
Motor van	2,000	
Motor expenses	95	
Sales		643
Purchases	800	
J. Eulie		800
Cash	40	
Cleaning	3	
	7,443	7,443

Question 3

(a) The transactions for the second week of trading by S. A. Nary are given below. Using the balances on the various accounts shown in Example 3 above, complete these accounts for the second week of trading.

Transaction number			
1	July	7	Purchased fish from market by cheque £185
2		7	Cash sales £210
3		8	Paid cash for petrol, etc., £8
4		8	Purchased fish from market; paid cash £150
5		8	Cash sales £192
6		9	Purchases made from market; paid cash £195
7		9	Paid J. Eulie by cheque £800

8	9	Cash sales £172
9	10	Paid cleaning £3 cash
10	10	Purchased fish from market; paid cash £200
11	10	Cash sales £274
12	10	Purchased selection of frozen foods from Hermos Ltd on credit—payable end of August £640
13	10	Paid for electricity by cheque £14
14	10	Paid salary for week £25
15	10	Banked £150 cash

(b) Prepare a trial balance after all the entries have been made. (The transactions have been numbered to aid identification in the book-keeping process.)

The ledger

All these transactions can be recorded in one book, the ledger, but owing to the large volume of transactions, certain accounts are kept in separate books of their own although remaining part of one notional ledger. An illustration of such a separation is set out in Fig. 1.1.

Fig. 1.1 Separation of types of accounts from general ledger into functional ledgers

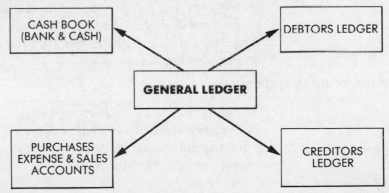

Question 4

(a) Write up the appropriate ledger accounts for the following entries which relate to the business of Sam Barker who owns a do-it-yourself store.

   (1) Opening balance at bank £5,321
   (2) Sold goods to J. Green for £65, allowed one month to pay
   (3) Purchased goods from the Timber Supply Co. Ltd for £974 on usual trade terms (net monthly)
   (4) Drew cash from bank £142 for wages
   (5) Sold goods for cash £74

(6) Returned some goods to Timber Supply Co. Ltd as poor quality valued at £38

(7) Sold goods on credit to Ace Hotel Co. Ltd £350

(8) J. Green paid £25 on account—cash

(9) Sold goods for cash £214

(10) Paid cheque for repairs to shop £27

(11) Sold goods for cash £118

(12) Banked £250 cash

(13) Paid cheque £2,000 for sawing equipment

(14) Sold goods to SBS (Decorators) Ltd £110 on credit terms

(15) Paid delivery expenses on goods to SBS (Decorators) Ltd cash £14

(16) Drew cash from bank £158 for wages

(b) After completing the entries, bring down the balances on all the accounts and draw up a trial balance. For this purpose, you are informed that the opening balance of assets amounted to £4,792. There were no outstanding liabilities at the beginning of the period.

(c) How much capital did Sam Barker have at the commencement of this period?

(d) How much does the business owe at the end of this period?

(e) How much is owed to the business at the end of the period?

(f) Indicate alongside the figure for each of the accounts in the trial balance which of the books would contain the account as suggested in Fig. 1.1.

The bookkeeping system

The outlines of the bookkeeping system and the relationship of the trial balance with this system is depicted in Figs 1.2 to 1.6 below. In practice, most accounting systems of varying degrees of complexity operate on the same principles.

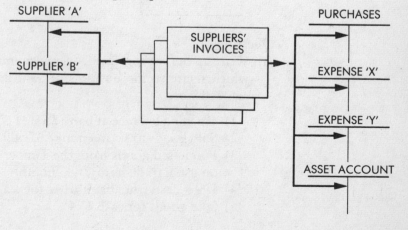

Fig. 1.2 Outline of double entry based on original source documents for goods and services purchased on credit

Fig. 1.3 Outline of double entry based on original documents for (a) sales made on credit and (b) cash sales

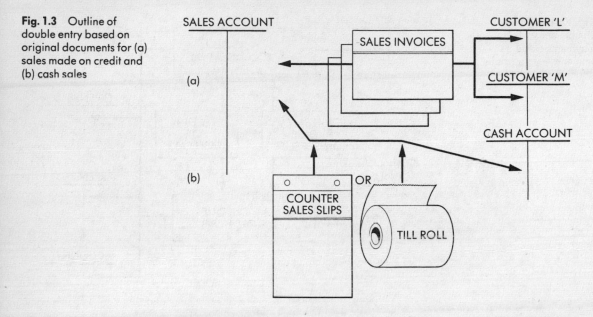

Fig. 1.4 Outline of double entry when payments made to creditors

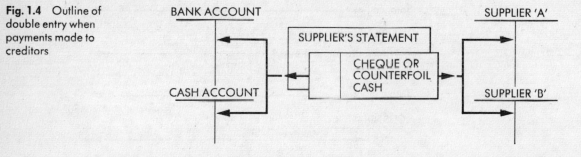

Fig. 1.5 Outline of double entry when debtors make payments to business

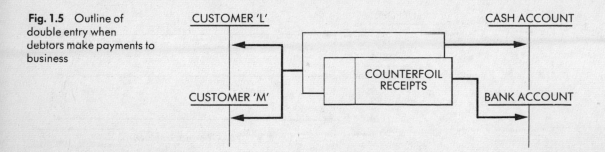

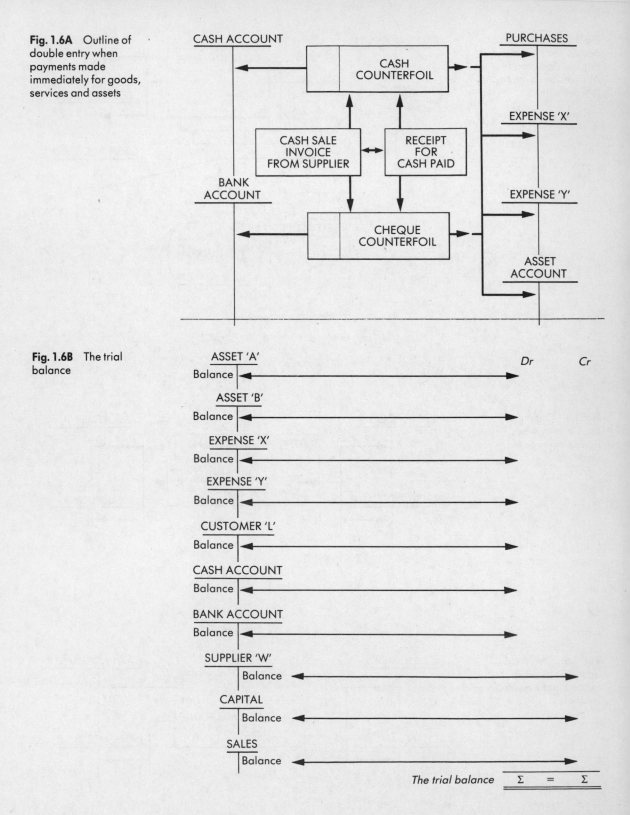

Fig. 1.6A Outline of double entry when payments made immediately for goods, services and assets

Fig. 1.6B The trial balance

Question 5
Prepare a trial balance from the list of balances shown below.

	Balance £	Dr £	Cr £
Trade creditors—Accounts payable	13,642		✓
Trade debtors—Accounts receivable	23,724	✓	
Wages paid	14,625	✓	
Rent and rates	6,520	✓	
Bank balance	1,590	✓	
Cash in hand	78	✓	
Sales	87,428		✓
Purchases—Goods for resale	34,697	✓	
Motor vehicles	18,620	✓	
Plant and machinery	15,000	✓	
Postage and printing	1,720	✓	
Advertising	3,450	✓	
Insurances	210	✓	
Motor expenses	1,836	✓	
Loan from bank	5,000		✓
Capital	16,000		✓

122070   122070

2 Profit Measurement and the Final Accounts

Chapter 1 dealt with the routine procedures for recording financial data, and with establishing the conceptual basis of the financial accounting process. It is evident, however, that the purpose of financial accounting information is not simply to record data, but, of much more importance, to provide information which will be useful in making business decisions. Accordingly, the usefulness of the financial data stored in the bookkeeping system may be established by considering the objectives of business activities. At the outset, it should be stated that the nature of business objectives is the subject of some considerable debate. For the purpose of this chapter, the issues involved in this debate are simplified to the extent that business is assumed to be conducted solely with a view to profit-making. This assumption conforms with a traditionalist view of the nature of business organization, and provides the rationale for conventional accounting practice.

This chapter is concerned, therefore, with the nature of profit. It is divided into the following sections:

The meaning of profit
Profit as a change in net worth
Profit measurement and the maintenance of capital
The profit and loss account
Preparing the profit and loss account
The trial balance and the preparation fo the profit and loss account and the balance sheet.

These sections investigate progressively the various concepts and problems involved in the process of profit measurement.

The meaning of profit

The salary or wage which an employee obtains from his employer is usually called his 'income' and it is easily measured by reference to the payment which is made to him at periodic intervals. The income which a businessman derives from his business is usually referred to as his 'profit'. The measurement of business profit raises complex issues, some of which relate directly to the meaning of profit itself.

If a person had, say, £5,000 which was to be utilized in a venture which involved committing the whole sum to the purchase of certain goods and, after reselling them, the total cash recovered from customers amounted to £6,500, then the profit would be £6,500 − £5,000 = £1,500. In such a simple situation, profit measurement, as the process is called, does not present any real difficulties. The conditions given in this example are, however, hardly likely to be found in the real business world. Nevertheless, it is important to note that profit is regarded as the excess recovered over and above the original amount invested.

Had the above example been posed in terms of the previous chapter, the amount available for purchasing goods for resale would have been termed 'capital'. Accordingly, profit could have been calculated by deducting the capital at the start of the venture from the capital at the end of the venture. This would accord with Hicks' definition of a man's income as the maximum value which he can consume during a period and still be as well off at the end of the period as he was at the beginning. The example given would state the situation in this way—£1,500 can be spent on personal satisfaction (i.e., non-business expenditure by the owner), leaving the business still worth £5,000.

Profit as a change in net worth

The use of the term 'well-off' creates difficulties for the accountant when determining business profit, for it immediately implies that valuation must take place when measuring profit. In effect, measuring profit as the difference in the net worth of a business at two different points in time raises a host of difficult questions about the manner in which the capital of a business should be valued. Nevertheless, it is accepted by accountants that one method of calculating profit is to compare the capital of the business at regular time intervals.

Fig. 2.1

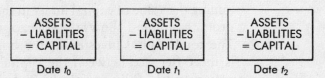

Using Fig. 2.1 as a representation of this method of determining profit, the capital at date t_0 is deducted from the capital at date t_1 to reveal the profit of the intervening period. Similarly, the capital at date t_1 is deducted from the capital at date t_2 to reveal that intervening period's profit.

It was noted above that these are only initial figures. Any fresh capital introduced or any withdrawals by the proprietor would affect the size of the capital calculated. Consequently, the profit determined by this process would need to be adjusted in these respects. Not to do so would conflict with the definition of income advanced by Hicks, as the following example will show.

Example 1

For simplicity, assume that the initial capital of a business was £5,000 in cash, and that this sum was wholly committed to the purchase of stock for resale. During the accounting period, further capital of £1,000 was introduced into the business and this sum was also committed to the purchase of additional stock. By the end of the accounting period, all the stock purchased had been sold for £8,000 cash.

On the basis of this information, the profit of the business could be calculated as follows:

		£
	Capital at the end of the accounting period	8,000
less:	Capital at the beginning of the accounting period	5,000
		3,000
less:	Capital introduced during the accounting period	1,000
	Income of the accounting period	2,000

To ignore the capital introduced during the period would have resulted in the overstatement of profit by £1,000. Equally, to ignore any withdrawals by the owner would result in an understatement of profit.

Profit measurement and the maintenance of capital

The foregoing example illustrates clearly a principle which has long been accepted by accountants as being fundamental to the process of profit measurement. This principle stresses the importance of maintaining the value of capital intact in the process of identifying periodic profit. Example 1 shows the effect of the application of this principle. The total capital invested in the business is clearly £6,000. Profit is the difference between the capital at the end of the accounting period and £6,000, namely £2,000. The owner of the business may withdraw £2,000 and in so doing would maintain the value of the business intact. If he withdrew £3,000, however, the capital of the business would be reduced by £1,000. The additional £1,000 withdrawn would be classified as a repayment of capital.

Example 1 is stated in cash terms only. Hence, many of the problems of valuation are assumed away since that example did not contemplate the possibility that the business may hold a variety of assets and may have liabilities to parties other than the owner of the business.

The process of measuring profit is much more complex than is suggested by Example 1.

A balance sheet showing all the assets owned by the business and all claims against the business could be drawn up at the beginning of the accounting period merely from the evidence adduced by appropriate documents and, where appropriate, by a physical check of the assets in the ownership of the firm. A similar balance sheet drawn up at the end of the accounting period would reveal the difference between the capital account at these two points in time. This difference would certainly be a measure of profit for that accounting period.

The drawbacks which accountants associate with this approach to profit measurement stem from the emphasis which it places on valuation and the failure to distinguish between realized gains stemming from transactions and holding gains stemming from unrealized increases in value. Accountants are particularly anxious that profit should be an operational concept; that is, it should be addressed to the problem of business efficiency Accordingly, the tradition in accounting has emphasized a transaction-based approach to profit.

The profit and loss account

The main criterion which accountants apply to the process of profit measurement is that the resulting numbers should be as objective as possible. The concept of objectivity has been given a restricted meaning in accounting and has been made synonymous with verifiability. From an accounting viewpoint, the advantage of a transaction-based approach to profit measurement is precisely that the accounting numbers derived from this approach are verifiable and hence satisfy the criterion of objectivity as understood in accounting. Nevertheless, valuation does enter into the process of profit measurement, particularly as regards such items as stocks of goods and raw materials unsold or unused at the end of the accounting period.

From a procedural viewpoint, the accounting approach to profit measurement relies on using the profit and loss account, rather than the balance sheet. Figure 2.2 below illustrates the relationship between a profit and loss account and a balance sheet.

The consequence of relying on the profit and loss account for the purpose of determining profit is to reduce the usefulness of the balance sheet in this respect. In effect, the balance sheet is by way of an appendix which collects the balances of the various accounts found in the bookkeeping system after the process of profit measurement has been completed. Hence, rather than being in reality a statement of financial position based upon a process of valuation, it is more

Fig. 2.2

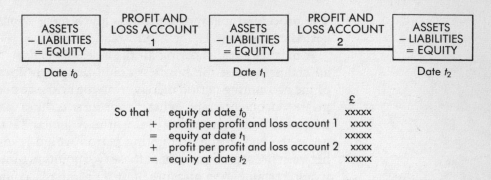

	So that	equity at date t_0	£ xxxxx
	+	profit per profit and loss account 1	xxxx
	=	equity at date t_1	xxxxx
	+	profit per profit and loss account 2	xxxx
	=	equity at date t_2	xxxxx

correctly described as a balance sheet which consists of the residual balances in the bookkeeping system.

In discussing the transaction-based approach to profit measurement, it is important to distinguish two different types of transactions which feature in the double-entry bookkeeping system. Profit results from *external transactions* in the course of which profit is realized. The transactions are those which occur *between* the accounting entity and external parties. The process of measuring profit involves the aggregation and the modification of data associated with external transactions. The process requires a series of transfers and adjustments *within* the accounting system. These may be regarded as *internal transactions* and are usually undertaken during the process of profit measurement.

It should be noted that the basic accounting equation applies to both external and internal transactions. The application of the accounting equation to the treatment of external transactions was considered in Chapter 1. In this chapter, it will be observed that the accounting equation is of central importance to the set of procedures used for ensuring that all internal transactions are properly made. In effect, the aggregation of accounting numbers found in several accounts takes place by means of transfers involving DEBIT and CREDIT entries.

Preparing the profit and loss account

In this section, the profit and loss account will be considered as one account which has been divided into two sections. The first section calculates the *gross margin* and the second section measures the *net profit*.

Calculating the gross margin

The first section of the profit and loss account, which has been known traditionally as the *trading account*, isolates the difference between the total money values of sales and the cost of goods sold during the accounting period. This difference is sometimes called the *gross profit* or the *gross margin*.

The data required to compute the total money value of sales is readily obtainable from the bookkeeping system, as is the total money value of goods purchased during the accounting period. This data will be shown on the trial balance drawn up on the last day of that period. However, the cost of goods actually sold during the accounting period may be determined only after the value of the closing stock has been ascertained.

It is very important to note that the value of the closing stock cannot be ascertained directly from the double-entry bookkeeping system. Stock has to be physically counted and then valued before it can be integrated into the bookkeeping system.

Example 2

Quentin owns and runs a small business which has the sole agency to distribute a single-size garden shed. During the year 19X7 he purchased from the manufacturer 140 of the sheds at a cost of £60 each. No sheds were on hand at the start of the year, 110 of the sheds at the agreed selling price of £85 each were sold during the year and the remainder were sold the following year.

The initial stage in the calculation of the gross margin involves transferring the balances on the purchases and the sales accounts to the trading section of the profit and loss account as follows:

Purchase account				Sales account			
	£		£		£		£
Cash	8,400	Transfer to profit and loss account	8,400	Transfer to profit and loss account	9,350	Cash	9,350
	8,400		8,400		9,350		9,350

Profit and loss account			
	£		£
Purchases	8,400	Sales	9,350

The second stage in the process of calculating the gross margin is to determine the value which should be placed on the closing stock of sheds at the end of the year. It is known that 30 sheds out of 140 purchased were unsold. To calculate the gross margin as being the difference between purchase and sales (£9,350 − £8,400 = £950) would imply that the closing stock had no value. This assumption would only hold good if the 30 sheds had no marketable value whatsoever. Given that the 30 sheds will be sold during the next accounting period, it must be considered whether they should be valued at their cost value to the business or at their market value.

Stock valuation

No value attached to closing stock

The failure to attach any value to the closing stock results in a distortion of the profits of successive accounting periods. Thus, the gross margin of years 1 and 2 for the foregoing example, assuming that no further purchases were made in year 2 and that the 30 sheds were sold for £85 each, would be as follows:

> Year 1: Sales £9,350 *minus* Purchases £8,400 = £950
> Year 2: Sales £2,550 *minus* Purchases   0 = £2,550

The extent of the distortion will be appreciated when it is recalled that 110 sheds were sold in year 1 for £85 each, whereas only 30 sheds were sold in year 2 at that price.

Closing stock shown at market value

The consequence of valuing closing stock at market value is to anticipate the profit of the succeeding year, and to bring that profit forward into the year in which the goods were purchased. Thus, the gross margin of years 1 and 2 would be:

Year 1	£	£
Sales 110 sheds @ £85 each		9,350
Purchases 140 sheds @ £60 each	8,400	
less:		
Closing stock 30 sheds @ £85 each	2,550	5,850
Gross margin		3,500

Year 2		
Sales 30 sheds @ £85 each		2,550
less:		
Value of stock brought forward from Year 1		2,550
Gross margin		—

It is clear, therefore, that this method of valuing closing stock also results in a distortion of the profit of successive accounting periods.

Closing stock shown at cost value

Accounting practice favours this method of valuing stock because it does prevent distortions in the profits over successive accounting periods as may be seen hereunder:

Year 1	£	£
Sales 110 sheds @ £85 each		9,350
Purchases 140 sheds @ £60 each	8,400	
less:		
Closing stock 30 sheds @ £60 each	1,800	6,600
Gross margin		2,750
Year 2		
Sales 30 sheds @ £85 each		2,550
less:		
Value of stock brought forward from Year 1		1,800
Gross margin		750

The result of this method of valuing closing stock is to smooth the profit of successive accounting periods by attaching a uniform gross margin to each unit of product sold. The gross margin per unit is £25 (selling price £85 minus purchase price £60). Hence, the gross margin of year 1 is £25 × 110 units sold = £2,750 and the gross margin of year 2 is £25 × 30 units sold = £750.

Although the cost-based method of valuing closing stock overcomes the difficulties associated with the other methods of stock valuation referred to, controversy has been revived as regards this method owing to its inability to reflect the impact of inflation. For the remainder of this chapter, however, and for the purpose of the questions posed hereunder, it will be assumed that closing stock should be valued at cost.

Question 1

Complete the following profit and loss accounts by calculating the missing data.

	A £	B £	C £	D £	E £
Sales	47,500	14,000	87,342	......	143,564
Opening stock	7,430	......	12,927	3,690	27,629
Purchases	30,100	8,490	......	21,347	82,231
Goods available for sale	......	......	......	......	......
Closing stock	8,910	710	14,250	2,190	......
Cost of sales	......	......	......	......	......
Gross margin	......	5,600	11,565	6,140	58,004
	47,500	14,000	87,342	......	143,564

Integrating closing stock in the bookkeeping system

Once the value of the closing stock has been determined by the method explained in the previous section, it must be integrated into the book-keeping system itself before the process of calculating the gross margin may be completed. The procedure is to open a *stock account* and to debit that account with the value of the closing stock. The accounting equation is maintained by crediting the value of the closing stock to the profit and loss account.

Example 3

Assume that at the end of the year 19X0, which was the first year of trading, the closing stock was valued at £1,540. The integration of this stock into the bookkeeping system would be effected as follows:

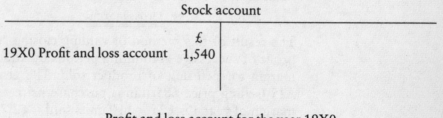

Stock account

	£
19X0 Profit and loss account	1,540

Profit and loss account for the year 19X0

	£
Closing stock	1,540

It should be particularly noted that the purchases for the year are debited in total to the purchases account and that no adjustment is made to that account in respect of goods unsold at the end of the accounting year. The sole adjustment for closing stock is that described above. However, it is evident that the effect on the gross margin of crediting closing stock to the profit and loss account is the same as if the purchases account had been credited with closing stock.

The closing stock for the year 19X0 becomes the opening stock for the year 19X1. Accordingly, the entry in the stock account is reversed by the transfer of the stock for 19X0 to the profit and loss account for the year 19X1. In effect, the goods available for sale in the year 19X1 comprise the opening stock and the purchases of the year 19X1 less the closing stock at the end of the year 19X1.

Assume that the closing stock at the end of the year 19X1 was £1,893. The stock account and the profit and loss account for the year ended 19X1 would be as follows:

Stock account

	£		£
19X0 Profit and loss account	1,540	19X1 Profit and loss account	1,540
19X1 Profit and loss account	1,893		

Profit and loss account for the year 19X1

	£		£
Opening stock	1,540	Sales	xxxxx
Purchases	xxxxx	Closing stock	1,893
Gross margin c/d	xxxxx		
	xxxxx		xxxxx
		Gross margin b/d	xxxxx

The profit and loss account forms part of the double-entry book-keeping system. Its essential purpose lies in the measurement of periodic profit. The objective of this process is to communicate information about the efficiency of a business enterprise interpreted in terms of its profit-earning ability. For the sake of clarity, it is usual to present the profit and loss account in a vertical form as illustrated below:

Profit and loss account for the year 19X1

	£	£
Sales		xxxxx
Opening stock	1,540	
Purchases	xxxxx	
	xxxxx	
Closing stock	1,893	
Cost of sales		xxxxx
Gross margin		xxxxx

Calculating the net profit

Once the trading section of the profit and loss account has been prepared and the gross margin ascertained, the data required to complete the second section may be collected together and the net profit calculated.

The usual practice for preparing the profit and loss account is to use the trial balance as a working paper. It should be noted that the various balances shown on the trial balance reflect the different classes of accounts found in the bookkeeping system and fall into the following classes:

(1) Assets.
(2) Liabilities.
(3) Capital.
(4) Expenses (purchases, rent, etc.).
(5) Revenue (sales, fees, etc.).

Since the bookkeeping system reflects the accounting equation when handling both external and internal transactions, it follows that the five classes of accounts stated above may be arranged to reflect the accounting equation. Generally, the arrangement would be as follows:

$$(\text{Capital} \pm \text{Profit or Loss for the year}) + \text{Liabilities} = \text{Assets}$$

It is clear, therefore, that the profit and loss account is a summary of all the changes which have occurred during the accounting period and which alter the value of the owner's equity in the business. Accordingly, the main procedural problem in computing the net profit is to identify those balances on the trial balance which are relevant to this purpose. Since the calculation of the gross margin has already taken care of purchases and sales, as well as the opening stock, it follows that the next stage is to transfer the remaining balances of the revenues and expenses accounts to the second section of the profit and loss account. The manner in which these balances are transferred is outlined in Figs 2.3 and 2.3A below.

Fig. 2.3 Formal presentation of profit and loss account

Profit and Loss Account for the year ended 31 March 19X2	£	£
Sales		285
Cost of sales		
Opening stock	32	
Purchases	141	
	——	
Value of disposable goods	173	
Closing stock	37	
	——	136
		——
Gross margin		149
Lighting and heating	10	
Rent and rates	16	
Advertising	20	
Wages	14	
Postages	12	
Repairs and renewals	8	
Delivery expenses	7	
	——	87
Net Profit transferred to Capital account		62
		═══

Opening Stock			*Profit and Loss Account year ended 31 March 19X2*				Sales		
Balance	32	Transfer to Profit and Loss A/c 32→	Opening stock	32	Sales Closing stock	285 ← 37	Transfer to Profit and Loss A/c	285	Cash 285
Purchases			Purchases	141					
Cash, etc.	141	Transfer to Profit and Loss A/c 141	Gross margin c/d	149					
				322		322	Stock (closing)		
Light and heat							Transfer to Profit and Loss A/c	37	
Cash, etc.	10	Transfer to Profit and Loss A/c 10→	→Light and Heat	10	Gross margin b/d	149			
Rent and rates			→Rent and Rates	16					
Cash, etc.	16	Transfer to Profit and Loss A/c 16→	→Advertising →Wagon	20 14					
Advertising			→Postage →Repairs and Renewals	12 8					
Cash, etc.	20	Transfer to Profit and Loss A/c 20→	→Delivery expenses →Net profit carried to Capital account	7 62					
Wages									
Cash, etc.	14	Transfer to Profit and Loss A/c 14→		149		149			
Postage									
Cash, etc.	12	Transfer to Profit and Loss A/c 12→							
Repairs and renewals									
Cash, etc.	8	Transfer to Profit and Loss A/c 8→							
Delivery expenses out									
Cash, etc.	7	Transfer to Profit and Loss A/c 7→							

Fig. 2.3A Outline of bookkeeping involved in preparation of the profit and loss account by the transfer of balance from the various accounts to the profit and loss account

The trial balance and the preparation of the profit and loss account and the balance sheet

Figures 2.3 and 2.3A above illustrate the manner in which the net profit may be calculated. Figures 2.4 and 2.4A below show how the trial balance may be used to draw up both the profit and loss account and the balance sheet. It should be noted that the opening stock always appears on the initial trial balance prepared before any adjustments are effected. Once the closing stock has been valued, the trial balance is adjusted to include the closing stock as well as

	Trial balance Dr £	Trial balance Cr £		Profit and loss account Dr £	Profit and loss account Cr £	Balance sheet Dr £	Balance sheet Cr £
Sales		36,422			36,422		
Purchases	20,100			20,100			
Opening stock	3,620			3,620			
Closing stock		*4,701			4,701		
			Gross margin	17,403			
				41,123	41,123		
			Gross margin		17,403		
Salaries	8,200			8,200			
Lighting and heating	910			910			
Printing and advertising	1,540			1,540			
Postages	320			320			
Rent and rates	2,060			2,060			
Repairs and renewals	624			624			
			Net profit	3,749			
				17,403	17,403		
Owners equity – capital		2,761			3,749		6,510
Creditors and accounts payable		5,627					5,627
Fixtures and fittings	1,500					1,500	
Closing stock	*4,701					4,701	
Debtors and accounts receivable	4,210					4,210	
Bank account	1,690					1,690	
Cash in hand	36					36	
	49,511	49,511				12,137	12,137

Fig. 2.4 Working paper: Final accounts for the year ended 31 December 19X6

the opening stock. However, since the profit and loss account has not yet been prepared, the only way to maintain the accounting equation when introducing the closing stock into the trial balance is to enter it twice as shown on Fig. 2.4. The asterisks on Fig. 2.4 show

Fig. 2.4A Formal presentation of the profit and loss account and balance sheet

Profit and Loss Account for the year ended 31 December 19X6		
	£	£
Sales		36,422
Cost of sales		
Opening stock	3,620	
Purchases	20,100	
	23,720	
Closing stock	4,701	
		19,019
Gross margin		17,403
Salaries	8,200	
Lighting and heating	910	
Printing and advertising	1,540	
Postages	320	
Rent and rates	2,060	
Repairs and renewals	624	
		13,654
Net profit transferred to Capital account		3,749

Balance Sheet as at 31 December 19X6		
Fixed assets		
Fixtures and fittings		1,500
Current assets		
Stocks	4,701	
Debtors	4,210	
Cash at bank	1,690	
Cash in hand	36	
	10,637	
Less: Current liabilities		
Creditors	5,627	
		5,010
		6,510
Capital		
Capital at 1 January 19X6		2,761
Profit for the year ended 31 December 19X6		3,749
		6,510

that the closing stock appears both as a debit balance and as a credit balance, so as to maintain the accounting equation.

Question 2

John Marly trading as a grocer extracted the following trial balance from his accounting records on the 30 September 19X5 at the close of one year's trading. The value of the closing stock at that date was determined to be £9,743 at cost.

Required

Prepare a profit and loss account for the year ended 30 September 19X5 and a balance sheet as at that date using the format illustrated in Figs 2.4 and 2.4A.

Trial balance as at 30 September 19X5

	Dr £	Cr £
Purchases	78,326	
Sales		105,290
Opening stock	8,425	
Employee's salaries	12,640	
Insurance	118	
Rent and rates	3,750	
Repairs	874	
Hire of freezers	1,050	
Postages	362	
Printing and advertising	1,822	
Bank charges	86	
Motor expenses	1,736	
Telephone	210	
Electricity	864	
Capital at 1 October 19X5		13,668
Creditors and accounts payable		5,624
Delivery van	3,500	
Shop fittings	4,000	
Debtors and accounts receivable	2,896	
Cash at bank	3,737	
Cash in hand	186	
	124,582	124,582

Question 3

Durant, a farmer, has asked for help in calculating his farming profit for the year ended 30 November 19X2. Owing to his preoccupation with farming operations, he claims to have been unable to maintain proper accounting records. Information obtained from Durant himself and from available records has enabled his accountant to prepare the following schedule of assets and liabilities at the beginning and close of the year.

Schedule of Assets and Liabilities

	1 December 19X1	30 November 19X2
	£	£
Cash in hand	24	36
Cash at bank	3,427	5,622
Tractor	5,000	3,500
Land Rover	2,100	1,600
Farm implements (valuation)	3,620	4,291
Dairy equipment (valuation)	7,200	6,000
Livestock	3,600	6,700
Due from Milk Marketing Board	842	720
Seeds and growing crops	2,100	4,850
Subsidies due from the government	1,450	1,725
Due to creditors:		
Feed and corn	1,897	2,624
Motor expenses	84	320
Bank loan	5,000	4,000

The following additional information is also obtained:

(1) Cash drawing is estimated to amount to £25 per week
(2) Mrs Durant has kept for her own use the proceeds from the sale of eggs, which are estimated to average £15 per week.

Required
Calculate Durant's profit for the year ended 30 November 19X2.

Question 4
Benham is planning to start trading as a bookseller. He has approached various publishers and learnt that he will be able to acquire his initial stock of books on credit. He estimates his initial requirement in this respect to be as follows:

	£
From Beta Books Ltd	350
Alpha Books Ltd	375
Prime Editions Co. Ltd	1,700
Paperbacks Reprints Ltd	875
Tutorial Texts Ltd	2,400
Leisure Classics Ltd	1,200

He estimates also that sales for the first two months of trading will allow him to repay this initial volume of credit. In addition, shelving for the shop is estimated to cost £900. Benham's father has agreed to lend him £500 towards his initial cash requirement of £2,000.

Required
Calculate how much capital is required to commence trading. (*Hint*: the accounting equation will be found useful for this purpose.)

Question 5
The following trial balance was extracted from the accounting records of the Bidston Boutique at the close of business on 30 June 19X6. The closing stock at that date was calculated as £4,390 on a cost basis.

Required
Prepare a profit and loss account for the year ended 30 June 19X6 and a balance sheet as at that date.

Trial balance as at 30 June 19X6

	Dr £	Cr £
Capital at 1 July 19X5		8,566
Freehold premises	15,500	
Fittings and display equipment	2,100	
Weldon Wholesale Clothing Ltd		840
Assistant's salaries	9,200	
Rates	785	
Monty's Model Gowns		190
Roscoe Denim Garments Ltd		1,243
Lighting and heating	674	
Purchases	35,319	
Opening stock 1 July 19X5	3,620	
Insurance	89	
Sundries and postages	146	
Telephone	103	
Sales		54,365
Cash in hand	48	
Cash at bank	2,620	
Loan S. Owens		5,000
	70,204	70,204

3   Periodic Profit Measurement: Some Further Adjustments

The purpose of Chapter 2 was to explain basic procedures involved in using the data recorded in the double-entry bookkeeping system in the process of profit measurement. Hence, the adjustments to the transactions already recorded are deliberately restricted to those essential to the determination of periodic profit, for example, the crucial adjustment for closing stock values.

The process of profit measurement is more complex than the simplified examples of Chapter 2 would imply, and the conceptual issues and practical problems involved remain the subject of considerable debate among accountants. Thus, our analysis of the problem of valuing closing stock was very much restricted to the elementary question of the need to make an adjustment and to pose some simple questions as to the appropriate basis for valuation.

In this chapter, we address ourselves to some further basic adjustments which must be made to the recorded data so that the process of profit measurement will reflect generally agreed and accepted principles relating to the nature of periodic profit. The adjustments which are now to be considered fall into two main categories. The first category relates to the timing of the recognition of revenues and expenses. The second category considers some accounting implications of credit trading, notably losses attributable to bad debts. Although these adjustments do raise issues which are fundamental to the process of profit measurement, the analysis in this chapter will once again be restricted to the mechanics of the adjustments.

This chapter is divided into three main topics as follows:

The accrual of revenue and expenses
The treatment of bad and doubtful debts
Adjustments and the extended trial balance

The accrual of revenue and expenses

The generalized use of credit trading as distinct from cash trading raises problems in the determination of periodic profit. Two alternatives are open to the accountant. First, it is possible to follow the most objective test and base the process of profit measurement solely on the cash receipts and cash disbursements of a particular accounting period, and this would result in a *cash flow statement of profit*. Second, it is possible to broaden the measurement base to recognize not just the cash receipts and cash disbursements of the period but also the *legal rights* to receive cash and the *legal obligations* to pay cash arising from the trading activities of that period. Conventional accounting profit is based on the second alternative, and is often referred to as *accrual accounting*. To retain the required degree of objectivity, the timing of the recognition of revenues and expenses must satisfy the criteria associated with the accruals convention.

The adjustments required to accommodate the accrual of revenue and expenses are the most frequently encountered adjustments to the data recorded in the accounts systems. Those relating to the accrual of expenses are more numerous and, therefore, will be considered first.

The accrual of expenses

Expenses paid in arrears

One of the most common consequences of period profit measurement is that expenses which are properly attributable to the operations of one accounting period are paid during the next accounting period. This arises either through the normal delay which occurs in the making of payments or because creditors delay in submitting their statements. Unpaid expenses must be accounted for in the particular period to which they relate, whether or not payment has actually been made. It is quite usual for accrual adjustments to be made in respect of unpaid telephone charges, rent, rates and electricity charges.

Example 1
At the close of the accounting year on 30 November 19X5, the electricity account of a business had been debited with the sum of £218 as follows:

Electricity account	
	£
Nov 30 Balance	218

On closer examination, it is found that the payments going to make up the balance of £218 were by cheque against demands for payment made by the electricity board. The last recorded payment of £43 was made on 23 September for electricity metered up to 31 August. If the balance of £218 were transferred to the profit and loss account as an expense without any modification, it would understate the true cost of the electricity consumed by the omission of the electricity used in the last three months. Obviously, the true cost for these last months would not be known until the electricity board presented its bill, but this does not prevent an adjustment being made, and a reasonable estimate based on past experience can be used. Suppose that on this basis the cost of electricity consumed in the three months to 30 November were estimated to be £110. The adjustment to the electricity account would be as follows:

Electricity account

	£		£
Nov 30 Balance	218	Nov 30 Profit and loss	
Nov 30 Accrual c/d	110	account	328
	328		328
		Dec 1 Accrual b/d	110

Note that this completes the double entry by a *debit* and a *credit* on the same account but with the *debit* in the first period and the *credit* in the second period. The account can now be transferred to the profit and loss account for the first period.

The sum of £328 is transferred to the profit and loss account as this is the cost of the electricity consumed (subject to the limits of accuracy of the estimate for the final three months) whether paid or not. The credit balance of £110 is included in the balance sheet as an accrued expense.

Two points should be noted:

(1) The accounting equation is maintained by the increase in external liabilities of £110 caused by the recognition of the debt owing to the electricity board and by the decrease of £110 in the net profit.

(2) If profit were calculated simply by measuring the changes in the capital between two dates, then the inclusion of this sum as a liability would obviously reduce the capital standing to the credit of the owner on the last date of the accounting period.

It will be appreciated that the accrual adjustment is made *solely* at the end of the accounting year in connection with the preparation of the annual profit and loss account. The question is—which accounts must be adjusted in practice? In fact, very few, since all suppliers will have invoiced the cost of purchases on a monthly basis.

Hence, the only accounts requiring adjustment are those for which sufficient time has not elapsed for accurate invoicing. Generally, these accounts are of the nature of insurance, electricity, rates, etc. Wages and salaries due but unpaid at the last day of the accounting year also would have to be accrued.

Example 2

A business obtains all its petrol and oil from Monton Garages Ltd. Invoices are received detailing the supplies and are paid at the end of the following month. In these circumstances the bookkeeping entries would be:

> Dr   Motor Expenses   } with the sums stated in
> Cr   Monton Garages Ltd } the invoices received

and later when the actual payment is made:

> Dr   Monton Garages Ltd } with the sum of the
> Cr   Bank account   } monthly settlement

If a less complete recording system is in use, as is the case with many small businesses which keep their accounts on a cash basis only, the accrual procedure is used to record amounts unpaid at the end of the year. Thus, it can be seen that this procedure has two uses. First, to correctly accrue expenses to an accounting period in the case of complete recording systems. Second, to correct less complete recording systems to take account of unpaid expenses at the end of the accounting period.

Expenses paid in advance

The complete reverse of an accrual occurs in those situations where expenses have to be paid in advance. The most common of these are rents and lease payments, rates and insurance premiums.

Example 3

Assume that a business leases shop premises at an annual rental of £2,400 payable in one sum in advance on 1 January each year. It is clear that one quarter of the rent would be 'unused' at 30 September, the date of the profit and loss account and would be shown as an asset. The rent account in the business books for the first year would be as follows:

Rent account

19X0	£	19X0	£
Jan 1 Bank[1]	2,400	Sept 30 Profit and loss	
		A/c[4]	1,800
		Sept 30 Prepayment c/d[2]	600
	2,400		2,400
Oct 1 Prepayment b/d[3]	600		

The following points should be noted:

(1) The rent paid on 1 January was paid by cheque;
(2) The prepayment is carried down and debited to the next account-ing period;
(3) The prepayment is shown on the balance sheet as an asset and is usually included with the balance of debtors;
(4) The rent appropriate to the period under review is transferred to the profit and loss account of that period.

Assuming that the rent due on the following 1 January remains unchanged, the rent account for the subsequent year will be as follows:

Rent account

19X0	£	19X0	£
Oct 1 Prepayment b/d	600	Sept 30 Profit and loss account	
			2,400
		Sept 30 Prepayment c/d	600
19X1			
Jan 1 Cash	2,400		
	3,000		3,000
Oct 1 Prepayment b/d	600		

The effect of these adjustments is to bring into coincidence the rental year which runs from 1 January with the accounting year which runs from 1 October. Thus, the rent transferred to the profit and loss account for the year ended 30 September 19X1 is in the form of a prepayment of £600 made in the previous year and a sum of £1,800 representing a portion of the payment of £2,400 made in the current year.

Two further points should be noted:

(1) The accounting equation is maintained by the increase of £600 in the assets caused by the creation of a debt to the business represented by the prepayment and by a decrease of £600 in the expenses charged against profit.

(2) If profit were calculated simply by measuring the changes in the capital between two dates, then the inclusion of this sum as an asset would obviously increase the capital standing to the credit of the owner on the last date of the accounting period.

Accrued expenses: summary

The adjustments required to deal with the accrual of expenses and the exclusion of prepayment in the process of determining the profit of a particular accounting period are in the nature of internal transactions. These adjustments are summarized below:

	£
Accured expenses	
Total expenses paid during the accounting period	xxxxx
add	
Accrual of expenses incurred but not yet paid	xxxxx
less	xxxxx
Expenses paid during the accounting period but accrued to the previous accounting period	xxxxx
Total expenses of the current accounting period	xxxxx
Prepaid expenses	
Total expenses paid during the accounting period	xxxxx
add	
Expenses prepaid in the previous accounting period and accrued to the current accounting period	xxxxx
less	xxxxx
Expenses prepaid in the current accounting period and accrued to the next accounting period	xxxxx
Total expenses of the current accounting period	xxxxx

Question 1

Complete the accounts shown below by calculating the missing numbers.

Accounts	Electricity Dr £	Electricity Cr £	Telephone Dr £	Telephone Cr £	Wages Dr £	Wages Cr £	Rates Dr £	Rates Cr £	Motor expenses Dr £	Motor expenses Cr £	Insurance Dr £	Insurance Cr £
Accrual/ Prepayment b/d		120	....		1,242		900			195	350	
Cash	800		654		....		2,700		799		....	
Profit and loss account	....			670		8,963		....	1,015			890
Accrual/ Prepayment c/d	70			47	1,380			600	....			420
	....		....		....		....		....		....	
	....		....		....	....			....		....	

The accrual of revenues

When a sale is made for cash over the counter in a store, the exchange of money and goods is immediately recognized as an event to be recorded in the bookkeeping system. If, however, a customer enters the store and says 'Will you keep that hifi set for me until next month?', it is less clear when the sale may be recognized as having been made.

The adjustments which the accountant makes to deal with the accrual or the prepayment of expenses are internal transactions which anticipate, in part, the eventual external recognition of a completed transaction. Normally, the external recognition is provided by an invoice or a formal demand for payment such as an electricity bill. Similarly, the accountant may have to come to a decision as to how far a sales transaction may be regarded as completed for the purpose of recording it in the bookkeeping system and making the required adjustments for the accrual of revenue. Hence, the accrual of revenue is also concerned with the correct determination of periodic profit.

The need for some consistency of treatment in the recognition of transactions is a critical requirement for the process of profit measurement.

Consider the following situations:

(1) The business receives a written order from a regular and valued customer for goods which are not on hand at the moment. The order is acknowledged, and in turn the business orders the goods from the supplier. Eventually they arrive, are despatched to the customer and an invoice is issued to him. The goods reach him two weeks after despatch from the business. When should the business enter the transaction as a sale?

(2) A customer enters a store, pays a deposit on a washing machine and agrees to buy it under a hire purchase agreement over the next twelve months, paying interest. The washing machine is delivered to the customer one week later. How much should be recorded as a sale and when?

(3) A small construction business agrees to build a new sea wall for the local authority. The job will take eighteen months to complete and the total contract price will be paid in three equal amounts at six-monthly intervals. After four months' work the business draws up its profit and loss account for the previous twelve months. Has any sale at all taken place? Has any profit been earned?

These examples illustrate the problems that may be encountered. In the first illustration it is usual to consider the legal transfer of ownership as marking the realization of the transaction, and this is usually on issue of an invoice to the customer.

Various treatments are suggested for the second type of transaction and, although the legal title may not pass until the final instalment has been paid, it is usual to recognize the sale as arising on the acceptance by both parties of the contract. The interest element is regarded as additional and is not recognized until paid, but it is assumed to be paid regularly, i.e., each instalment is assumed to include a partial payment of the pure sale price of the goods and a part of the interest payable.

In the final case, the business may assume that 4/18ths of the work is done and that the local authority was a debtor to that extent. The proportion of work done may not necessarily be 4/18ths and some certified proportion may have to form the basis of any entries in the accounting system.

Question 2
C. Aspin, a jobbing carpenter, undertakes work for small builders. He commenced business on 1 July 19X2 with a van which he had just bought for £2,800, tools worth £235 and cash at the bank of £2,100.

A summary of his transactions for the year is as follows:

	£
Purchased timber for various jobs	3,670
Received from Reed & Co (Builders) Ltd for work done on new houses	1,650
Received from Studio Holiday Homes Ltd for work on the conversion of old houses	4,620
Cash received for casual small jobs undertaken	1,246
Motor expenses paid during the year	930
Replacement of tools	65
Paid for casual labour	750
Withdrew per week from the bank for personal expenses	30
Received from Melvin Estates for various repairs to property	2,400
Entered into a contract with Studio Holiday Homes Ltd for further conversion work. Payment is to be made on the completion of the work, which was half completed on 30 June 19X2. Payment due on completion	3,500

Required
(1) Prepare a trial balance as at 30 June 19X3.
(2) After making the necessary adjustments in respect of the items detailed below, prepare a profit and loss account for the year ended 30 June 19X3 and a balance sheet as at that date

	£
(a) Motor expenses due but not yet paid	46
(b) Closing stock of timber at cost	1,643
(c) Reed and Co., are dissatisfied with work done and are demanding a refund of	1,500

Note
The adjustment for drawings should be by way of a credit to the bank account ($£30 \times 52 = £1,560$) and a corresponding debit to the capital account. The usual practice is to debit drawings to a drawings account which is transferred at the end of the accounting period to the debit of the capital account. Hence, the procedure suggested above is a shortcut for the purpose of this question only.

(3) Assume that C. Aspin has to use the accounts you have prepared for the following purposes:
  (a) to apply to his bank for a loan,
  (b) to attach to his income tax return.

Examine the various items appearing on the profit and loss account and discuss any alternative treatment which could apply to the manner in which they could be represented to the bank and the income tax authorities, respectively.

The treatment of bad and doubtful debts

When goods are sold by a business to customers on credit terms there is always the potential hazard of not collecting the cash due. In accounting, this hazard is considered as involving two types of debts: those which may be classified as bad debts and those which may be classified as doubtful debts.

Bad debts

When a customer does not pay his account and circumstances indicate that no recovery is possible, the business patently has an asset in its books which is valueless. When this occurs and all recovery methods have been tried without success, or are too costly in relation to the value of the debt, there is no alternative but to write off the debt.

This is done by the simple process of transferring the balance on all such debtors accounts to a bad debts account and then transferring the total to the profit and loss account where it will be treated as an expense. As far as the accounting equation is concerned, this is maintained by the effect of a reduction in the assets of the business and an equal reduction (eventually) in the capital.

The accounting entries are as follows:

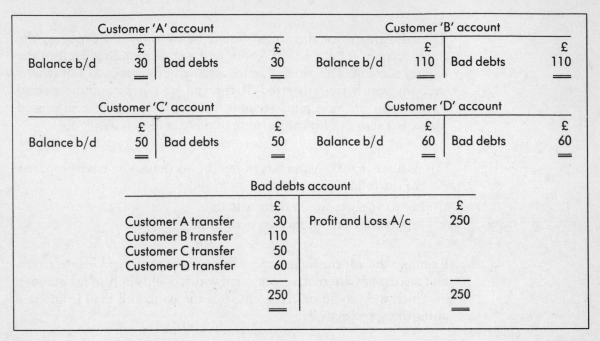

Fig. 3.1

Notes
(1) The balance on the customers' accounts are debts to the business in respect of credit sales to these customers. Hence, prior to being written off as bad debts, these debtor balances would have been classified as asset balances.
(2) The bad debts account is a summary account to which all bad debts are transferred and aggregated in one total before being transferred to the profit and loss account.

Doubtful debts

In addition to the problem of dealing with debtor balances which will clearly not be recovered, there is the separate question of debtor balances which are doubtful of payment. Underlying the approach to doubtful debts is the conservatism which surrounds all accounting activities, and the need to keep a balance between optimism and pessimism. Doubtful debts are debts which, at the close of the accounting period, are not considered as being bad debts, although there is sufficient evidence to suggest that they may eventually prove to be such. When the evidence available is inconclusive that debts are good or bad, treating them as doubtful enables a decision to be deferred till the position becomes clear. Further, the doubtful debts account is also a safeguard against the excessive optimism of treating such debts as good, since it creates a provision against the likelihood that they may turn out to be irrecoverable.

There are two methods of estimating doubtful debts:

(a) to inspect each and every debtor account and to estimate the extent to which each debt may be doubtful, or
(b) to rely on statistical evidence of past experience to reveal some consistent percentage of total debtors which ultimately proves to be irrecoverable.

The former method takes the form of a specific provision for doubtful debts, and the latter takes the form of a general provision for doubtful debts. In the United Kingdom, there are taxation objections to the use of a general provision inasmuch as they are not usually allowed in calculating taxable profit, whereas specific provisions are allowed within reason. It is, of course, much easier to rely on the second method and to create a general provision, but large numbers of accounts are needed before any statistical method of determining doubtful debts can be argued to have any degree of reliability.

The necessary bookkeeping entries are as follows:

Dr Profit and loss account ⎱ with the total amount of all
Cr Provision for doubtful debts ⎰ debtors considered doubtful

These entries effectively take some of the profit out of the profit and loss account and place it as a credit balance in the provision for doubtful debts account. For balance sheet purposes, this provision is deducted from the total of debtors. It is essential to note that when doubtful debts are being examined in this way, no entries or adjustments are made to individual debtors' accounts until the point at which they are declared to be completely bad and irrecoverable. The provision for doubtful debts appears on the balance sheet as follows:

	£	£
Debtors (accounts receivable)	14,624	
less Provision for doubtful debts	348	14,276

Example 4

A business which commenced on 1 January 19X1 had accumulated the following total of debtors in respect of each accounting period ended on the following dates:

	£
31 December 19X1	60,000
„ 19X2	80,000
„ 19X3	90,000
„ 19X4	75,000

Relying on experience gained in the particular area of trading activity, it is believed appropriate to create and maintain a general provision for doubtful debts at the rate of 6%. Accordingly, the provision for doubtful debtors is as under:

Provision for doubtful debts account

		£			£
Dec 31 19X2	Balance c/d	4,800	Dec 31 19X1	Profit and loss a/c	3,600
			Dec 31 19X2	Profit and loss a/c	1,200
		4,800			4,800
Dec 31 19X3	Balance c/d	5,400	Jan 1 19X3	Balance b/d	4,800
			Dec 31 19X3		600
		5,400			5,400
Dec 31 19X4	Profit and loss a/c	900	Jan 1 19X4	Balance b/d	5,400
19X4	Balance c/d	4,500			
		5,400			5,400
			Jan 1 19X5	Balance b/d	4,500

Bad and doubtful debts: additional considerations

Before leaving the question of bad debts, a further matter should be considered. The methods described for the treatment both imply that bad debts and the provision for doubtful debts should be treated as expenses charged against the profit of the year in which the decision was taken to treat such debts as bad and doubtful respectively.

It may be argued that no event has really taken place in the current period that affects the profit measurement process of this period.

If we attempt to analyse the situation in this way the following conclusions may be drawn.

Bad debts

(a) By the very nature of the processes involved in the recovery of bad debts, the date when the debt is regarded as irrecoverable may be in a completely different accounting period from that which includes the date on which the sale took place.

(b) It would be more appropriate to adjust the profit and loss accounts of prior periods rather than to charge and hence 'distort' the net profit for the current period under review. This, it will be found, is mentioned in a 'Standard' about which more will be said in a later chapter. (A 'Standard' in this context is, briefly, an agreed method of dealing with certain transactions where more than one such method exists.)

(c) The above treatment may not be necessary if the amounts are so small as not to be material

Doubtful debts

The following suggested treatment of doubtful debts would be considered appropriate also for bad debts when the sale and the decision to regard the consequent debt as bad take place in the same period.

(a) Since a provision for doubtful debts implies that some part of the transfer of goods to debtors was not, in fact, true sales, it could be considered more correct to regard the adjustment as a deduction from sales rather than as an expense.

(b) The disclosure of the provision would still be achieved by the suggested following presentation:

Profit and loss account for the year ended ....

	£
Gross sales	xxxxx
less Deduction for doubtful debts	xxxx
Net sales	xxxxx

Adjustments and the extended trial balance

In Chapter 2 use was made of the technique of extending the figures from the trial balance into additional columns in order to produce a rough draft form of the profit and loss account and balance sheet. This enables a check to be kept on all the figures on one work sheet, and the formal presentation of the profit and loss account and balance sheet is reduced to a simple task of copying out. This method of using the trial balance may be extended to deal with all the required adjustments.

The extended trial balance

In the previous use of this technique no adjustments were made to the figures actually recorded as a result of external transactions. Now, in order to incorporate these adjustments, an additional column is interposed between the trial balance and the profit and loss account. As there may well be a need to distinguish between the profit and loss account to the point of the gross margin and the profit and loss account to net profit, there are two columns devoted to the profit and loss accounts, one for each aspect.

The basic procedure still remains the same. Every item in the trial balance must be transferred to either the profit and loss account or the balance sheet columns, but now incorporating any necessary modifications in the adjustment column.

Example 5

The following trial balance was extracted from the books of J. Halsall trading as a retail haberdasher:

Trial balance as at 31 December 19X1

	Dr £	Cr £
Stock	3,670	
Sales		28,620
Purchases	13,745	
Rent	1,000	
Rates	240	
Electricity	127	
Wages	4,600	
Motor expenses	824	
Motor cars	5,200	
Fixtures and fittings	1,400	
Debtors	6,210	
Creditors		2,450
Drawings	2,500	
Capital at 1 January 19X1		8,446
	39,516	39,516

In additional, the following information is available:

(1) The closing stock at 31 December 19X1 at cost is £4,340.
(2) No provision has been made for due and unpaid rent amounting to £250.
(3) Rates prepaid totalled £60.
(4) No provision has been made for the usage of electricity estimated to cost £46.
(5) Bad debts abount to £185.

It is required to prepare a profit and loss account for the year ended 31 December 19X1 and a balance sheet as at that date.

The first step is to enter all the adjustments in both the debit and the credit side of the adjustment column so as to maintain the accounting equation. Thus, the closing stock is shown once as a debit which will go into the balance sheet as an asset and once as a credit which will go into the profit and loss account. Note 2 regarding £250 rent due will need an adjustment which (Dr) increases rent and (Cr) increases creditors. Once all the adjustments are entered and the columns added to see if the debit and credit sides agree, the next column is added, and the difference between the totals is the gross margin

	Trial balance		Adjustments			Profit and loss account				Balance sheet	
	Dr £	Cr £	Note	Dr £	Cr £	Dr £	Cr £	Dr £	Cr £	Dr £	Cr £
Opening stock	3,670		Note 1	4,340	4,340	3,670	4,340			4,340	
Sales		28,620					28,620				
Purchases	13,745		Gross margin			13,745					
Gross margin						15,545			15,545		
Rent	1,000		Note 2	250				1,250			
Rates	240		Note 3		60			180			
Electricity	127		Note 4	46				173			
Wages	4,600							4,600			
Motor expenses	824							824			
Motor cars	5,200									5,200	
Fixtures and fittings	1,400									1,400	
Debtors	6,210		Note 5		185					6,025	
Creditors		2,450	Note 2 / Note 4		250 / 46						2,746
Drawings J. Halsall	2,500									2,500	
Capital J. Halsall		8,446									8,446
Prepayments			Note 3	60						60	
Bad debts			Note 5	185				185			
Net profit			Net profit					8,333			8,333
	39,516	39,516		4,881	4,881	32,960	32,960	15,545	15,545	19,525	19,525

of £15,545. This figure is entered on the debit side of the gross margin column of the profit and loss account and the credit side of the profit and loss account and the process is repeated to find the net profit. This net profit figure is transferred to the balance sheet where it should cause the two sides to be equal.

Question 3

You are required to enter the following transactions in the records of M. Plant, who started trading as a shoe retailer on 1 July 19X4 with a capital of £8,000 in cash.

19X4

July	1	Purchased shop fittings for £1,500 by cheque
	2	Bought goods to the value of £2,400 on credit terms from D. K. Ltd
	3	Paid £75 being three months' advance rent for the shop
	4	Cash sales £85
	5	Sold boots on credit to the Hamilton Construction Co. Ltd for £350
	6	Cash sales £84
	6	Paid wages of £22 to shop assistant
	8	Purchased goods for £270 by cheque
	9	Paid postage £3 cash
	10	Paid £500 to D. K. Ltd
	11	Received cheque for £200 from the Hamilton Construction Co. Ltd
	13	Weekly cash sales £242
	13	Paid wages £22
	20	Weekly cash sales £384
	20	Paid wages £22
	23	Sold sports shoes on credit to the Midborough Education Committee for £330
	23	Paid £23 for fuel supplies
	24	Paid £12 to Shop Cleaners Ltd for cleaning
	27	Weekly cash sales £170
	27	Paid wages £22
	29	Received an invoice for £28 for wrapping paper from B. W. Paper Ltd
	30	Paid £8 for deliveries to customers
	31	Weekly cash sales £142

After recording these transactions, prepare a trial balance as at 31 July 19X4 and, using the extended trial balance method, prepare a profit and loss account for July 19X4 and a balance sheet as at 31 July 19X4. The additional information required for this purpose is that the closing stock at 31 July 19X4 was valued at £1,210 at cost. Unrecorded use of electricity was estimated at £25.

Question 4

Norman Coates commenced business as a furniture dealer on 1 October 19X2 with £11,000 in the bank. Transactions for October 19X2 were as follows:

			£
Oct	1	Bought goods by cheque	510
	2	Bought goods on credit from Dobson	945
		Bought goods on credit from Bridges	1,422
		Bought goods on credit from Gates	365
		Bought goods on credit from Ryan	850
	3	Bought packaging from Boxed Ltd on credit	510
	6	Sold goods on credit to Murgatroyd	212
		Sold goods on credit to Archer	400
		Sold goods on credit to Hornby	700
		Sold goods on credit to Atkins	605
	7	Paid rent for October and November	200
	8	Bought fittings on credit from Sampson	1,400
	9	Paid salaries	310
	15	Goods returned to Dobson	210
	15	Bought van by cheque	2,300
	16	Received loan from S. Small	1,800
	16	Goods returned by Archer	40
	16	Goods returned by Atkins	110
	19	Cash sales	270
	20	Sold goods on credit to Archer	300
		Sold goods on credit to Atkins	940
		Sold goods on credit to Smart	420
	21	Paid by cheque outstanding accounts of Dobson and Bridges	
	22	Received cheques from Smart and Archer in settlement of their accounts	
	26	Paid electricity account by cheque	80
	27	Received further loan from S. Small	200
	28	Received cheque from Atkins	1,000

Required

(1) Enter these transactions in the books of the business.
(2) Prepare a trial balance as at 31 October 19X2.
(3) Using the extended trial balance method, prepare a profit and loss account for the month of October 19X2 and a balance sheet as at 31 October 19X2. For this purpose the following additional information is provided:

   (a) The closing stock at 31 October 19X2 was valued at cost at £1,500
   (b) The unrecorded usage of electricity was estimated at £70
   (c) Wages due but not paid at 31 October 19X2 amounted to £200.

Question 5

The following trial balance was extracted from the books of P. Earnshaw.

Trial balance as at 31 May 19X5

	£	£
Purchases	67,800	
Sales		112,960
Stock	16,540	
Postages and telephone	912	
Motor expenses	1,596	
Salaries	17,456	
Sundry expenses	332	
Rent	1,560	
Rates	620	
Debtors	28,792	
Creditors		16,696
Premises at cost	30,000	
Motor vehicles at cost	9,400	
Fixtures and fittings at cost	4,480	
Bank overdraft		1,832
Drawings	15,400	
Capital at 1 June 19X4		63,400
	194,888	194,888

The following additional information is available:

(1) Closing stock at 31 May 19X5 was valued at cost at £13,436
(2) Expenses owing were: Sundry expenses £95
                         Motor expenses £121
(3) Expenses prepaid: Rates   £90
                      Telephone £35
(4) Bad debts totalled £624

Required

(a) Prepare a profit and loss account for the year ended 31 May 19X5.
(b) A balance sheet on that date.

Question 6

The following trial balance was extracted from the books of C. Hopley.

Trial balance as at 31 December 19X1

	£	£
Capital at 1 January 19X1		20,932
Furniture and fittings	1,450	
Motor vans	4,160	
Purchases	122,400	
Sales		153,000
Stock	14,000	
Trade debtors and creditors	16,300	13,228
General expenses	4,400	
Bank balance	1,930	
Lighting and heating	642	
Drawings	4,200	
Wages and salaries	13,498	
Bad debts	1,132	
Provision for bad debts at 1 January 19X1		300
Motor expenses	1,350	
Rent and rates	1,650	
Printing and stationery	180	
Insurances	168	
	187,460	187,460

The following additional information is given:

(1) Closing stock at the 31 December 19X1 was valued at cost at £13,200.
(2) Wages and salaries unpaid at 31 December 19X1 amounted to £116.
(3) Insurance paid in advance at 31 December 19X1 amounted to £40.
(4) The provision for bad debts is to be increased to £500.

Required
(a) Prepare a profit and loss account for the year 19X1, and
(b) A balance sheet as at 31 December 19X1.

Question 7

H. Latham started business on 1 January 19X4 by paying £6,000 into a business bank account. He rented premises and purchased fittings and furniture for £3,000 and paid by cheque.

At 31 December 19X4 the following figures were available from his records for the year.

	£
Sales on credit	44,800
Purchases on credit	39,300
Cost of goods sold	33,600
Receipts from trade debtors	39,936
Payment to trade creditors	32,408
Business expenses paid	5,500
Business expenses due but not paid	212
Business expenses prepaid	144
Drawings	4,400

There were no cash sales and all amounts received were paid into the bank. All payments were made by cheque.

Required

(a) Calculate the cost value of the stock at 31 December 19X4.
(b) Calculate the balance of trade debtors at 31 December 19X4.
(c) Calculate the balance of trade creditors at 31 December 19X4.
(d) Calculate the balance at the bank at 31 December 19X4.
(e) Show the business expense account as it would appear at the close of business on 31 December 19X4.
(f) Prepare a profit and loss account for the year 19X4.
(g) Prepare a balance sheet as at 31 December 19X4.

4 Assets: Recognition and Depreciation

This chapter is addressed to one of the most important areas of financial accounting, namely the recognition and treatment of asset values. Accounting for asset values impinges on the problems of profit measurement in a number of ways. First, the recognition of expenditure involving the acquisition of assets means that such expenditure must be excluded from expenses charged against revenue in arriving at periodic profit. Second, certain assets are taken into account in the calculus of periodic profit. Thus, stocks of raw materials existing at the end of the accounting period are taken into account in the calculation of the gross margin of the following period. Third, certain fixed assets are depreciated over time. In effect, this means that the process of depreciation is a method of allocating the cost of acquiring fixed assets over the economic life of these assets, which will span a number of years. Finally, the disposal of assets may involve a gain or loss which will appear in the profit and loss account.

A number of other problems exists in relation to the treatment of assets, which this chapter introduces. These problems include the selection of the appropriate basis for depreciation, and the financial implications of provisions for depreciations.

This chapter is divided into the following sections:

The meaning and nature of assets
The concept of depreciation
Depreciation and profit measurement
Methods of depreciation
Depreciation and the valuation of assets
The economic life of an asset
The disposal of fixed assets
Asset values and cash flows

The meaning and nature of assets

The term 'asset' is usually associated with proprietary rights, both tangible and intangible; that is, rights to tangible property such as motor cars, plant and machinery, and rights to intangible property such as rights to the enjoyment of land, trade marks and patents.

Accounting has its traditional concern with recording rights of property and the control of such rights, and in the exercise of this concern it follows the law as regards the interpretation of the term 'asset'.

The purpose of this section is to examine in detail the importance of asset definition in accounting, and in particular to analyse the distinction between different forms of assets and the manner in which these distinctions are significant to the accounting process. Lying at the root of much of the accounting debate about the meaning of asset is the process of profit measurement. In this context, the term 'asset' has a strict meaning in accounting which is associated with the 'use' of assets in an operational sense. In this analysis, the existence of 'asset values' on the balance sheet is conditional upon an expectation of future benefits to the firm arising from such values. Hence, the exact meaning of the term 'asset' is a conditional interpretation of a legal concept.

From the foregoing, the term 'asset' is used in accounting to refer to a legal right which offers the prospect of future benefits to the accounting entity in which the right is vested. Initially, therefore, the recognition of an asset in accounting depends upon a transaction which confers legal rights to the entity to the use of the asset in its business operations. Next, the continued recognition of an asset depends upon the possibility that it will continue to have a use in the profit-generating process.

It is important to note, however, that asset recognition in accounting is *generally* limited to a range of economic resources over which ownership rights *can* be acquired and *are* acquired by contract. Accounting theory, however, does not recognize as assets an important class of economic advantages of crucial importance to the profitability of a business. The technical expertise of the employees of the firm, a monopoly position in the market, good industrial relations, etc., are all economic advantages which are not formally expressed in accounting as 'assets', although in nearly every case they depend upon a legal contract; for example, employees have contracts of employment and the conditions attached to such contract may well be crucial to good industrial relations. Monopoly rights may arise from patents, but may well be associated with distribution agreements.

Finally, it is important to note that asset recognition is *generally* limited to the payments made for the acquisition of the legal rights implied in the term 'asset'. Thus, accountants have difficulty in recognizing assets except by the process of acquisition by purchase. The need to revalue the historic cost of acquisition to reflect a revised realizable and revised replacement cost is the subject matter of inflation accounting.

The meaning of the term 'asset' is extended by the classification systems adopted for accounting purposes. Fixed assets are distinguished from current assets, and this distinction has particular significance in explaining the operational context in which the assets are intended to be employed. In general terms, fixed assets represent the collection of assets which provide the *profit-generating structure* of the business and have a degree of permanence in that role. By contrast, current assets represent the collection of assets which are associated with *profit-generating operations*.

Fixed assets

The association of fixed assets with the profit-generating structure of the business hinges to a considerable extent upon the distinction between capital and revenue expenditure which is central to the process of profit measurement. Essentially, fixed assets represent expenditure which has been capitalized in the process of determining the profit of the current or previous years. The concepts of accounting which are related to the recognition of expenditure as representing the acquisition of fixed assets provide a set of elementary rules of thumb to guide accountants in bookkeeping and in the preparation of annual financial statements. The simple rule is to recognize a series of assets as appertaining to a class denoted fixed assets. Among these assets are land and buildings, plant and equipment, motor vehicles, tools, furniture and fittings, etc. Their common characteristic lies in their *long-term* use in the operations of the business. It is for this reason principally that they are regarded as providing the capital structure of the business. Accordingly, the reason which underlines the simple rule associates the term 'fixed assets' with all expenditure that is incurred in the acquisition of assets which will have a use in the business extending beyond one year.

At a more sophisticated level, the term 'fixed asset' may be seen as representing an implicit forecast of future net cash flows flowing to the firm associated with expenditure which has been capitalized rather than written off against revenues.

From a practical viewpoint, it is sometimes difficult to identify particular items of expenditure. An additional factor in this problem are the rules applied by the income tax authorities towards classes of expenditure. For example, it is possible to undertake repairs either through the activity of restoring an asset by repair or simply by replacement. Often, it is cheaper to replace than to repair. Expenditure on repairs is written off against profit, but expenditure on replacement is capitalized both under accounting and taxation rules. Difficulties arise, moreover, where there is both an element of repair and improvement; for example, when in the course of repairing an entire central heating system, a new boiler is installed. Is the expenditure on the boiler a part of repairing the central heating system or should it be treated as an item separate from the system? Some typical problem areas are listed below, with a brief note on the reasoning involved in a decision to treat the item as involving capital or revenue expenditure.

Transaction	Discussion
1 Purchase of secondhand machine.	So long as the acquisition implies future usefulness, it does not matter that the item purchased is new or secondhand. Hence, in this case, the machine must be treated as a fixed asset.
2 Repair a secondhand machine which has just been purchased in order to use it in the business.	The act of repairing disguises the true purpose of the expenditure which is to improve the item purchased. Hence, the repair must be capitalized and added to the value of the machine.
3 Transport and installation costs of machinery.	*All* costs normally associated with putting an asset into a condition ready for use are capitalized and added to the purchase cost of the asset.
4 Painting and partitioning new offices.	Any initial expenditure carried out on an asset, which would otherwise be treated as current expenditure, must be capitalized when it relates directly to placing an asset into use.
5 Hire purchase charges of £1,000 involved in the purchase of machinery costing £10,000, and included in the total price of £11,000.	The asset value is recorded as £10,000 and the charges of £1,000 are treated as an immediate financial expense related to the credit service rendered to the business.

6 During a slack period of trading, employing staff on the construction of a new warehouse, rather than laying them off. An outside contractor has quoted £25,000 for the construction of the warehouse.

Under normal circumstances, the wages would be treated as revenue expenditure. But since the men are employed in creating a capital asset, their wages and all other expenditure related to constructing the warehouse should be capitalized. The outsider quotation of £25,000 is irrelevant for accounting purposes.

From the foregoing discussion, it is clear that the nature of expenditure is only prima facie evidence of its correct accounting definition and of the manner in which it should be recorded and treated in the process of profit measurement. A business may choose to use its labour to build its own factory or machinery, and the labour and other costs which would otherwise be included under wages, purchases and other expenses should be capitalized under the heading of the appropriate asset account. In the case of a warehouse, for example, all associated labour and material expenses would merely appear as debits to warehouse building account. In this connection, it should be noted that both capital and current expenses involve debit entries in the books. Hence, the process of using the double-entry bookkeeping system for measuring profit requires the ability to distinguish the debit entries, which should be classified as assets and excluded from expenses chargeable against revenues, from those debit entries which are properly chargeable against revenues in the process of profit measurement.

Current assets

Current assets are closely associated with the profit-earning process and are involved in the cycle of activities implied by that process. They include stocks of raw materials and finished goods, trade debtors, payments in advance and cash. Their recognition in some cases depends purely on the concept of measuring profit periodically, for example, stocks arise purely as the result of the practice of excluding the cost of goods unsold at the end of the accounting period from the expenses of that period. The association of fixed assets with the capital structure of a business provides a useful analogy for a definition of current assets. The latter may be associated with the notion of circulating capital. For example, when they are realized as sales, stocks are transformed into either cash or deferred cash in the form of debtors. Cash is used to finance the purchase of further stocks or to finance the recycling of trade creditors where stocks are acquired on credit terms.

The identification of current assets with the concept of circulating capital provides another useful accounting concept—working capital. This is defined as the excess of current assets over current liabilities. A further analysis of working capital is provided in Chapter 6. Figure 4.1 below illustrates the concept of current assets as circulating capital.

Fig. 4.1 Elementary outline of the flow of current assets and current liabilities

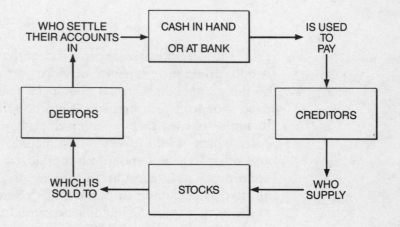

The concept of depreciation

The concept of depreciation raises a number of complex issues in accounting. The issues which are discussed in this section relate to the notion of capital maintenance in the process of profit measurement, the manner in which depreciation should be represented, the financial implication of depreciation, and the problem of allocating costs over time.

The maintenance of capital

The problems involved in the maintenance of capital are illustrated in Example 1 below.

Example 1
James Cavendish started business on 1 April 19X0 as a hot-dog vendor. His initial capital was £2,600. He purchased a van already converted for use as a hot-dog stall at a cost of £2,400 and applied the balance of £200 to the purchase of foodstuff for sale. Hence, the van represented the fixed capital and the £200 represented the

working capital of the business. Each day, he would acquire £200-worth of foodstuff for sale during that day. For reasons of hygiene, Cavendish never bought more than he required, since the foodstuff purchased was of a perishable nature. Hence, no stock of unsold foodstuff remained at the close of each day's trading. Cavendish's policy was to treat as profit any surplus over £200 which was left after meeting daily expenses and to withdraw that surplus immediately for his own private use. The balance sheet on the 1 April 19X0 was as follows:

Assets	=	Capital account
Van £2,400 + Cash £200	=	£2,600

In view of the policy adopted by Cavendish, it is evident that his balance sheet at the end of any day would be exactly as above. His capital account would remain at £2,600 since profit is immediately withdrawn.

At the end of the fourth year of trading, the van fails to pass a road test and is pronounced unroadworthy. Owing to its particular features, it had no scrap value. The balance sheet at 31 March 19X4 is as follows:

Assets	=	Capital account
Cash £200	=	£200

In effect, Cavendish has failed to maintain the value of the business and the value of the capital invested in that business, since over the period of four years that value has dropped from £2,600 to £200. The difference of £2,400 represents the original value of the van. Hence, the failure to maintain the value of capital is caused by the failure to provide for the depreciating value of the van out of annual profit. Hence, the sums withdrawn daily by Cavendish represented not only profit but also a withdrawal of capital. To restore the value of the capital invested in the business to the position existing at 1 April 19X0, Cavendish would have to invest a further £2,400.

It is evident that the perception of the gradual loss in value of the van over its life in use would have induced Cavendish to make an appropriate provision out of profit for the replacement of the van at the end of its life. Assuming constant prices over the four-year period, the replacement cost of the van is equal to its historic cost. Had Cavendish estimated the life of the van at four years, he should have created a reserved of £2,400/4 = £600 per annum and reduced his withdrawals by that sum annually. Accordingly, the accounting equation would have been maintained by a decreasing value of the van and a corresponding increase in the amount reserved out of profit. Assuming that this reserve is held in cash, the revised balance sheets for each of the four years to 31 March 19X4 would have been as follows:

		Assets				Capital account
		£		£		£
31 March 19X1	Van	1,800	+ Cash	800	=	2,600
31 March 19X2	Van	1,200	+ Cash	1,400	=	2,600
31 March 19X3	Van	600	+ Cash	2,000	=	2,600
31 March 19X4	Van	0	+ Cash	2,600	=	2,600

Providing for depreciation

The provision for depreciation in the accounts system deals with the replacement of fixed assets at the termination of their useful life. It should be noted that its purpose is limited to fixed assets which experience a loss in value through use. For example, plant and machinery are fixed assets which generally lose their usefulness through use, whereas land may well retain its value and indeed increase in value in relation to other assets.

The procedure involved in creating a provision for depreciation is relatively simple as regards bookkeeping:

> Dr   Profit and loss account   ⎱ with the annual amount
> Cr   Provision for depreciation account ⎰ of depreciation

The debit to the profit and loss account reduces the net profit of the business and hence the amount which may be withdrawn. The credit is normally shown as a deduction from the relevant asset account on the balance sheet.

The provision for depreciation account increases yearly by the amount transferred from the profit and loss account as depreciation.

Example 2
The creation of a provision for depreciation of the van used by Cavendish in Example 1 would be as follows:

Provision for depreciation—motor van

	£		£
31 March 19X1 Balance c/d	600	31 March 19X1 Profit and loss a/c	600
31 March 19X2 Balance c/d	1,200	1 April 19X1 Balance b/d	600
		31 March 19X2 Profit and loss a/c	600
	1,200		1,200
31 March 19X3 Balance c/d	1,800	1 April 19X2 Balance b/d	1,200
		31 March 19X3 Profit and loss a/c	600
	1,800		1,800
31 March 19X4 Balance c/d	2,400	1 April 19X3 Balance c/d	1,800
		31 March 19X4 Profit and loss a/c	600
	2,400		2,400
		1 April 19X4 Balance b/d	2,400

The entry on the motor van account remains as £2,400, being the acquisition cost, for the four-year period involved, as follows:

Motor van account

	£		£
1 April 19X0 Cash	2,400	31 March 19X1 Balance c/d	2,400
1 April 19X1 Balance b/d	2,400		
	....		
	....		
1 April 19X4 Balance b/d	2,400		

The balance sheet for each of the four years would reflect the following positions:

	Balance sheets as at 31 March			
	19X1	19X2	19X3	19X4
	£	£	£	£
Fixed assets				
Motor van at cost	2,400	2,400	2,400	2,400
Accumulated depreciation	600	1,200	1,800	2,400
	1,800	1,200	600	0
Current assets				
Cash	800	1,400	2,000	2,600
	2,600	2,600	2,600	2,600
Financed by				
capital account	2,600	2,600	2,600	2,600

Financial implications of depreciation

Although the foregoing example shows a connection between the depreciation and an increase in the cash balance, this situation is unlikely ever to be found in practice. Indeed, there is no reason why depreciation should be associated with a provision out of profit in the form of cash. Depreciation is not a source of funds, and it is misleading to consider it as such.

Example 3

Assume for simplicity that at the end of an accounting period in which all transactions were conducted in cash, that the net income is £100. Evidently, this income is reflected in a cash balance of £100. A decision to create a provision for the depreciation of fixtures and fittings of £50 does not result in a decrease in the cash balance from £100 to £50, though it results in a decrease in the net profit from £100 to £50. The effect of the decision to introduce a provision for depreciation of £50 is to restrict the distributable profit to £50 from £100.

Depreciation and the allocation of costs over time

An important aspect of the concept of depreciation is the allocation of the cost of fixed assets over the several accounting periods during which they are used in the production of profit.

Example 4

A newly formed mining company requires substantial supplies of electricity, and is faced with two alternative means of obtaining those supplies. The first alternative is to enter into a contract with the local electricity supply board and buy electricity on a metered basis. The second alternative is to install an electricity generating plant and to produce the electricity required.

Clearly, the outcome of the first alternative method of obtaining electricity would be the receipt of periodic bills which would be debited to the electricity account. As regards the second alternative, the only visible cost associated with the periodic supply of electricity would be in the form of the costs of operating the electricity generating plant. The major costs would be involved in the installation of the plant, and the problem is how to represent those costs as part of the cost of obtaining supplies of electricity? This problem arises in every case where assets are purchased. This is because the services associated with the use of assets may be obtained either by the purchase of the assets or by leasing or buying the services themselves.

Accordingly, the depreciating value of the electricity generating plant may be seen as representing an annual charge for the provision of the services implied in the acquisition of the asset.

The recognition of assets as representing the acquisition of service potential and the treatment of depreciation as a charge for the periodic services provided by assets is an indication of the manner in which accounting theory is moving from a strictly legal base to an economic interpretation of the nature of assets. The bookkeeping entries for dealing with depreciation in this way are the same as shown earlier.

Depreciation and profit measurement

Depreciation is concerned with two critical issues regarding the measurement of profit:

(1) The maintenance of capital.
(2) The allocation of costs over different accounting periods.

The useful economic life of an asset is an important consideration in both cases, and the failure to take account of the economic life of an asset when calculating depreciation may lead to underestimating the required provision for depreciation with consequential effects on the maintenance of capital and the allocation of fixed asset costs over time.

Accounting practice is to rely on technical estimates of the life of an asset as a basis for allocating the cost of the asset against the profits of different accounting periods. These are discussed below.

It should be noted, however, that depreciation is only one element of the cost of obtaining asset services. Running costs and the cost of repairs should be included perhaps in the overall consideration of the relationship between depreciation and profit measurement. For example, the effective economic life of an asset may be shortened if running costs suddenly were to increase, whereas—given that running costs remain at a normal and expected level—the economic life of an asset may well be prolonged by careful maintenance.

Methods of depreciation

The various methods for dealing with depreciation are set out below. It is important to note that whichever methods are used, the net figures shown on the balance sheet do not necessarily indicate that the realizable or replacement values of the assets involved correspond with the actual market values. Tables 1 and 2 briefly describe methods of depreciation and Table 3 presents the formulae for calculating depreciation.

Table 1 Depreciation methods which depend on a prior estimate of asset life

Method	Annual depreciation	Comment
(1) Straight line	Equal amount per annum	Implies that the routine operating efficiency of the asset remains constant throughout its life and that repairs are also constant. Much used for plant and machinery.
(2) Declining balance	Highest in the first year and declining year by year	Implies that operating efficiency is declining and that repairs are increasing. Frequently adopted for motor vehicles, fixtures and fittings.
(3) Sum-of-years digits	Very high in the first few years but declining rapidly	A method of providing a rapid build-up in the provision for depreciation, and is a more extreme form of the declining balance method. Considered to be appropriate for assets with high risks of obsolescence.
(4) Annuity	Lowest in first year but increasing year by year	Introduces the time value of money into the depreciation concept. This method is the reverse of the declining balance and the sum-of-years digits methods, which is unlikely to represent reality for most assets. It is considered appropriate for assets, such as property, with a long life.

Variants of the methods described in Table 1 do exist, but the fundamental purpose of all methods of depreciation in accounting is to allocate costs over different time periods.

Table 2 Depreciation methods which depend upon technical knowledge of the usage capacity of an asset

Method	Annual depreciation	Comment
(1) Production	Varies with production	Used where an asset has an expected total output, for example stamping and pressing machines. Repairs do not enter into the choice of this method.
(2) Revenue	Varies with revenue raised	May be appropriate for assets used directly in raising revenue, such as assets hired out.
(3) Depletion	Varies with extraction	Relevant to dealing with natural resources, such as mines and oil wells, where the life of the asset is related to the known mineral reserves.

The formulae for computing depreciation under the methods described in Tables 1 and 2 are shown in Table 3 below. The following symbols are used in these formulae:

C = Origin cost of the asset
D = Annual charge for depreciation
A = Accumulated depreciation
S = Scrap value
n = Number of years of expected life of asset

Table 3 Formulae for depreciation methods

Method	Formula
(1) Straight line	$D = \dfrac{C - S}{n}$
(2) Declining balance	(a) To determine the rate r to be applied in the formula: $r = 1 - \sqrt[n]{\dfrac{S}{C}}$ (b) $D = r(C - A)$
(3) Sum-of-years digits	$D = \dfrac{t}{n(n + 1)/2} \times (C - S)$ where t = number of years of asset life left.

(4) Annuity

$$D = \frac{C}{\overline{a_n}|^i} - i(C - A)$$

where $\overline{a_n}|^i$ is the present value factor of an annuity of £1 discounted at $i\%$ for n years, and i is the appropriate interest rate for the business. The scrap value is ignored in this example as it introduces a minor difficulty which is beyond the scope of this text.

(5) Production

$$D = \frac{\text{No of units produced}}{\text{Total potential usage}} \times (C - S)$$

(6) Revenue

$$D = \frac{\text{No of units sold}}{\text{Total potential sales}} \times (C - S)$$

(7) Depletion

$$D = \frac{\text{No of units extracted}}{\text{Total potential output}} \times (C - S)$$

Depreciation and the valuation of assets

A few brief examples are given below of the manner in which the charge for depreciation affects the written-down value of assets. For the sake of completeness, an example is given of the manner in which the annuity method affects the written-down value of assets, but the implications of this method are not pursued.

Table 4 Written-down asset values under various depreciation methods (*Note:* The figures given below assume that the original asset cost is £12,000, the expected life 5 years and the expected scrap value is £2,000)

Method	Written-down values

(1) Straight line

(a) Depreciation $= \dfrac{C - S}{n}$

$$= \frac{£12,000 - 2,000}{5}$$

$$= £2,000 \text{ per annum}$$

(b) Written-down value

Year	Original cost £	Annual depreciation £	Accumulated depreciation £	Written-down value at year end £	
1	12,000	2,000	2,000	10,000	
2	—	2,000	4,000	8,000	
3	—	2,000	6,000	6,000	
4	—	2,000	8,000	4,000	
5	—	2,000	10,000	2,000	= Scrap value

(2) Declining balance

(a) Rate r

$$= 1 - \sqrt[n]{\frac{S}{C}}$$

$$\sqrt[5]{\frac{2,000}{12,000}}$$

$$= 0.31 \text{ or } 31\%$$

Depreciation $= r(C - A)$
$$= 0.31$$
(12,000 − Accumulated depreciation at the end of each year, namely 31% of £12,000 at end of year 1, etc.)

(b) Written-down value

Year £	Original cost £	Annual depreciation £	Accumulated depreciation £	Written-down value at year end £
1	12,000	3,720	3,720	8,280
2	—	2,567	6,287	5,713
3	—	1,770	8,057	3,943
4	—	1,222	9,279	2,721
5	—	721*	10,000	2,000

* This figure is adjusted to account for approximations

(3) Sum-of-years digits

(a) Depreciation $= \dfrac{t}{n(n+1)/2} \times (C - S)$

Year 1 $= \dfrac{5}{5(5+1)/2} \times (12,000 - 2,000)$

$$= £3,333$$

Year 2 $= \dfrac{4}{5(5+1)/2} \times (12,000 - 2,000)$

$$= £2,666$$
etc.

(b) Written-down value

Year £	Original cost £	Annual depreciation £	Accumulated depreciation £	Written-down value at year end £
1	12,000	3,333	3,333	8,667
2	—	2,666	5,999	6,001
3	—	2,000	7,999	4,001
4	—	1,333	9,332	2,668
5	—	668*	10,000	2,000

* Adjusted for approximation

(4) Annuity

(a) Depreciation $= \dfrac{C}{a_{\overline{n}|}^i} - i(C - A)$

(*Note:* for simplicity, it is assumed that $C = £10,000$, thereby eliminating the scrap value, and that $i = 12\%$).

The calculation of depreciation involves two stages:

(1) calculating the annual depreciation
(2) calculating the annual interest imputed against the written-down value of the asset.

The annual depreciation is calculated as follows:

$$\frac{10,000}{a_{5|}^{0.12}} = \frac{10,000}{3.605} \text{ (from tables)} = £2,774$$

The annual interest imputed against the written-down value of the asset is shown below in the valuation of the written-down value.

(b) Written-down value

Year £	Original cost £	Annual depreciation £	Interest Base £	Rate %	Imputed interest £	Net depreciation £	Written-down value at year end £
1	10,000	2,774	10,000 ×12		1,200	1,574	8,426
2	—	2,774	8,426 ×12		1,011	1,763	6,663
3	—	2,774	6,663 ×12		800	1,974	4,689
4	—	2,774	4,689 ×12		563	2,211	2,478
5	—	2,774	2,478 ×12		296	2,478	0

The method of calculating the depreciation charge under the production, revenue and depletion methods are similar. The following example illustrates the depletion method.

Example 5

The Longlump Slate Company purchased a quarry for £100,000 having estimated reserves of 500,000 tons. The output of the quarry in the first year was 25,000 tons and it rose to 50,000 tons in the second year. The following depreciation calculated on the depletion method should be charged against the profits of years 1 and 2 respectively:

$$\text{Depreciation} = \frac{\text{No. of units extracted}}{\text{Total potential output}} \times (C - S)$$

$$\text{Year 1} = \frac{25,000}{500,000} \times £100,000$$

$$= \underline{\underline{£5,000}}$$

$$\text{Year 2} = \frac{50,000}{500,000} \times £100,000$$

$$= \underline{\underline{£10,000}}$$

The economic life of an asset

Accounting practice relies on a technical estimate of the life of an asset. Thus, a lorry may be given a life of five years on the basis that it will be worn out by the end of that period. The analysis of the effective life in use of an asset must obviously take into consideration its potential physical life. It is also clear that other factors impinge upon the analysis of the economic life of an asset. Such factors as obsolescence resulting from technological improvement, falling output associated with increasing repairs are typical considerations indicating the need to view the problem of assessing the economic life of an asset as being associated with establishing a cycle of asset renewal aimed at securing the lowest overall annual asset cost.

Example 6

Consider the case of a small engineering firm faced with the problem of buying a new lathe, which has a technical life of four years. The following data is available:

	£
Cost of lathe	10,000
Estimated annual repairs:	
Year 1	900
Year 2	1,300
Year 3	1,600
Year 4	3,000
Estimated disposal value at end of·	
Year 1	5,000
Year 2	4,000
Year 3	600
Year 4	—

The total average cost per year of operating the lathe may be calculated as follows:

At end of:	Year 1 £	Year 2 £	Year 3 £	Year 4 £
Original cost	10,000	10,000	10,000	10,000
Repairs: Year 1	900	900	900	900
Year 2	—	1,300	1,300	1,300
Year 3	—	—	1,600	1,600
Year 4	—	—	—	3,000
Net cost	10,900	12,200	13,800	16,800
Disposal value	5,000	4,000	600	0
Annual cost	5,900	8,200	13,200	16,800
Average annual cost	5,900	4,100	4,300	4,200

It is clear that since the lowest average annual cost of operating the lathe occurs over a two-year period, the firm should adopt an economic life for the lathe of two years and replace the lathe at the end of each two-year period.

The disposal of fixed assets

Fixed assets are either sold or scrapped at the end of their useful life. The accounting implications are twofold. First, entries are required to record the sale of scrapping of the assets in the appropriate accounts. Second, any difference between the disposal value and the written-down book value is regarded either as a profit or loss, as may be, on the disposal of assets and is shown on the profit and loss account in the year of disposal.

Example 7
During the year ended 31 March 19X7, a business sold a typewriter for £70 which originally cost £300, and in respect of which the provision for depreciation stood at £250.

The bookkeeping entries required to record the disposal of the typewriter are concerned with the following three points:

(a) Removing the asset from the office equipment account.
(b) Eliminating the provision for depreciation in respect of the asset.
(c) Posting the difference between the written-down book value and the disposal value to the profit and loss account of the year 19X7.

The means by which these three objectives are met is through an asset disposal account, as follows:

(a) Transfer the original cost of the typewriter from the office equipment account to the asset disposal account as follows:

Debit   Asset disposal account ⎫
Credit   Office equipment account⎬ with £300

(b) Transfer the provision for depreciation in respect of the typewriter from the provision for depreciation—office equipment account to the asset disposal account as follows:

Debit   Provision for depreciation office ⎫
         equipment account   ⎬ with £250
Credit   Asset disposal account   ⎭

(c) Record the sale of the typewriter in the asset disposal account and transfer the difference between the disposal value and the written down value to the profit and loss account as follows:

Debit   Cash
Credit   Asset disposal account } with £70

Debit   Asset disposal account } with £20 being gain on
Credit   Profit and loss account } disposal

The bookkeeping entries are as follows:

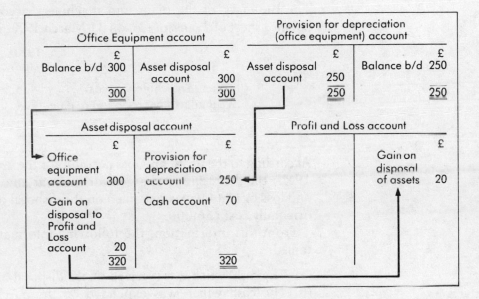

Notes
(1) The only external transaction is the receipt of cash from the sale of the typewriter.
(2) The gain or loss on disposal represents the final adjustment for depreciation. A true gain would only arise where the asset is sold for more than it originally cost.
(3) With rare exceptions, assets are found in accounts for whole categories of assets. Equally, the provision for depreciation applies to all assets in the category denoted. Thus, all motor vehicles will be found in the Motor Vehicle account, and there will not be an account for each individual motor vehicle. Similarly, the Provision for Depreciation (Motor Vehicle) account will relate to all motor vehicles.

Asset values and cash flows

Transactions concerned with the acquisition and disposal of assets give rise to cash flows and non-cash flows. Thus, the sale of a typewriter which had already been substantially depreciated gives rise to a net non-cash flow of £20 shown as a gain on disposal in the profit and loss account, where the cash flow associated with the actual sale of the typewriter was £70, which was the sum of money received. It is important, therefore, to distinguish these different accounting flows that lie behind the aggregated asset figures on the balance sheet.

Example 8

The summary of the plant and machinery account shown on the balance sheet of Transcot Co. on 31 March 19X1 is as follows:

	19X0 £000	19X1 £000
Plant and machinery at cost	424	506
Accumulated depreciation to date	214	282
	212	224

According to the profit and loss account for the year ended 31 March 19X1, the depreciation charged for the year amounted to £105,000 and loss of £8,000 was sustained on the disposal of machinery which originally cost £56,000.

From this information, the following information may be ascertained:

(a) The cash which was received on the disposal of the machinery.
(b) The cash which was expended on the purchase of new plant and machinery during the year ended 31 March 19X1.

The procedure relies on a reconstruction of the accounts lying behind this data.

Asset disposal account

	£		£
Plant and machinery	56,000	Provision for depreciation	37,000
		Loss on disposal	8,000
		Cash (b)	11,000
	56,000		56,000

Plant and machinery account

	£		£
Balance b/d	424,000	Asset disposal account transfer	56,000
Cash (c)	138,000	Balance c/d	506,000
	562,000		562,000
Balance b/d	506,000		

Provision for depreciation—Plant and machinery account

	£		£
Asset disposal account transfer (a)	37,000	Balance b/d	214,000
Balance c/d	282,000	Profit and loss account	105,000
	319,000		319,000
		Balance b/d	282,000

Notes
(a) The amount of depreciation transferred out relates to assets sold. This figure is obtained from the opening and closing figures and the amount added to the provision by the depreciation charged in the profit and loss account for the year ended 31 March 19X1.
(b) Cash received from plant and machinery sold is derived from the other three components in the asset disposal account.
(c) Cash paid for new plant and machinery is derived from the other known figures in the plant and machinery account.

Question 1
Indicate how you believe the following transactions should be treated in the accounting records. State the reasons for your decision.

(a) Delivery van with a written down value of £260 traded in for an allowance of £400 against the purchase of a new van costing £2,800.
(b) Overhaul of machinery costing £1,500 which has extended its working life.
(c) The purchase of three old cars for £100 each for use as spares by a garage.
(d) The construction of new storage bins from metal which was regarded as scrap.
(e) The replacement of all the mechanical adding machines used in the offices of a business by electronic calculators at a net cost of £950.
(f) Repainting all the delivery vans of a business to conform with a new and distinctive style at a cost of £2,600.
(g) Replacement of a factory heating system, from coal-fired steam boilers to a hot-air ducted system costing £3,200 and the sale of scrap from the old system resulting in the receipt of £850 although the written down value of the old system was zero.
(h) Build a new fire escape to comply with office safety regulations at a cost of £985.

Question 2

Ron Stalker, the owner of a printing firm, is contemplating the purchase of new printing machinery costing £8,000, and having a technical life of four years. The following estimates of repairs and maintenance costs over a four-year period have been prepared from experience of similar machines in the past.

	£
Year 1	200
Year 2	850
Year 3	1,200
Year 4	1,300

The disposal value of the new machinery has been estimated as follows:

	£
At the end of year 1	3,500
At the end of year 2	2,800
At the end of year 3	2,000
At the end of year 4	0

Required

(1) Advise Stalker on the length of economic life which he should attach to the machinery which he proposes to purchase.
(2) Suggest a method of depreciation which would be appropriate to your recommendation. (Support your recommendation with the calculations you have made.)

Question 3

You are required to show the provision for depreciation (fixed assets) account in respect of the machine mentioned below as it would appear in the accounting records of the business during the five relevant years by each of the following methods:

(a) Straight line.
(b) Decreasing balance.
(c) Sum-of-years digits.
(d) Production usage.

The machinery was bought for £12,000 on 1 January 19X2, and at that date it was estimated that the scrap value at 31 December 19X6 would be £1,500. The number of operating hours per annum were:

Year ended 31 December:	Hours
19X2	2,500
19X3	5,000
19X4	3,000
19X5	3,000
19X6	1,500

It may be assumed that the useful life of the machine is represented by the total hours shown above.

Question 4

On 1 January 19X4, a manufacturer acquired two identical machine tools at a cost of £8,000 each, and a reprographic machine for the office at a cost of £4,000. The machine tools are depreciated at 25% per annum on a declining balance basis, and the reprographic machine, which has an estimated residual value of £400 and a life of six years, is depreciated on a straight line basis. On 1 January 19X5, one of the machine tools was sold for £4,500 and a new one acquired for £11,000.

Required

(1) Prepare the relevant asset accounts, the provision for depreciation accounts and the asset disposal account, for the year ended 31 December 19X5.

(2) The manufacturer, observing the data given in the asset disposal account and noting the cost of the new machine, ruled that 'in future we must increase the depreciation rate because we under-estimated the amount of cash needed to replace the asset'. Discuss this statement.

Question 5

On 1 January 19X1, a manufacturing business bought three machines at a cost of £20,000 each. The business normally provided depreciation at 20% per year on the declining balance basis. On 1 January 19X3, a further machine was acquired at a cost of £22,000. On 30 June 19X3, one of the machines originally acquired on 1 January 19X1 was sold for £8,000. A full year's depreciation is charged in the year of purchase of any asset, but none is charged in the year of disposal.

Required

(1) Prepare the following accounts for each of the years ended 31 December 19X1, 19X2, and 19X3:
  (a) Machinery account.
  (b) Provision for depreciation (machinery) account.
  (c) Asset disposal account.

(2) According to the owner of the business, 'if depreciation had not been charged in 19X3, then the loss for the year could have turned into a profit which would have been much better for the business. Why, therefore, do we have to charge depreciation?'
Write a brief memorandum in reply to this question.

Question 6

J. Martin commenced business as a house builder on 1 January 19X0 with a capital of £70,000. A summary of the transactions for the year ended 31 December 19X0 is given below:

		£
(1)	Purchased:	
	Fixed assets	36,000
	Materials	92,046
(2)	Payments made	
	Creditors	120,722
	Wages	37,168
	General expense	5,838
(3)	Drawings by Martin for his own use	8,234

(4) Details of work undertaken by Martin on contract were as follows:

	Materials used £	Wages incurred £	Sales invoiced £	Cash received £
Moss Estates	19,296	14,932	40,698	40,698
Waverly Homes	23,960	12,126	42,172	42,172
Gorse Hill	14,910	4,702	22,614	14,068
Rush Homes Ltd	17,584	3,528	—	—
Poole Villas	10,288	2,464	—	10,000
	86,038	37,752	105,484	106,938

The Rush Homes Ltd and Poole Villas contracts were uncompleted at 31 December 19X0.

(5) At 31 December 19X0:
   the balance of cash in hand and at the bank was £4,976,
   the stock of work-in-progress is to be valued on the basis of the cost of materials used and wages incurred plus 25% of wages for general expenses.

(6) Depreciation is to be provided on fixed assets at the rate of 10% per annum on cost for a full year.

Required

Prepare a profit and loss account for the year ended 31 December 19X0 and a balance sheet as at that date.

Question 7

S. Cummins traded as a merchant. His trial balance at 31 December 19X6 revealed the following:

	£
Capital account as at 1 January 19X6	67,042
Trade debtors	19,200
Rent and rates	1,676

Fittings and equipment at cost	35,200
Provision for depreciation	5,292
Purchases	117,354
Drawings	5,000
Trade creditors	14,864
Provision for doubtful debts	754
Stock	13,868
Motoring expenses	832
Sales	136,426
Advertising	2,750
Delivery vans at cost	6,000
Provision for depreciation	1,500
Salesmen's salaries	10,524
Lighting and heating	1,982
Bad debts	152
Audit and professional charges	86
Cash at bank and in hand	10,296
Postage and office expenses	958

The following adjustments are to be made:

(1) The closing stock at 31 December 19X6 at cost was estimated at £7,832

(2) Depreciation is to be provided at 10% on fittings and equipment and at 25% on delivery vans

(3) Prepayments at 31 December 19X6 were:

	£
Rates	120
Motoring expenses (insurance for van)	116

(4) Accruals at 31 December 19X6 were:

	£
Rent	200
Electricity	54
Repairs to delivery vans	78
Audit fee	210
Telephone	56

(5) The provision for doubtful debts is to be made equal to 5% of trade debtors.

Required
Prepare a profit and loss account for the year ended 31 December 19X6 and a balance sheet as at that date.

Question 8

The following balances were extracted from the books of B. Baker, timber importer, on 30 September 19X1:

	£
Capital account at 1 October 19X0	48,478
Office furniture and equipment	2,880
Drawings	9,776
Stock	29,944
Purchases	335,520
Sales	409,600
Rent	2,700
Lighting and heating	950
Insurances	608
Salaries	12,704
Stationery and printing	1,474
Telephone and postages	1,034
General expenses	5,122
Travellers' commission and expenses	19,850
Bad debts	662
Trade debtors	38,200
Trade creditors	16,324
Cash at bank	13,208
Cash in hand	58
Provision for doubtful debts	288

The following additional information is given:

(1) Closing stock at 30 September 19X1 was estimated at cost at £12,972

(2) Provision is to be made for the following accrued expenses at 30 September 19X1:

	£
Rent	900
Lighting and heating	272
Travellers' commission and expenses	900
Audit charge	400

(3) The provision for doubtful debts is to be raised to 3% of closing debtors

(4) Office furniture and equipment is to be depreciated by 10% on book value

(5) B. Baker has withdrawn goods costing £112 for his own use during the year.

Required

Prepare a profit and loss account for the year ended 30 September 19X1 and a balance sheet as at that date.

5　Partnership and Limited Companies

The purpose of the previous chapters was to examine in detail the procedures associated with double-entry bookkeeping and the basic problems to which financial accounting is addressed. For this purpose, reference was made to the most simple form of accounting entity described as the sole trade. This form of business organization is very prevalent, but the more significant forms of business organizations from the accounting viewpoint are those which have harnessed much greater capital, and control much greater economic resources. Such organizations pose complex financial accounting problems. These problem will form the substance of the rest of this part.

The initial expansion of a business organization is often by the way of an extension to the sole trader form of organization effected by the admission to the business of a co-owner, who is known as a partner. Partnerships remain the most common form of business organizations for a variety of activities, including those represented by the professions, such as doctors, dentists, architects, stockbrokers and accountants. It is the limited liability company, however, which has assumed the greater significance from an economic and accounting point of view.

The purpose of this chapter, therefore, is to examine the financial accounting implications of partnerships, and to proceed to discuss the most important aspects of the financial accounting problems and procedures associated with limited liability companies. Accordingly, this chapter is divided into two main topics as follows:

> Financial accounting for partnerships
> Financial accounting for limited liability companies.

Financial accounting for partnerships

The financial accounting aspects of partnerships are concerned with the following problems:

(1) The formation of a partnership and the admission of a new partner.

(2) The division of partnership profit among the partners and the subdivision of the equity in the partnership to reflect the rights of individual partners.

(3) The dissolution of a partnership or the retirement of a partner.

The problems really fall into two categories. The first category is concerned with reflecting changes in ownership and include both (1) and (3) above. These important events occur infrequently. The second category is concerned with profit measurement and the concept of capital and includes (2) above. The measurement of partnership profit is an on-going process. Since this text is concerned emphatically with the problem of profit measurement, attention will be focused on the implications of the partnership form of organization for process of profit determination.

The proprietary theory and partnerships

In the case of the sole trader form of business, the owner's equity is represented by the capital account and is the residual balance expressed in the accounting equation as follows:

$$\text{Capital} = \text{Assets} - \text{Liabilities}$$

The capital account is used to aggregate the accounting numbers which affect the value of the owner's equity. Thus, the opening and closing balances on the capital account are reconciled by taking into account the net profit and drawings made during the accounting period as follows:

Summary of Account	
J. Bloggs—Capital as at 1 January 19X1	32,467
Net profit for the year	8,620
	41,087
Drawings	7,400
Capital as at 31 December 19X1	33,687

In the case of a partnership, the equity of the partners is analysed in order to distinguish:

(a) the original capital brought into the partnership by each partner,

(b) any loans by a partner to the partnership over and above the agreed capital,

(c) the net profit accruing to each partner less drawings.

Three separate accounts must be maintained to reflect these requirements, as follows:

(a) a capital account for each partner showing the original capital contributed,
(b) a loan account when a partner makes a loan to the partnership,
(c) a current account for each partner to which his share of the partnership is credited and to which his drawings are debited.

The appropriation of net profit

In the case of the sole trader form of business, the whole of the net profit is deemed to be attributable to the owner and his capital account is automatically credited with the net profit of the business. An important distinction introduced by the partnership and the limited liability company forms of business is the manner in which the net profit is appropriated. In both cases, a new section is added to the profit and loss account which will be referred to as the appropriation section.

The formula for apportioning the net profit between the partners is normally detailed in the partnership agreement. This formula may take a variety of forms. Thus, a partnership agreement between A, B and C may provide that A is to be paid a salary of £4,000 per annum, that interest at the rate of 10% per annum is to be allowed on capital, and that the balance of net profit is to be divided in the ratio of 2:3:5. It is clear, however, that despite the terms used in this type of agreement, the designation of particular payments as being 'salary' and 'interest on capital' merely represent a formula for dividing the net profit among the partners. Such payments should not be treated as normal expenses in calculating the net profit, but should be shown in the appropriation section of the profit and loss account.

Example 1
Ash, Birch and Cedar trading in partnership as timber importers realized a net profit of £24,150 for the year ended 30 June 19X3. The condensed trial balance as at 30 June 19X3 shown below reflects the balances in the books after the calculation of the net profit but before its appropriation among the partners.

The partnership agreement provides that the net profit is to be divided in the ratio Ash 4 : Birch 4 : Cedar 2, after allowing them interest at the rate of 12% per annum on the original capital subscribed and crediting Cedar with salary of £2,500 per annum.

The appropriation section of the profit and loss account for the year ended 30 June 19X3 and the resulting balance sheet as at that date are set out below:

Trial balance as at 30 June 19X3

			£	£
Capital account 1 July 19X2	Ash			10,000
	Birch			8,000
	Cedar			6,000
Current account 1 July 19X2	Ash			800
	Birch			1,000
	Cedar			550
Drawings for year to 30 June 19X3	Ash		4,000	
	Birch		3,500	
	Cedar		3,000	
Fixed assets at cost			35,000	
Provision for depreciation to 30 June 19X3				8,000
Current assets			25,000	
Current liabilities				12,000
Net profit for year ended 30 June 19X3				24,150
			70,500	70,500

Appropriation of profit
for the year ended 30 June 19X3

			£	£
Net profit				24,150
less: Interest on capital:	Ash		1,200	
	Birch		960	
	Cedar		720	2,880
				21,270
less: Salary—Cedar				2,500
				18,770
Balance to Ash 4/10ths			7,508	
Birch 4/10ths			7,508	
Cedar 2/10ths			3,754	18,770
				—

Balance sheet as at 30 June 19X3

	Ash £	Birch £	Cedar £	Total £
Capital accounts	10,000	8,000	6,000	24,000
Current accounts at 1 July 19X2	800	1,000	550	
add: Interest	1,200	960	720	
Salaries			2,500	
Share of net profit	7,508	7,508	3,754	
	9,508	9,468	7,524	
less: Drawings	4,000	3,500	3,000	
	5,508	5,968	4,524	16,000
Partners' funds employed				40,000

Represented by:	Cost	Depreciation	
	£	£	£
Fixed assets	35,000	8,000	27,000
Current assets		25,000	
less: Current liabilities		12,000	13,000
			40,000

The undermentioned points should be noted with particular care:

(a) The amount to be apportioned between the partners in accordance with the agreed profit-sharing ratio is the residual amount *after* all other appropriations by the way of interest and salary have been made. Thus, in the example above, the residual amount to which the profit-sharing ratio is to be applied is £18,770 and *not* £24,150.
(b) The interest to be credited to each partner is a percentage of the capital invested in the partnership and *not* a percentage of net profit.
(c) The salary payable to any partner should be debited to his current account. No separate salary account should be opened for a partner.

The control of partnerships

Where an agreement exists between the partners, such provisions as are necessary for the conduct of business affairs should normally be included as terms of the partnership agreement. These will be legally binding on all partners. Where no partnership agreement exists, or where the partnership agreement is silent on a point at issue, United Kingdom legislation provides that the rules contained in the Partnership Act of 1890 are to apply. One important feature of the Partnership Act 1890 is that if offers a definition of what constitutes a partnership. As a result, whenever two or more persons are engaged in any form of mutual activity which falls within the definition of a partnership within the meaning of the Partnership Act 1890, a partnership is deemed to exist and the provisions of the Act apply.

Question 1
Cabernet, Pinot and Gamay trade in partnership under the name Western Wines. The partnership agreement allows for the payment of 15% per annum on capital, and the payment of a salary of £3,500 per annum to Pinot. The balance of the net profit or loss is to be apportioned in the ratio of Cabernet 5:Pinot 2:Gamay 3.

Required
Using the trial balance as the 30 September 19X7 given below, prepare a profit and loss account for the year ended 30 September 19X7 and a balance sheet as at that date. The additional information which is required for this purpose is as follows:

(a) The closing stock as at 30 September 19X7 is valued at £21,234 at cost.
(b) Bad debts amounting to £625 should be written off.
(c) Depreciation is to be provided as follows:

(1) Racks and fittings at the rate of 25% using the declining balance method.
(2) Delivery vans on the basis of a 5-year life using the straight line method and assuming no scrap value at the end of 5 years.
(3) Cooling equipment on the basis of a 10-year life using the straight line method and assuming no scrap value at the end of 10 years.

(d) Rates are prepaid to the extent of £500.
(e) Telephone charges due and unrecorded amount to £120.

Trial balance as at 30 September 19X7

		£	£
Capital accounts 1 October 19X6	Cabernet		18,000
	Pinot		12,000
	Gamay		10,000
Current accounts 1 October 19X6	Cabernet		4,600
	Pinot		3,760
	Gamay		2,640
Drawings for year to 30 September 19X7	Cabernet	4,800	
	Pinot	5,200	
	Gamay	3,850	
Warehouse and shop at cost		27,500	
Racks and fittings		8,300	
Provision for depreciation			1,100
Delivery vans		7,400	
Provision for depreciation			1,020
Cooling equipment—at cost		4,400	
Provision for depreciation			3,960
Salaries to employees		16,422	
Rates, lighting and heating		3,412	
Advertising		3,685	
Stock		18,347	
Motor expenses		3,210	

Insurances	318	
Repairs and renewals	410	
Telephones and postage	586	
Printing and stationery	214	
Purchases	114,210	
Sales		168,111
Debtors and accounts receivable	8,614	
Creditors and accounts payable		7,197
Balance at bank	1,327	
Cash in hand	183	
	232,388	232,388

Question 2

Jill and Dora run a small clothing boutique in partnership, Jill, having completed a secretarial course some time ago, has prepared the following current accounts and balance sheet.

	Jill £	Dora £		Jill £	Dora £
Drawings	6,320	7,920	Opening balance	2,280	1,560
Closing balance	1,960	1,440	Interest on capital	1,000	800
			Share of profit	5,000	4,000
			Salary	—	3,000
	8,280	9,360		8,280	9,360

Balance Sheet as at 31 October 19X5

	£	£		£	£
Capital accounts			Shop—at cost	16,000	
Jill	10,000		less Depreciation	3,120	
Dora	8,000				12,880
		18,000	Fittings	10,000	
Current accounts			less Depreciation	4,100	5,900
Jill	1,960				
Dora	1,440		Stock		4,180
		3,400	Debtors		4,220
Loan—Jill's uncle		4,000	Prepayments—Expenses		280
			Cash in hand		320
Creditors—Goods		1,660			
Accrued expenses		180			
Bank overdraft		540			
		27,780			27,780

Investigating further, you discover the following:

(1) Part of the closing stock which had been included at cost of £440 had badly faded in storage and could only be expected to realize £160.

(2) Dora had introduced £4,000 of her capital on 30 April 19X5 but had been credited with interest for a whole year.

(3) Bank charges had been overlooked and amounted to £140 for the year.

(4) Depreciation of £900 on fittings had been omitted for the year.

(5) A creditor for goods for £740 had been omitted from both purchases and creditors although the goods had been correctly included in closing stock.

(6) A charge of £1,200 for rates was in the profit and loss account but £160 of this applied to the period after 31 October 19X5.

(7) Jill's uncle had made the loan to the business at the concessional interest rate of $7\frac{1}{2}\%$ per annum but this had not been included in the profit and loss account.

(8) Dora's salary should have been £2,800 and not £3,000 as shown.

Required

(a) Prepare a statement showing the true net profit before appropriation.

(b) Prepare the revised current accounts of Jill and Dora.

(c) Redraft the balance sheet as at 31 October 19X5.

(d) Explain why, in the case of partnerships, the treatment of (i) interest paid to a partner and interest paid to a third party and (ii) the salary of a partner and the salary of an employee is different.

Financial accounting for limited liability companies

The growth of limited liability companies has been a feature of Western industrialized society. The size of the corporate sector in Western countries, its contribution to national economic well-being and development, the employment that it provides and the burden of taxation which it assumes merely underline the economic importance of this form of business organization.

The limited liability company developed out of the pursuit of wealth through larger economic units than could be financed by partnerships. The legislation which governs limited liability companies is addressed to the legal problems arising from their business activities, and particularly from the desire of legislators to regulate their conduct.

The Companies Acts of 1948, 1967, 1976, 1980 and 1981, which were consolidated in 1985, contain the specific legislation which applies to United Kingdom companies. These Companies Acts contain provisions which apply to financial accounting procedures, and to the information which companies are required to publish in profit and loss accounts, balance sheets and other documents published for shareholders and other users.

This section deals with the financial accounting requirements of the Companies Acts.

Formal requirements for company status

The registration of a company with limited liability under the Companies Act 1985 results in the creation of a legal entity having an independent legal existence from the individual persons who own its capital, who are known as shareholders.

The procedure to be followed for registration begins with the submission of a number of legal documents to the Registrar of Companies, prior to receiving a Certificate of Registration, which marks the legal birth of the company. The Certificate of Registration shows the date of incorporation, the name of the company, and the registration number.

The two most important documents filed with the Registrar of Companies are the Memorandum of Association and the Articles of Association.

The Memorandum of Association defines the relationship between the company and external parties. In particular, it states the company's objectives. It is illegal for a company to exceed those objectives. For example, a company registered with the objective of dealing in wine and spirits would be acting illegally if it were to set up a business as electrical engineers. The Memorandum of Association also state the capital of the company. A company is not entitled to raise capital in excess of the amount stated in the capital clause, without seeking an amendment to that clause. The balance sheet is required to show the issued share capital, and a supplementary note must disclose the authorized capital and in this way indicate what further margin is left for raising additional capital.

The Articles of Association regulate the internal affairs of a company. They define the rights of various classes of shareholders, the rules for the conduct of meetings, and the rights and duties of members and officers of the company. The Companies Act 1985 has a model form of Articles of Association, which most companies adopt sometimes with minor modifications.

Companies fall into two classifications:

(a) Public limited companies, which consist of companies which issue shares to the public and comprise essentially companies quoted on the Stock Exchange. Public companies are required to disclose their status by adding the suffice 'plc' behind their name.

(b) Private companies, which do not issue shares to the public at large but restrict the issue of shares. The comprise a large number of companies operated by individuals and families for their own private benefit. Private companies are required to disclose their status by adding the suffice 'ltd' behind their name.

Share capital and shareholders' equity

The capital of the company is divided into separate units known as shares. Thus, the capital of a company may be 100,000 shares of £1 each representing a total of £100,000. A shareholder who has purchased and paid for his share cannot be called upon to contribute further to the company's capital in respect of his shareholding. In effect, his liability to contribute to the company's debts in the case of insolvency is limited to the amount which he has agreed to pay for his shares. This is the strict meaning of limited liability. Accordingly, the most important difference in this context between the owner of a business which is not a limited liability company and the owner of shares in a limited liability company is that the former is liable at law for the debts of his business to the extent of his personal property whereas the latter is liable at law only to the extent of the amount unpaid, if any, on the shares which he holds.

Whereas shares are initially purchased from a company at the price stipulated by the company, all subsequent transactions in these shares take place between buyers and sellers usually through the medium of a stock exchange, which is a formalized market for share dealings. Thus, a company may make a public offer of a parcel of 100,000 shares at a price of £1 each, and will receive £100,000 from various buyers. Subsequently, however, the market price of the shares may rise to £2, which is the price which an existing shareholder will obtain if he seeks to sell his shares to another person through the Stock Exchange.

From the foregoing, the shareholders' equity consists essentially of the total sum which the company has itself received in respect of the shares which have been issued and of the net profit of the company which has not been paid out to shareholders as dividends.

Types of shares

The flexibility introduced into the capitalization of a company by the subdivision of the capital into shares of small denominations is further enhanced by the ability of a company to attach different rights to these shares. As a result, shares having different rights appeal to different classes of investors and broaden the base from which the company may acquire its capital.

The main types of shares are:

(a) Preference shares.
(b) Ordinary shares.
(c) Deferred shares.

In the United Kingdom, shares of whatever class must be stated in terms of a fixed nominal amount, irrespective of the price which the company may have obtained for such shares. The net profit of the company which it is decided to distribute to shareholders as dividends may be declared as a percentage of the nominal value of the shares or as x pence per share. In the United States, however, shares are not required to have a nominal or par value. They are issued as shares of no par value. As a result, such shares simply represent a unit of ownership and are issued and recorded at whatever price is decided upon by the directors.

Preference shares

Preference shares are preferential over other classes of shares in a company in respect of profit distribution, and usually as regards the repayment of capital when a company is dissolved. The main feature of preference shares is their entitlement to a fixed rate of dividend before any dividends are declared in favour of other classes of shareholders. When a company is wound up, preference shareholders receive the refund of the capital they have subscribed immediately after preferred, secured and unsecured creditors have been paid, if the preference shares are preferential as to capital as well as profit.

Preference shares generally fall into three main classes:

(a) *Cumulative preference shares*. Where the net profit of a company is insufficient in any year to declare a dividend in favour of holders of cumulative preference shares, the right of such shareholders to receive a dividend in respect of that year is carried over and accumulates until the company has sufficient net profit to pay the accumulated dividend entitlement.

   Preference shares are now deemed to be cumulative unless expressly issued by a company as non-cumulative preference shares.

(b) *Participating preference shares*. In addition to being cumulative, preference shares may also participate in the net profit available for distribution after other shareholders have received a stated dividend percentage. Thus, such preference shareholders receive not only their fixed dividend entitlement which will be cumulative, but in a good year will also receive a further dividend after ordinary and deferred shareholders, as may be, have received a dividend. For example, the conditions of issue attached to participating preference shares may state that an extra 1% dividend, as well as the fixed dividend, will be paid to participating preference shareholders for every 1% by which a dividend declared for the ordinary shareholders exceeds 12%. In this way, preference shareholders can benefit from their investment in successful companies.

Business opportunities may arise and induce a company to seek further capital. Where such capital is needed only for a reasonably short period but where it would be disadvantageous to undertake an indefinite commitment to pay dividends, a company may issue redeemable shares.

(c) *Redeemable preference shares*. A number of restrictions are attached to the issue of redeemable preference shares, for example, the shares must be stated to be redeemable, the earliest date of redemption must also be stated and the terms of redemption must be clearly given. Moreover, redeemable preference shares may be redeemed only out of the proceeds of a fresh issue of shares or from a reserve created by the company.

The attraction of preference shares from the viewpoint of an investor is that they offer a less risky investment than ordinary shares, but less opportunity for gains. They do not usually carry voting rights, except when the non-payment of dividend or alteration of class rights entitles them to vote at a meeting of preference shareholders.

Ordinary shares

Ordinary shares are the most important class of shares, for not only do they represent the risk capital invested in a company but they carry voting rights conferring control over the company's affairs through the right to elect its directors.

Ordinary shareholders are also entitled to the balance of the company's net profit after payment of interest on loans, taxation and dividends on preference shares. It is the usual practice for companies to declare only a portion of the net profit as dividends and to retain the balance of undistributed profit to provide further capital for investment purposes. The dividend is recommended by the board of directors to the shareholders at their annual general meeting, and paid once it has been approved by vote.

As is the practice with other types of shares, ordinary shares issued in the United Kingdom bear a fixed nominal value. The company may, nevertheless, attach any selling price to such shares, save that shares may not be issued at a discount. There is only one exception to this rule, and it requires the consent of the court.

It is quite commonplace for shares to be issued at a premium, that is, at a price in excess of the fixed nominal value. Following the Companies Act 1981 ordinary shares may now be issued as redeemable ordinary shares.

Example 2

Unac Limited issued 100,000 ordinary shares having a nominal value of £1 each at a price of £2.50 each. All the shares offered for sale were subscribed for by the public.

The result of this sale is shown in the books of Unac Limited as follows:

	£	£
Debit cash	250,000	
Credit ordinary share capital		100,000
Credit share premium account		150,000

It should be noted that the ordinary share capital account is credited only with the nominal value of the shares issued, and that the premium received in excess of this value is credited to a share premium account. Any dividend subsequently paid by the company is declared as a percentage of the nominal value of the shares or as xp per share.

Deferred shares

These are shares which have the opposite characteristics of preference shares, for holders of these shares are not entitled to receive dividends until ordinary shareholders have received a stated dividend percentage. Moreover, in the event of a liquidation, ordinary shareholders usually also have a priority as regards the return of capital.

Deferred shares are now seldom issued. Their original intention was to indicate confidence in the company, and for this reason they tended to be subscribed for by the founder members or the management of the company. For this reason, they are sometimes referred to as 'founders' or 'management' shares. Under conditions of prosperity, holders of deferred shares received considerable benefits in the form of a high dividend rate, and in some cases, the voting rights attached to such shares gave their holders virtual control over the company. Deferred shares may now be issued as redeemable deferred shares.

Share capital transactions

Share capital transactions may be regarded as being limited to the issue of shares. The accounting equation holds good as shown in Example 2 above, even when shares are issued at a premium. This section is concerned with the application of the accounting equation to share capital transactions and will be limited to what is considered to be relevant to identify the results of the issue of capital.

The formation of a company by the acquisition of a business

Companies often originate from partnerships or from the business of sole traders. It is common practice for the business of the partnership or of the sole trader to be sold as a going concern to a company formed specifically to take over the business. The arrangement in these cases is for the company to take over the assets and liabilities of the business in return for the issue of shares.

Example 3

Having successfully operated and expanded his business for some years, Ronald Champion has decided to form a limited liability company and to transfer his business to the company. As at the date of transfer the balance sheet of the business is as follows:

Ronald Champion
Balance sheet as at 1 April 19X7

	£	£
Capital		54,700
Represented by:		
Fixed assets at written down value		36,800
Current assets	29,200	
less: Current liabilities	11,300	17,900
		54,700

The new company is to be called Ronchamp Limited. The authorized share capital is to amount to £100,000 consisting of 10,000 12% preference shares of £1 each and 90,000 ordinary shares of £1 each.

The business is to be transferred to Ronchamp Ltd for £54,700 and Ronald Champion is to receive all the preference shares which the company is authorized to issue and the balance of the consideration in the form of ordinary shares. In order to conform with the requirements of the Companies Act 1985 that the minimum number of shareholders in a company shall be two, he transfers 100 of the ordinary shares to his wife. In this connection, it may be noted that companies which issue shares to the public at large, must also have at least two shareholders.

Ronchamp Limited

	£	£
Fixed assets		36,800
Current assets	29,200	
less: Current liabilities	11,300	
Net current assets		17,900
		54,700
Share capital		
12% preference shares of £1 each		10,000
Ordinary shares of £1 each		44,700
		54,700

Example 4

Suppose that the business of Ronald Champion in the previous example had included under fixed assets premises at cost of £22,000. Assume that the market value of these premises was £29,500. A revaluation of these premises immediately prior to transfer of the business to Ronchamp Ltd would have been effected in the books of Ronald Champion as follows:

	£	£
Debit premises account	7,500	
Credit capital account		7,500

being the increased value of the premises on revaluation.

The result of the revaluation would have been that the assets sold to the company would have been increased in value by £7,500 and Champion would have received a further 7,500 ordinary shares of £1 each.

Goodwill

It frequently happens that the vendor of a business believes that the value of the business transferred to a company is greater than that shown in his books. In Example 4, this increased value is due to a higher market value than that recorded. However, even after specific assets have been revaluated to take account of their current market value, the vendor may still insist that the global value of the business is higher than that shown by a market valuation of its individual assets. This additional value is referred to as goodwill. Statement of Standard Accounting Practice No. 22, *Accounting for Goodwill* deals with the accounting procedure relating to goodwill.

In accounting, goodwill is treated as an intangible asset associated with the total or global value of all other assets employed by a business. Goodwill often arises as an element of added value which is specific to the business, and is often taken to represent some trading advantages which it enjoys. For this reason, goodwill is often associated with marketing advantages in the form of the goodwill of a clientele, a trade mark or a monopoly or quasi-monopoly position in the market. It is usually recognized when businesses are sold or acquired. Thus, if in the course of negotiating a price at which a business is to be acquired, the company pays a sum which is greater than the market value of the net assets, the difference is referred to as goodwill and is shown as a separate asset.

One of the reasons why ordinary shares may be issued initially at a premium is related to goodwill. Under normal circumstances, it might be thought that if a company issues a share having a nominal of £1, the buyer expects to acquire a share having a 'real' value of £1. Companies are able to issue shares at a price higher than the nominal value because such shares have a value that is higher than £1.

Example 5
Paul Emmerson, a wholesale clothing merchant, wishes to retire and has been offered the sum of £128,000 for his business by the Handbridge Clothing Co. Ltd. Emmerson's balance sheet as at 30 June 19X5 is as follows:

Balance sheet as at 30 June 19X5

	£
Fixed assets	73,040
Net current assets	21,320
	94,360
Capital	94,360

All the assets in the balance sheet are deemed to be correctly valued and Emmerson accepts the offer.

Handbridge Clothing Company Ltd had been formed for the purpose of carrying on the business once Emmerson had accepted the offer. The share capital issued was 128,000 ordinary shares of £1 each and so immediately before transfer the balance sheet of the company was as follows:

Handbridge Clothing Company Ltd
Balance sheet as at 30 June 19X5

	£
Cash at Bank	128,000
Share capital	
Ordinary shares of £1 each	128,000

Immediately after the transfer of the business to the company, the balance sheet of Handbridge Clothing Company Ltd would appear as follows:

Handbridge Clothing Company Ltd
Balance sheet as at 30 June 19X5

		£
Fixed assets		
Intangible—Goodwill		30,640
Tangible		73,040
		103,680
Net current assets (21,320 + 3,000 cash)		24,320
		128,000
Share capital		
128,000 ordinary shares of £1 each		128,000

When a partnership is formed into a limited company it must be noted that in deciding how many shares are to be given in exchange for each partner's equity in the partnership, any surplus on valuation, and this includes goodwill, will be credited to the partners' current accounts in proportion to their net-income-sharing ratios. Any partner's equity in the partnership consists of both the capital and the current account.

Loan capital

So far, it has been assumed that the capital provided to a company is obtained from shareholders in return for shares in the company. However, many firms—particularly larger firms—tend to finance a significant proportion of their capital needs by means of long-term borrowing. Such borrowings exclude routine overdraft facilities from banks which are essentially short-term by nature.

Since shareholders have no liability for the debts of the company, except in so far as there may be an unpaid amount on the shares which they hold, safeguards are required to protect the interests of creditors. In this context, it should be stated that it is a rare occurrence to find a company which has outstanding calls in respect of issued shares. The first line of protection afforded to creditors is a limitation on the power to borrow which is found in the Memorandum and Articles of Association. Thus, the power to borrow money must be stated in the Memorandum of Association and the maximum limit of borrowing must be stated in the Memorandum of Association and the maximum limit of borrowing must be stipulated in the Articles of Association.

Although long-term borrowings may be obtained from financial institutions such as banks, the conventional method of obtaining long-term loan capital is by means of the issue of debentures. A debenture is a fixed interest security issued by a company, and is usually secured on the assets of the company. Unsecured debentures which are often described as unsecured notes, may be successfully issued by large companies.

Debentures are usually issued in larger monetary units than shares, frequently in £100 units. They are normally redeemable at clearly stated dates and on predetermined terms. Occasionally, they are redeemable by a right of conversion into shares, when they are known as convertible debentures.

The security provided is either by creating a fixed charge on the specific assets of the company or by creating a floating charge over all its assets. Both charges are the result of a legal process, usually associated with drawing up a trust deed on behalf of the debenture holders. The creation of a fixed charge identifies specific assets which are reserved as security: a floating charge does not identify any particular assets and only crystallizes when the company is in breach of a condition of the trust deed. The security granted to debenture holders under either a fixed charge or a floating charge is realizable by the trustees for the debenture holders, and the assets charge as security may be sold on behalf of the debenture holders. This extreme situation would only usually arise in the case of an insolvency.

The conditions attached to the debentures are stated in the trust deed, which provides not only for the rate of interest payable, the date of redemption, etc., but also grants the trustees for the debenture holders power to act on behalf of the body of the debenture holders, even to the extent of calling meetings of the debenture holders, and conduct negotiations with the company on their behalf over any question affecting their interests. The power of the trustee is clearly defined in the trust deed.

It is important to note the difference between the fixed rate of dividend payable in respect of a preference share and the fixed rate of interest payable in respect of debentures. This difference stems from the fact that a preference shareholder is in fact a member of the company and the owner of a share in the company. Hence, the preference dividend is a distribution of profit. By contrast, a debenture holder is not a member of the company but a creditor of the company whose rights against the company are stated in the form of a debenture. The debenture interest is a charge against the company's profit and must be treated as an expense in the process of profit determination.

The profit and loss account of a company

The basic principles associated with the determination of profit apply to all forms of business organizations. Hence, the rules for aggregating revenues and expenses and classifying assets and liabilities are the same for a company as they are for a sole trader or a partnership. Equally, the accounting equation provides the fundamental logic to the presentation of company profit and loss accounts and balance sheets. Such marginal modifications as are required to reflect the separate legal entity of a company do not disturb the financial accounting principles which have been examined so far, or the conventions attached to the application of these principles.

The appropriation of profit

Once the net profit has been determined, a company proceeds to appropriate this profit to the following purposes:

(a) Taxation.
(b) Dividends.
(c) Reserves.

Taxation

Companies are liable to corporation tax on their net profit. The exact amount of the corporation tax assessment will be determined by the Inland Revenue after it has received the annual accounts and calculated the corporation tax due and payable. At the close of the accounting year, the company makes provision for corporation tax on the net profit on the basis of its own estimate of the amount due. When the corporation tax assessment is eventually received, any difference between the provision for corporation tax created and the corporation tax due is adjusted through the corporation tax account.

The profit and loss account shows the provision for corporation tax established in relation to the net profit figure.

Example 6

The profit and loss account for the year ended 31 December 19X6 for Paddock Ltd showed a profit on ordinary activities before taxation of £246,000. Paddock Ltd's estimate of corporation tax due was £118,000, and a provision for corporation tax in that sum was made. During the year ended 31 December 19X6, the formal assessment to corporation tax for the year ended 31 December 19X5 was received and showed that corporation tax for that year had been overprovided by £10,000. This information will be shown in the profit and loss account for the year ended 31 December 19X6 in the following form:

Paddock Ltd
Profit and loss account for the year ended 31 December 19X6

(extract)	£000	£000
Profit on ordinary activities before taxation		246
Taxation on profit on ordinary activities		
Corporation tax for the year	118	
Overprovided in previous year	(10)	108
Profit on ordinary activities after tax		138

Dividends

The appropriation of profit to dividends is effected by formal declarations of dividend in favour of shareholders of different classes. For example, where preference shares as well as ordinary shares have been issued, there will be separate dividend declarations in their favour reflecting the dividend rights which are associated with these classes of shares.

The conditions of issue of preference shares entitle them to a fixed percentage rate of dividend to be paid out of profits before any dividends are declared in favour of ordinary shareholders.

Profits remaining after taxation and preference dividends have been met may be distributed to ordinary shareholders. Articles of association may allow the Board of Directors to declare interim dividends to ordinary shareholders during the accounting year in anticipation of the final net profit. The final dividend rate to ordinary shareholders takes the form of a proposed ordinary dividend presented to the Annual General Meeting of Shareholders, which ordinary shareholders are asked to approve. Ordinary shareholders do not have the power to increase the rate of dividend proposed by the Board of Directors. The interim and the final dividends to ordinary shareholders amount to a portion of the net profit available for distribution and are normally expressed as a rate of pence per share. The Board of Directors has powers to appropriate net profits to reserves for the purposes of financing the activities of the company, and to limit the proportion distributed to shareholders. The only exception to their powers in this regard are the rights of preference shareholders to the payment of the rate of annual rate of dividend to which they are entitled in terms of the conditions of issue of these shares.

Example 7

The issued share capital of Edcomm plc consists of 500,000 preference shares of £1 each having a right to an annual dividend rate of 12%, and 12 million ordinary shares of 25p each. The preference dividend is paid in two instalments of 30 June and at 31 December each year. The company's financial year runs to 31 December. In the year ended 31 December 19X7, an interim dividend was paid to ordinary shareholders at the rate of 2.5p per share on 27 August 19X7, and a final dividend of 4.0p per share was proposed at the close of the year for approval at the Annual General Meeting due to take place in May 19X8.

The accounting entries relating to these dividends are as follows:

(a) Preference dividend	Debit	Credit
19X7	£000	£000
June 30 Preference dividend account	30	
Bank		30
Dec 31 Preference dividend account	30	
Bank		30
Dec 31 Profit and loss account	60	
Preference dividend account		60

(b) Ordinary share dividend		
19X7		
Aug 27 Ordinary dividend account	300	
Bank account		300
Payment of interim dividend of 2.5p per share		
Dec 31 Ordinary dividend account	480	
Dividend payable account		480
Proposed final dividend of 4.0p per share		
Dec 31 Profit and loss account	780	
Ordinary dividend account		780

The proposed dividend of £480,000 would appear as a current liability in the balance sheet presented to the shareholders and the full dividend would appear in the profit and loss account for the year end.

Reserves

The model balance sheet given in the Companies Act 1985 requires capital and reserves to be shown in published accounts as follows:

	£
1. Called up share capital	x
2. Share premium account	x
3. Revaluation reserve	x
4. Other reserves	x
5. Profit and loss account	x
	x

The share premium account records premiums arising from the issue of shares at a premium. The revaluation reserve arises from the accounting procedures for revaluing fixed assets, and crediting the increased value to the revaluation reserve. The profit and loss account represents the accumulated surplus accruing to shareholders out of which dividends may be paid to them should the directors consider it prudent to make such distributions and should adequate liquid funds be available out of which such distributions may be paid.

The balance sheet of a company

The only difference between the balance sheet of a company and other forms of business organizations such as sole traders and partnerships relates to the manner in which the ownership in the company is portrayed. As will be shown below, the shareholders' equity consists of the share capital account plus the various reserves representing a cumulative total of retained earnings.

It was noted in the previous section that reserves may be created as appropriations of the net profit of a company. These reserves are described under the heading of general reserves. It is permissible for a company to reduce these reserves, if it wishes, by the declaration of dividends or the distribution of what are termed 'bonus shares'. The latter are shares issued freely to existing shareholders and are, in effect, paid out of undistributed earnings. The issue of 'bonus shares', therefore, circumvents the declaration and payment of dividends out of retained earnings and the reinvestment of those dividends in shares of the company.

In addition to reserves created out of profit, a company may also have capital reserves. These reserves are treated, in general, as if they were part of the capital of the company and, therefore, not available for distribution to shareholders as dividends. Capital reserves include the share premium account, which is the excess over the nominal value of shares paid to the company in respect of issued shares, and the capital redemption reserve which represents the amount equal to the value of redeemable preference shares actually redeemed and not covered by a fresh issue of shares.

The disclosure of accounting information

The amount of information which should be contained in the accounts laid by the board of directors before shareholders has always been a contentious issue. The view which company directors and managers have traditionally held is that the disclosure of information is potentially harmful to the interests of the company and its shareholders if used by competitors. There is little evidence of any real substance in this view and competitors generally know a great deal more of the company's affairs than could possibly be revealed in financial accounts. Some critics of existing legislation argue that the restriction of information disclosure serves rather to protect the interests of directors and management rather than those of shareholders and the investing public at large.

In effect, the history of the development of legal obligations upon companies to disclose accounting information is a history of a conflict between businessmen operating as company directors and those who have provided capital in the form of subscriptions for shares and loans to the company.

Parliament has intervened to require the minimum disclosure of certain transactions and items in the accounts of companies. The reason underlying this minimum disclosure requirement may best be explained in terms of a demand that the accounts should be relevant for the purpose of indicating that the directors have properly discharged their functions as stewards of the shareholders' property and that they have honestly discharged their obligations as such. It should be stressed that this requirement does not extend to a requirement that the accounts should be relevant to assessing their efficiency as managers of the company's business. In this respect, shareholders have to form their own judgement of the effectiveness with which their affairs have been handled by the directors. Accordingly, the disclosure requirements are essentially addressed to establishing that these affairs have been handled in an honest manner.

Although companies are free to disclose as much information as they wish to shareholders, the general tendency as far as financial information is concerned is to satisfy merely the minimum disclosure requirements established by law.

The Companies Acts 1967, 1976, 1980 and 1981, which were consolidated by the 1985 Acts, show a considerable increase in the minimum disclosure requirements imposed upon companies. All companies are required to lodge annually a profit and loss account and a balance sheet with the Registrar of Companies. Any member of the public is able to examine these documents upon payment of a small fee. To protect small and medium-sized companies from giving away too much information to persons other than their own shareholders, the Companies Act 1985 allow them to file shortened financial reports, which limit the amount of information that may come into public notice. Large companies, however, have to file with the Registrar of Companies the same information that is given to shareholders in annual financial reports.

The three categories of companies that have been established are as follows:

(a) Small-sized company, defined as one which satisfies at least two of the following three conditions:
  (i) has a turnover up to £1.4 million,
  (ii) has gross assets up to £0.7 million,
  (iii) has average employees per week up to 50 employees.
(b) Medium-sized company, defined as one which satisfies at least two of the following three conditions:
  (i) has a turnover up to £5.75 million,
  (ii) has gross assets up to £2.8 million,
  (iii) has average employees per week up to 250 employees.
(c) Large company, defined as one which satisfies at least two of the following three conditions:
  (i) has a turnover of £5.75 million,
  (ii) has gross assets over £2.8 million,
  (iii) has average employees per week over 250 employees.

The Companies Act 1985 has developed the information disclosure requirements to the point of prescribing models for the presentation of the balance sheet and the profit and loss account.

Two alternative formats are proposed for the balance sheet—one being a vertical presentation (format 1) and the other a horizontal presentation (format 2). Notes to the balance sheet that explain the amounts stated thereon are required in both cases. The vertical presentation (format 1) has been widely followed. The extent of the information disclosure required for companies may be judged from the reproduction below of the format 1 model.

Companies Act 1985: format for vertical balance sheet

		£	£	£
A	CALLED UP SHARE CAPITAL NOT PAID*			X
B	FIXED ASSETS			
	I Intangible assets			
	1. Development costs	X		
	2. Concessions, patents, licences, trade marks and similar rights and assets	X		
	3. Goodwill	X		
	4. Payments on account	X̲	X	

---

* These items may be shown in either of the positions indicated.

	£	£	£
II Tangible assets			
1. Land and buildings	X		
2. Plant and machinery	X		
3. Fixtures, fittings, tools and equipment	X		
4. Payments on account and assets in course of construction	<u>X</u>	X	
III Investments			
1. Shares in group companies	X		
2. Loans to group companies	X		
3. Shares in related companies	X		
4. Loans to related companies	X		
5. Other investments other than loans	X		
6. Other loans	X		
7. Own shares	<u>X</u>	<u>X</u>	
			X
C CURRENT ASSETS			
I Stocks			
1. Raw materials and consumables	X		
2. Work in progress	X		
3. Finished goods and goods for resale	X		
4. Payments on account	<u>X</u>	X	
II Debtors			
1. Trade debtors	X		
2. Amounts owed by group companies	X		
3. Amounts owed by related companies	X		
4. Other debtors	X		
5. Called up share capital not paid*	X		
6. Prepayments and accured income*	<u>X</u>	X	
III Investments			
1. Shares in group companies	X		
2. Own shares	X		
3. Other investments	<u>X</u>	X	
IV Cash at bank and in hand	<u>X</u>	X	
D PREPAYMENTS AND ACCRUED INCOME*	<u>X</u>	—	

* These items may be shown in either of the positions indicated.

		£	£	£
E	CREDITORS: AMOUNTS FALLING DUE WITHIN ONE YEAR			
	1. Debenture loans	X		
	2. Bank loans and overdrafts	X		
	3. Payments received on account	X		
	4. Trade creditors	X		
	5. Bills of exchange payable	X		
	6. Amounts owed to group companies	X		
	7. Amounts owed to related companies	X		
	8. Other creditors including taxation and social security	X		
	9. Accruals and deferred income*	X		
			(X)	
F	NET CURRENT ASSETS (LIABILITIES)			X
G	TOTAL ASSETS LESS CURRENT LIABILITIES			X
H	CREDITORS: AMOUNTS FALLING DUE AFTER MORE THAN ONE YEAR			
	1. Debenture loans	X		
	2. Bank loans and overdrafts	X		
	3. Payments received on account	X		
	4. Trade creditors	X		
	5. Bills of exchange payable	X		
	6. Amounts owed to group companies	X		
	7. Amounts owed to related companies	X		
	8. Other creditors including taxation and social security	X		
	9. Accruals and deferred income*	X		
			X	
I	PROVISIONS FOR LIABILITIES AND CHARGES			
	1. Pensions and similar obligations	X		
	2. Taxation, including deferred taxation	X		
	3. Other provisions	X		
			X	
J	ACCRUALS AND DEFERRED INCOME*		X	
				X
				X

* These items may be shown in either of the positions indicated.

	£	£	£
K CAPITAL AND RESERVES			
I Called up share capital			X
II Share premium account			X
III Revaluation reserve			X
IV Other reserves:			
1. Capital redemption reserve	X		
2. Reserve for own shares	X		
3. Reserves provided for by the articles of association	X		
4. Other reserves	X		
			X
V Profit and loss account			X
			£X

The Companies Act 1985 provides two horizontal and two vertical formats for the presentation of the profit and loss account. Essentially, the two formats may be distinguished by the way in which costs are analysed. Format 1 analyses costs by type of operation, while format 2 analyses costs by type of expenditure. The vertical formats of these two different types of analyses are given below.

Format 1   Operational format

	£	£
1. Turnover		X
2. Cost of sales		(X)
3. Gross profit (or loss)		X
4. Distribution costs	X	
5. Administrative expenses	X	
		(X)
		X
6. Other operating income		X
		X
7. Income from shares in group companies	X	
8. Income from shares in related companies	X	
9. Income from other fixed asset investments	X	
10. Other interest receivable and similar income	X	
		X
		X
11. Amounts written off investments	X	
12. Interest payable and similar charges	X	
		(X)
Profit on ordinary activities		X
13. Tax on profit (or loss) on ordinary activities		(X)

	£	£
14. Profit (or loss) on ordinary activities after taxation		X
15. Extraordinary income	X	
16. Extraordinary charges	(X)	
17. Extraordinary profit (or loss)	X	
18. Tax on extraordinary profit (or loss)	(X)	
		X
		X
19. Other taxes not shown under the above items		(X)
20. Profit (or loss) for the financial year		£X

Format 2   Type of expenditure format

	£	£	£
1. Turnover			X
2. Change in stocks of finished goods and work in progress			(X)
3. Own work capitalized			X
4. Other operating income			X
			X
5. (a) Raw materials and consumables	X		
(b) Other external charges	X		
		X	
6. Staff costs:			
(a) Wages and salaries	X		
(b) Social security costs	X		
(c) Other pension costs	X		
		X	
7. (a) Depreciation and other amounts written off tangible and intangible fixed assets	X		
(b) Exceptional amounts written off current assets	X		
		X	
8. Other operating charges		X	
			(X)
			X
9. Income from shares in group companies		X	
10. Income from shares in related companies		X	
11. Income from other fixed asset investments		X	
12. Other interest receivable and similar income		X	
			X
			X
13. Amounts written off investments		X	

		£	£
14.	Interest payable and similar charges	<u>X</u>	
			(X)
	Profit on ordinary activities		X
15.	Tax on profit (or loss) on ordinary activities		(X)
16.	Profit (or loss) on ordinary activities after taxation		X
17.	Extraordinary income	X	
18.	Extraordinary charges	(X)	
19.	Extraordinary profit (or loss)	X	
20.	Tax on extraordinary profit (or loss)	(X)	
			X
			X
21.	Other taxes not shown under the above items		(X)
22.	Profit (or loss) for the financial year		£X

The Companies Act 1985 requires disclosure of the following items on the face of the profit and loss account although they do not appear in the formats:

(a) Profit and loss account on ordinary activities before taxation,
(b) Transfers to and from reserves, and
(c) The aggregate amount of dividends paid and proposed.

Example 8
The trial balance of Trelon plc as at 31 December 19X1 is given below, and is used to prepare the profit and loss account for the year ended 31 December 19X1 and the balance sheet as at that date.

Trial balance as at 31 December 19X1

	£	£
Ordinary share capital		500,000
9% Preference shares		100,000
12% Debentures		50,000
Share premium		35,000
Retained earnings (profit and loss account)		137,000
Fixed assets	650,000	
Provision for depreciation at 1 January 19X1		214,500
Stock	482,250	
Debtors and creditors	280,000	190,550

	£	£
Provision for doubtful debts		10,450
Cash in hand	3,650	
Bank overdraft		35,450
Purchases and sales	1,160,500	1,610,500
Wages and salaries	62,750	
Rent, rates and insurances	46,100	
Administration expenses	19,450	
Lighting and heating	38,450	
Advertising	56,300	
Bad debts	17,050	
Packing materials	28,400	
Carriage on sales	32,050	
Bank interest	3,500	
Debenture interest	3,000	
	2,883,450	2,883,450

The following additional information is available:

(1) Stock at 31 December 19X1 was valued at £568,250.

(2) The authorized share capital of Trelon plc consists of 1,250,000 ordinary shares and 150,000 9% preference shares of £1 each.

(3) The provision for doubtful debts is to be maintained at 5% of the total of debtors.

(4) Rates of £4,250 and insurance of £1,550 are prepaid.

(5) Provision for depreciation for the year for fixed assets amounts to £57,500.

(6) The following expenses have been incurred in the year ended 31 December 19X1 and have not been included in the trial balance figures:

Rent	£5,500
Telephone	£650 (part of the administration expense)
Audit fee	£1,250
Debenture interest	£3,000

(7) The preference dividend and a proposed ordinary dividend of 10% are to be provided for.

(8) Taxation is estimated to be £37,000.

(9) The debentures are secured against land and buildings in the fixed assets and are redeemable on 1 January 1995.

The first step is to prepare a fully detailed profit and loss account.

Trelon plc
Profit and loss account for the year ended 31 December 19X1

	£	£	£	£
Sales				1,610,500
less Cost of sales				
Opening stock			482,250	
Purchases			1,160,500	
			1,642,750	
Closing stock			568,250	1,074,500
Gross profit				536,000
less Selling and administration expense				
Packing		28,400		
Carriage outwards		32,050		
Advertising		56,300	116,750	
Administration expenses				
Wages and salaries		62,750		
General		20,100		
Audit fee		1,250	84,100	
Establishment expenses				
Rent, rates and insurance		45,800		
Lighting and heating		38,450		
Depreciation		57,500	141,750	
Financial expenses				
Bad debts	17,050			
Provision for doubtful debts	3,550	20,600		
Bank interest		3,500		
Debenture interest		6,000	30,100	372,700
Net profit before tax				163,300
Provision for taxation				37,000
Net profit after tax				126,300
Retained profit at 1 January 19X1 brought forward				137,000
				263,300
Dividends: 9% Preference			9,000	
Proposed ordinary at 10%			50,000	59,000
Retained profit carried forward				204,300

From this detailed profit and loss account the following condensed profit and loss account is prepared suitable for publications to shareholders.

Trelon plc
Profit and loss account for the year ended 31 December 19X1

	£	£
Turnover		1,610,500
Cost of sales		1,074,500
Gross profit		536,000
Distribution costs	116,750	
Administrative expenses	246,450	363,200
Operating profit		172,800
Interest charges		9,500
Profit on ordinary activities before taxation		163,300
Taxation on profit on ordinary activities		37,000
Profit on ordinary activities after taxation		126,300
Retained earnings brought forward		137,000
		263,300
Dividends: 9% Preference	9,000	
Proposed ordinary at 10%	50,000	59,000
Retained profit carried forward		204,300

The balance sheet does not differ much in detail between the full internal version and the prescribed disclosure model.

Trelon plc
Balance sheet as at 31 December 19X1

	£	£
Fixed assets		378,000
Current assets		
Stock	568,250	
Debtors	266,000	
Prepayments	5,800	
Cash in hand	3,650	
	843,700	
Creditors: amounts falling due within one year	332,400	
Net current assets		511,300
		889,300
Creditors: amounts falling due after more than one year		50,000
		839,300
Share capital and reserves		
Called up share capital		600,000
Share premium account		35,000
Profit and loss account		204.300
		839,300

Working notes:
Profit and loss account

	£	£
Distribution costs		
Packing	28,400	
Carriage outwards	32,050	
Advertising	56,300	116,750
Administrative expenses		
Wages and salaries	62,750	
General	20,100	
Audit fee	1,250	
Rent, rates and insurance	45,800	
Lighting and heating	38,450	
Depreciation	57,500	
Bad debts	17,050	
Provision for doubtful debts	3,550	246,450

	Cost	Depreciation	Net
Balance sheet			
Fixed assets	650,000	568,300	378,000

Creditors: amounts falling due within one year—	£
Creditors	190,550
Accrued expenses	10,400
Dividends	59,000
Provision for taxation	37,000
Bank overdraft	35,450
	332,400

Creditors: amounts falling due
after more than one year—
    12% Debenture (secured) redeemable
       1 January 1995   £50,000

Question 3

Frank Graine, a seed merchant, has received an offer for his business from a large agricultural supply company. His balance sheet as at 31 December 19X0 is as follows:

Balance sheet as at 31 December 19X0

	£	£
Fixed assets		
Freehold warehouse at cost		8,210
Warehouse fittings—written-down value		1,500
Motor vans—written-down value		6,350
		16,060
Current assets		
Stock	18,621	
Debtors	12,190	
Bank balance	3,547	
	34,358	
less Current liabilities	7,640	
Net current assets		26,718
		42,778
		£
Capital—F. Graine		42,778

After details had been examined, the following terms were decided upon: (i) Morgain plc, the buying company, would issue 15,000 ordinary shares of £1 each to Graine. The ordinary shares of Morgain plc are presently quoted on the Stock Exchange at £3 each, (ii) Morgain plc would take over all assets and liabilities except the bank balance. (iii) The value of the warehouse was to be taken as £13,500. (iv) Fittings were only valued at £1,250 and the vans at £6,000. (v) Inspection revealed that of the stock, seeds costing £890 had deteriorated and were worthless. (iv) Experience led Morgain plc to believe that £1,000 of the debts would not be recoverable. (vii) A creditor for £310 had been omitted.

Required
(a) Calculate the value of goodwill in the business as a result of the purchase.
(b) Show how much will appear in the share premium account of Morgain plc as a result of his purchase.
(c) Prepare a schedule of the assets and liabilities taken over by Morgain plc at the new values.
(d) Prepared a statement for Frank Graine showing the value to him of the business as a consequence of the offer.

Question 4
Owen and Arthur were trading in partnership as suppliers of sporting goods, sharing net income in the ratio of 6:4 respectively and allowing

interest on capital at the rate of 10% per annum. The trial balance at the close of the trading year is shown below:

Trial balance as at 30 September 19X7

	£	£
Capital account—Owen		9,000
Arthur		6,000
Current account—Owen		1,210
Arthur		462
Freehold shop at cost	12,300	
Fittings at cost	2,500	
Depreciation to 30 September 19X6		1,500
Delivery van at cost	3,800	
Depreciation to 30 September 19X6		1,520
Stock	4,632	
Advertising and stationery	750	
Accountancy fees	250	
Rates and insurances	1,480	
Assistant's wages	2,650	
Electricity	860	
Postages and telephone	734	
Motor expenses	1,648	
Purchases	58,124	
Creditors		1,625
Balance at bank and cash in hand	6,869	
Sales		85,962
Debtors	2,894	
Drawings for year—Owen	4,130	
Arthur	3,658	
	107,279	107,279

To ensure the continuity of the business in the event of the death of one partner, they propose to form a limited liability company under the name of Waverton (Sports) Limited and to transfer the business to that company. At the time when consideration is being given to this question, the partners have just completed a year's trading and wish to ascertain the net income of the partnership prior to proceeding with the formation of the company.

The following additional information is available:
(1) Closing stock at 30 September 19X7 is valued at cost at £5,321
(2) Rates prepaid amount to £360
(3) Electricity used and unrecorded is estimated at £74
(4) Depreciation is to be provided on the straight line method. Fittings are assumed to have a 10-year life and the delivery van a 5-year life. No scrap value is anticipated in either case.

For the purposes of the formation of the limited company, both Owen and Arthur agree that the value of the shop should be increased to £16,000 and that Waverton (Sports) Ltd should offer £35,000 to Owen and Arthur in ordinary shares of £1 each from their authorized share capital of £50,000.

Required

(a) Prepare a profit and loss account and appropriation statement for the year ended 30 September 19X7 for the partnership.
(b) Prepare a balance sheet as at 31 September 19X7 for the partnership.
(c) Prepare a statement showing how many shares Owen and Arthur receive respectively following the transfer of the business of Waverton (Sports) Ltd.
(d) Show the balance sheet of Waverton (Sports) Ltd after the transaction has been completed.

Question 5

The following balances were extracted from the ledger of Portlin plc at 30 June 19X4 after the profit and loss account for that year had been prepared and all the relevant adjustments had been made.

Balances as at 30 June 19X4

	£000
Freehold land and building at cost	1,600
Bank overdraft	1,360
Cash in hand	84
Stock	3,720
Creditors	928
10% Debentures	1,700
Dividends Proposed—8% Preference shares	80
10% Ordinary shares	300
Accrued expenses	120
General reserves (at 1 July 19X3—£400,000)	1,000
Share capital—1 million 9% Preference shares of £1 each	1,000
3 million Ordinary shares of £1 each	3,000
Investments at cost	740
Motor vehicles at cost	1,860
Provision for depreciation at 1 July 19X3	280
Plant and machinery at cost	3,748
Provision for depreciation at 1 July 19X3	604
Profit and loss account (at 1 July 19X3, £1,400,000)	1,640
Share premium	712
Sundry debtors	1,776

Required
(1) Prepare the balance sheet of Portlin Limited as at 30 June 19X4.
(2) Ascertain the net profit for the year.

Notes
(1) The authorized share capital consist of 2 million 8% preference shares of £1 each and 6 million ordinary shares of £1 each.
(2) The investments should be shown as a separate asset and inserted on the balance sheet after fixed assets and before current assets.

Question 6

Following the completion of the accounting year on 31 March 19X5, a junior member of the Accounts Department has produced a rough set of accounts to show the results of the year for his company, Quillan plc. These are shown below.

Quillan plc
Profit and loss account year ended 31 March 19X5

	£	£000		£000
Cost of sales		35,100	Turnover	59,500
Wages and salaries		6,300		
Administration expenses		4,550		
Motor expenses		7,450		
Depreciation				
Motors	650			
Fixtures and fittings	55	705		
Advertising		475		
Audit fee		175		
Debenture interest		160		
Preference dividend		525		
Surplus for year		4,060		
		59,500		59,500

Balance Sheet as at 31 March 19X5

	£000		£000
Ordinary share capital	10,000	Freehold land and buildings	8,500
Preference shares	10,000	Fixtures and fittings	2,060
8% Debentures (1990/1995)	2,000	Motor vehicles	1,265
Creditors	9,100	Debtors	16,995
Provision for doubtful debts	725	Stock	10,300
Profit and loss account	8,605	Balance at bank	5,715
General reserve	4,500	Cash in hand	95
	44,930		44,930

The following additional information is available:

(1) The nominal value of the company's shares was £1 each and the authorized share capital has been fully issued and paid.
(2) Additional fees of £6,000 are to be provided for the chairman of the company.
(3) A provision of £1,800,000 is to be made for Corporation Tax.
(4) The original cost of fixed assets is as follows:

	£000
(a) Freehold land and buildings	8,500
(b) Fixtures and fittings	3,230
(c) Motor vehicles	1,960

(5) The provision for doubtful debts should have been adjusted to £900,000.
(6) A dividend of 7% is proposed in respect of the ordinary shares.

Required
Redraft the profit and loss account and the balance sheet in a more useful and regular form, making such adjustments as are required in terms of the additional information given in notes (1) to (6) above.

Question 7
The following trial balance as at 30 September 19X0 relates to Linthal Limited, a wholesale food company.

Trial balance as at 30 September 19X0

	£	£
Ordinary shares of 25p fully paid		20,000
Profit and loss account		8,700
Fixtures and fittings at cost	7,400	
Provision for depreciation		2,600
Delivery vans at cost	10,800	
Provision for depreciation		3,240
Stock	6,390	
Purchases and sales	110,430	143,690
Rent and rates	5,500	
Advertising	1,400	
Lighting and heating	960	
Motor expenses	2,340	
Telephone and postages	930	
Salaries	14,000	
Directors' fees	6,000	
Debtors and creditors	11,210	7,480
Balance at bank	8,350	
	185,710	185,710

The following additional information is given:

(1) The closing stock was valued at cost at £9,430.
(2) Rates repaid amounted to £750.
(3) Telephone expenses due and not yet paid amounted to £130.
(4) Depreciation for the year to be provided as follows:

Delivery vans	£1,200
Fixtures and fittings	£600

(5) A dividend of 20% on the ordinary shares is proposed.
(6) The authorized share capital consisted of 100,000 ordinary shares of 25p each.

Required

Prepare a profit and loss account for the year ended 30 September 19X0 and a balance sheet as at that date.

Question 8

The balance sheet of Bargemon Limited, a wholesale company, as at 31 December 19X0 was as follows:

	Cost £	Depreciation £	£
Fixed assets	221,352	82,412	138,940
Current assets			
Stock		128,154	
Sundry debtors	103,046		
less Provision for doubtful debts	2,216	100,830	
Prepaid business expenses		1,086	
Cash at bank		19,722	
		249,792	
Creditors: amounts falling due due within one year			
Sundry creditors	82,558		
Business expenses accrued	3,446		
Proposed dividend	40,000	126,004	123,788
			262,728
Capital and reserves			
Called up share capital			200,000
Profit and loss account			62,728
			262,728

The following are the summarized transactions and other decisions of Bargemon Limited during the year 19X1:

(1) Sales on credit amounted to £526,016 and the cost of stock sold was £396,676.
(2) Sales returns amounted to £5,066 and the cost of the items (all taken back into stock) was £3,830.
(3) Debtors paid £460,674.
(4) Bad debts amounting to £1,952 were written off.
(5) In settling their accounts, debtors set off sums due to them as creditors amounting to £42,000.
(6) Purchases on credit amounted to £426,174 gross.
(7) Purchases returns were £4,008.
(8) Payments totalling £362,432 were made to creditors.
(9) Fixed assets were purchased for cash for £12,844.
(10) Fixed assets which originally cost £10,758 were sold for £1,000 cash, and the aggregate depreciation on them to the date of sale was £9,182. Any gain or loss on sale should be taken to the profit and loss account as a separate item.
(11) Depreciation on fixed assets (including those sold) amounted to £24,528.
(12) Business expenses of £67,410 were paid (including actuals at 31 December 19X0). At 31 December 19X1, prepaid business expenses amounted to £1,164 and business expenses accrued were £3,798.
(13) The provision for doubtful debts is to be made equal to £2,458.
(14) A physical check of the stock at 31 December 19X1 gave a value that was identical with the book value of stock at that date.
(15) The proposed dividend at 31 December 19X0 was paid during the year. At 31 December 19X1, the directors recommended that a dividend of £30,000 was to be paid out of the net profit and that the date of payment should be 28 February 19X2.
(16) The authorized share capital of Bargemon Limited consisted of 300,000 ordinary shares of £1 each.

Required
(1) Show the following accounts as they would appear in the ledger of Bargemon Limited for 19X1.

   (a) Cash at bank
   (b) Sundry debtors
   (c) Sundry creditors
   (d) Fixed assets at cost
   (e) Provision for depreciation of fixed assets

    (f) Gain or loss on sale of fixed assets

    (g) Provision for doubtful debts

    (h) Stock

    (i) Business expense

(2) Prepare a profit and loss account for the year ended 31 December 19X1 and a balance sheet as at that date.

6 Control of Working Capital

Financial accounting plays an important role in the financial management of organizations. Previous chapters have been concerned with the analysis of financial accounting method and its procedures for recording transactions, the use of recorded data for the determination of profit and the presentation of financial accounting information in the form of a profit and loss account and a balance sheet. Underlying this activity is the fundamental objective of accounting information, namely, its use and relevance to the financial management of organizations.

The financial management of an organization may be interpreted as being essentially concerned with the problem of control, and with using accounting data to establish standards of performance and to monitor results. Profitability, as measured by net profit, provides an overall measure of financial performance by which to assess the efficiency of use of organizational resources. Financial accounting records are critically important for the control of assets and liabilities. Financial statements in the form of profit and loss accounts and balance sheets provide the basis for the accountability of business managers to shareholders and investors.

The purpose of this chapter is to examine specifically the application of financial accounting data for the control of working capital. In a very real sense, the management of working capital is central to profitability for it is concerned with the control of the financial resources committed to supporting current levels of operations. Thus, it includes the control of stock, debtors and cash as well as the control of short-term indebtedness to creditors. In addition to being critically important to profitability, the control of working capital is centrally important for the financial stability and solvency of a business enterprise. Thus, the failure to control the level of short-term debt in relation to the level of available funds may rapidly produce a situation in which the firm could be made insolvent by its inability to meet its debts.

The control of working capital requires additional financial accounting procedures. In particular, to facilitate the control of large numbers of debtor and creditor accounts, use is made of control accounts for providing a central point of reference and control. In order to explain the procedures underlying the entries to control accounts, reference will be made to the journal as an originating source of data.

This chapter contains the following topics:

The journal

The concept of working capital

The control of debtors

The control of creditors

Stock control

Funds flow and cash flow accounting.

The journal

It has been a traditional rule in bookkeeping not to make entries direct into the ledger, but to require all transactions to be recorded initially in the journal or day book prior to posting to the ledger. The journal was a device to enable transactions to be checked prior to being formally recorded in the ledger. With the segregation of the purchases day book and the sales day book, as well as the cash book, from the journal, its use became restricted to recording miscellaneous transactions which did not fall within any specified category prior to these being entered in the ledger. It is used particularly for such transactions as recording depreciations, bad debts, and for the preparation of the profit and loss account.

Journal entries are in the form illustrated below. It should be noted that each entry has an explanatory note of the circumstances attaching to the event being recorded.

Date	Detail		folio	Dr	Cr
19X4				£	£
Jan 18	S. Green	Dr	DL145	114	
	To Bank account				114
	Being cheque dishonoured received from S. Green		CB 67		
				114	114
19X4				£	£
Jan 30	Bad Debts account	Dr	GL 36	65	
	To L. Brown				65
	Being amount owing by L. Brown now written off as irrecoverable		DL 92	65	65
19X4				£	£
Jul 1	Bank account	Dr	CB 89	250,000	
	To Ordinary Share Capital account		GL 8		100,000
	Share Premium account		GL 14		150,000
	Being cash received on issue of 100,000 Ordinary Shares of £1 each at £2.50 per share—per order of the board—				
	31 May 19X4			250,000	250,000

* DL = Debtor's Ledger   CB = Cash Book   GL = General Ledger

The concept of working capital

Working capital is conventionally defined as the net assets available to meet all current expenses and liabilities due for payment. It is measured as the difference between current assets and current liabilities. It is essentially a static concept. Occasionally, it is referred to as circulating capital.

The main components of working capital are illustrated in Diagram 1 below:

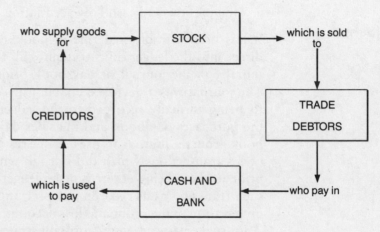

Diagram 1   Simplified flow of working capital

The control of working capital does not rely simply on recording the flow of the key components illustrated above. Thus, the control of debtors involves policy considerations such as the creditworthiness of potential customers, the credit limit to be granted and time limit imposed for payment in individual cases. Accounting procedures for the control of debtors are designed to keep a record of individual debts to ensure that policy decisions are being applied, and to keep a running total of outstanding debts due to the firm to ensure that the firm is not investing in debtors beyond the limit of its ability.

The control of the major components of working capital presents problems of some complexity from the viewpoint of financial management policy. Financial accounting procedures, therefore, provide a data source to enable sound financial management decisions to be made and to ensure that they are implemented.

The control of debtors

The expansion of sales generally involves a significant increase in the proportion of credit sales to cash sales, and gives rise to the creation of substantial balances of trade debts at any given time. The existence of a considerable volume of credit sales gives rise to the following accounting problems:

(a) What procedures should be applied to facilitate the process of recording credit sales?
(b) What procedures should be applied to facilitate the control of total debtor balances?

The means of solving both problems are found in segregating the individual debtor accounts from the general ledger, and substituting a debtors control account in the general ledger for the individual debtor accounts which would otherwise have been shown in the general ledger. The debtors control account is, in effect, a summary or total of all the transactions effected in the debtors ledger. These procedures are based on the use of individual sales invoices which indicate both the amount of the sale and the customer's indebtedness for this amount. It is evident that the process of entering each transaction invoice by invoice would become an onerous burden on the accountant's department. To streamline the recording process, all invoices are entered in the sales journal or sales day book as it is sometimes called. The accounts of individual debtors in the debtors ledger are debited directly from the sales journal to provide an accurate record of individual indebtedness at any time. The cash book contains an additional column to record cash receipts from debtors, thereby distinguishing them from other receipts.

The exclusion of individual debtor accounts from the general ledger enables the control account to be used to represent the total balance of debtors outstanding. Figure 6.1 below illustrates the use of the debtors control account in the general ledger as representing the total transactions recorded in the individual debtor accounts found in the debtors ledger. The debtors control account shows at a glance the total balance of debtors outstanding as well as the level of cash receipts from debtors in relation to the total debtors outstanding.

A number of other transactions affect the balances on debtors accounts, among which are the following:

(a) Discounts allowed for prompt payment of invoices.
(b) Credits allowed in respect of goods returned,
   (i) other items,
   (ii) dishonoured cheques,
   (iii) bad debts written off.

These transactions affect not only individual debtors accounts but also the total balance shown in the debtors control account.

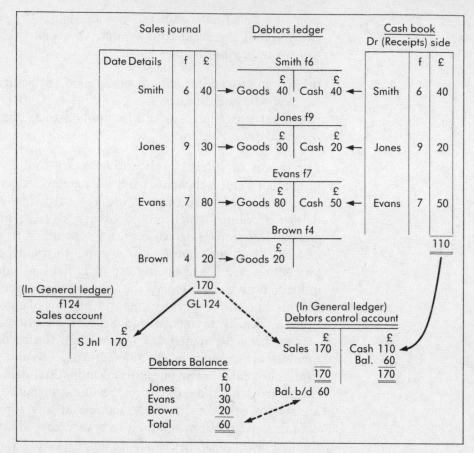

Fig. 6.1 Schematic outline of a debtors control system

Discounts allowed

Cash discounts are inducements to customers to settle their accounts promptly, and should be distinguished from trade discounts, which are reductions allowed to dealers as distinct from consumers. They have the effect of reducing the debtor balance.

Example 1

J. Berg, a customer of Midtown Supplies Company Ltd, has bought goods on credit for £100. To encourage prompt payment, Midtown Supplies Company Ltd allows a cash discount of 5%. Accordingly, Berg pays £95 in settlement of his account. The entry in the company's books would be:

J. Berg account

		£		£
Goods		100	Cash	95

To close the account, an entry must be effected in respect of the discount allowed as follows:

Debit   Discount allowed account ⎫
Credit   J. Berg account ⎬ with £5

Accordingly, J. Berg's account would be closed as follows:

J. Berg account

		£			£
Goods		100	Cash		95
			Discount allowed		5
		___			___
		100			100

The procedure used to streamline the recording of discounts allowed is simply to add an additional column on the debit side of the cash book and to record only the discounts allowed in that column. The cash book may be used as a basis for posting the details of receipts from debtors and discounts allowed to individual debtors accounts, and for posting the total receipts and discounts allowed to the debtors control account in the general ledger. Thus, the debtors control account continues to reflect accurately the balance of debtors outstanding.

Other items

(i) **Sales Returns**
Sales returns are recorded in the sales returns journal, and the procedures applied to the entries in this journal follow the same pattern as those applied to recording sales. Thus, individual debtor accounts are credited with the value of goods returned, and the total sales returns are credited to the debtors control account.

(ii) **Dishonoured Cheques**
On receipt of a cheque from a debtor, his account is credited with the value of the cheque and the cash book is debited with that amount. Upon notification by the bank that the cheque has not been honoured, the debt has to be re-established as follows:

Debit   Debtor's account ⎫ with the amount of the disho-
Credit   Cash account ⎬ noured cheque.

Corresponding entries will be made in the debtors control account, and the journal will be used in this instance to record the event.

(iii) **Bad Debts**

The journal is used to record the transfer of the balance on a debtor's account to the bad debts account. As indicated in Chapter 3, the debtor's account is closed. Corresponding entries will be made in the debtors control account.

The different types of entries to be found in the debtors control account are illustrated below together with explanatory notes.

Debtors control account (dates omitted)

		£			£
(1)	Balance b/d	14,732	(5)	Cash received	80,320
(2)	Goods—sales	83,214	(6)	Discount allowed	843
(3)	Cash refund	62	(7)	Returns	1,714
(4)	Dishonoured cheques	117	(8)	Bad debts	620
			(9)	Contra items— creditors	540
			(10)	Balance c/d	14,088
		98,125			98,125
Balance b/d		14,088			

Notes

(1) The opening balance would have been reconciled with the total extracted from the debtors ledger.

(2) The sales total is recorded from the sales journal.

(3) Occasionally, a customer may have paid for goods which are subsequently returned as faulty and his cash may be refunded. Sometimes accidental overpayment occurs as when an invoice is paid twice. The journal is used to provide the information needed for the purposes of the debtors control account.

(4) Dishonoured cheques can be ascertained as a total by inspection of the journal.

(5) Cash received as a total is found in the cash book column reserved for that purpose.

(6) The total discounts allowed is recorded in the discount-allowed column of the cash book.

(7) The sales returns total is recorded from the sales returns journal.

(8) Bad debts are recorded from the journal.

(9) Occasionally, transactions involving both purchases from and sales to the same person are conducted. To streamline the recording process and eliminate the need to record in full amounts

paid to and amounts received from the same person, the mutual debt is set off and only the difference is actually paid or received. The set-off procedure requires that the various amounts which are set off in the respective accounts should be eliminated by the use of 'contra' entries. The journal will normally supply the details of the totals of contra entries to be made in the ledgers.

(10) The closing balances of debtors outstanding in the debtors control account must agree with the sum of the individual balances extracted from the individual debtor accounts in the debtors ledger.

Example 2

The following information is available from the books and records of Friedel and Company Limited as at 31 December 19X8:

	£
Total debtors outstanding at 1 January 19X8	64,369
Sales for the year to 31 December 19X8	237,426
Returns for the year to 31 December 19X8	2,690
Cash received from debtors during year	214,894
Discount allowed to debtors during year	8,316
Bad debts written off in the year	975
Settlements by contra—Suppliers' accounts	2,810

The total debtors outstanding at the 31 December 19X8 may be obtained from the debtors control account as follows:

Debtors control account

19X8		£	19X8		£
Jan 1	Balance b/d	64,369	Dec 31	Returns	2,690
Dec 31	Sales	237,426	.. 31	Cash	214,894
			.. 31	Discounts allowed	8,316
			.. 31	Bad debts	975
			.. 31	Contras	2,810
			.. 31	Balance c/d	72,110
		301,795			301,795
19X9					
Jan 1	Balance b/d	72,110			

The balance of outstanding debtors of £72,110 should agree with the total of the balances of the individual debtor accounts in the debtors ledger.

The control of creditors

The procedure for facilitating the process of recording credit purchases and for the process of controlling total creditor balances is similar in nature to that applied to debtors. An additional problem is involved in the need to distinguish creditors in respect of goods supplied and creditors in respect of services provided. This distinction is required since total credit purchases are included in the total purchases shown in the trading section of the profit statement for the purpose of calculating the gross margin, whereas the various expenses charged in the computation of net profit includes services rendered but unpaid at the end of the accounting period. This additional problem is resolved by using an extended column analysis in the purchases journal to classify the nature of the goods or services supplied. The totals of the various columns are debited to the different expense accounts, and the total of goods purchased is debited periodically to the purchases account. Postings to the individual creditors accounts in the creditors ledger and the posting of the total credit balance to the creditors control account in the general ledger are also made periodically.

Discounts for prompt payment may also be received as well as allowed. A separate column is required in the cash book to record discounts received, the total of which is credited to the discount received account and shown as a debit in the creditors control account. The discount received from individual creditors is debited to their account in the creditors ledger.

Example 3

A typical creditors control account is set out below with notes on the origins of the entries.

Creditors control account (dates omitted)

19X8	£	19X8	£
(3) Returns	4,620	(1) Balance b/d	74,691
(4) Cash	218,110	(2) Purchases and	
(5) Discounts received	6,180	supplies	210,360
(6) Contras (debtors)	1,470		
(7) Balance c/d	54,671		
	285,051		285,051
		Balance b/d	54,671

Notes
(1) The balance brought down will have been agreed with a list of balances extracted from the creditors ledger.
(2) Purchases, etc., will be obtained from the total in the purchase journal which itself uses the suppliers' invoices as a basis for entries.

(3) The total purchases returned is obtained from the purchases returns journal which is based on suppliers' credit notes.
(4) Cash will be the figure shown as a total in the cash paid to creditors column in the cash book.
(5) The total discounts received are recorded in the cash book, as explained earlier.
(6) The 'contra' entries arise from the cancellation of mutual indebtedness.
(7) The balance of total creditors outstanding must agreed with the total extracted from the creditors ledger.

A schematic outline of a creditors control system is shown in Fig. 6.2 below.

Question 1

The following balances, details and totals were taken from the various books of Baker Bargains Ltd as at 30 September 19X4.

	£
Debtor balances at 1 October 19X3	6,120
Cash paid to creditors	29,600
Bad debts written off	380
Sales returns	810
Purchases	36,114
Discount allowed	1,440
Debtor balances at 30 September 19X4	7,830
Creditor balances at 1 October 19X3	4,390
Discounts received	967
Cash received from debtors	42,150
Contra items—purchases and sales	870
Sales	47,360
Purchases returns	1,960
Creditor balances at 30 September 19X4	7,107

Required

Prepare the debtors control and the creditors control accounts for the year to 30 September 19X4.

Question 2

The following balances appear in the general ledger of a company as at 1 July 19X3.

	£
Debtors control account	60,000
Creditors control account	32,000
Provision for doubtful debts	2,000

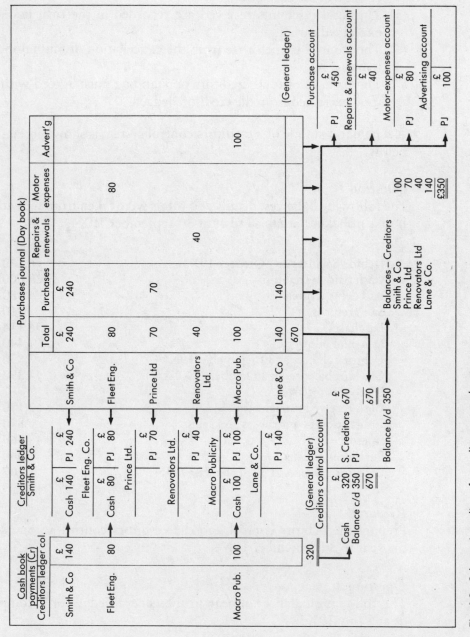

Fig. 6.2 Schematic outline of a creditors control system

The following transactions occurred during the year ended 30 June 19X4:

	£
Credit sales	380,000
Return of goods previously sold on credit	14,000
Cash received from sundry debtors	285,400
Discounts allowed	5,600
Bad debts written off	5,000
Debtors and creditors accounts settled by contra	50,000
Credit purchases	186,000
Return of goods previously bought on credit	3,800
Discount received	2,200
Cash paid to sundry creditors	122,000

The balance on the provision for doubtful debts account at 30 June 19X4 is to be made equal to 5% of the balance on the total sundry debtors at that date.

Required

Using the information given, prepare the following accounts for the year ended 30 June 19X4:

(1) Debtors control account
(2) Creditors control account
(3) Provision for doubtful debts account.

Question 3

The following entries appear in the debtors ledger of a company for the year ended 31 December 19X4:

	£
Sales as per posting summaries	149,506
Receipts from debtors	138,942
Discounts allowed	3,634
Balance on control account as at 1 January 19X4	17,904

The clerk in charge of the debtors ledger listed the balances outstanding on 31 December 19X4 as amounting to £19,326, but this did not agree with the balance on the debtors control account. There were no credit balances on the ledger cards.

Investigation of the differences revealed the following:

(i) The bank statement showed cheques received from debtors amounting to £396 which had been completely overlooked.

(ii) The following journal entries had been correctly posted to the debtors ledger but had not been posted to the debtors control account in the general ledger:

	£
Debtor balances set off against creditor balances	5,792
Bad debts written off	1,280

(iii) When listing the debtor balances in the debtors ledger, the clerk had overlooked three debtor accounts with debit balances totalling £382.

(iv) An opening debit balance of £427 on a debtor account in the debtors ledger had been discovered by the clerk in charge as having been included as £27 only.

(v) A receipt of £2,346 from J. Spruce had been recorded in the debtors' column of the cash book, but had not been posted, since no account under that name could be traced. On investigation, it was discovered that it was in payment for a car used by the sales department and which had been sold to Spruce.

Required

(a) Prepare the debtors control account for the year ended 31 December 19X4, taking into account the above adjustments.

(b) Reconcile the clerk's balance of £19,326 with the corrected balance on the debtors control account in the general ledger.

(c) Explain the benefits that accrue from using control accounts.

Question 4

The offices of Tullins Groceries Ltd were broken into during the night of 24 March 19X3 and the safe was stolen. In the safe were the day's takings, the cash book and the ledgers.

From the remaining books and other records left on the premises, the following information was available:

	£
Total debtors at 1 January 19X3	38,541
Total debtors at 24 March 19X3	63,783
Total creditors at 1 January 19X3	11,115
Total creditors at 24 March 19X3	18,828
Purchases from 1 January to 24 March 19X3	262,902
Sales from 1 January to 24 March 19X3	428,547
Expenses from 1 January to 24 March 19X3	86,238
New vans purchased 28 February 19X3	7,500
Salaries paid from 1 January to 24 March 19X3	44,586
Dividend paid to shareholders on 10 February 19X3	2,520
Balance at bank in hand 1 January 19X3	4,494

The bank informed Tullins Groceries Ltd that the balance at the bank on 24 March 19X3 was £7,848. Cheques issued by the company prior to 24 March 19X3 amounting to £342 were subsequently presented for payment. All takings prior to the theft had been banked with the exception of the takings for 24 March 19X3.

Required
Calculate how much cash had been stolen in the safe.
Hint: Prepare control accounts for debtors and creditors.

Stock control

The objective of a stock control system is to provide means of exercising a close control over the flow of materials or goods into stock and the flow of stock into production or sales, thereby not only preventing losses but also ensuring that adequate stock levels are maintained. The purpose of this section is to focus on the procedures applied to the control of stock on a daily basis. Policy decisions affecting minimum stock levels will not be discussed.

A feature of stock control systems is the need to maintain records of both quantities and values. In this respect, it will be recalled that stock valuations depend upon a physical stocktake combined with a valuation base, such as unit cost or unit market value. Stock control systems increase in complexity with the number of different items held. Indeed, in the case of large firms, stock control systems are completely computerized. In this section, it will be assumed for simplicity that only one item is held in stock. Moreover, this section is concerned only with trading enterprises and the control of stock of finished goods purchased for resale. The more complex stock control problem facing manufacturing firms which hold stocks of raw materials and work-in-progress as well as finished goods will be discussed in Part 2.

Controlling the flow of stock

The flow of stock through an accounting system is as follows:

Purchases

Purchases of goods for resale are recorded in the *purchases account*, as follows:

Dr   Purchases account   } with the cost of
Cr   Creditor account or cash book } the goods bought.

It should be noted particularly that the purchases account is only used for the purpose of recording the purchase of trading stocks, and is not used to record acquisitions of such items as plant, equipment and supplies. The purchases account provides a record of all purchases during the accounting period, supporting evidence for which is found in the invoices received from suppliers which will have been entered in the purchases day book.

Stock

There are two methods of recording stock flows:

 (i) the periodic inventory method,
(ii) the perpetual inventory method.

(i) Periodic inventory

Under this method of accounting for the flow of stock, no record of stock is maintained during the accounting period. At the end of the accounting period, the purchases account is closed. Those purchases remaining unsold are transferred to the *stock account:* the balance representing the goods which have been sold is transferred to the *cost of goods sold account*.

The periodic inventory method requires a count of all the items unsold on the last day of the accounting period to determine the closing stock. Little is known about the exact content of the stock during the course of the year. Thus, items in the opening stock or purchased during the year which are not found present in the closing stock are presumed to have been sold.

In effect, the periodic inventory method provides virtually no control over the flow of stock. The closing stock on the last day of the accounting period becomes the opening stock on the first day of the *next* accounting period, and remains in the stock account throughout that period. Acquisitions and disposals of stock are not recorded. The only check which is made is the physical stocktake on the last day of the accounting period.

The cost of goods sold under this method is determined as follows:

$$\text{Cost of goods sold} = \text{Opening stock} + \text{Cost of purchases} - \text{Closing stock}$$

(ii) Perpetual inventory

The object of this method of stock control is to maintain a continuous record of acquisitions, disposal and balances of stock throughout the accounting period. It is to be noted particularly that under this method of stock control no separate account is kept for purchases.

Instead, each purchase is recorded as an increase in the stock account, and the following entries are made:

Dr   Stock account   } with cost of
Cr   Cash or creditor } goods purchased.

When goods are sold, the following entries are now made:

Dr Cost of goods sold account } with the cost of
Cr Stock account   } the goods sold.

It is evident, therefore, that the result of this method of recording both purchases and the cost of sales through the stock account means that the stock account shows the cost of stock on hand at any particular time. A further advantage of the perpetual inventory method is that the cost of goods sold account can provide a direct means of calculating the gross margin on sales, without the necessity of formally preparing a profit and loss account. Thus, a partial profit and loss account based on details available in the sales account and the cost of goods sold account can take the following simple form:

	£
Sales	800,000
Cost of goods sold	600,000
Gross margin	200,000

It should also be noted that since the perpetual inventory provides up-to-date information on the quantities and value of stock on hand, the importance of the physical count of stock is reduced to one of checking the accuracy of the information contained in the stock account. The detailed records of inflow and outflow of stock is maintained as subsidiary record to the Ledger. As may be seen from Fig. 6.3 below, the perpetual inventory shows quantities, unit costs and

Date	Received			Sold			Stock		
19X4	Quantity	Unit cost	Total cost	Quantity	Unit cost	Total cost	Quantity	Unit cost	Total cost
		£	£		£	£		£	£
Jan 1							200	4	800
Feb 21				120	4	480	80	4	320
Mar 24	300	4	1,200				380	4	1,520
Apr 11				250	4	1,000	130	4	520
Aug 28	150	4	600				280	4	1,120
Sep 14				100	4	400	180	4	720
Oct 19	200	4	800				380	4	1,520
Nov 23	350	4	1,400				730	4	2,920
Dec 10				200	4	800	530	4	2,120

Fig. 6.3 Example of a perpetual inventory account

total costs of each transaction relating to the acquisition and disposal of stock. In the simplified illustration shown above, it is assumed that the firm only carries one item in stock. Where many items are involved, a record would be maintained for each item.

Figure 6.3 shows how the perpetual inventory facilitates the control of stock by showing (a) the quantity of stock which should be on hand, and (b) the cost of that stock.

The valuation of stock

Stock valuation is of considerable significance for profit determination and the valuation of the business. The closing stock is often large in proportion to other items appearing on the balance sheet. Any understatement or overstatement in the valuation of closing stock will affect the measurement of the cost of goods sold, the gross margin on sales, the net profit for the period, as well as affecting the valuation of current assets and the value of the equity in the firm.

Errors in stock valuation not only affect accounting measurements relating to the period concerned, but also they spread over into the next accounting period. Thus, if the closing stock of the current period is overstated, the gross margin will also be overstated, and, since the closing stock is the opening stock of the next period, it follows that the gross margin of that period will be understated by reason of the overvaluation of the opening stock. Accordingly, the consequential effect will reach as far as the measurement of the net profit of the following period.

In the examples given above, stock has been shown at cost, and it has been assumed that the acquisition cost of stock remained constant. Clearly, the assumption is unreal and it is likely that costs will fluctuate as well as rise through time. As a result, the transfer of stock to the cost of goods sold account poses a difficulty as to the value which should be attached to individual items transferred. This difficulty also affects the valuation of closing stock.

A ruling convention among accountants is that closing stock should be valued at the 'lower of cost or net realizable value'. Unfortunately, there are many pitfalls in the application of this rule. First, there are difficulties in defining the cost of closing stock. Secondly, the rule reflects the conservatism of accountants concerned that closing stock should not be overvalued and that, therefore, the net profit should not be overstated. Thirdly, the rule may be applied consistently and yet permit a great variety of procedures for valuation.

There are three generally accepted methods for valuing the cost of stock, which reflect different treatments of the changing cost of acquisition of stock. These methods are commonly referred to as

FIFO (First In First Out), LIFO (Last in First Out), and AVCO (Average Cost).

FIFO

This method assumes that the oldest goods on hand are those which are first to be sold. The cost of goods sold, therefore, is determined by reference to the price at which the earliest items in the stock were purchased. Consequently, the closing stock is valued at the most recent purchase price, as the most recent purchases are deemed to be still on hand. It should be noted, therefore, that FIFO reflects a traditional view of the flow of stock.

The following example illustrates the application of the FIFO method.

Example 4

The following data relates to the Marford Supply Co. Ltd for April 19X0.

Opening stock 1 April 19X0   100 units at a cost of £4 each.

Purchases				£
April 2	200 units @	4.15		830
.. 7	200 .. @	4.20		840
.. 15	300 .. @	4.30		1,290
.. 22	100 .. @	4.40		440
.. 28	200 .. @	4.65		930
				4,330

During April the company sold 800 units. The cost of goods sold and the value of the closing stock are as follows:

	Units	Costs		
		£	£	
Cost of sales	100	4.00	400	(Opening stock)
	200	4.15	830	(Bought April 2)
	200	4.20	840	(Bought April 7)
	300	4.30	1,290	(Bought April 15)
	800		3,360	
Closing stock	100	4.40	440	(Bought April 22)
	200	4.65	930	(Bought April 28)
	300		1,370	

LIFO

This method assumes that the most recently acquired goods are the first to be sold. It assumes, therefore, an opposite viewpoint of the flow of stock to that assumed by FIFO. Under the LIFO method, the cost of goods sold is determined by reference to the price of the latest acquisitions.

The following example illustrates the application of the LIFO method.

Example 5

By taking the same data given in the previous example and using the LIFO as distinct from the FIFO method, the cost of goods sold and the value of the closing stocks are as follows:

	Units	Costs		
		£	£	
Cost of sales	200	4.65	930	(Bought April 28)
	100	4.40	440	(Bought April 22)
	300	4.30	1,290	(Bought April 15)
	200	4.20	840	(Bought April 7)
	800		3,500	
Closing stock	200	4.15	830	(Bought April 2)
	100	4.00	400	(On hand April 1)
	300		1,230	

AVCO

This method avoids the extreme assumptions of the FIFO and LIFO methods and attempts to avoid the excessive distortions in either the cost of goods sold or the the value of closing stock implied by these methods. This method is at best an expedient which does not really solve the problems of valuing stock.

Example 6

The first step is to calculate the weighted average cost of goods available for sale in the period under review. Using the data for the Marford Supply Co. Ltd, the weighted average cost is as follows:

		Units	Price	
			£	£
April 1	Opening stock	100	4.00	400
2	Purchases	200	4.15	830
7	..	200	4.20	840
15	..	300	4.30	1,290
22	..	100	4.40	440
28	..	200	4.65	930
		1,100		4,730

The weighted average cost is £4730/1100 = £4.30 per unit

Cost of sales is therefore: $\quad$ 800 × 4.30 = 3,440
and closing stock: $\qquad\qquad$ 300 × 4.30 = 1,290

$$\underline{\qquad 1,100 \qquad\qquad 4,730 \qquad}$$

The balance of the stock going into the next period will be used as part of the data used in arriving at the weighted average cost for that period.

Retail price less gross margin

Many businesses and, in particular large stores, find it convenient to value stock at selling price and to reduce this valuation by the amount of the gross margin to obtain the cost value. The advantage of this method is that it avoids a considerable amount of record keeping although weakening the stock control system. Since the gross margin is fairly stable for individual classes of goods, it can be applied to the selling prices to obtain a reliable valuation of stock. For this purpose, the gross margin ratio is calculated as follows:

$$\frac{\text{Gross margin}}{\text{Sales}} \times 100$$

Example 7

The gross margin ratio expresses the relationship between the selling price and the cost of the goods sold. Consider the following data:

	£
Selling price of goods	100
Cost of goods	80
Gross margin	20

The gross margin ratio is:

$$\frac{20}{100} \times 100 = 20\%$$

It is evident on the data given above that a gross margin of 20% on sale is equivalent to 25% on cost. Expressing these relationships as fractions, if the gross margin on sales is 1/5, then it is 1/4 on cost. Accordingly, the following generalization may be made:

If the gross margin on sales is $\frac{1}{x}$, then it is $\frac{1}{x-1}$ on cost.

Similarly, if the gross margin is expressed as $\frac{1}{y}$ on cost,

then it is $\frac{1}{y+1}$ on sales.

Selecting the method of valuation

Since the value of the closing stock has an immediate impact on the measurement of the net profit it is important to understand the reasons for adopting one method of valuation rather than another.

FIFO

As indicated earlier, FIFO seeks to emulate the physical flow of goods in and out of the business. This method is used by the majority of companies in the United Kingdom. During periods of inflation, however, the value of the closing stock under this method is likely to approximate current replacement cost. Whilst this characteristic is relevant to the correct valuation of closing stock on the balance sheet, it leads to an overstatement of reported profit.

LIFO

Under LIFO valuation procedures, the closing stock will be at the value of the earliest purchases constituting stock. Accordingly, stock values tend to be progressively understated. Advocates of this method claim that the most current costs are being matched against revenue, leading to more accurate representation of stock. Changes in stock levels, however, can lead to fluctuations in the cost of sales. This system is rarely used in the United Kingdom. The Inland Revenue does not regard it as an acceptable basis for tax purposes.

AVCO and retail price

These methods usually have the merit of requiring fewer clerical processes and are easy to operate. AVCO may be appropriate where purchase prices fluctuate, but seems to have little merit for dealing with conditions of constantly rising prices.

The retail price method is widely used. Its use produces valuations which are closer to FIFO than other methods, particularly when selling prices and cost are moving in the same direction.

Stock control and stock valuation

So far valuations have been placed on stock at the end of a financial period leaving the Cost of Sales as a residual. This application of the method is known as *periodic inventory*. Thus, when a valuation procedure as stated as being FIFO, LIFO or AVCO, then it must be further qualified to indicate whether the periodic inventory method is being used. This is necessary because the flow assumption underlying FIFO, etc., can be applied in an alternative way which is called *perpetual inventory*. This method requires an accounting system which not only fully records each acquisition of stock in the way explained above, but also identifies, and places a value on, each withdrawal of goods from stores on the date of withdrawal. If this is done then, the closing inventory is the residual, unlike the results of periodic inventory.

The valuation of the goods withdrawn for sale, processing, etc., is based on the same ideas of FIFO, LIFO and AVCO, whichever method has been adopted. The distinction is that the rule is applied in the light of knowledge at the date of the withdrawal. It will be apparent that in order to use this method a control system must be in force which identifies goods withdrawn from stores. This normally takes the form of an authorized requisition note which is then used as the basis for an accounting entry, which will be:

Dr   Cost of sales account   }   with cost value of
Cr   Stock   }   goods withdrawn

and similar in the case of items withdrawn for further processing in the manufacture of a final product. Under perpetual inventory, the following consequences emerge when the method is compared with periodic inventory.

(a) *FIFO*. Under the assumption of this method of valuation, there will be no difference between the value of goods transferred out of stock and the value of goods remaining in stock, irrespective of which stock control system is used.

(b) *LIFO*. The application of LIFO to the perpetual inventory method requires the strict observance of the rule that transfers out of stock must be valued at the most recent purchase price. During periods of rising prices, the cost of goods transferred out of stock will have a total value which will be smaller in the case of the perpetual inventory method than in that of the periodic inventory method. This is because the closing stock under the latter method will be valued at the latest purchase price, whereas under the former method, it will reflect a series of progressively increasing purchase prices rather than the latest purchase price.

(c) *AVCO*. Under this method, the transfers of goods out of stock to sales must be based on the most recent weighted average cost. This means that the average cost must be calculated at the time of purchase and not at the time of sale. The application of this method under conditions of rising prices will lead to smaller valuations of the closing stock when using the perpetual inventory as distinct from the periodic inventory method.

Example 8
The following data was given in Example 4:

Opening stock 1 April 19X0   100 units at a cost of £4 each.

Purchases			£	£
April	2	200 units @	4.15	830
..	7	200 .. @	4.20	840
..	15	300 .. @	4.30	1,290
..	22	100 .. @	4.40	440
..	28	200 .. @	4.65	930
				4,330

Sales for April totalled 800 units, and the goods transferred out of stock were as follows:

April	3	250 units
..	10	200 ..
..	16	250 ..
..	23	100 ..

The stock records based on the perpetual inventory method under the different valuation procedures are as follows:

(a) *FIFO.* As stated earlier, no difference exists in the valuation of cost of sales and closing stock as between the two methods of stock control.

(b) *LIFO.* The effect of using the perpetual inventory method is to produce the following valuations:

	£
(1) Total cost of goods sold	3,385
(2) Closing stock	1,345

Figure 6.4 below shows how these valuations are produced. The corresponding valuation using the periodic inventory method is as follows:

	£
(1) Total cost of goods sold	3,500
(2) Closing stock	1,230

(c) The effect of the AVCO method is to produce the following valuations:

	£
(1) Total cost of goods sold	3,366
(2) Closing stock	1,364

The corresponding valuations under the periodic inventory method are as follows:*

	£
(1) Total cost of goods sold	3,440
(2) Closing stock	1,290

* See page 139

Date	Received			Sold			Stock balance		
19X0	Quantity	Unit cost	Total cost	Quantity	Unit cost	Total cost	Quantity	Unit cost	Total cost
		£	£		£	£		£	£
Apr 1							100	4.00	400
2	200	4.15	830				200	4.15	830
3				200	4.15	830	100	4.00	400
				50	4.00	200	50	4.00	200
7	200	4.20	840				200	4.20	840
10				200	4.20	840	50	4.00	200
15	300	4.30	1,290				300	4.30	1,290
16				250	4.30	1,075	50	4.00	200
							50	4.30	215
22	100	4.40	440				100	4.40	440
23				100	4.40	440	50	4.00	200
							50	4.30	215
28	200	4.65	930				200	4.65	930
					Total cost of sales	3,385	300	Closing stock	1,345

Fig. 6.4 Perpetual inventory—using LIFO

(d) *Comparison of valuations*. Figure 6.6 below summarizes the differing valuations of the cost of goods sold and of the closing stock using the three alternative valuation methods, under the perpetual inventory method.

Periodic or perpetual control?

Two separate problems should be recognized in considering the choice between the two alternative methods of stock control. The need to establish close control over stock and the possibility of computerizing and programming stock control decisions is a major advantage in favour of perpetual inventory control. The valuation problem is extremely complex, and cannot easily be resolved. The process of profit determination requires cost measurements which realistically reflect the cost of goods sold. Likewise, representations of the value of closing stock should produce realistic valuations. The problem of valuation is very controversial and will be examined further in Chapter 8.

Date	Received			Sold			Stock balance		
19X0	Quantity	Unit cost	Total cost	Quantity	Unit cost	Total cost	Quantity	Unit cost	Total cost
		£	£		£	£		£	£
Apr 1							100	4.00	400
2	200	4.15	830				200	4.15	830
							300	4.10	1,230
3				250	4.10	1,025	50	4.10	205
7	200	4.20	840				200	4.20	840
							250	4.18	1,045
10				200	4.18	836	50	4.18	209
15	300	4.30	1,290				300	4.30	1,290
							350	4.28	1,499
16				250	4.28	1,071	100	4.28	428
22	100	4.40	440				100	4.40	440
							200	4.34	868
23				100	4.34	434	100	4.34	434
28	200	4.65	930				200	4.65	930
				Total cost of sales		3,366			
				Closing stock			300	4.55	1,364

Fig. 6.5 Perpetual inventory—using AVCO

	FIFO £	LIFO £	AVCO £
Perpetual inventory			
Cost of goods sold	3,360	3,385	3,366
Closing stock	1,370	1,345	1,364
Periodic inventory			
Cost of goods sold	(Example 4) 3,360	(Example 5) 3,500	(Example 6) 3,440
Closing stock	(Example 4) 1,370	(Example 5) 1,230	(Example 6) 1,290

Fig. 6.6 Comparison of valuations

Question 5
The following information relates to one of the items carried by the Houlgate Co. Ltd.

Purchases record of Item No A.312 for October 19X5

		£	£
Balance on hand at start	250 units @ 1.60 =		400
October 8 Purchases	800 .. @ 1.70 =		1,360
.. 13 ..	400 .. @ 1.75 =		700
.. 20 ..	350 .. @ 1.80 =		630
.. 29 ..	200 .. @ 1.85 =		370

During October 1,700 units were sold.

Required
Calculate the cost of sales for October and the value of closing stock based on each of the following methods:

(a) FIFO   (b) LIFO   (c) AVCO

Question 6
In addition to the data given in Question 5 above, you are given the following information concerning the dates and quantities of Item No A.312 transferred to the cost of goods sold account:

October 5 Sales	200 units
.. 10 ..	700 ..
.. 15 ..	450 ..
.. 23 ..	300 ..
.. 30 ..	50 ..

Required
(i) Calculate the cost of sales and the value of closing stock using perpetual inventory applied to

(a) FIFO   (b) LIFO   (c) AVCO

(ii) Prepare a perpetual inventory for each method of valuation.

Question 7

On 9 August 19X7, a fire completely destroyed the shop and warehouse of the Portal Home Decorating Co. Ltd. The stock of goods was destroyed, but the basic ledgers of the company, which were kept in a fireproof safe, were recovered. From the ledgers, the following information was extracted:

	£
Opening stock on 1 January 19X7	35,612
Purchases at cost to 9 August 19X7	134,364
Sales to 9 August 19X7	187,200

The company's policy was to fix selling price as a mark-up on one-third on cost.

Required

Calculate the cost of the stock destroyed for the purpose of an insurance claim against the Fire Insurance Co. Ltd.

Question 8

The miscellaneous section of the stock of the Speedwell Engineering Company Ltd as at 30 June 19X4 consisted of the following items:

Parts	Quantity	Unit price Cost	Market value
		£	£
Sprockets	2,000	2.00	2.15
Flanges	1,500	3.10	3.00
Gear wheels	3,000	1.60	1.75
Drive chains	1,000	4.30	4.00
Clamps	4,000	1.20	1.25

Required

Calculate the total value of the stock for this section at 30 June 19X4 applying the following bases of valuation:

(a) Cost base only.
(b) Lower of cost or market value by total.
(c) Lower of cost or market value by item.

Question 9

Solo Ltd, who only deal in one product, have produced the following schedule of their transactions for purchases and sales of goods during 19X6.

			Purchases			Sales			Balance		
			Qty	Unit cost £	Total £	Qty	Unit cost £	Total £	Qty	Unit cost £	Total £
Jan	1	Stock							600	2.10	1,260
	8	Sales				400					
	23	Purchases	300	2.15	645						
Feb	2	Sales				240					
	18	Purchases	700	2.20	1,540						
	23	Sales				500					
Mar	14	Purchases	250	2.30	575						
	23	Purchases	300	2.35	705						
	27	Sales				200					
Apr	3	Sales				260					
	10	Purchases	400	2.40	960						
	15	Sales				500					
May	28	Purchases	200	2.30	460						
Jun	18	Purchases	200	2.35	470						
	24	Sales				400					
Jul	17	Purchases	300	2.40	720						
Aug	2	Sales				500					
	30	Purchases	600	2.45	1,470						
Sep	18	Sales				200					
	30	Purchases	400	2.50	1,000						
Oct	10	Sales				600					
Nov	9	Purchases	400	2.55	1,020						
	28	Sales				300					
Dec	1	Purchases	200	2.70	540						
	23	Sales				100					

The selling price up to June 30 was £5 per unit but was raised to £5.50 for the rest of the year.

Required

Prepare the profit and loss account up to the gross margin under the following cost flow assumptions.

(a) Periodic inventory
    (i) FIFO   (ii) LIFO   (iii) AVCO
(b) Perpetual inventory
    (i) FIFO   (ii) LIFO   (iii) AVCO
(c) Using the form shown above as your example, complete the column for sales and balance in accordance with perpetual inventory assumptions, using
    (i) FIFO   (ii) LIFO   (iii) AVCO

Funds flow accounting

Financial accounting may be said to be concerned with the control of three types of flows—profit flows, funds flows and cash flows. Previous chapters have been concerned with profit flows and their resulting effects on the financial position of an enterprise, which is reflected in the balance sheet.

Statements of source and application of funds

Traditionally, firms have been content to prepare annual financial reports on the basis of a profit and loss account for the year and a balance sheet as at the close of the year. The objective of the profit and loss account is to show the profit or loss earned during the year, and the balance sheet to show the financial status of the firm at the year end. The profit and loss account is concerned with financial performance, and the balance sheet with financial status.

The financial status of an enterprise changes over time. Its growth will be manifested in the increase of total assets and total liabilities. Clearly, a successful business will be making profits and reinvesting a portion of profits in the form of further acquisition of fixed or current assets, or the reduction of debts or current liabilities.

Example 9

The profit and loss account of Manuel plc for the year ended 31 December 19X1 showed a net profit of £1,500. The balance sheets as at 1 January 19X1 and 31 December 19X1 were as follows:

	Balance sheet as at	
	1 January 19X1	31 December 19X1
	£	£
Fixed assets	2,500	3,500
Net current assets	1,000	1,500
	3,500	5,000
Capital and reserves	£	£
Called up share capital	2,000	2,000
Other reserves	1,500	1,500
Profit and loss account	—	1,500
	3,500	5,000

It is evident in this example that the net profit for the year ended 31 December 19X1 has been retained in the business, and has been applied to financing the acquisition of additional fixed assets of £1,000 and of additional net current assets of £500.

The statement of source and application of funds for the year ended 31 December 19X1 could be expressed as follows:

Statement of source and application of funds for the year ended 31 December 19X1

Source of funds	£	Application of funds	£
Net profit for the year	1,500	Purchase of fixed assets	1,000
		Increase in net current assets	500
	1,500		1,500

In this example, the increased size of the firm in terms of larger assets during the year ended 31 December 19X1 is entirely explained by reference to the retained profits which have financed this expansion.

The growth of an enterprise as a result of profitability only is a rare phenomenon. Successful businesses are able to grow at a faster rate than improving profits allow because they are able to attract further funds in the form of borrowings and additional capital.

Example 10

The profitability of Manuel plc during the year ended 31 December 19X1 has encouraged the directors to seek to expand the business more rapidly than could be financed out of profits. The shareholders were asked to subscribe further capital of £5,000 in the ensuing year, and a debenture loan of £5,000 was also obtained in that year. The net profit for the year ended 31 December 19X2 amounted to £4,000, and the opening and closing balance sheets were as follows:

	Balance sheet as at	
	1 January 19X2	31 December 19X2
	£	£
Fixed assets	3,500	11,500
Net current assets	1,500	7,500
	5,000	19,000
Less:		
Creditors: amounts falling due after more than one year		
Debenture loan	—	5,000
	5,000	14,000
	£	£
Capital and reserves		
Called up share capital	2,000	7,000
Other reserves	1,500	1,500
Profit and loss account	1,500	5,500
	5,000	14,000

The statement of source and application of funds for the year ended 31 December 19X2 could be shown as follows:

Statement of source and application of funds for the year ended
31 December 19X2

Source	£	Application	£
Net profit for the year	4,000	Purchase of fixed	
Additional share capital	5,000	assets	8,000
New debenture loan	5,000	Increase in net current	
		assets	6,000
	14,000		14,000

Consequently, the profit and loss account only partially explains changes in the size of a business between two successive balance sheets. A complete explanation can only be given by also taking into account other sources of funds than those coming out of profits.

Moreover, given that a firm has had additional sources of funds available to it during an accounting period, there is interest in having explanations of the manner in which those funds have been applied in its business. Example 10 shows how the statement of source and application of funds explains not only the total additional sources of funds obtained during the accounting period, but also how they have been applied.

Funds may be applied in increasing the asset side of the balance sheet. In the foregoing example, it has been assumed that the additional sources of funds have been applied to increasing the total assets, and therefore the size of the balance sheet has been increasing.

Funds may also be applied to reducing repayment debts, without there being any increase in assets.

Example 11

During the year ended 31 December 19X3, the continued success of Manuel plc was shown in a bumper profit of £10,000. The directors decided to distribute an interim dividend of £5,000 out of these profits and also to repay the debenture loan of £5,000 before maturity. These transactions took place on the 31 December 19X3. The balance sheets as at 1 January 19X3 and 31 December 19X3 were as follows:

	Balance sheet as at	
	1 January 19X3	31 December 19X3
	£	£
Fixed assets	11,500	11,500
Net current assets	7,500	7,500
	19,000	19,000

Less:
Creditors: amounts falling due
after more than one year
     Debenture loan

Debenture loan	5,000	—
	14,000	19,000

Capital and reserves	£	£
Called up share capital	7,000	7,000
Other reserves	1,500	1,500
Profit and loss account	5,500	10,500
	14,000	19,000

The statement of source and application of funds plays a special role in the supply of information to shareholders and investors, and for this reason, it became usual practice for it to be included with the profit and loss account and the balance sheet in annual published company reports.

The nature of funds flows

The purpose of the statement of source and application of funds is to provide the following information:

(a) The additional sources of funds which the firm has obtained during the accounting period.
(b) How these additional sources of funds have been applied during the accounting period.

The statement of source and application of funds may be compared with the balance sheet, in the sense in which the statement of source and application of funds deals with the changes in the financial structure of a business over *one* accounting period, whilst the balance sheet is a cumulative statement showing the totality of such changes over the life of the enterprise to the date of the balance sheet.

A major difference, however, between the items shown on the balance sheet and those appearing on the statement of source and application of funds lies in the 'funds' concept used by the latter.

The nature of the funds flows depicted in the statement of source and application of funds is associated with the idea of 'funds' expressed as 'liquid funds'. For example, if a firm raises a loan of £1,000, the liquid funds resulting from that loan are £1,000. Similarly, if an asset is sold for £1,000, the liquid funds flowing to the firm amount to £1,000. Conversely, if there is a repayment of a loan, the liquid funds applied to the debt reduction amount to £1,000.

Sources of liquid funds result, typically, from additional capital, new loans, the sale of fixed assets, the reduction of working capital and, of course, operating profits.

Applications of liquid funds are, typically, the purchase of fixed assets, the repayment of loans, the increase in working capital, the payment of dividends and taxes on profits.

Measuring funds flows

The information required for the preparation of the statement of source and application of funds is obtainable by first comparing the relevant balance sheets for the accounting period to be covered. This comparison will highlight the changes in the balance sheet which are to be explained by the statement of source and application of funds.

Example 12

The following balance sheets relate to Marterey plc:

	Balance sheet as at			
	31 December 19X4		31 December 19X5	
	£	£	£	£
Fixed assets				
Land and buildings	20,000		22,000	
Plant and machinery	15,000	35,000	13,000	35,000
Current assets				
Stocks	30,000		25,000	
Debtors	27,000		23,000	
Cash at bank and in hand	5,000		7,000	
	62,000		55,000	
Creditors: amounts falling due within one year				
Trade creditors	(32,000)		(25,000)	
Taxation	(15,000)		(10,000)	
Net current assets		15,000		20,000
		50,000		55,000
Capital and reserves	£	£	£	£
Called up share capital		10,000		12,000
Other reserves	30,000		30,000	
Profit and loss account	10,000	40,000	13,000	43,000
		50,000		55,000

Summary of balance sheet changes

	£	£	£ +	£ −
Fixed assets				
Land and buildings	20,000	22,000	2,000	
Plant and machinery at cost less depreciation	15,000	13,000		2,000
Current assets				
Stocks	30,000	25,000		5,000
Debtors	27,000	23,000		4,000
Cash at bank and in hand	5,000	7,000	2,000	
	62,000	55,000		
Creditors: amounts falling due within one year				
Trade creditors	(32,000)	(25,000)	7,000	
Taxation	(15,000)	(10,000)	5,000	
Net current assets	15,000	20,000		
	50,000	55,000		
Capital and reserves				
Called up share capital	10,000	12,000	2,000	
Other reserves	30,000	30,000		
Profit and loss account	10,000	13,000	3,000	
	50,000	55,000		

Explanation of balance sheet changes

The changes emerging from a straight comparison of the two balance sheets are not sufficient in themselves for the purpose of measuring funds. Further information is required.

Fixed assets: The changes in these accounts are analysed as follows:

Land and buildings—cost of installing partition £2,000, Plant and machinery—the net decrease of £2,000 is explainable in terms of the disposal of old equipment originally costing £2,000 and written down to £1,000 in the books, the acquisition of new equipment for £3,000, and the depreciation for the year of £4,000. The old equipment realized £1,200. There was a gain on asset realization of £200 shown on the profit and loss account.

The funds flow relating to fixed assets are:

	£	£
Application of funds: Land and buildings	2,000	
Plant and machinery	3,000	
		5,000
Source of funds: funds realized from disposals		1,200

Note

The gain on asset realization of £200 shown in the profit and loss account is an accounting gain. The funds flow resulting from the disposal is the sale value realized of £1,200.

Current assets: In terms of funds flow analysis, the reductions in stocks of £5,000 and of trade debtors of £4,000 are considered as sources of funds. They result from the partial liquidation of funds that had been invested in stocks and trade debtors. Conversely, increases in these items would be treated as applications of funds.

Changes in cash at bank and in hand may be explained as follows:

Increases are treated as *applications* of funds
Decreases are treated as *sources* of funds.

It may be noted, therefore, the cash balances are treated in the same way as other current assets as regards funds flow analysis. In this example, the increase of £2,000 in the cash balance is an *application* of funds during the accounting year ended 31 December 19X5.

Creditors: Increases in creditor balances are treated as *sources* of funds during the year in which they occur, and decreases in these balances are treated as *applications* of funds. In the logic of funds flow analysis, creditors represent sources of finance, and the reimbursement of the credits obtained are application of funds. Accordingly, the decrease in trade creditors of £7,000 is interpreted as an application of funds.

The taxation account is an exception of this practice. The taxation account is credited with the amount provided for taxation in respect of the current financial year and debited with tax payments made. The tax payments themselves may relate to the current financial year and also to preceding financial years. The amount credited to the taxation account, representing an amount owing to the Inland Revenue, is not treated as a source of funds as would be the case if the Inland Revenue were treated as a trade creditor. This is because the statement of source and application of funds shows net profits *before* taxation as the originating source of funds from operations. It would be double counting, therefore, to show an increase in the balance on the taxation account on the balance sheet as a source of funds. Taxes on profits are regarded as application of funds *only* when they are paid. In the example shown, the change in the taxation account balance is ignored for the purposes of the statement of sources and application of funds.

Capital: Additional injections of capital are sources of funds. In this example, the additional capital subscribed of £2,000 is a source of funds.

Reserves: Changes in reserves result merely from book transactions— they do not give rise to funds flows. Reserve accounts, as well as similar book transactions such as provision accounts, are used in connection with the transfer of accounting balances.

Profit and loss account: The profit and loss account balance of £13,000 represents the retained profits as at 31 December 19X5. To ascertain the funds flowing from operations, it is necessary to refer to the profit and loss account results from accounting practice in which book gains and losses on asset disposal will be included in the calculation of the net profit or loss, and in which non-cash expenses in the form of provisions will have been debited. Some important items, such as provisions for depreciation of fixed assets, for doubtful debts, etc., do not create cash outflows. Accordingly, the net profit or loss for the year has to be adjusted and recalculated in terms of funds flows from operations.

Assume that in the example of Marterey plc, the profit and loss account for the year ended 31 December 19X5 is as follows:

	£
Turnover	125,000
Cost of sales	75,000
Gross profit	50,000
Other costs and expenses	25,000
	25,000
Gain on asset disposal	200
Profit on ordinary activity	25,200
Tax on ordinary activity	10,000
Profit for the year	15,200
Profit for the year	15,200
Balance b/f	10,000
	25,200
Dividend paid	12,200
Balance c/f	13,000

The provision for depreciation of fixed assets for the year amounted to £4,000. The tax actually paid during the year was £15,000, shown as outstanding at 31 December 19X4.

The funds flow from operations is calculated as follows:

	£	£
Profit for the year before tax		25,200
Adjustment for items not involving the movement of funds:		
Depreciation of fixed assets	4,000	
Gain on asset disposal	(200)	
		3,800
Funds generated from operations		29,000

Calculating the funds flow from operations before taxation and dividends allows these latter two items to be shown as applications of funds as and when they are paid. Amounts shown on the balance sheet as provisions for taxation and provisions for proposed dividends are ignored when examining the balance sheet for changes susceptible of giving rise to funds flows.

Preparing the statement of source and application of funds

The sources and application of funds calculated above may now be represented in a statement of source and application of funds as follows:

Statement of source and application of funds for the year ended
31 December 19X5

Source	£	Application	£
Funds from operations	29,000	Purchase of fixed assets	5,000
Additional capital	2,000	Taxes paid	15,000
Sale of fixed assets	1,200	Dividend paid	12,200
Decrease in stocks	5,000	Decrease in creditors	7,000
Decrease in debtors	4,000	Increase in cash	2,000
	41,200		41,200

The statement of source and application of funds may be presented in different ways. In the United Kingdom, companies are required to follow SSAP 10 *Statements of Source and Application of Funds*, when publishing their financial reports to shareholders.

SSAP 10 *Statements of Source and Application of Funds*

SSAP 10 was published in January 1976, some two and a half years before the release of the EEC Fourth Directive which contained a requirement for the publication of statements of source and application of funds by companies registered within member countries of the EEC. SSAP 10 prescribes rules for the presentation of such statements which conforms to the requirements of the EEC Fourth Directive, and accordingly remains valid today.

SSAP 10 does not define funds, but indicates that the statement of source and application of funds should have as a bottom line the notion of liquid funds. According to SSAP 10,

> a funds statement should show the sources from which funds have flowed into the company and the way in which they have been used. It should show clearly the funds generated or absorbed by the operations of the business and the manner in which any resulting surplus of liquid assets has been applied or any deficit of such

assets has been financed, distinguishing the long term from the short term. The statement should distinguish the use of funds for the purchase of new fixed assets from the funds used in increasing the working capital of the company.

SSAP 10 requires the following information to be disclosed:

(1) The profit or loss for the period.
(2) An adjustment for items charged in the profit and loss account which do not involve the movement of funds, for example, depreciation and other provisions.
(3) Dividends paid.
(4) Acquisitions and disposals of fixed assets and other non-current assets.
(5) Funds raised or expended in increasing or redeeming issued share capital, long-term or medium-term loans.
(6) Increases or decreases in working capital, subdivided into components.
(7) Movements in net liquid funds, defined as cash at bank and in hand, as well as cash equivalents (investments held as current assets). Included under this heading are bank overdrafts and other borrowings.

SSAP 10 provides the following model for the statement of source and application of funds.

Statement of source and application of funds for the year ended
31 December 19X

	£	£	£
Sources of funds			
Profit before tax			xxxx
Adjustments for items not involving the movement of funds:			
Depreciation		<u>xxxxx</u>	
			<u>xxxx</u>
Total generated from operations			xxxx
Funds from other sources			
Issue of shares for cash			xxxx
Application of funds			
Dividends paid		(xxxx)	
Tax paid		(xxxx)	
Purchase of fixed assets		<u>(xxxx)</u>	
			(xxxx
			A
Change in working capital			
Increase in stocks		xxxx	
Increase in debtors		xxxx	
(Increase) decrease in creditors, excluding taxation and proposed dividends		xxxx	
Movement in net liquid funds			
Increase (decrease) in			
Cash balances	xxxx		
Short term investments	<u>xxxx</u>		
		<u>xxxx</u>	
			<u><u>A</u></u>

The model layout proposed by SSAP 10 highlights the following:

(1) The net flow, taking into account funds from operations and other sources of funds and applications of funds.
(2) Increases/decrease in working capital.
(3) Movement in net liquid funds.

It is particularly important to note that the layout explains the net funds flow in terms of changes in working capital, and in that context gives a separate emphasis to movements in liquid funds.

Example 13
The statement of source and application of funds for Marterey plc for the year ended 31 December 19X5 shown in Example 12 above resulted in the following presentation:

Statement of source and application of funds for the year ended
31 December 19X5

Source	£	Application	£
Funds from operations	29,000	Purchase of fixed assets	5,000
Additional capital	2,000	Taxes paid	15,000
Sale of fixed assets	1,200	Dividend paid	12,200
Decrease in stocks	5,000	Decrease in creditors	7,000
Decrease in debtors	4,000	Increase in cash	2,000
	41,200		41,200

Redrafting this statement in the form required by SSAP 10 results in the following presentation:

Marterey plc
Statement of source and application of funds for the year ended
31 December 19X5

	£	£
Source of funds		
Profit before tax		25,200
Adjustments for items not involving the movement of funds:		
Depreciation	4,000	
Gain on asset disposal	(200)	
		3,800
Total generated from operations		29,000
Funds from other sources		
Issue of shares for cash		2,000
Sale of fixed assets		1,200
Application of funds		
Dividends paid	(12,200)	
Tax paid	(15,000)	
Purchase of fixed assets	(5,000)	
		(32,200)
		—
Change in working capital		
Decrease in stocks	(5,000)	
Decrease in debtors	(4,000)	
Decrease in creditors, excluding taxation and proposed dividends	7,000	
Movement in net liquid funds		
Increase in:		
Cash balances	2,000	
Short-term investments	—	
		—

Question 10

The balance sheet for Schurig plc for the years ended 19X1, 19X2 and 19X3 are as follows:

Schurig plc
Balance sheets as at 31 December

	19X1 £000s	19X2 £000s	19X3 £000s
Fixed assets			
Plant and equipment	13,200	16,110	16,410
Current assets			
Stocks	2,190	2,280	2,490
Debtors	2,040	2,100	2,430
Short-term investments	4,200	1,800	1,290
Cash at bank and in hand	1,920	2,010	2,580
Creditors: Amounts falling due within one year			
Short-term loans	(2,340)	(2,580)	(2,550)
Trade creditors	(2,760)	(2,610)	(2,670)
	(5,100)	(5,190)	(5,220)
Net current assets	5,250	3,000	3,570
Total assets *less* current liabilities	18,450	19,110	19,980
Capital and reserves			
Called up share capital	4,500	4,500	4,500
Share premium account	9,000	9,000	9,000
Profit and loss account	4,950	5,610	6,480
	18,450	19,110	19,980

Other Data:	19X1 £000s	19X2 £000s	19X3 £000s
Profit before tax	960	1,020	1,230
Annual depreciation	645	780	900
Dividends declared and paid	360	360	360

In 19X2, equipment was sold at a loss of £210,000. New plant in 19X2 cost £5,100,000 and in 19X3 cost £1,200,000.

Required

Prepare a statement of source and application of funds for 19X2 and 19X3 in compliance with SSAP 10.

Question 11

Set out below are the condensed balance sheets for Glazings plc for 19X1 and 19X2, and a profit and loss account for the year ended 31 December 19X2.

Glazings plc
Balance sheet as at 31 December

	19X1		19X2	
	£000s	£000s	£000s	£000s
Fixed assets				
Land and buildings at cost	240		240	
Accumulated depreciation	30	210	40	200
Plant and machinery at cost	262		694	
Accumulated depreciation	42	220	84	610
Motor vehicles	60		60	
Accumulated depreciation	30	30	34	26
		460		836
Current assets				
Stocks	204		234	
Trade debtors	360		432	
Cash at bank and in hand	276		10	
	840		676	
Creditors: Amounts falling due within one year				
Trade creditors	(144)		(192)	
Taxation	(60)		(80)	
Proposed dividend	(16)		(20)	
	(220)		(292)	
Net current assets		620		384
Total assets *less* current liabilities		1,080		1,220
Creditors: Amounts falling due after one year				
7% Debenture loans		140		200
		940		1,020
Capital and reserves				
Called up share capital		600		600
Share premium account		100		100
Other reserves		80		100
Profit and loss account		160		220
		940		1,020

Summarized profit and loss account for the year ended
31 December 19X2

	£000s	£000s
Turnover		1,324
Cost of sales		936
Gross profit		388
Distribution costs	98.8	
Administrative expenses	100	198.8
Profit on ordinary activities		189.2
Taxation on ordinary activities		80
		109.2
Loss on the sale of assets		9.2
Profit for the financial year		100
Ordinary dividend proposed		(20)
Transfer to reserves		(20)
Retained profit for the financial year		60

Plant and machinery recorded at cost of £28,000 and at written down value of £16,000 was sold for £6,800.

Required
Prepare a statement of source and application of funds for the year ended 31 December 19X2 in conformity with SSAP 10.

7 Accounting Concepts and the Need for Standards ——

Previous chapters have been concerned with the examination of the practices of financial accounting, and in particular those relating to record keeping and the use of recorded data for profit measurement, representations of asset values and the control of working capital.

Underpinning these practices are a set of concepts which not only have a deterministic influence on the manner in which accounting procedures are carried out but also have a profound influence on the meaning and usefulness of the information resulting from these procedures.

Some of the most important concepts have already been mentioned, for example, the entity concept, the concept of periodicity, the accruals and the matching concepts. It has been noted that they lend a particular characteristic to the manner in which accountants treat accounting events.

In the search for rationality which is a feature of the scientific method increasingly applied in the study of accounting, many authors have been concerned by the evident lack of *general* theory of accounting which would provide a coherent framework of reference for the continued development of accounting knowledge. In particular, such a theory would assist in the analysis of the objectives of accounting and would provide criteria for evaluating the validity of accounting practices. As a result, it is argued, accounting would become more 'scientific' in its approach to the analysis of its problems and in the formulation of appropriate solutions and methods.

Recent criticisms of financial accounting information have drawn public attention to what accountants were content to regard as matters of purely professional interest and concern. Criticism has centred particularly on the treatment of inflation, the representation of asset values, and the wide variations in the measurement of the profits of the *same* company resulting simply from the application of different valuations concepts.

In essence, the debate has now focused on the need to re-examine the substance of some important accounting concepts and to provide *standards* for regulating the manner in which they are applied in the practice of accounting. The significance of such standards, therefore, lies in the fact that they act as a substitute for rules which would otherwise emanate from a *Theory* of Accounting in which rationality rather than consensus would act as the deterministic influence.

In this chapter we summarize and discuss the substance of some of the most important accounting concepts, such as those referred to in the third paragraph above, and the need to provide adequate standards with which to regulate accounting practice. This chapter is therefore divided into four sections as follows:

Accounting concepts
Accounting standards
International accounting standards
Statements of standard accounting practice.

Accounting concepts

Accounting is a man-made discipline. Its methods cannot be validated by reference to 'natural laws' as in the physical sciences or to the internal logic of numbers as in mathematics. Yet, accountants cannot avoid the need for reference to rules which not only provide a unity of understanding but also a uniformity of approach in the practice of accounting. The significance of such rules is evident when one considers that accountants attach meaning to events by representing them as numbers. Such meaning would be lost entirely if the compilation and the communication of accounting numbers did not conform to a generally accepted set of rules. Accounting rules are sometimes referred to as 'concepts'.

The entity concept

The entity concept defines the limits of the financial accounting process by its identification with an organization deemed to have a separate existence from its owner(s). The accounting process is concerned with the activities of the entity and not the activities of its owner or other persons.

There are two interpretations of the entity concept:

(i) The proprietary concept which views the entity as a vehicle through which the owner engages in economic activity with a view to profit. Assets are regarded as belonging to the owner, and the balance sheet reflects the owner's interest in the entity as being the net worth stated as the owner's equity.

(ii) The entity concept, as distinct from the proprietary concept, views the entity as having a separate identity with its own objectives. This interpretation may be termed the pure entity concept. Hence, the owner is treated as being merely another interested party having claims against the entity. In line with this view, the assets are regarded as belonging properly to the entity, and the claims against it are all classified as equities.

The sole trader is the best example of the manifestation of the proprietary concept, and the limited liability company is the foremost example of the pure entity concept.

The money measurement concept

This important concept limits the recognition of accounting events to those which may be described in money terms. As a result, many factors of considerable economic importance to the entity are not recorded, for example, management expertise, technical competence of employees, good industrial and customer relations.

The failure to recognize these factors arises principally from the fact that the accounting process is transaction-based, and money value tends to arise mainly from transactions giving rise to rights and obligations susceptible of expression in money values.

Accounting does not preclude entirely the use of non-monetary measurements. As will be seen in Part 2, measurement of physical quantities are used in costing, and statistics are often found in explanations put forward by accountants in appendices to financial reports.

Although non-monetary measurements bring further clarity and meaning to purely monetary measurements, the major obstacles to widening the basis of the accounting process in this respect are as follows:

(i)   monetary measurements have a unity of meaning which makes them readily understood when communicated as information,

(ii) monetary measurements provide a basis for quite complex financial analyses which rely on numbers having a common denominator,

(iii) non-monetary measurements cannot be integrated meaningfully with monetary measurements to provide a generalized calculus of the value of the firm and its activities.

Nevertheless, there is an active interest in non-monetary measurements in the current debate about social responsibility accounting. This subject is beyond the scope of this text, but reference should be made to *Accounting Theory and Practice* for a discussion of this development.

Question 1

Jeremy and Irene Bownus have been equal partners for the last seven years in a successful interior design consultancy firm. They employ four assistants who are competent to work without supervision in the firm's business.

A large manufacturer of wallpaper and paint has expressed interest in purchasing the partnership business. Jeremy and Irene are concerned that the balance sheet of the business may be used as the basis for calculating a price. Since they have always operated from rented premises, and have no fixed assets of significant value, they feel that this may affect any offer that is made.

The balance sheet at 31 August 19X8 being the most recent one was as follows:

Balance sheet as at 31 August 19X8

	J. Bownus £	I. Bownus £	Total £
Capital account	3,500	3,500	7,000
Current account	4,400	3,050	7,450
	7,900	6,550	14,450

Represented by:

Furniture at written down book value		1,190
Office equipment at written down book value		1,480
Motor vehicles at written down book value		7,000
Cameras		1,200
		10,870
Debtors	2,200	
Cash at bank	2,010	
	4,210	
less: Creditors	630	3,580
		14,450

The net profit of the partnership for the last seven years prior to any distribution to the partners was as follows:

	£		£
19X2	6,200	19X6	13,800
19X3	9,400	19X7	15,760
19X4	11,150	19X8	16,940
19X5	12,400		

Required

Write a report to Jeremy and Irene Bownus suggesting (i) why their fears may be unfounded and (ii) the reasoning which may be behind any offer. *Note*: Do not attempt to suggest a price, though you may indicate the factors relevant to the valuation of the firm.

The dual aspect concept

The essence of double-entry bookkeeping is the concept that all transactions are classified twice. The manifestation of this concept is the fact that they are entered twice: once as debits and once as credits. This allows the accounting equation to be maintained throughout the bookkeeping system.

The detailed application of this concept has been examined in preceding chapters. Although advanced data recording systems based on computers have been developed to process accounting information in great detail and integrate the activities of complex organizations, these systems still rely on the dual aspect concept.

Although the dual aspect concept relies on faultless mathematical principles, which we noted ensured that the total debit and credit entries balance when extracted in the form of a trial balance, errors may still occur even in computerized data-processing systems. These errors may not only be attributed to input errors but also to erroneous interpretations of the economic events which accounts purport to show.

The cost concept

In seeking for objectivity in attaching values to inputs of economic resources, accountants use the acquisition price as the most objective measurement since it is supported by the evidence of a transaction. Accountants have been accused of confusing verifiability with objectivity. Nevertheless, the cost concept provides uniformity in the treatment of inputs and provides a reliable valuation under conditions of stable prices. Price instability associated with specific inflation and the debasement in the value of money associated with general inflation undermine the validity of the assumptions upon which the cost concept is based. In particular, it leads to serious distortions in the measurement of profit when historic costs are allocated against current revenues. As a result, this concept has suffered increasing criticism when used for financial reporting purposes, and an alternative system based on replacement cost has been recommended for adoption in the United Kingdom.

The going concern concept

This concept is of great importance for asset valuation, for it reflects the assumption that the firm is to be valued on the basis that it is a going concern, and is not likely to terminate in the period immediately ahead. In effect, this concept underpins the asset values shown on the balance sheet and the other concept associated with the representation of liabilities. To abandon this concept would imply that assets should be valued on a realizable value basis. Nevertheless, the following observations may be made:

(i) It is not necessarily true that firms do not cease trading. Therefore, balance sheet valuation based on the going concern assumption may give investors an incorrect view of the value of assets, particularly when firms cease trading shortly after the last published balance sheet. In this connection, decisions to cease trading may be taken quite abruptly in the face of a perception of radically changed circumstances.

(ii) It is misleading to suppose that the going concern concept applies equally to continuity in the firm's operations in a particular sector or as regards a particular product. In this respect, the going concern concept finds no support in any other formal study of economic behaviour.

(iii) The concept precludes the consideration of alternative courses of action and prevents the provision of relevant accounting information for this purpose.

The realization concept

The realization concept influences financial accounting in two ways. First, it acts to mark the recognition of an accounting event and to regulate the timing of entries in the bookkeeping system. Second, it prevents undue optimism in business affairs by restricting the recognition of gains to those which have been actually realized through a transaction giving rise to legal rights to receive monetary payments.

In essence, the realization concept reflects the spirit of caution and conservatism which marks the accountant's approach to the analysis of business activities. It reinforces the cost concept by requiring costs to be accumulated until they may be allocated to the revenues with which they are associated.

The realization concept is criticized because it may distort the process of profit determination in cases where gains may have accrued over a long period but are not recognized until a sale has occurred. By refusing to recognize 'holding gains', it is argued that the accounting process rejects a cardinal feature of profit measurement which is to measure increases in wealth between two points in time.

To prevent excessive distortions in certain cases, the realization concept is modified. This is particularly the case in large building and engineering projects, where gains are accrued on the certification of work. As regards routine trading operations involving the receipt of an order, the issue of an invoice, the despatch of goods and the receipt of payment, the issue of the invoice marks the timing of an entry in the bookkeeping system.

The concept of periodicity

It may be argued that the only correct measure of enterprise profit is the surplus arising over its entire life and determined at that point of time when all business transactions have been completed and the only remaining asset is cash. This view would be inconsistent with the going concern concept and with the need to assess the financial status and performance of the firm from time to time.

Hence, an arbitrary time period, usually a year, is chosen as a basis for the measurement of *periodic* profit. The assumption underlying the concept of periodicity is that business events can be identified with particular periods.

This concept induces the necessity for supporting concepts for example, the realization, the matching, and the accruals concept which have their logic in the measurement of periodic profit.

The concept of periodicity assumes a degree of homogeneity in the pattern of business activities and a corresponding smoothness in the time profile of a periodic profit stream. Neither of these assumptions is confirmed by the evidence of business activities.

The additional problem induced by this concept relates to the depreciation of fixed asset values over successive accounting periods. As we noted in Chapter 5, depreciation poses complex theoretical and practical problems.

The matching concept

This concepts supports that of periodicity in assuming that particular items of expense can be associated with the revenues of particular periods. It also subscribes to the accounting view that cost is an appropriate measure of economic value. Moreover, it assumes that cost flows parallel the physical flow of goods, thereby inducing the various stock valuation methods discussed in Chapter 6.

Cost allocation procedures implicitly required by the matching concept results in a great variety in cost numbers matched against periodic revenue. Thus, the allocation of fixed asset costs and other costs incurred over protracted time make it impossible to cost numbers which are free of bias. Indeed, as will be seen in Part 2, accounting procedures for allocating and apportioning *current* production costs are themselves the source of distortions in cost measurements. These costing procedures are directly related to the matching concept and result from the application of this concept to the measurement of product costs.

The accruals concept

Together with the realization and the matching concept, the accruals concept has its origin in the concept of periodicity. It requires that revenues and expenses associated with a particular accounting period be brought into the calculus of the profit of that period *whether or not* cash has been received or paid.

The importance of the accruals concept has already been made explicit in earlier chapters. From a bookkeeping point of view, recorded receipts and expenditure must be carefully scrutinized in the process of determining periodic revenues and expenses. Payments in advance, both of the nature of revenue and expense, must be excluded and carried forward to the next accounting period to which they belong. Amounts receivable and payable in respect of which no entries in the books have been made must be accrued at the close of the accounting period so that they may be reflected in the revenues and expenses of the year to which they properly belong. As a result, payments received and made in respect of amounts accrued in the previous period are treated as payments from debtors and payments to creditors, and do not affect the measurement of current profit. Accrual accounting represents the conventional accounting approach to profit determination.

Criticisms of the accruals concept are that it introduces complexity into accounting numbers and renders accounting results difficult to interpret by users who are non-accountants. Accordingly, proponents of cash flow accounting argue that it reduces complexity and allows a more general understanding of accounting information. Moreover, they argue that cash flow accounting is more relevant to the decisions which businessmen and investors wish to make. In this connection, it should be noted that one important attribute of the accruals concept is that it smoothes the time profile of periodic cash flows and for this reason alone provides a more accurate view of the trend of periodic profit.

The concept of consistency

This concept is directed at providing a degree of uniformity in accounting numbers to enable realistic comparisons to be made by requiring that methods of treating particular items should be followed consistently once they have been adopted.

Uniformity is required in accounting for two reasons. First, to permit comparisons to be made by reference to the results of previous years by a company in the process of evaluating its own performance and making decisions about the future. Second, to permit useful inter-firm comparisons to be made by investors in the process of selecting and evaluating investment alternatives.

The concept of consistency is at variance with the practice of accounting in several important respects. First, accounting practice permits alternative valuation methods to coexist within the same firm and as between different firms. For example closing stock may be valued at the 'lower of cost or net realizable value'. Additionally, different firms may select entirely different valuation methods in the allocation and apportionment of costs of stock values. Second, the practice of accounting requires the exercise of judgement in considering the manner in which particular events should be represented. This has led to serious misunderstanding in the past as regards, for example, the valuation of stock items. It is possible for one firm of accountants to give a radically different treatment to a stock item from that of another firm called to give an opinion on the same matter. As a result, disputes have occurred in which the accounting profession has suffered a measure of criticism for not seeming able to keep its own house in order. These criticisms have led to a demand for some degree of standardization of accounting practice, and the establishment of the Accounting Standards Committee to deal with this problem.

The concept of prudence

This concept has a pervasive influence on accounting practice. As regards financial accounting, it is manifested in the following propositions:

(a) the accountant should under no circumstances anticipate profit but should provide for potential losses,
(b) where alternative valuation methods are available that method should be selected which leads to the lowest value.

In a real sense, the concept of prudence reflects the social role which accountants play in providing information to businessmen and investors. Excessive optimism may bias the judgement of businessmen. The accountant acts as a foil by discounting risk factors in any information which he provides.

Question 2

David Lawrence owns 5 houses which he leases to students on an annual basis. The rentals fixed for the year ending 30 June are as follows:

Properties 1 and 2	£1,000 per annum each
Properties 3 and 4	£1,500 per annum each
Property 5	£2,000 per annum

Lawrence prepared his profit and loss account for every year to 30 June for the purpose of computing his tax liability. The following information is available at 30 June 19X7:

(1) Rates paid in full for 19X7/19X8, i.e. to 31 March 19X8 to rating year:

	£
Properties 1 and 2	320 each
Properties 3 and 4	360 each
Property 5	420

The balance of prepaid rates at 30 June 19X6 was £1,080.

(2) Repairs and renewals paid for the year to 30 June 19X7	267
(3) Insurance paid for the year to 30 June 19X7	68
(4) Electricity paid for the year to 30 June 19X7	492
Estimate of electricity used and unpaid at 30 June 19X6	118
Estimate of electricity used and unpaid at 30 June 19X7	78
Estimate of monies collectable from metered coin boxes at 30 June 19X7	95

(5) All rents due for the year ended 30 June 19X7 had been collected with the exception of the rent for the last quarter on property 4 which had been occupied by third-year students who had graduated and left. The students in property 5 had paid a quarter in advance for the period to 30 September 19X7 to secure the tenancy for the next year.

Required

Prepare a profit and loss account for the year to 30 June 19X7 on

(1) an accrual basis
(2) a cash basis

Question 3

Bond Ltd and Enlaye Ltd are two companies which have been in existence for approximately the same duration of time and are engaged in importing and distributing food products. Their profit for the year ended 31 December 19X3 is exactly similar in the sum of £120,000 each.

The following information is available:

(a) Bond Ltd was originally financed by the issue of 100,000 ordinary shares of £1 each which were fully paid, whilst Enlaye Ltd was financed by the issue of 40,000 ordinary shares of £1 each fully paid and a debenture issue of £60,000 at 11%.

(b) Bond Ltd have written off against profit the sum of £8,692 which was incurred on research into food storage. Enlaye Ltd had treated the sum of £9,500 incurred on new product research as an asset acquisition.

(c) Bond Ltd have charged depreciation against their profit on the basis of straight line method in respect of fixed assets costing £80,000 and having a 5-year life with no residual value. Enlaye Ltd have exactly the same asset structure and fixed asset values of £80,000 but have given their assets an 8-year life.

(d) Bond Ltd have used a FIFO stock valuation system giving stock a value of £34,000, where a LIFO valuation would have given a value of £23,000. Enlaye Ltd have used a LIFO stock valuation system giving stock a value of £18,000, where a FIFO valuation would have given £27,000.

Required
Calculate

(i) the net profit of Enlaye Ltd if they had applied the same methods used by Bond Ltd for measuring profit.

(ii) the net profit of Bond Ltd if they had applied the same methods used by Enlaye Ltd for measuring profit.

Question 1
On 1 January 19X1, George Frobisher commenced business as a market gardener with an initial injection of capital of £5,000 in cash, and using land which he had purchased three years ago for £6,500. The following summary relates to transactions for the six months to 30 June 19X1:

	£
Purchased seeds—lettuce, radish, etc.	150
Purchased sunflower seeds	500
Purchased manure and fertilizer	300
Purchased van	1,600
Purchased tractor and implements	2,000
Purchased herb plants	250
Withdrawn for personal use £50 per week	1,300
Sold to local health store—herbs, etc.	600
Sold to greengrocers—lettuce, etc.	1,200
Motor and tractor expenses paid	610

On 30 June 19X1, Frobisher received his bank statement which showed that he had only £50 left in hand. Realizing that he would

have to borrow from the bank, Frobisher drew up the following profit and loss account to 30 June 19X1:

Profit and loss account for the period ended 30 June 19X1

		£	£
Income:	Herbs $\frac{1}{2}$ sold	600	
	$\frac{1}{2}$ to be sold	600	1,200
	Lettuces, etc. $\frac{1}{3}$ sold	1,200	
	$\frac{2}{3}$ to be sold	2,400	3,600
	Sunflower seeds—expected to be sold for:		3,500
	Increase in the value of land £(9,000 − 6,500)		2,500
			10,800
Expenses:	Cost of seeds and manure	1,200	
	Motor and tractor expenses	610	
	Loss in value of:		
	(i) Van £(1,600 − 1,500)	100	
	(ii) Tractor £(2,000 − 1,750)	250	
	Wages—self	1,300	
			3,460
	Net profit		7,340

Having prepared the profit and loss account Frobisher asks for your comments, and in particular for your opinion as to his chances of obtaining borrowing facilities from the bank on the basis of the information shown in that statement. During conversation with Frobisher, you learn that some people have become mildly ill after consuming herbs which he had sold to the health store and that the store was now asking Frobisher for a refund.

Required

Redraft Frobisher's profit and loss account to 30 June 19X1 in accordance with recognized accounting concepts.

Question 5

George Whiteside graduated from university with a degree in business studies, and an idea for putting his recently acquired knowledge of computers to profitable use. Using £250 which he had saved from vacation earnings and £1,000 borrowed from his mother, he commenced business under the name 'Mainchance Computer Dating'. This business offered to pair couples by scientific matching.

He leased premises on 1 September 19X9, the day on which he commenced trading, and paid £200 being six months' rent in advance. He then inserted advertisements in various student magazines and placed cards in shop windows, all of which cost £620. He paid £480 immediately and secured monthly credit terms for the balance which was to be paid at the end of October 19X9.

To his delight, within a fortnight he had received over 600 replies of which 400 contained the requested fee of £6. Quickly settling down to the job of classifying the applications, he proceeded to set up the necessary programs and, buying computer time for £500 which he paid at once, he matched up the applicants and wrote to them all giving them a selection of suitable persons with the address and the relevant information.

In the course of the following week, he received the following information:

(a) Eight of the cheques for £6 each had been returned marked 'unpaid'.

(b) Six couples had met and come to immediate matrimonial arrangements. His fee for this additional success was to be £25, but none of the couples had yet paid.

(c) Fourteen people had turned up for appointments which had not been kept by the other party, and George Whiteside had promised to arrange alternative dates or refund the fee.

(d) One retired businessman was so delighted with his date that a marriage had been arranged and he promised to send a cheque for £1,000 to Mainchance Computer Dating out of gratitude.

(e) Thirty men had turned up to one date organized by George's program and fighting had broken out in the pub when just one girl appeared. Two broken noses had been reported so far and property in the pub had been damaged. A preliminary estimate of claims against the service came to £75.

(f) Inexplicably, George's mother's name had been included in the computer program, and she was demanding to know why so many men were calling at her flat. She asked him for an account of his business to 31 October 19X9.

Required

Prepare an accounting statement in any suitable form in respect of the activities of Mainchance Computer Dating, and explain your reason for the treatment of all items shown on this statement.

Accounting standards

The variety of different procedures and valuations permitted under generally accepted accounting practice which has given rise to the problems referred to in the previous section, has eroded to some extent their basic accounting purpose. This purpose is to provide a set of rules for ensuring that accounting information has an identity of meaning to all its users. A prerequisite to this condition is that accounting procedures should themselves be standardized in such a way as to guarantee that the information resulting from the application of these procedures to data will be identical in meaning to all users.

Underlying the debate about accounting standards are a number of very important issues for the accounting profession. These issues are as follows:

(1) *Reliability* Accounting information should be reliable in use. This implies that users should be able to rely on some basic assumptions about the quality of accounting information produced by accountants. The ultimate criterion of reliability is one which satisfies the following conditions:

   (a) that users know precisely the meaning of information, and are not deceived in their analysis of its relevance to their own needs,
   (b) that users know precisely the limits to the knowledge content of the information provided.

   It is evident that in considering the range of public expectations from accounting information, a degree of reliability which satisfies the minimum conditions stated above must be regarded as a fundamental requirement.

(2) *Uniformity* Accounting information is used for making informed judgements about the affairs of a business, and also for making informed comparisons between the performance of different businesses. Where these judgements are used by the public for the purpose of making investment decisions, it follows that the degree of uniformity which is required should enable *reliable comparisons* to be made. The pressure for the standardization of accounting practices is to ensure a uniformity of treatment of data and hence an identity of the meaning of information.

(3) *Comparability* Reliability and uniformity are integrated in the notion of comparability. This debate about comparability is more complex than is implicit in the assumption that uniformity of accounting practice will secure perfect comparability. In a real sense, the activities and the circumstances of different firms are not comparable because they are not identical. Indeed, the activities and the circumstances of the same firm may not be identical from year to year. Hence, the issue of comparability is not really concerned with discovering an *identity* of meaning about the activities and circumstances of firms, but it is concerned with

revealing the *differences* between them. Some assert, therefore, that these differences may well be lost to view if accountants are not allowed to select their own procedure for revealing these differences.

(4) *Judgement* Accountants assert that they should be allowed to exercise some judgement in interpreting data. This implies that some variety should be allowed for in the procedures available for transforming data into information. This point is made particularly as regards alternative valuation methods and ways of treating depreciation.

These several issues do not form part of a restricted discussion within the accounting profession. Both in the USA and in the UK, the criticisms levelled in the press against the accounting profession has been associated with the failure to disclose important information to investors about the true state of affairs in a number of celebrated company reports. Although accountants have been able to formulate their own rules about what is 'true and fair', their interpretation of truth and fairness has not seemed convincing to the public. In the wake of public concern and the fear that governments might intervene to impose a measure of state control in the affairs of the profession, the pressure for standardization has become overwhelming.

The discussion of accounting standards has taken place at a national and at an international level. Given the growing interdependency of nation states, the appearance of unified capital markets and supranational bodies to formulate international laws, it is to be expected that there will ultimately be a set of international accounting standards which will be universally applicable. The processes by which these international accounting standards are currently being forged are interesting in themselves. Some countries, for example the USA and the UK, have a long tradition of professional independence. Others, for example France, have a long experience of state control.

In the USA, an early interest in accounting standards resulted from the Securities Exchange Commission (SEC) which was established under the Securities Exchange Act of 1934. It has power to intervene in the accounting practices adopted by corporations seeking listings on the stock exchanges. Although the SEC has a powerful influence in this respect, it has been concerned essentially with the protection of shareholders and investors and fair dealings on the stock exchanges rather than with accounting theory as such. At a professional level, the American Institute of Certified Public Accountants formed the Financial Accounting Standards Board (FASB) in 1973 with the objective of formulating financial accounting standards. Indications so far are that a pragmatic approach will be adopted towards pressures for standards emanating from different sources. The possibility of intervention by Congress either directly or through empowered agencies does exist.

In the UK, too, an early interest in accounting standards is evident in previous endeavours by the Institute of Chartered Accountants in England and Wales to obtain a measure of agreement on accounting principles. A series of Recommendations on Accounting Principles has been issued on matters of professional interest. This endeavour was never a comprehensive approach to the problem, nor did it produce anything comparable in scope to the Inventory of Generally Accepted Accounting Principles of Business Enterprise issued by the American Institute of Certified Public Accountants in 1965. In 1971, the Accounting Standards Committee was established and has since issued a series of Statements on Standard Accounting Practice (SSAPs). These will be discussed in the final section of this chapter.

At an international level, progress has been made and agreement has been reached in several areas and a number of International Accounting Standards have been published since the International Accounting Standards Board was established in 1973.

An important influence on the development of international accounting standards within the European Economic Community has been the Fourth Directive issued in 1978 by the European Economic Commission. The Fourth Directive, which is obligatory on member countries, emphasized the four concepts stated in SSAP 2 (discussed hereinafter), namely accruals, prudence, consistency and going concern. Additionally, it prescribed two alternative formats for the presentation of the balance sheet and the profit and loss account and their required content. It obliged countries which did not already do so to legislate for the publication of funds flow statements and notes to the accounts, in addition to balance sheets and profit and loss accounts. Finally, it declared that the 'true and fair view' audit certification followed in United Kingdom practice should be a universal standard in the EEC. Some minor alterations to English company law were required as a result of the Fourth Directive, and these were enacted in the Companies Act 1981. In so far as the Fourth Directive applies, all countries within the EEC are now on the same basis of accounting for companies.

The Seventh Directive dealing with the consolidated accounts of groups of companies was finally published in 1983, and is in the process of becoming law in the member countries of the EEC.

It is evident that the issues involved in the debate about accounting standards have deeper roots than the superficial absence of uniformity in accounting procedures. It is clear that it is really the absence of a *theory of financial accounting* which is the root cause of problems. There is already evidence of a search towards a methodology essential to the formulation of such a theory in current discussions about the objectives of financial reporting. A theory of financial accounting would provide a framework for evaluating alternative accounting practices in a systematic and coherent manner consistent with the scientific method used in other sciences for formulating theories. In this analysis, the approach to the superficial absence of uniformity by the diktat of accounting standards would not appear to be an appropriate way of solving the more fundamental problem. Nevertheless, it may be regarded as affording partial solutions to problems which cannot be presently solved, bearing in mind the current state of the art.

International Accounting Standards

There are several influences at work in the process of welding together an international set of agreed standards of accounting practice. These reflect a tendency towards a common view of the problems involved. In many cases, it is obvious that legislation governing the disclosure of accounting information to shareholders in the form of annual balance sheets and profit statements has a broad similarity from country to country. Tax laws also tend to develop a set of rules for the assessment of taxable corporate profit, and these laws have a degree of similarity. The existence of capital markets and the operation of stock exchanges also have an influence on the nature of published financial accounting information.

It is really at the level of professional practice, and in particular where accounting conventions allow scope for the discretionary treatment of data, that the formulation of International Accounting Standards has a particular significance. In addition to laying down a framework of basic rules, their influence for the evolution of an integrated European Common Market where eventually the executive function for regulating a unified European accounting profession may rest with the European Commission.

The initial impetus for the establishment of the International Accounting Standards Board came from the accounting profession itself. Its founder members were predominantly representative of advanced industrial nations, excluding the Communist bloc, as follows:

Australia	Japan
Canada	Mexico
France	Netherlands
Germany	United Kingdom and Ireland
	United States of America

Many countries have subsequently associated themselves with the International Accounting Standards Board, ranging alphabetically from Bangledesh to Zambia, and including economies as diverse as those of Fiji and Finland, Tobago and Yugoslavia.

The formulation of International Accounting Standards may be seen as a process emanating from the efforts of individual countries in formulating accounting standards. Given the interest of the IASB in the future development of International Accounting Standards, it follows that no country which is associated with IASB will proceed to formulate standards which will directly conflict with possible future IAS. Obviously, the possibility of conflict and redundancy cannot be overlooked.

Statements of Standard Accounting Practice (SSAPs)

The approach to the formulation of SSAPs in the United Kingdom may be taken as representative of a conscious development of accounting standards in keeping with the spirit with which the IASB has adopted. The accounting bodies in the United Kingdom formed an Accounting Standards Committee with technical support staff. The deliberations of topics has led to the issue of a series of Exposure Drafts (ED) setting forth the particular solutions recommended by the ASC and inviting comment. After the elapse of sufficient time for comment and discussion, the Exposure Draft is re-examined and modified as required, and formally issued as a Statement of Standard Accounting Practice (SSAP) which members of the profession are expected to observe.

The uneasy reception which has been accorded to some of the SSAPs which have been issued in the United Kingdom presages the difficulties facing the IASB. The dangers in the approach adopted are:

(a) The response by a professional body to an external need may be slow,
(b) It may be difficult for a professional body to institute disciplinary procedures against its members who do not conform to an accounting standard in respect of which there is not unanimous agreement. This problem has manifested itself already in the United Kingdom.
(c) In an extreme case, a professional body may be forced to expose an SSAP to an adoption or rejection decision by its members. Issues of importance should be decided by force of argument and logic rather than a straight vote in which other influences may be at work.

To date, the ASC has issued the following standards:

SSAP 1 *Accounting for the Results of Associated Companies*
SSAP 2 *Disclosure of Accounting Policies*
SSAP 3 *Earnings Per Share*
SSAP 4 *The Accounting Treatment of Government Grants*
SSAP 5 *Accounting for Value Added Tax*
SSAP 6 *Extraordinary Items and Prior Year Adjustments*
SSAP 8 *The Treatment of Taxation under the Imputation System in the Accounts of Companies*
SSAP 9 *Stocks and Work in Progress*
SSAP 10 *Statements of Source and Application of Funds*
SSAP 12 *Accounting for Depreciation*
SSAP 13 *Accounting for Research and Development*
SSAP 14 *Group Accounts*
SSAP 15 *Accounting for Deferred Taxation*
SSAP 16 *Current Cost Accounting*
SSAP 17 *Accounting for Post Balance Sheet Events*
SSAP 18 *Accounting for Contingencies*
SSAP 19 *Accounting for Investment Properties*
SSAP 20 *Foreign Currency Translation*
SSAP 21 *Accounting for Leases and Hire Purchase Contracts*
SSAP 22 *Accounting for Goodwill*
SSAP 23 *Accounting for Acquisitions and Mergers*

The prime concern underlying these SSAPs is with quoted companies, and the procedures adopted to report financial information to investors.

Perhaps the most useful SSAP for the purpose of this text is SSAP 2 *Disclosure of Accounting Policies*, which is reproduced in its entirety below.

SSAP 2: Disclosure of Accounting Policies

Contents   *Paragraphs*

2. Disclosure of accounting policies (issued November 1971)

© The Institute of Chartered Accountants in England and Wales.

It is fundamental to the understanding of financial accounts that those who use them should be aware of the main assumptions on which they are based. The purpose of the Statement which follows is to assist such understanding by promoting improvement in the quality of information disclosed. It seeks to achieve this by establishing as standard accounting practice the disclosure in financial accounts of clear explanations of the accounting policies followed in so far as these are significant for the purpose of giving a true and fair view. The Statement does not seek to establish accounting standards for individual items; these will be dealt with in separate Statements of Standard Accounting Practice issued from time to time.

PART 1—EXPLANATORY NOTE

Fundamental accounting concepts, accounting bases and accounting policies

1   In accounting usage terms such as 'accounting principles', 'practices', 'rules', 'conventions', 'methods' or 'procedures' have often been treated as interchangeable.[1] For the purpose of this Statement it is convenient to distinguish between *fundamental accounting concepts, accounting bases* and *accounting policies*.

2   *Fundamental accounting concepts* are here defined as broad basic assumptions which underlie the periodic financial accounts of business enterprises. It is expedient to single out for special mention four in particular: (a) the 'going concern' concept (b) the 'accruals' concept (c) the 'consistency' concept and (d) the 'prudence' concept.[2] The

[1] In this series 'accounting practices' has been adopted as a generic term to encompass all aspects of financial accounting methods and presentation.

[2] It is emphasized that it is not the purpose of this Statement to develop a basic theory of accounting. An exhaustive theoretical approach would take an entirely different form and would include, for instance, many more propositions than the four fundamental concepts referred to here. It is, however, expedient to recognize them as working assumptions having general acceptance at the present time.

use of these concepts is not necessarily self-evident from an examination of accounts, but they have such general acceptance that they call for no explanation in published accounts and their observance is presumed unless stated otherwise. They are practical rules rather than theoretical ideals and are capable of variation and evolution as accounting thought and practice develop, but their present generally accepted meanings are restated in paragraph 14 below.

3   *Accounting bases* are the methods which have been developed for expressing or applying fundamental accounting concepts to financial transactions and items. By their nature accounting bases are more diverse and numerous than fundamental concepts, since they have evolved in response to the variety and complexity of types of business and business transactions, and for this reason there may justifiably exist more than one recognized accounting basis for dealing with particular items.

4   *Accounting policies* are the specific accounting bases judged by business enterprise to be most appropriate to their circumstances and adopted by them for the purpose of preparing their financial accounts.

Particular problems in application of the fundamental concepts

5   The main difficulty in applying the fundamental accounting concepts arises from the fact that many business transactions have financial effects spreading over a number of years. Decisions have to be made on the extent to which expenditure incurred in one year can reasonably be expected to produce benefits in the form of revenue in other years and should therefore be carried forward, in whole or in part; that is, should be dealt with in the closing balance sheet, as distinct from being dealt with as an expense of the current year in the profit and loss account because the benefit has been exhausted in that year.

6   In some cases revenue is received for goods or services the production or supply of which will involve some later expenditure. In this case a decision must be made regarding how much of the revenue should be carried forward, to be dealt with in subsequent profit and loss accounts when the relevant costs are incurred.

7   All such decisions require consideration of future events of uncertain financial effect, and to this extent an element of commercial judgements is unavoidable in the assessment.

8   Examples of matters which give rise to particular difficulty are: the future benefits to be derived from stocks and all types of work in

progress at the end of the year; the future benefits to be derived from fixed assets, and the period of years over which these will be fruitful; the extent to which expenditure on research and development can be expected to produce future benefits.

Purpose and limitations of accounting bases

9   In the course of practice there have developed a variety of accounting bases designed to provide consistent, fair and as nearly as possible objective solutions to these problems in particular circumstances; for instance bases for calculating such items as depreciation, the amounts at which stocks and work in progress are to be stated, and deferred taxation.

10   Accounting bases provide an orderly and consistent framework for periodic reporting of a concern's results and financial position, but they do not, and are not intended to, substitute for the exercise of commercial judgement in the preparation of financial reports. Where a choice of acceptable accounting bases is available judgement must be exercised in choosing those which are appropriate to the circumstances and are best suited to present fairly the concern's results and financial position; the bases thus adopted then become the concern's accounting policies. The significance of accounting bases is that they provide limits to the area subject to the exercise of judgement, and a check against arbitrary, excessive or unjustifiable adjustments where no other objective yardstick is available. By definition it is not possible to develop generalised rules for the exercise of judgement, though practical working rules may be evolved on a pragmatic basis for limited use in particular circumstances. Broadly, the longer a concern's normal business cycle—the period between initiation of business transactions and their completion—the greater the area subject to judgement and its effect on periodic financial accounts, and the less its susceptibility to close regulation by accounting bases. These limitations to the regulating powers of accounting bases must be recognized.

Significance of disclosure of accounting policies

11   In circumstances where more than one accounting basis is acceptable in principle, the accounting policy followed can significantly affect a concern's reported results and financial position and the view presented can be properly appreciated only if the policies followed in dealing with material items are also explained. For this reason adequate disclosure of the accounting policies is essential to the fair presentation of financial accounts. As accounting standards become

established through publication of Statements of Standard Accounting Practice, the choice of accounting bases regarded as generally available will diminish, but it has to be recognized that the complexity and diversity of business renders total and rigid uniformity of bases impracticable.

12 The items with which this Statement is mainly concerned are those which are subject to the exercise of judgement as to how far they should be dealt with in the profit and loss account for the period under review or how far all or part should be carried forward in the balance sheet as attributable to the operations of future periods. The determination of the annual profit or loss of nearly every business substantially depends on a systematic approach to a few material items of this type. For the better appreciation of the view they give, annual accounts should include a clear explanation of the accounting policies followed for dealing with these few key items (some examples of which are given in paragraph 13 below). The intention and spirit of this Statement are that management should identify those items of the type described which are judged material or critical for the purpose of determining and fully appreciating the company's profit or loss and its financial position, and should make clear the accounting policies followed for dealing with them.

Examples of matters for which different accounting bases are recognized

13 Significant matters for which different accounting bases are recognised and which may have a material effect on reported results and financial position include:

—depreciation of fixed assets
—treatment and amortization of intangibles such as research and development expenditure, patents and trademarks
—stocks and work in progress
—long-term contracts
—deferred taxation
—hire-purchase or instalment transactions
—leasing and rental transactions
—conversion of foreign currencies
—repairs and renewals
—consolidation policies
—property development transactions
—warranties for products or services.

This list is not exhaustive, and may vary according to the nature of the operations conducted.

PART 2—DEFINITION OF TERMS

14   *Fundamental accounting concepts* are the broad basic assumptions which underlie the periodic financial accounts of business enterprises. At the present time the four following fundamental concepts (the relative importance of which will vary according to the circumstances of the particular case) are regarded as having general acceptability:

(*a*) The 'going concern' concept: the enterprise will continue in operational existence for the foreseeable future. This means in particular that the profit and loss account and balance sheet assume no intention or necessity to liquidate or curtail significantly the scale of operation;

(*b*) the 'accruals' concept: revenue and costs are accrued (that is, recognised as they are earned or incurred, not as money is received or paid), matched with one another so far as their relationship can be established or justifiably assumed, and dealt with in the profit and loss account of the period to which they relate; provided that where the accruals concept is inconsistent with the 'prudence' concept (paragraph (*d*) below), the latter prevails. The accruals concept implies that the profit and loss account reflects changes in the amount of net assets that arise out of the transactions of the relevant period (other than distributions or subscriptions of capital and unrealised surpluses arising on revaluation of fixed assets). Revenue and profits dealt with in the profit and loss account are matched with associated costs and expenses by including in the same account the costs incurred in earning them (so far as these are material and identifiable);

(*c*) the 'consistency' concept: there is consistency of accounting treatment of like items with each acounting period and from one period to the next;

(*d*) the concept of 'prudence': revenue and profits are not anticipated, but are recognized by inclusion in the profit and loss account only when realized in the form either of cash or of other assets the ultimate cash realization of which can be assessed with reasonable certainty; provision is made for all known liabilities (expenses and losses) whether the amount of these is known with certainty or is a best estimate in the light of the information available.

15   *Accounting bases* are the methods developed for applying fundamental accounting concepts to financial transactions and items, for the purpose of financial accounts, and in particular (*a*) for determining the accounting periods in which revenue and costs should be recognized in the profit and loss account and (*b*) for determining the amounts at which material items should be stated in the balance sheet.

16   *Accounting policies* are the specific accounting bases selected and consistently followed by a business enterprise as being, in the opinion of the management, appropriate to its circumstances and best suited to present fairly its results and financial position.

PART 3—STANDARD ACCOUNTING PRACTICE

Disclosure of adoption of concepts which differ from those generally accepted

17   If accounts are prepared on the basis of assumptions which differ in material respects from any of the generally accepted fundamental concepts defined in paragraph 14 above, the facts should be explained. In the absence of a clear statement to the contrary, there is a presumption that the four fundamental concepts have been observed.

Disclosure of accounting policies

18   The accounting policies (as defined in paragraph 16 above) followed for dealing with items which are judged material or critical in determining profit or loss for the year and in stating the financial position should be disclosed by way of note to the accounts. The explanations should be clear, fair, and as brief as possible.

Date from which effective

19   The accounting practices set out in this statement should be adopted as soon as possible and regarded as standard in respect of reports relating to accounting periods starting on or after 1st January, 1972.

Question 6
Discuss the influence of accounting concepts on the nature of accounting information. Illustrate your analysis by reference to any three concepts.

Question 7
'Accounting concepts reflect the result of long experience of the complexity of business life acquired by accountants. They offer guidelines for dealing with situations in which there are no simple answers. They permit the exercise of judgement and they allow the necessary variety in current accounting practice. Accordingly, the standardization of accounting practices is a negation of accumulated wisdom.' Discuss this comment.

Question 8

'Accounting standards are concerned with establishing an underlying identity of meaning in the information produced by accountants. They should not be concerned with establishing a rigid uniformity in accounting practices which would rob accountants of the ability to interpret accounting events.' Evaluate this comment.

> This chapter is concerned with the three fundamental account-
> ing purposes for using financial data which are as follows:
>
> (1) *Appraisal of past performance*. The decision maker assesses
>   the success of the business and the effectiveness of the man-
>   agement by considering information such as the return on
>   investment earned, sales, volume, and working capital and
>   cash flows. It also helps him compare one business with
>   another.
> (2) *Evaluation of present condition*. The decision maker
>   requires information such as the cash position, the stock
>   position, the types of assets owned and the debt/equity ratio.
> (3) *Prediction of future potential*. This necessitates the provision
>   of information which provides the decision maker with a
>   base from which to predict the future and supply insights
>   as to how the firm may respond to future economic develop-
>   ments.

The purpose of previous chapters has been to analyse the functions
which may be properly attributed to financial accounting. These have
been stated as being as follows:

(1) To provide a methodical system of recording financial accounting
    data.
(2) To use the financial accounting data to determine periodic profit
    and to ascertain the financial status of an enterprise at the end
    of the accounting period.
(3) To provide an information basis for the control of financial assets
    and liabilities.

The notion of financial control lies at the root of conventional
accounting. It is concerned with the use and allocation of resources
with a view to profit. Financial control is emphatically addressed
to the problem of profitability, and may be seen as having two dimen-
sions. First, internal financial control may be defined as the process
of rationing funds within the firm to projects and activities which
will be most profitable. Thus, a firm is concerned with seeking the
most profitable employment of its resources for two reasons, namely,
to provide a sufficient return on the capital invested by shareholders
and to provide a sufficient level of internally generated funds to allow

the firm to finance its own expenditure plans. Second, external financial control may be viewed as the process by which scarce financial resources are rationed between competing firms on the basis of their profitability. Investors (both present and potential shareholders) must decide whether to buy, sell or retain their ownership interests in a business entity. Loan creditors must decide whether to make loans and in what amounts and on what terms. Government agencies decide whom to tax and whom to subsidize. Labour unions make decisions on wage bargaining tactics.

Interpretation

Users of financial statements generally desire information about the profitability, efficiency and financial soundness of the business under study, whatever their time perspectives. Within these three areas, however, the type of financial analysis that takes place depends on the particular interest that the user has in the enterprise. For example short term creditors, such as banks, are primarily interested in the ability of the firm to pay its currently maturing obligations. The composition of the current assets and their relation to short-term liabilities are examined closely to evaluate the short-term solvency of the firm. Debenture holders, on the other hand, look to more long-term indicators, such as the enterprise's capital structure, past and projected profits and changes in financial position. In the long-run a firm that continually operates unprofitably will inevitably encounter difficulty in acquiring financial capital to remain solvent. Shareholders, present or prospective, are also interested in many of the features considered by a long-term creditor. They are interested in profitability because this affects the market price of their investment. Nevertheless, they are also interested in the financial stability of the firm. Management are interested in all three areas in making internal operating decisions.

Limitations of conventional financial analysis

The major limitations to conventional methods of interpreting financial statements are to be found in the problems inherent in accounting practice. These are:

(a) Limitations stemming from conventions associated with the measurement of periodic profit and the representation of balance sheet values. These limitations undermine the usefulness of accounting numbers for the valuation of the enterprise. In this connection, the Institute of Chartered Accountants in England and Wales has been at pains to stress on repeated occasions that financial reports are not intended to be used for the purpose of valuing the enterprise.

(b) Limitations stemming from the restrictions on the disclosure of information to shareholders and investors. This problem has been examined earlier, and it may be mentioned that as a result of the restricted information disclosures required by the Companies Act financial statements are not generally regarded as providing the only source of information of immediate relevance to investors. By and large, financial statements have a temporary impact when they are published, but form a very small part of the total information flow used, for example, on the Stock Exchange.

Interpretation by ratio analysis

The object of financial analysis is to establish the pattern of key variables which are otherwise concealed in the information aggregated in the profit and loss account and balance sheet. The usefulness of ratio analysis in this context is twofold. First, aggregate numbers are reduced into numbers which may provide a basis for comparing the results of the current year with those of previous years, and for comparing the results of different companies for the same year. Second, flexibility is given to financial analysis by allowing information reported in the profit and loss account to be integrated with information disclosed on the balance sheet, thereby giving a broader dimension to the analysis of results.

Ratio analysis is the application of a complex number of different ratios which focus on the several aspects of a firm's financial status. These ratios fall into two broad categories. The first group consists of accounting ratios which rely upon the information disclosed in the financial statements themselves. The second group consist of market ratios which integrate the information contained in the financial statements of a company with information relating to the Stock Exchange valuation of the company's shares. Accordingly, they apply only to companies whose shares are quoted on a stock exchange.

Accounting ratios

Accounting ratios may be grouped into four categories as follows:

(a) *Profitability ratios* which attempt to measure the efficiency of the enterprise in the generation of profit.

(b) *Activity ratios* which attempt to indicate the relative efficiency with which the firm's resources have been employed.

(c) *Solvency ratios* which attempt to predict the firm's ability to meet

its financial obligations and so prevent the possibility of insolvency.

(d) *Gearing ratios* which attempt to determine the financial implications of the firm's capital structure.

Profitability ratios

Profitability ratios are classified into two categories: ratios which
express profit as a percentage of sales, and ratios which express profit
as a yield associated with the employment of resources. For the purpose of the analysis of profitability, profit is generally expressed as
profit before interest and tax (PBIT). The reason for excluding interest
paid on borrowing from profitability ratios lies in the intention that
they should focus on the result of operating decisions rather than
financing decisions. The capital structure of different firms will generally reflect a different mix of equity and debt capital. Hence, it would
not be possible to compare the profitability of different firms unless
their results are calculated on the same basis. Profitability ratios are
also generally based on profit before taxation in order to exclude
the distortion which would result from the application of taxation
rules in the computation of the taxable income of different companies.
In this regard, it should be noted that taxation is not neutral when
comparing different companies. Indeed, it is often used to encourage
companies to follow certain policies, in particular those relating to
investments. Companies engaged in the expansion of capital expenditure often may lay claim to accelerated depreciation allowances which
have the effect of reducing their taxable profits and tax payable.
As a result, such companies would show comparatively higher after-
tax earnings than similar companies not engaged in heavy capital
expenditure. For these various reasons, therefore, taxation is also
excluded from the profit figures used in profitability ratios.

Ratios of profit as a percentage of sales

Two important profitability ratios are the gross profit ratio and the
net profit ratio.

(1) *Gross profit ratio*
This ratio is also commonly known as the gross margin ratio.
It expresses the gross profit as a percentage of sales and is calcu-
lated as follows:

$$\frac{\text{gross profit}}{\text{sales}} \times 100 = \ldots \%$$

The gross profit ratio is widely used to check the stability of
market conditions for the only two operative factors are sales

and the cost of sales. Under normal conditions, the gross profit ratio should show little change from year to year.

(2) *Net profit ratio*
This ratio shows the net profit resulting from sales. It is calculated as follows:

$$\frac{\text{PBIT}}{\text{sales}} \times 100 = \dots \%$$

It is usual to express the net profit ratio in terms of each £100 of sales. This ratio tends to fluctuate as between different companies operating in the same market owing to the variations in overhead expenses such as advertising, depreciation and management costs. Since companies are required to disclose their total sales revenue, the net profit ratio may be used as a significant ratio of profitability.

Ratios of return on resources employed
The essential purpose of these ratios is to measure profitability as a return or yield on the resources employed by an enterprise. These resources have alternative interpretations as follows:

Net asset value.
Total assets.
Gross assets.

These alternative interpretations give rise to three ratios, the most commonly used of which is the return on capital employed (ROCE).

(3) *Return on capital employed (ROCE)*
This ratio interprets the capital employed as being the net asset value which is found by adding the value of fixed assets to that of current assets and deducting the total of current liabilities. In effect, it interprets the resources employed as being equivalent to the sharesholders' equity *plus* long-term borrowings. It is calculated as follows:

$$\frac{\text{PBIT}}{\text{NAV}} \times 100 = \dots \%$$

(4) *Return on total assets*
This ratio interprets the value of the resources employed as the total assets employed in the business to give a view of the efficiency with which assets are employed by management. It is calculated as follows:

$$\frac{\text{PBIT}}{\text{fixed} + \text{current assets}} \times 100 = \dots \%$$

(5) *Return on gross assets*

This ratio requires a modification to the calculation of PBIT by adding back the depreciation charges against assets in the period under review. The reason for this adjustment is to exclude the distortion introduced into profit measurement by different methods of computing depreciation. Hence, its purpose it to obtain a more reliable basis of comparison between companies. It is calculated as follows:

$$\frac{\text{PBIT} + \text{depreciation for the period}}{\text{fixed assets at cost} + \text{current assets}} \times 100 = \ldots\%$$

The objection to using this method of calculating the return on assets employed is that depreciation is intended to ensure the maintenance of capital. To exclude depreciation, therefore, leads to erroneous conclusions as regards calculations of the asset base.

The return on capital employed (ROCE) is regarded as being the most significant ratio of profitability, and it is widely used by businessmen and financial analysts. Its limitations are mainly to be found in its reliance upon accounting conventions for measuring profit and the absence of any verifiable basis for assessing the value of net assets.

Activity ratios

Activity ratios are intended to analyse the use made of resources by the enterprise. Four important activity ratios are as follows:

Stock turnover.
Collection period for debtors.
Ratio of net asset value to sales.
Ratio of total asset value to sales.

(6) *Stock turnover*

The rate at which a business converts stock into sales is a critical indicator of business activity. The stock turnover indicates the number of times the stock is completely sold and replaced by purchases during the accounting period. Given complete data about the cost of sales, the stock turnover may be calculated as follows:

$$\frac{\text{cost of sales}}{\text{average stock}} = \text{number of times stock is turned over}$$

Since an external user of financial reports may not be given data relating to the cost of sales, the following formula is commonly used:

$$\frac{\text{sales}}{\text{average stock}} = \text{number of times stock is turned over}$$

The natural trading cycle for different types of businesses will obviously not be similar. Hence, it must be expected that the stock turnover will be characteristic of the type of trading operations in which a firm is engaged. Moreover, the trading cycle may be cyclical, resulting in peak and low stock levels. Without knowledge of seasonal variations in stock levels, the stock turnover based on the average of opening and closing stock will not provide an accurate analysis of stock levels throughout the period. This is an important consideration when examining the financial implications of stock levels and the need to minimize investments in stock. In this connection, the holding time in the case of engineering products may well be appreciably longer and will require a higher level of net investment than that associated with a supermarket where stock may be sold within the normal credit period allowed.

(7) *Average debtor collection period*

The careful control of debtor levels is an important aspect of good financial management. The average length of time for the payment of debts owing to the business is an important indicator of the efficiency of management. It is found by dividing the average daily *credit* sales into the total debtors outstanding as follows:

$$\frac{\text{debtors}}{\text{Cr sales}/365} = \text{average number of days for payment}$$

This formula may be restated as follows:

$$\frac{\text{debtors}}{\text{Cr sales}} \times 365 = \text{average number of days for payment}$$

The average debtor collection period is only a first indicator to be used in the analysis of debtors. Debt age schedules and other data would be used for further analysis.

(8) *Ratio of asset values to sales*

This ratio has two alternative expressions based on different interpretations of asset values. These are (i) net asset value (NAV), and (ii) total asset value (FA + CA), as follows:

$$\text{(i).} \ \frac{\text{sales}}{\text{NAV}} \quad \text{or} \quad \text{(ii)} \ \frac{\text{sales}}{\text{FA} + \text{CA}}$$

Both ratios are concerned with assessing the rate at which asset values are converted into sales revenue. They are indicative, therefore, of the ability of assets to generate profits. The most commonly used ratio is the ratio of net asset value to sales.

The return on capital employed (ROCE) mentioned earlier is derived by associating the net profit ratio with the ratio of net asset value to sales as follows:

$$\frac{\text{PBIT}}{\text{sales}} \times \frac{\text{sales}}{\text{NAV}} \times 100$$

The ROCE links profitability with activity ratios to provide an integrated view of profitability which is based on the profitability of sales and the profitability of assets. Total assets may be substituted for net assets if it is wished to express the rate of return on that basis.

Example 1

The financial statement of Cornerstores Ltd for the year ended 31 December 19X8 showed the following data:

	£
Sales for the year	5,000,000
Net profit for the year	100,000
Net assets employed	500,000

The net profit ratio is as follows:

$$\frac{\text{PBIT}}{\text{sales}} \times 100 = \frac{100,000}{5,000,000} \times 100 = 2\%$$

Thus, by itself the rate of profitability on sales would appear to be quite low. The ratio of net asset values to sales, however, is much greater as follows:

$$\frac{\text{sales}}{\text{NAV}} = \frac{5,000,000}{500,000} = 10$$

Combining these two ratios, the ROCE shows that the overall profitability expressed as a return on capital employed is:

$$2\% \times 10 = 20\%$$

or, more formally:

$$\frac{\text{PBIT}}{\text{sales}} \times \frac{\text{sales}}{\text{NAV}} \times 100 = \frac{\text{PBIT}}{\text{NAV}} \times 100$$

$$= \frac{100,000}{500,000} \times 100 = 20\%$$

Solvency ratios

Solvency ratios are addressed to the analysis of the ability of a business to meet its immediate financial obligations and thus avoid the possibility of insolvency. Two ratios in common use are the current ratio and the quick or acid test ratio.

(9) *The current ratio*

A general indication of a firm's ability to meet its current liabilities is found in the current ratio, which is calculated as follows:

$$\frac{\text{current assets}}{\text{current liabilities}}$$

This ratio assumes that current assets could be converted into cash to meet current liabilities. There is no general rule as to the dimension of this ratio which may vary from industry to industry, though any ratio less than 1 would indicate that the firm might have a potential problem in meeting creditors' claims. By contrast, a number significantly greater than one would imply that current assets were being underemployed.

(10) *The acid test ratio*

A limitation of the current ratio is the assumption that all current assets could readily be converted into cash. The acid test ratio focuses on this problem by recognizing that stock is not easily converted into immediate cash. It is calculated as follows:

$$\frac{\text{current assets} - \text{stock}}{\text{current liabilities}}$$

It remains true, however, that other current assets, for example prepayments, are also not readily convertible into cash and should not be regarded as available to meet current liabilities. When using the acid test ratio, care should be taken to exclude from current liabilities such claims as are not immediately payable.

The concern with the problem of solvency should not hide the fundamental purpose for borrowing money, namely using borrowed funds to generate profits. A ratio which expresses the relationship between profit and borrowed funds is the following:

(11)
$$\frac{\text{long-term debt} + \text{current liabilities} - \text{current assets}}{\text{profit after interest and tax}}$$

This ratio expresses the length of time it would take to repay indebtedness out of net profit after interest and tax. The reason for this formulation of net profit stems from the fact that debt repayments have to be made from the balance of profit after interest and tax obligations have been met.

In conclusion, it must be stressed that the relevance of solvency ratios in the analysis of potential insolvency is controversial. Hence, care should be taken when applying them to the circumstances of particular companies.

Gearing ratios

The proportion of a company's fixed interest capital to total capital is of considerable importance to ordinary shareholders. The gearing or leverage of a company is defined as the ratio of preferred share capital and loan capital to ordinary share equity. Two formulas are used to express gearing or leverage. The first shows long-term debt (D) as a fraction of capital expressed as long-term debt (D) plus ordinary share equity (S) as follows:

$$(12) \quad \text{gearing or leverage} = \frac{D}{D + S}$$

The second formula shows long-term debt (D) as a fraction of ordinary share equity (S) as follows:

$$(13) \quad \text{gearing or leverage} = \frac{D}{S}$$

The first formula is generally found to be more useful since it will always produce a result which is less than one, whereas the second formula will produce a much greater range of answers.

Example 2

Compoost plc has a capital structure which includes £2,000,000 of 11% debenture and 400,000 ordinary shares of £1 each fully paid. Accordingly, the gearing or leverage is:

$$\frac{D}{D + S} = \frac{2,000,000}{6,000,000} = 0.33$$

The values expressed in the gearing ratio of 0.33 have been obtained directly from the balance sheet. In the case of a company whose shares are quoted on the Stock Exchange, it would be more useful to investors to use the market values of the debentures and shares. These market values would be significantly different from those based on accounting procedure.

The capital structure of a company reflects the financial strategy adopted for financing the company's activities. The analysis of the optimal financial structure is the subject of considerable literature and debate. In simple terms, the advantage to be gained from borrowing capital rather than raising capital by the issue of ordinary shares is found in the difference between the company's internal rate of return and the cost of borrowed money. Thus, if the company's rate of return on capital employed is 12% and the interest payable on borrowing is, say 9%, there is a distinct advantage to the ordinary shareholders of borrowing money rather than raising further equity capital. However, the introduction of debt capital into the capital structure increases the degree of risk attached to the expectations of ordinary shareholders. This is because the payment of interest on borrowed money is a prior charge on the company's assets. The more obvious effects of debt capital on the income of shareholders from the company are seen when the company's profit is fluctuating. Thus, when the company's profit falls, the dividends payable to ordinary shareholders are restricted by the amount of interest payable on debt capital. When the company's profits are expanding, the proportional burden of debt is considerably reduced, and the dividends payable to ordinary shareholders increases correspondingly.

An additional ratio which is quite useful is to express the total liabilities of a company as a percentage of total assets as follows:

$$(14) \qquad \frac{\text{long-term debt capital} + \text{current liabilities}}{\text{fixed assets} + \text{current assets}} \times 100$$

Moreover, gearing or leverage can be used as a profit ratio to indicate the extent to which the company's profit covers its interest obligations. The following ratio expresses the interest coverage:

$$(15) \qquad \text{Interest coverage} = \frac{\text{PBIT}}{\text{debt interest}}$$

Finally, the leasing of plant and machinery can produce misleading ratios in so far as lease payments are written off as expenses against profits and there is no asset base against which to measure profitability. Ratio (15) may be expanded to cover this problem by including the fixed charges incurred under leasing and hiring agreements as follows:

$$(16) \qquad \text{Interest and fixed charges coverage}$$

$$= \frac{\text{PBIT} + \text{fixed charges}}{\text{debt interest} + \text{fixed charges}}$$

Ratio analysis and public quoted companies

A number of additional ratios are applied to the analysis of the results of public quoted companies. The following ratios are frequently used in this respect:

Dividend yield.
Dividend coverage.
Earnings yield.
Earnings per share.
Price/earnings.

(17) *Dividend yield*
The practice in the United Kingdom is to declare dividends by reference to the nominal value of shares. The dividend yield expresses the dividend as a return on the current share price, as follows:

$$\text{dividend yield} = \text{declared dividend rate} \times \frac{\text{nominal value of share}}{\text{market price of share}}$$

(18) *Dividend coverage*
As a guide to the company's ability to sustain dividend payments, the dividend coverage indicates the ratio of distributable earnings to actual dividends as follows:

$$\text{dividend coverage} = \frac{\text{net profit after interest and tax}}{\text{dividend payable}}$$

(19) *Earnings yield*
This ratio simply expresses the earnings of the company (net profit after interest and tax) as a percentage of the market price of the share. It can be derived by two alternative methods:

(i) dividend yield $\times$ dividend cover

or

(ii) $\dfrac{\text{net profit after interest and tax}}{\text{market price of share} \times \text{number of shares issued}} \times 100$

(20) *Earnings per share (EPS)*
This ratio is the most commonly used ratio for valuing shares. It represents the earnings of the company, *whether or not they are declared as dividends*, as earnings derived from each ordinary share held in the company. It is calculated as follows:

$$\text{earnings per share} = \frac{\text{net profit after interest and tax}}{\text{number of ordinary share issued}}$$

Some complications arise in the calculation of this ratio in the treatment of extraordinary items which may have affected the company's earnings for one year only, as well as the impact of Corporation Tax on earnings. These complexities are examined in Statement of Standard Accounting Practice 3.

(21) *Price/earnings ratio*

This ratio is widely used by financial analysts and journalists as a capitalization factor for use in establishing the market value of a company. A capitalization factor may be defined as a number which is applied to periodic profit for arriving at a capital sum representing the value of a company or other asset. The market value so derived represents the price which the market would be prepared to pay for a company.

Example 3

A company having in issue 200,000 ordinary shares with a nominal value of £1 each and a market price of £3.20 per share on the basis of earnings per share of 40p on the last reported results would be valued as follows:

$$\text{price/earnings ratio} = \frac{\text{price per share}}{\text{earnings per share}}$$
$$= \frac{£3.20}{40p}$$
$$= 8$$

value of the company = capitalization factor × net profit after interest and tax
$$= 8 \times (40p \times 200,000)$$
$$= \underline{£640,000}$$

This valuation is exactly the same as would be derived directly from the market price of the company's shares as follows:

value of the company = market price of shares × number of shares in issue
$$= £3.20 \times 200,000$$
$$= \underline{£640,000}$$

The importance of the P/E ratio lies in its association with expectations about a company's prospects. Changes in the company's earnings generally result in corresponding changes in the share price

The following example is a comprehensive ratio analysis applied to a quoted company.

Example 4

The following ratio analysis is based on the profit and loss accounts of Edbark plc for the years ended 31 December 19X7 and 19X8, the balance sheets as at those dates, and market data available on 31 January 19X9.

Edbark plc
Profit and loss accounts for years to 31 December

	19X7	19X8
	£000s	£000s
Sales	1,270	1,480
Gross profit	664	760
Net profit for year before tax	120	164
Corporation Tax	60	80
Net profit after tax	60	84
Dividend proposed	16	40
Retained profit	44	44

Notes

(1) 90% of all sales were on credit
(2) The accounts are truncated and are not meant to show conformity with standards or legal disclosure requirements
(3) The only interest paid was debenture interest.

At the end of January 19X9 the following information was available from the market:

Quoted price of ordinary shares of Edbark (ex div) £3.20 each

Quoted price of £100 units of debenture £105 (for the sake of simplicity these are treated as irredeemable).

Edbark plc
Balance sheets as at 31 December

	19X7			19X8		
	£000s	£000s	£000s	£000s	£000s	£000s
Fixed assets	Cost	Depn		Cost	Depn	
Freehold property	60	—	60	210	—	210
Fixtures and fittings	240	56	184	300	70	230
Motor vehicles	70	34	36	70	40	30
	370	90	280	580	110	470
Current assets						
Stock		90			164	
Debtors		130			188	
Bank		136			24	
		356			376	

Creditors—amounts falling due within one year					
Trade creditors	70			142	
Proposed dividend	16	86		40	182
Net current assets			270		194
Total assets less current liabilities			550		664
Creditors—amount falling due after more than one year					
12% Debentures			120		120
Capital and reserves					
Called up share capital		150		200	
Share premium account		—		20	
Profit and loss account		280		324	
			430		544
			550		664

[*The ratio analysis appears on pages 204–5*]

Valuation

Valuation is a controversial, complex and problematical issue in accounting theory and practice. *It is controversial* because many accountants would argue that they are not concerned with valuation but with cost allocation. Others would argue, however, that accounting representations which attach financial measurements to assets and liabilities revenue and expense cannot avoid the implication that such representations have the characteristic of valuation. *It is complex* because valuation itself is complex subject. Valuation is essentially a subjective process. The value of an object to oneself may be greater than its value in exchange for a variety of reasons. Once it is decided to attempt to make an objective valuation of an object, the valuation process inevitably appears as a price determined between a willing buyer and a willing seller. *It is problematical* because any representation of value should be specific to the needs to users of that information. Hence, a number of important issues are found in the accounting debate in this respect. Accountants would assert that the values represented on the balance sheet cannot be used to derive the value of a business. The cost allocation process results in balances which cannot be used to represent either the value in use of the assets represented, their realizable value or their replacement cost. Hence, there is no obvious mechanism in the accounting process which would permit any valuation of assets to be derived. Accountants would hold that they are not concerned with providing valuations which would be relevant to the most important and fundamental need of investors and other users of accounting information, namely a valuation of the firm. The report of the Sandilands Committee went only so far as to state that assets should be represented at their value to the business, but limited this interpretation to their current cost.

Edbark plc
Ratio analysis 19X7 and 19X8

Profit ratios:	Formula	Year 1	Year 2	Ratios Year 1	Ratios Year 2	Industry average	Comment
(1) Gross profit ratio	$\dfrac{\text{gross profit}}{\text{sales}} \times 100$	$\dfrac{644}{1270} \times 100$	$\dfrac{760}{1480} \times 100$	51%	51%	48%	This ratio is not available to shareholders as the gross margin is not disclosed
(2) Net income ratio	$\dfrac{\text{PBIT}}{\text{sales}} \times 100$	$\dfrac{120 \times 14.4}{1270} \times 100$	$\dfrac{644 + 14.4}{1480} \times 100$	10.5%	12%	10%	

These results indicate that the amount of margin, both gross and net, is in line with the average for the industry.

	Formula	Year 1	Year 2	Ratios Year 1	Ratios Year 2	Industry average	Comment
(3) Return on capital employed	$\dfrac{\text{PBIT}}{\text{NAV}} \times 100$	$\dfrac{134.4}{550} \times 100$	$\dfrac{178.4}{664} \times 100$	24%	27%	20%	Only the version based on NAV is given

The return on capital employed (net asset value) shows that the company is using its assets efficiently when compared with the industry average. This could be due to a lower expenditure on fixed assets or, perhaps, using assets over a longer life than the average.

Activity ratios

	Formula	Year 1	Year 2	Ratios Year 1	Ratios Year 2	Industry average	Comment
(6) stock turnover	$\dfrac{\text{sales}}{\text{average stock}}$	$\dfrac{1270}{90}$	$\dfrac{1480}{(90+164)/2}$	14 times	12 times	11 times	

This ratio indicates that the company turns over its stock rather more rapidly than the average. They may have secured a more rapid replacement system with suppliers, thereby enabling lower stocks, on average, to be carried. Efficient re-order systems would seek to minimize stock carrying whilst not risking stock-outs (i.e., not being able to meet customer demand immediately).

	Formula	Year 1	Year 2	Ratios Year 1	Ratios Year 2	Industry average	Comment
(7) Debtors collection period	$\dfrac{\text{debtors} \times 365}{\text{credit sales}}$	$\dfrac{130 \times 365}{0.9 \times 1270}$	$\dfrac{188 \times 365}{0.9 \times 1480}$	42 days	51 days	32 days	

The average for the industry looks very low. The general proportion of cash sales to credit sales would need to be established. If net monthly credit terms are advanced to customers (which is payment at end of month following that of delivery of goods), then 42 days would be very good indeed.

	Formula	Year 1	Year 2	Ratios Year 1	Ratios Year 2	Industry average	Comment
(8) Sales to NAV Number of times covered	$\dfrac{\text{sales}}{\text{NAV}}$	$\dfrac{1270}{550}$	$\dfrac{1480}{664}$	2.3 times	2.2 times	1.9	Only the version based on NAV is given
Note ROCE = net profit ratio × sales value to NAV	$\dfrac{\text{PBIT}}{\text{sales}} \times \dfrac{\text{sales}}{\text{NAV}}$	$\dfrac{134.4}{1270} \times \dfrac{1270}{550} \times 100$	$\dfrac{178.4}{1480} \times \dfrac{1480}{664} \times 100$	24%	27%	20%	

Profit ratios:	Formula	Year 1	Year 2	Ratios Year 1	Ratios Year 2	Industry average	Comment
Solvency ratios							
(9) Current ratio	$\dfrac{\text{current assets}}{\text{current liabilities}}$	$\dfrac{356}{86}$	$\dfrac{376}{182}$	4.1	2.1	2.9	
(10) Acid test ratio	$\dfrac{\text{current assets less stock}}{\text{current liabilities}}$	$\dfrac{356-90}{86}$	$\dfrac{376-164}{182}$	3.1	1.2	1.4	
(11) Time to repay liabilities from profit	$\dfrac{\text{long-term debt plus current liabilities minus current assets}}{\text{profit after interest and tax}}$	$\dfrac{120+86-356}{60}$	$\dfrac{120+182-376}{84}$	-2.5	-0.9	1.5	

The solvency ratios indicate that the company is able to meet its forthcoming payments with little difficulty. The current and acid test ratios have slipped somewhat from year 1 to year 2 but still seem good. The recovery of indebtedness by profit shows a very wide safety margin.

Gearing ratios							
(12) Basic gearing ratio	$\dfrac{\text{long-term debt}}{\text{equity}}$	$\dfrac{120}{430}$	$\dfrac{120}{544}$	1:3.6	1:4.5	$-1:4$	
Ratio of borrowed funds to total funds	$\dfrac{\text{long-term debt}}{\text{long-term debt plus equity}}$	$\dfrac{120}{550}$	$\dfrac{126}{664}$	1:4.6	1:5.3	$-1:5$	
(14) Percentage claims against business	$\dfrac{\text{long-term debt plus current liabilities}}{\text{total assets}}\times 100$	$\dfrac{120+86}{280+356}\times 100$	$\dfrac{120+182}{470+376}\times 100$	32%	36%	-38%	
(15) Times interest covered	$\dfrac{\text{PBIT}}{\text{interest}}$	$\dfrac{134.4}{14.4}$	$\dfrac{178.4}{14.4}$	9×	12×	8×	

The gearing ratios of Edbark plc indicate that the company is not heavily financed by debt. It seems to be about meeting the industry average.

In view of the foregoing introduction to this topic, it is evident that valuation cannot be dealt with satisfactorily at an elementary level of argument. Certainly, it is beyond the scope of this text to do more than introduce a few of the salient points in issue.

The objectives of valuation

The fundamental objective of any representation of value is to provide information for decision-making. Applying the proprietorship concept of the firm, shareholders may be assumed to be interested basically in the value of the firm to them. On the basis of the going-concern convention, the value may be derived as follows:

(1) By using the reported profit for the purpose of calculating the value of the firm as a profit-yielding asset. That value would be derived in the same way as any other asset would be valued, namely by establishing the present value of the stream of future income flowing from that asset.

Example 5

A property yields an annual rent of £1,000. Given that the current rate of interest is 10%, the capitalized value of the rent is:

$$\frac{£1,000}{0.10} = \underline{£10,000}$$

Similarly, if the net profit of a business is £1,000 and is expected to continue at that level in perpetuity, and given that the current rate of interest is 10%, the capitalized value of the firm is:

$$\frac{£1,000}{0.10} = \underline{£10,000}$$

(2) By using the reported net asset values to calculate the capitalized value of the firm. In this context, it is evident that—if it is accepted that the value of assets is related to the net profit which they produce—then the net asset value should be equal to the capitalized value of net profits.

It should be noted that all references here to discounting 'profits' to arrive at capital value should really refer to net cash flows generated. Profit is used as a shorthand term for this although technically this is incorrect.

Investors attempt to establish the value of a business by reference to the profit yield rather than by reference to any accounting representation of asset value. Thus, the objective of ratio analysis in the case of quoted companies is to use such ratios as earnings per share and price earnings ratio to calculate the value of the company's shares and hence the value of the company. No reference is made to the value of assets shown on the balance sheet, except where the company might be in liquidation or might hold valuable assets which are currently considerably undervalued or unused. In such a case, the market price of the shares would reflect an adjustment to the valuation which would be derived more directly from reported earnings.

Given that investors are able to establish a value for a company, the decision which they have to make is typically an investment decision, namely to buy or hold shares in the company or to sell the shares which they currently hold.

Seen in the context of a society having broader social objectives than satisfying the needs of investors for a rational system for investment decision-making, the objectives of valuation may be interpreted again in terms of establishing the value of any enterprise to society. In this sense, the use of scarce national resources in the form of human skills, government and private funds and other resources should be allocated to those firms which are most efficient in utilizing such resources. It is true that profitability remains the key success factor in judging the performance of business enterprises. Therefore, it may be argued that the basic objective of valuation is to provide a value of the business as a going concern in terms of the present value of future net profit flows. The objective of the balance sheet may be interpreted in this context as providing a verification of the valuation so derived.

The valuation of assets

The accounting process does not attempt to value the business as a going concern. Nevertheless, considerable attention is given to the valuation of individual assets without relating the problems involved to the valuation of the business. In strict terms, a rational theory of asset valuation cannot escape the conclusion that the sum of the value of the net assets of a business should be equal to the present value of the future stream of its net profit. The reasoning for this statement is in itself unexceptional, and may be found in the decision to invest and hold individual assets. Given that a firm has to finance the acquisition of assets, the cost of finance to the firm is equivalent to a given rate of interest. Hence, unless the stream of future income associated with the purchase of any asset has a present value which is *at least equal* to the current acquisition cost, the firm should not acquire that asset.

Example 6

Suppose that a company's cost of capital is 10%, and that the purchase of an asset costing £1,000 is contemplated. In deciding whether or not to purchase that asset, the company is required to assess if the present value of the future net income generated by means of that asset is worth at least £1,000. This means evaluating that stream of future net income as being at least £100 per annum, for the present value of £100 per annum discounted at 10% is £1,000.

From the foregoing example, the generalized proposition which may be advanced is that the sum of the value of the net assets of the company should be equal to the present value of its future net income. This proposition provides a rational framework not only for the purpose of management decisions regarding the acquisition of assets but also for the purpose of financial reporting concerned with providing a basis for rationing scarce funds to competing firms.

Most accountants would probably agree that the present value of assets provides the optimal valuation basis if it is assumed that the objective of financial statements is to facilitate decision-making by the users of those statements. The problem lies in estimating the present value of assets, for this involves forecasting future income. Moreover, it would be wellnigh impossible in practice to forecast the incremental net future income associated with the purchase of most assets.

Alternative valuation methods

Controversy in accounting circles has not been addressed to the problem of selecting the optimal valuation basis relevant to the need of investors to formulate informed judgements about the value of a business and the efficiency of its management in allocating and using scarce funds in the process of managing the asset base. On the contrary, the debate has been concerned with the comparative merits of alternative valuation methods. These are as follows:

Historical cost.
Realizable value.
Replacement cost.
Current cost.

Historical cost

The most commendable virtue from an accounting viewpoint is that it is supported by documentary evidence in the form of invoices and, therefore, has the attribute of being verifiable by audit. It is also sometimes argued that since all valuations are at best reasoned guesses, historical cost values could well be retained in view of their familiarity to accountants.

Historical cost valuation represents the accounting tradition based on conservatism, and the maintenance of capital concept implicitly reflected by historical cost is the original money contribution by share-holders.

The major drawback of historical cost valuation stems from rapid inflation which distorts money values leading to an understatement of the real value of the non-monetary assets of the firm and an over-statement of the net profit.

Realizable value

This concept of valuation is based on the money value of assets if they were sold. Thus, whereas historical cost valuations reflect entry values, realizable values represent exit values. Realizable values emphasize the liquidation rather than the use of the company's assets. Hence, they are criticized for representing an unrealistic view of the firm. Supporters of realizable value accounting argue as follows:

(a) It does not pre-empt any decision as to whether or not the enter-prise should continue.
(b) Economic theories of the firm portray the firm as an adaptive opportunity-seeking organism. Hence, a measure of its ability to switch resources and activities is relevant to users of financial reports.
(c) Realizable values are the best indicators of the sacrifice made by the firm in holding assets and, therefore, are the best measures of the opportunity cost involved.
(d) Realizable values are the most easily understood values.
(e) Realizable values do not invoke the future to measure the present.

Replacement cost

This is the cost of replacing the services of the existing asset. Given that changes in technology occur it should not be thought of simply in terms of replacement by a physically identical asset. Rather it should be thought of as the cost of replacing the service potential of the existing asset.

Current cost

This concept combines the realizable and replacement cost methods and adopts a 'value to the business' or 'deprival value' approach to valuation. In order to value any individual asset it is necessary to ask the question: If the firm were to be deprived of the asset what sum of money would this loss represent? The value to the business approach has been adopted by the Accounting Standards Committee and is considered in depth in the following section.

Inflation

Until the advent of the rapid inflation of the 1970s, it was assumed that the money standard of measurement had a relatively stable value and that historical cost accounting provided an accurate and objective method for measuring profit and for balance sheet representations.

The accounting approach to profit determination stresses the maintenance of capital concept, which is understood to apply to the original money contribution made by the proprietors or shareholders. Accordingly, the objectives of historical cost accounting are concerned with ensuring that the expenses charged against revenues in the process of determining periodic profit will be adequate to maintain the value of capital intact. Inflation erodes the value of the original capital in three important respects:

(a) The provision for the depreciation of fixed assets under conditions of inflation is totally inadequate to provide for the replacement of such assets. This is because the replacement cost rises with inflation.

(b) Equally, the cost of replacing the stock sold rises directly with inflation and is greater than the original cost of acquiring the stock. The FIFO method of stock valuation which is generally applied in the United Kingdom results in the *undervaluation* of the cost of goods sold under conditions of increasing replacement costs. As a result the gross profit is correspondingly *overstated*.

(c) Finally, there is need to cover changes in the purchasing power of contractual obligations stated in money terms.

The general consequence of inflation as regards the determination of profit is to lead to an overstatement of net profit, and the danger that a dividend policy relying on such measurements could result in a repayment of capital. From the viewpoint of management, the replacement of stocks under conditions of ever rising prices could result in the firm having to obtain further capital simply to maintain the same physical volume of business.

The search for the most appropriate method of accounting for inflation took the form of a protracted debate which began officially in the United Kingdom with the publication in 1974 of SSAP 7, *Accounting for Changes in the Purchasing Power of Money*, and led in 1980 to the issue of SSAP 16, *Current Costing Accounting* (*CC Accounting*).

SSAP 16 applies to quoted companies and entities with a turnover of £5 million or more. It does not apply to insurance companies, property investment companies, unit trusts, and to entities such as building societies, trade unions and pension funds.

SSAP 16 allows historical cost accounts to be retained, but requires current cost accounts consisting of a Profit and Loss Account and a Balance Sheet with explanatory notes to be published along with the traditional historical costs reports.

SSAP 16 profit and loss accounts provide adjustments to the following items:

(a) Depreciation.
(b) Cost of sales.
(c) Monetary working capital.
(d) Gearing.

Additionally, CC accounts should contain explanatory notes dealing with earnings per share calculations and setting out the basis and methods used in preparing these accounting.

In 1985 the Accounting Standards Committee announced that SSAP16 was no longer mandatory and that it intended to develop a new accounting standard on accounting for the effects of changing prices to take the place of SSAP16 in due course. It is intended that the proposed new standard will allow more choice of method than SSAP16 and that the SSAP16 methodology will be one of those that would comply with the new standard.

Fixed assets and depreciation

Current cost accounting is an adaptation of historical cost accounting. It has the objective of converting the valuation of fixed assets from that based on their acquisition cost to the firm (historic cost) to a valuation of such assets based on their current cost to the firm. SSAP 16 defines the current cost of assets as the net current replacement cost, applying in this manner the concept of 'value to the business' as the basis of asset valuation. Where it is evident that the asset concerned has suffered a permanent diminution in value in the hands of the business below its net current replacement cost, the basis of valuation used is the recoverable amount. For example, if the net replacement cost of an asset is established at £1,000 by reference to official statistics, but it is evident that excessive use or other reason has permanently reduced the value of the asset held by the firm to below that figure and the sum which could be recovered through sale is only £400, then the valuation to be shown on the current cost balance sheet is to be £400 and not £1,000.

For the purpose of CC accounting, fixed assets have been grouped into three main categories:

(a) Plant and machinery.
(b) Land and buildings.
(c) Wasting assets and intangibles.

The net current replacement cost of plant and machinery is relatively easier to ascertain than is that of the other two categories. Special valuation procedures are adopted for the latter two categories of fixed assets. The most common valuation procedure followed for plant and machinery is a reference to a published index, by means of which a single item of machinery or a whole plant may be revalued at the net current replacement cost. The revaluation is obtained by the application to the historic cost of the asset of a factor derived from the index at the current balance sheet date and the index at the acquisition date. This factor is calculated as follows:

$$\frac{\text{index at balance sheet date}}{\text{index at acquisition date}}$$

The revised value of the asset is shown on the current cost balance sheet. Where the net current replacement cost is higher than the historical cost, as will be usually the case under inflation, the difference will be debited to the CC fixed asset account and a corresponding credit shown on the CC reserve account.

Example 7
A machine purchased in 19X1 for £18,000 is being depreciated on a straight-line basis over ten years. The Index for Machine Classification at 31 December 19X1 and at 31 December 19X4 is 140 and 180 respectively. Assuming that CCA is applied for the first time in 19X4, the accounting procedure will require the revaluation of the machine account to the current cost value at 19X4, as follows:

(a) Written down value in HC records:

$$£18,000 - (1,800 \times 4) = £10,800$$

(b) Adjusted CCA value:

$$£10,800 \times \frac{180}{140} = £13,886$$

(c) Accounting entries:

> CC Machine account   Dr £3,086
> CC Reserve account   Cr £3,086

These entries deal with the difference between the HC and the CC asset values.

It may be expected that most accounting systems will show assets recorded at their historical cost. Accordingly, the provision for depreciation account will also require adjustment, when CCA is introduced. In the case of the figures shown in this example, the net adjustment of £3,086 takes account of the adjustment for CCA depreciation as follows:

(a) Increase in asset value on introduction of CCA:

$$£18,000 \times \frac{180-140}{140} = £5,143$$

(b) Increase in provision for depreciation on introduction of CCA:

$$£7,200 \times \frac{180-140}{140} = £2,057$$

where £7,200 is the provision for depreciation under HC for the four years 19X1 to 19X4 inclusive.

(c) Accounting entries adjusting both the asset account and the provision for depreciation account would be as follows:

		£	£
Machine account	Dr	5,143	
Provision for depreciation account	Cr		2,057
Current cost reserve account	Cr		3,086
		5,143	5,143

Example 7 shows the accounting adjustments required to be made to HC records on the introduction of CCA. A feature of inflation is that the replacement cost value of assets will continue to increase through time. The adjustments shown above would bring the HC figures up to date as at the end of the year 19X4. In subsequent years, the annual depreciation on a CC basis would be calculated by reference to the actual replacement cost established at the end of each accounting year, on the basis of the Index of Replacement Cost Values. Therefore, while the provision for depreciation under CCA for the actual year under review would be correct, the provision for depreciation accumulated for prior years would require to be increased. The amount of this increase would depend on the rate at which the replacement costs themselves are increasing. In addition to the annual provision for depreciation which would be charged in the profit and loss account a further charge—known as backlog depreciation—has to be made. In effect, the backlog depreciation is equal to the difference between current replacement cost of the asset and the total current cost depreciation already charged.

It follows that, under CCA, the adjustment for depreciation has two elements:

(a) An adjustment to bring the HC provision for depreciation account up to the CC provision for depreciation *for the year under review.*
(b) An adjustment required to bring the shortfall of previous years' CCA depreciation up to the required accumulated provision for depreciation as at the beginning of the year under review.

The first element (a) is charged in the profit and loss account for the year under review, thereby reducing the net profit for that year, and the second element (b) is transferred directly to the current cost reserve account.

Example 8

Equipment purchased for £10,000 on 1 January 19X0 is depreciated on a straight line basis over five years. The company's financial year ends on 31 December.

After applying the appropriate indices, the following replacement cost values are determined:

		£
At 31 December 19X1		11,000
..	19X2	12,000
..	19X3	15,000
..	19X4	16,000
..	19X5	17,500

The following table shows the figures which will be involved under CCA. (HC depreciation = £2,000 per year).

End of year	Replacement cost (£)	Transfer to credit of CC reserve (£)	CCA depreciation (£)	CCA adjustment to P & L A/C (£)	Required accumul. CCA depn (£)	Actual accumul. CCA depn (£)	Backlog (£)
1	11,000	1,000	2,200	200	2,200	2,200	0
2	12,000	1,000	2,400	400	4,800	4,600	200
3	15,000	3,000	3,000	1,000	9,000	7,800	1,200
4	16,000	1,000	3,200	1,200	12,800	12,200	600
5	17,500	1,500	3,500	1,500	17,500	16,300	1,200
				4,300			3,200

The accounts for CCA would appear as follows (remember: companies would keep these as separate working documents).

Equipment account

			£
19X1	Cash		10,000
19X1	Current cost reserve		1,000
19X2	..	..	1,000
19X3	..	..	3,000
19X4	..	..	1,000
19X5	..	..	1,500
			17,500

HC provision for depreciation account

					£	Cumulative £
Year 1	Profit and loss account				2,000	2,000
2	..	..	..	..	2,000	4,000
3	..	..	..	..	2,000	6,000
4	..	..	..	..	2,000	8,000
5	..	..	..	..	2,000	10,000
					10,000	

Current cost reserve account

			£				£
19X2	Backlog depreciation		200	19X1	Equipment		1,000
19X3	..	..	1,200	19X2	..		1,000
19X4	..	..	600	19X3	..		3,000
19X5	..	..	1,200	19X4	..		1,000
		..		19X5	..		1,500
			3,200				7,500

CCA depreciation adjustment account

		£	Cumulative CC reserve £	P & L A/C £
19X1	Profit and loss account	200		200
19X2	Profit and loss account	400		600
19X2	CC reserve account	200	200	
19X3	Profit and loss account	1,000		1,600
19X3	CC reserve account	1,200	1,400	
19X4	Profit and loss account	1,200		2,800
19X4	CC reserve account	600	2,000	
19X5	Profit and loss account	1,500		4,300
19X5	CC reserve account	1,200	3,200	
		7,500		

The cost of sales adjustment (COSA)

The purpose of the COSA is to charge against sales the current cost of the goods sold rather than the original cost of acquisition of manufacture, as would be the case under historical cost accounting and the FIFO assumption which applies to stock valuation in the United Kingdom. In the examples given hereunder, all stock movements are assumed to reflect FIFO.

Example 9

A company purchased goods in January for £2,500 and resold them in the following November for £3,500. In the meantime, the replacement cost of these goods increased by £400 to £2,900, which was the amount incurred by the company in November. Under HC accounting, the profit and loss account reflecting these transactions would be as follows:

	£	£
Sales		3,500
Purchases (2,500 + 2,900)	5,400	
less: Closing stock	2,900	2,500
Gross profit		1,000

Once the true effects of price changes on these transactions are admitted, it is evident that the gross profit of £1,000 consists of two separate elements. First, there is a gain associated simply with holding the goods from January to November when their value increased by £400 (£2,900 − £2,500). This holding gain should be distinguished from the gain made on the sale itself, namely the realization gain, amounting to £600 (£3,500 − £2,900). The realization gain is linked to the trading activity. Under CCA, the Profit Statement would be as follows:

	£
Sales	3,500
Cost of sales—at current cost	2,900
Gross profit	600

Analysing these transactions in cash-flow terms, the resulting situation would be:

		£
Cash balance	January	2,500
Goods purchased	..	2,500
		—
Sales of goods	November	3,500
Goods purchased	..	2,900
Cash balance		600

Comparing the gross profit under HC and CCA with the cash balance, it is evident that a distribution of £1,000 as dividends—which HC accounting would permit—could not be made without further funds of £400 being subscribed to the company as capital or as a loan.

The purpose of the COSA is to avoid the overstatement of profit under inflation, and in this sense, prevent the distribution of what would be the capital of the business.

Identifying the cost of sales

Normal trading operations prevent firms from systematically relating goods sold with their costs. To overcome this problem, it is necessary to establish an averaging process having two components. First, averaging the acquisition of stock in terms of time, to derive an average quantity and average acquisition cost. Second, by using average index numbers, to determine the average cost of sales in terms of their current cost. As in the case of the depreciation adjustment, it is necessary to use an appropriate index for the industrial sector in which the company is operating and establish:

(i) The index at the start of the accounting period to apply to the opening stock.
(ii) The average index for the entire accounting period.
(iii) The index at the close of the accounting period to apply to the closing stock.

Assuming that the goods are purchased evenly across the accounting period, both opening and closing stock shown in terms of HC can be converted into current costs by the use of the following index numbers:

$$\frac{\text{average index for the period}}{\text{index at date of purchase}}$$

Example 10

A company had opening stock at 1 January 19X7 of £2,692,000 and closing stock at 31 December 19X7 of £5,374,000—both figures being stated at HC. The opening stock represented two months' purchases and the closing stock three months' purchases. The related current cost index, all stated at month-end were:

19X6	November	146.3
	December	148.2
19X7	October	162.6
	November	168.4
	December	170.2

The average index for 19X7 on a full year basis is, therefore,

$$\frac{(148.2 + 170.2)}{2} = 159.2$$

The calculation of the cost of sales involves three steps:

(1) Restate the closing stock at average cost. Since this represented three months' supply, the mid-point is found at mid-November 19X7. At this date, the index is:

$$\frac{162.6 \text{ (end October)} + 168.4 \text{ (end November)}}{2} = 165.5$$

Accordingly, the closing stock revalued at average cost is:

$$£5,374,000 \times \frac{159.2}{165.5} = £5,169,430$$

(2) Restate the opening stock at average cost. In this instance, since the opening stock represented two months' purchase, the end of November 19X6 index will represent the mid-point index for the purpose of comparing the index at the close of the year 19X7 with that at the beginning of the year 19X7, and determining thereby the current cost of the opening stock as follows:

$$£2,692,000 \times \frac{159.2}{146.3} = £2,929,367$$

(3) Calculate the difference between the opening and closing stock in current cost terms. The stock increase is:

	£
Closing stock at current cost	5,169,430
Opening stock at current cost	2,929,367
	2,240,063

The calculation of the stock variation in current cost terms will reflect a volume change. To establish the cost change associated with inflation, it is necessary to compare the stock variation at HC with that at CC. In the example given above, the price change is as follows:

	£
Stock variation at HC (£5,374,000 − £2,692,000) =	2,682,000
less: stock variation at CC	2,240,063
Cost variation	441,937

The figure of £441,937 derived in this manner is the COSA, which in this case is deducted from the HC profit to arrive at the CC profit, this debit being reflected in a credit to the current cost reserve account.

The formula for calculating the COSA is:

$$COSA = (C - O) - I_a \left(\frac{C}{I_c} - \frac{O}{I_o} \right)$$

where C is the closing stock at HC, O is the opening stock at HC, I_a is the average index for the year, I_c is the index at average purchase date of the closing stock and I_o is the index at average purchase date of the opening stock.

Balance sheet representation of stock under CCA

The COSA is an adjustment to HC profit which has the purpose of adding cost variations resulting from inflation to the cost of goods sold in calculating CC profit. This cost variation reflects the additional amount which the enterprise has to finance when replacing stock under conditions of inflation.

The principle of restating assets at current cost for balance sheet purposes raises additional problems when dealing with closing stock. In the simplest case, where year-end stocks are low and the stock turnover is high, the difference between the historical cost and the replacement cost of stock is immaterial and no further adjustment to HC stock valuation is really needed. In all other cases, adjustments are required when converting HC stock valuation to CCA figures.

Example 11

Assume, as in Example 10 above, that opening stock at HC at 1 January 19X7 was £2,692,000 and closing stock at HC at 31 December 19X7 was £5,374,000 and that the month-end index numbers were as follows:

19X6	November	146.3
	December	148.2
19X7	October	162.6
	November	168.4
	December	170.2

Assume now that CCA was applied to the year ended 31 December 19X6, as a consequence of which a credit was passed to the current cost reserve account at 31 December 19X6 in respect of the COSA for that year. As it will have been seen in Example 10, the COSA involves the revaluation of both the opening and the closing stock of the accounting period at CC, and comparing the stock variation with that obtained from HC valuations. The closing stock at CC as at 31 December 19X6 was derived from an average index, and not the index at end December 19X6. Therefore, there already exists in the opening stock at 1 January 19X7 an unrealized gain. The procedure for establishing the balance sheet stock valuation at 31 December 19X7 and adjusting the current cost reserve at that date is as follows.

(1) Calculate the unrealized gain included in the opening stock at CCA valuation:

CCA opening stock $2,692,000 \times \dfrac{\text{index at end of period}}{\text{index at average purchase date}}$

$$\text{or } 2,692,000 \times \frac{148.2}{146.3}$$

$$= 2,762,960$$
$$- \text{HC opening stock} \quad \underline{2,692,000}$$
$$= \text{unrealized gain} \quad \underline{\underline{34,960}}$$

(2) Calculate the unrealized gain included in the closing stock at CCA valuation:

CCA closing stock $=$ HC $\times \dfrac{\text{index at end of period}}{\text{index at average purchase date}}$

£

$$= 5,374,000 \times \frac{170.2}{165.5} \text{ (see Example 10 above)}$$

$$= 5,526,615$$
HC closing stock $\underline{5,374,000}$
Unrealized gain $\underline{\underline{152,615}}$

(3) The balance sheet stock value under CCA will be as follows:

Current assets—(extract)

	31 December 19X6	31 December 19X7
Stock	£2,726,960	£5,374,000

The adjustments to the balance standing to the credit of the current cost reserve account are as follows:

	£	£
Debit current cost reserve account	34,960	
Credit opening inventory being the unrealized gain existing in opening stock at 1 January 19X7		34,960
Debit closing inventory	152,615	
Credit current cost reserve account being the unrealized gain existing in closing stock at 31 December 19X7		152,615

The net increase in the current cost reserve account is:

	£
Unrealized revaluation surplus as at 1 January 19X7	34,960
Unrealized revaluation surplus as at 31 December 19X7	152,615
Net increase	117,655

The net increase in the current cost reserve account in respect of the year ended 31 December 19X7 will consist of the COSA adjustment calculated above amounting to £466,006, and the balance sheet adjustment to the closing stock at 31 December 19X7 calculated above amounting to £117,655:

	£
COSA	466,006
Balance sheet	117,655
Net increase	583,661

The Monetary Working Capital Adjustment (MWCA)

Inflation hits the firm by raising the replacement cost of assets used in the business, and requires that extra cost to be financed if the firm is to maintain its operating capacity. The depreciation and the cost of sales adjustments allowed under CC accounting charge that extra cost against current profits, thereby financing such cost out of profits.

A further financial problem resulting from inflation is that other costs of doing business are also affected by price changes. One important consequence of credit trading is that as credit sales increase in monetary terms (without necessarily increasing in volume terms), firms have to find extra finance to provide this facility. For example, if annual sales give rise to average debtor balances of £50,000, and inflation is running at 20% as regards the business, then the annual increase in the average debtor balances—without any increase at all in the volume of sales—will be £10,000. This figure will continue to rise with inflation. Unless the firm can obtain additional finance to continue to maintain its existing credit practices, it will be forced to curtail credit and, ultimately will lose business.

The MWCA has the purpose of allowing a firm to finance the impact of inflation on working capital requirements out of profits. The MWCA takes into account the impact of inflation on both debtors' and creditors' balances, but excludes the impact of volume changes on these balances. It is calculated by taking the average monetary working capital, defined as above, and multiplying it by the increase in the index of inflation, divided by the average index, as follows:

$$MWCA = \text{average MWC} \times \frac{\text{increase in index}}{\text{average index}}$$

It may be noted that the MWCA requires a strict definition of the items included as trade debtors and trade creditors, and relies also on an averaging process.

The MWCA applies only to items used in the day to day operating activities of the business. Trade debtors are defined to include, in addition to those listed as such in the debtors ledger, trade bills receivable, prepayments and VAT recoverable. Trade creditors are defined to include, in addition to those listed as such in the creditors ledger, trade bills payable, accruals, expense creditors and VAT payable. Creditors and debtors associated with fixed assets transactions should not be included.

Example 12

Assume that the opening balance of trade debtors and trade creditors at 1 January 19X7 amounted to £836,420 and £420,140, respectively, and that the closing balances at 31 December 19X7 were £1,568,760 and £736,290, respectively. Assume, too, that included in trade debtors and trade creditors were the totality of items falling to be considered in the MWCA. The average age of all items included in trade debtors and trade creditors is one month.

Assume also that the relevant index numbers that apply to the MWCA items are those which applied to the COSA in Example 11, namely,

Opening MWCA items	30 November 19X6	146.3
Closing MWCA items	30 November 19X7	168.4
Average for the year ended	31 December 19X7	159.2

(1) Ascertain the relevant monetary working capital:

		£
Opening MWC	(£836,420 − 420,140)	= 416,280
Closing MWC	(£1,568,760 − 736,290)	= 832,470

(2) Calculate the variation in the MWC during the period:

	£
Closing MWC	832,470
Opening MWC	416,280
Increase in MWC	416,190

This increase represents the unadjusted change in the volume of MWC.

(3) Restate the closing and opening MWC in terms of average value and thereby identify the *effect* of the change in the volume of MWC in adjusted terms:

$$\text{adjusted closing MWC} = \frac{\text{closing MWC at HC}}{\text{closing index}} \times \text{average index}$$

$$\text{adjusted opening MWC} = \frac{\text{opening MWC at HC}}{\text{opening index}} \times \text{average index}$$

Using the above formulae, the net effect of the volume change in MWC is:

		£
Adjusted closing MWC $= \dfrac{£832,470}{168.4} \times 159.2$		$= 786,990$
less: Adjusted opening MWC $= \dfrac{£416,280}{146.3} \times 159.2$		$- 452,985$
Adjusted increase in MWC		$334,005$

(4) The MWCA may now be calculated by deducting the adjusted increase in MWC from the unadjusted increase, thereby reflecting the impact of inflation on the amount invested in the MWC. On the basis of the above figures, the MWCA is:

	£
Unadjusted increase in MWC	416,190
Adjusted increase in MWC	334,005
MWCA	82,185

The formula used for calculating the MWCA is similar in nature to that used for the COSA, as follows:

$$\text{MWCA} = (C - O) - I_a \left(\frac{C}{I_c} - \frac{O}{I_o} \right)$$

where O is the opening MWC, C is the closing MWC, I_a is the average index for the period, I_o is the index number appropriate to opening MWC and, I_c is the index number appropriate to closing MWC.

The gearing adjustment

The capital structure of a company describes the manner in which the cost of assets has been financed: the gearing represents the relative proportion of shareholders' capital to loan capital in the capital structure. A company which is highly geared will have a relatively high proportion of loan capital in its capital structure.

Shareholders tend to gain at the expense of lenders under inflation, since the loan capital is repayable in fixed monetary terms, that is, loan repayments are fixed at the amount originally borrowed, and are not adjusted for inflation. Inflation acts to transfer wealth from lenders to shareholders, and effectively helps shareholders to finance the cost of maintaining the operating capability of the business by replacing assets at the expense of lenders.

The purpose of the gearing adjustment is to calculate the current cost accounting profit attributable to shareholders by *adding* the benefit flowing to them from the extent of gearing to the current cost profit.

The gearing adjustment is calculated in three stages: first, the net borrowings, second, the gearing proportion and third, the gearing adjustment itself.

Net borrowings are defined in SSAP 16 as:

> the aggregate of all liabilities and provisions fixed in monetary terms (including convertible debentures and deferred tax but excluding proposed dividends) other than those included within monetary working capital which are, in substance, equity capital,

over

> the aggregate of all current assets other than those subject to a cost of sales adjustment and those included within monetary working capital.

This defininition is wider than the conventional definitions used for the purpose of establishing the gearing, including as it does such items as deferred taxation—implicitly interpreted as financing by the government, and hire purchase creditors as well as the more usual long-term loan commitments such as debentures.

Example 13

The following CCA balance sheets as at 31 December 19X6 and 19X7 are used to calculate the gearing adjustment:

	December 31 19X6 £	December 31 19X7 £
Share capital and reserves	16,325,000	21,470,000
Proposed dividends	495,000	650,000
Total shareholders interest the average of which = S	16,820,000	22,120,000

Net borrowings:

Debentures	5,000,000	5,000,000
Deferred taxation	830,000	900,000
Bank overdraft	2,600,000	2,100,000
Taxation	510,000	614,000
Monetary assets	(1,600,000)	(2,100,000)
Total net borrowing the average of which = L	7,340,000	6,514,000
Total, the average of which = L + S	24,160,000	28,634,000

Using the figure for net borrowings shown above, the gearing proportion may be calculated as follows:

$$\text{average } S = \frac{(£16,820,000 + 22,120,000)}{2}$$

$$= £19,470,000$$

$$\text{average } L = \frac{(£7,340,000 + 6,514,000)}{2}$$

$$= £6,927,000$$

Using the formula $L/(L + S)$, the gearing proportion is:

$$\frac{£6,927,000}{£6,927,000 + 19,470,000} \times 100\% = 26.2\%$$

To ascertain the gearing adjustment, apply the percentage obtained to the full adjustment made to allow for the effect of price changes made under:

(1) The depreciation adjustment.
(2) The COSA.
(3) The MWCA.

Assume for the purpose of this example that for the period under review the depreciation adjustment was £276,000 and that the COSA and MWCA were as shown above. The calculation is then:

Total adjustment

	£
Depreciation	276,000
COSA	441,937
MWCA	82,185
	800,122

$$£800,122 \times 26.2\% = £209,632$$

This final figure of £209,632 represents the amount of capital maintenance reserve which is effectively freed for the equity shareholders from the overall total of £800,122 and to that extent it limits the amount transferred to current cost reserve account.

Using an assumed HC profit and interest figures, the following sets out the impact of all the adjustments on the profit and loss account.

		£
HC profit before interest		4,638,000
less: Current cost adjustment		800,122
		3,837,878
Interest payable	285,000	
Gearing adjustment	209,632	75,368
Current cost profit before taxation		3,762,510

Note
Throughout these various calculations there has been a large number of 'averaging' assumptions. Accordingly, it is unlikely that, in practice, any attempt to refine the actual figures down to anything less than the nearest thousand in this example would be undertaken.

Question 1
What do you understand by 'value'?

Question 2
Suggest different concepts which render meaningful the notion of the 'value of an enterprise'.

Question 3
Discuss the objectives of valuation from an accounting viewpoint.

Question 4
Examine the relationship between the concept of profit and the value of a business derived from balance sheet numbers.

Question 5
Compare and contrast alternative valuation bases and discuss their advantages and disadvantages when used for the purpose of deriving accounting measurements.

Question 6
Using the profit and loss accounts and balance sheets given below of G. E. & Main Co. plc, wholesale fashion clothes distributors, you are required to:

(1) Prepare a statement of sources and application of funds for the year ended 30 September 19X7.
(2) Calculate those ratios which would be helpful in further interpretation of the results and financial position

Profit and loss accounts for years ended 30 September

	19X6		19X7	
	£000s	£000s	£000s	£000s
Sales		635		740
less: Cost of sales: Opening stock	37		45	
Purchases	321		397	
	358		442	
Closing stock	45	313	82	360
Gross profit		322		380
less: Wages	122		138	
Advertising	25		26	
Printing, post and stationery	12		14	
Motor expenses	20		26	
Audit fees	8		9	
Directors' remuneration	34		38	
Interest payment including debenture	12		18	
Rent and rates	25		7	
Lighting and heating	8		12	
Telephones	6		8	
Depreciation—Motors	4		3	
Depreciation—Fixtures and fittings	14		22	
Insurance	2		3	
Loss on sale of fixtures	—		24	
		292		348
Net profit for the year		30		32
Balance brought forward		118		140
		148		172
Dividend proposed		8		10
Balance carried forward		140		162

G. E. & R. Main Co. plc
Balance sheets as at 30 September

	19X6			19X7		
	£000s	£000s	£000s	£000s	£000s	£000s
	Cost	Depn		Cost	Depn	
Fixed assets						
Freehold property	—	—	—	90	—	90
Fixtures and fittings	120	28	92	150	35	115
Motor vehicles	35	17	18	35	20	15
	155	45	110	275	55	220

G. E. & R. Main Co. plc
Balance sheets as at 30 September (cont.)

| | 19X6 | | | 19X7 | | |
	£000s Cost	£000s Depn	£000s	£000s Cost	£000s Depn	£000s
Current assets						
Stock		45			82	
Debtors		65			94	
Bank		68			2	
		178			178	
Creditors—amounts falling due within one year						
Trade creditors	35			71		
Proposed dividend	8	43		10	81	
Net current assets			135			97
Total assets less current liabilities			245			317
Creditors—amounts falling due after more than one year						
12% Debentures			30			45
Capital and reserves						
Called up share capital		75			100	
Share premium account		—			10	
Profit and loss account		140			162	
			215			272
			245			317

Note
During the year to 30 September 19X7 some fitting were sold which originally cost £70,000.

Question 7
The following condensed accounting statements for the years ended 31 December 19X2 and 19X3 relate to Domestic Equipment Company plc, manufacturers of kitchen equipment.

Condensed profit and loss accounts for the years
ended 31 December

	19X2 £000s	19X3 £000s
Sales	2,000	2,400
Cost of sales	1,200	1,400
Gross profit	800	1,000
Expenses	400	440
Profit before taxation	400	560
less Taxation	170	252
Profit after taxation	230	308
Dividends	160	160
Income retained	70	148

Condensed balance sheet as at 31 December

	19X2 £000s	19X3 £000s		19X2 £000s	19X3 £000s
Share capital—issued and fully paid ordinary £1 share	800	800	Fixed assets (net of depreciation)		
Retained earnings	200	348	Plant and equipment	600	800
9% debenture	100	100	Motor vehicles	200	300
	1,100	1,248		800	1,100
Current liabilities			Current assets		
Creditors	270	300	Stock	400	540
Taxation	170	252	Debtor	180	200
Dividends proposed	160	160	Bank	320	120
	1,700	1,960		1,700	1,960

Note

In the expense figures for 19X3 is included depreciation of £60,000 on plant and equipment and £40,000 for motor vehicles.

Required

Prepare:

(a) A statement of sources and application of funds.
(b) Such ratios as you may be able to calculate and which you believe would aid in the interpretation of these figures.
(c) Present your interpretation of the results obtained from (a) and (b).

Question 8

Set out below are the trading results, balance sheets and certain other data of the Bigdeal Stores plc for the years to 30 September 19X2 and 19X3. The company owns and operates a chain of department stores throughout the country and is quoted on the London Stock Exchange.

		19X2 £000s		19X3 £000s
Turnover		178,392		191,423
Trading profit after charging the following		12,314		9,503
Depreciation	6,211		8,312	
Interest	1,500		2,050	
Directors' remuneration	64		86	
Audit fees	62		70	
Taxation		5,710		6,117
Profit after taxation		6,604		3,386
Dividend on ordinary shares		2,000		2,500
Transfer to retained earnings		4,604		886
Ex div price of £1 share on results declared in October		£4.20		£5.00

Balance sheets as at 30 September

	£000s	£000s	19X2 £000s	£000s	£000s	19X3 £000s
Fixed assets						
Goodwill			27			—
Shop and properties			42,310			68,810
Fixtures and equipment			12,110			16,834
Vehicles			610			582
			55,057			86,226
Current assets						
Stock		27,142			34,836	
Debtors and prepayments		1,237			2,142	
Bank		8,629			340	
		37,008			37,318	
Creditors—amounts falling due after more than one year						
Trade creditors	16,927			24,113		
Dividends	2,000			2,500		
Taxation	5,710	24,637		6,117	32,730	
Net current assets			12,371			4,588
Total assets less current liabilities			67,428			90,814
Creditors—amounts falling due after more than one year						
10% Debentures			15,000			15,000
11% Debentures			—			5,000
Capital and reserves						
Called up share capital			20,000			20,000
Share premium account			13,500			13,500
Revaluation reserve			—			17,500
Profit and loss account			18,928			19,814
			67,428			90,814

Required

Prepare an analysis of the information supplied above by means of appropriate ratios. Comment upon the implications of your analysis.

PART 2
Accounting for Planning and Control —

Introduction

To this point, our discussion of accounting has been limited to service and trading businesses. A trading business buys merchandise in a finished form and sells it in the same form. In contrast, manufacturing firms employ labour and use machinery to convert materials into finished products. This results in a corresponding difference between the methods of accounting for the cost of goods sold of the two types of businesses. The measurement of cost of goods sold is more complicated in a manufacturing company, because additional accounts are necessary to record the activities involved in converting raw materials into finished goods. In a merchandising company this cost is normally obtained direct from invoices. The process by which manufacturing companies collect and aggregate the several elements of manufacturing cost is discussed in Chapter 9.

In Part I we discussed the role of accounting in establishing the financial position of the firm in relation to its environment. The information presented in the profit and loss account, the balance sheet and funds flow statement is critical to the assessment of financial performance in terms of profitability and financial status expressed in terms of gearing and solvency. In this part we shall be concerned with the role of cost accounting information in securing the internal efficiency of the use of resources which is reflected in overall profitability. One main objective of a cost accounting system is to ascertain the cost of manufacturing or providing individual products and services. By contrast, the emphasis in the financial accounts is to assess the effect of total costs on overall profitability.

Assume a company has three product lines. Information relating to the products and to the company as a whole is given below:

	Total (£)	Products A (£)	B (£)	C (£)
Sales	100,000	50,000	20,000	30,000
Cost of Sales	50,000	32,000	8,000	10,000
Gross profit	50,000	18,000	12,000	20,000
Selling expenses	20,000	11,000	5,000	4,000
Administrative expenses	20,000	9,000	4,000	7,000
Net profit	10,000	(2,000)	3,000	9,000
Net profit/sales	10%	(4%)	15%	30%

These figures illustrate the importance of a costing system to the management of the company concerned. The financial accounting system is of little use for providing information to management who require to know how the overall profitability of the company was achieved.

The above example illustrates how cost accounting data puts more meaning into historical data. However, the main interest of management lies in the future, not the past. Thus, management is concerned with planning and control and with the fixing of responsibility for meeting objectives. It is seeking quantitative data which will be helpful in solving the many problems encountered in manufacturing and selling the company's products. The accounting department must be organized to meet these needs.

The three broad objectives of cost and management accounting which are considered in this Part are:

(1) To provide data for profit measurement and stock valuation (profit and loss account and balance sheet). A major function of cost accounting is the attachment of costs to products manufactured and the matching of these product costs with the revenue derived from their sale. Two basic systems—job order and process—which each use a different method of cost accumulation, are discussed in Chapter 9. A job, or made to order, type of system provides for a separate record of the cost of each particular quantity of product that passes through the factory. In contrast, a process system accumulates costs by processes or departments and is employed where a uniform type of product is produced during a continuous production process.

(2) To provide data for management planning and decision making. One aspect of planning requires management to evaluate alternative proposals to reach decisions on appropriate action. The accountant marshals relevant data for such purposes which include long run decisions, such as capital investment plans (Chapter 10) and short run tactical decisions, for example, certain production and pricing decisions (Chapter 12). Another aspect of managerial planning involves the making of the economic forecast for the coming year and the plans based on that forecast. The accountant contributes by co-ordinating plans made by functions, such as sales and production, and in analysing their interrelationships (Chapter 11).

(3) To provide information for the management control of the firm's operations and activities. The accountant compares performance with operating plans and standards and reports and interprets the results of operating to all levels of management. Aspects of control are discussed in Chapter 13.

9 Basic Cost Accounting

The purpose of this chapter is to examine the manner in which the flow of costs through an industrial process is recorded. This area of accounting knowledge is commonly referred to as 'cost accounting', so that it may be distinguished from 'management accounting' which is concerned with the role of accounting information for planning and control purposes. Given the evident emphasis which management accounting attaches to cost planning and cost control, this distinction is probably not helpful to the appreciation of the critical importance of cost accounting in providing the information base on which management accounting relies. For this reason, we begin this Part with an analysis of basic cost accounting with a view to establishing a framework within which the provision of accounting information for management purposes may be considered.

The cost accounting system is not independent of the financial accounts. Rather, it represents an elaboration of the basic financial accounting system. Cost accounting procedures are superimposed upon the general accounting system to provide a greater degree of cost classification and to allow a closer control over costs. Therefore, through these records the cost accounting system is able to contribute to the control over the resources of a firm.

This chapter is divided into the following six sections:

Manufacturing accounting.
Predetermined overhead costing.
Job order costing.
Process costing.
Joint costs and by-product costs.
Recording cost and financial transactions:
(a) Separate cost and financial accounting systems.
(b) Integrated cost and financial accounting systems.

Manufacturing accounting

Unlike a trading firm which ordinarily stocks and sells the same items which it originally bought, a manufacturing firm purchases raw materials and, through a production process, transforms their physical nature into new items which are to be sold. Because of this difference, a manufacturing firm requires additional asset and expense accounts in respect of (1) stocks (raw materials, work-in-progress and finished goods), (2) plant and equipment and (3) manufacturing or production costs.

The main difference between a trading and a manufacturing firm is apparent from the abbreviated financial statements shown below:

Profit and loss account					
Trading firm			Manufacturing firm		
	£	£		£	£
Sales		500	Sales		500
Cost of goods sold:			Cost of goods sold:		
Opening stock of merchandise	100		Opening stock of finished goods	100	
Net cost of merchandise purchased	400		Cost of goods manufactured	400	
Available for sale	500		Available for sale	500	
Closing stock of merchandise	200		Closing stock of finished goods	200	
Cost of goods sold		300	Cost of goods sold		300
Gross profit margin		200	Gross profit margin		200

Balance sheet			
Trading firm		Manufacturing firm	
	£		£
Current assets		Current assets	
Stocks of merchandise (i.e. finished goods)	200	Stocks of raw materials	200
		Stocks of work-in-progress	500
		Stocks of finished goods	200

In the factory at any one time, such as the end of the accounting period, there may be materials which are only partially converted into finished goods. This incomplete production is known as work-in-progress. Completed production which is awaiting sale to customers is called finished goods stock. Notice that the cost of goods manufactured on the manufacturing firm's profit and loss account corresponds to the net cost of merchandise purchased on the trading firm's profit and loss account. In both cases, these amounts represent the cost of goods which form part of the total available for sale. In contrast to the trading firm, however, the manufacturing firm has to establish the cost of converting raw materials into finished goods.

The flow of costs

Figure 9.1 illustrates the flow of costs associated with a manufacturing firm and their classification for profit measurement purposes.

Fig. 9.1   Flow of costs

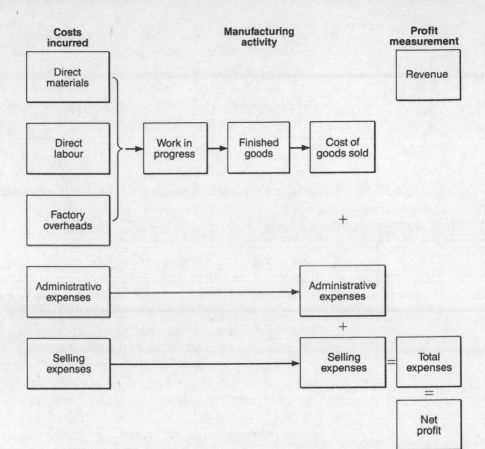

For product costing purposes the adjective *direct* indicates the relationship of these cost elements to the product being produced. *Direct materials* represents that portion of materials used in the manufacturing process that is clearly traceable or readily identifiable in the goods produced. Materials put into the process that cannot meet this criterion are treated as indirect material, a part of manufacturing overhead. However, where the cost per unit may be too insignificant to measure as direct materials cost, e.g. glue and thread used in manufacturing furniture, these materials may be classified as indirect. *Direct labour* represents those labour costs that are clearly traceable or readily identifiable with the product. *Factory overhead* consists of all those costs put into the manufacturing process that cannot be classified as either direct material or direct labour. Depreciation of factory buildings and equipment, heat, light and power are examples of factory overhead. In Fig. 9.1 both direct and indirect factory costs are shown as included in the cost of completed products. Figure 9.1 distinguishes between factory costs which are attached to particular products and administrative and selling overhead expenses which are not included in cost of goods sold. These two categories of expenses are treated as expenses in the period incurred and appear, as we see later, in the profit and loss account.

In Chapter 11 we consider the construction of profit statements which distinguish between variable and fixed costs. *Variable costs* are those costs that change proportionately with changes in volume of activity. Direct material cost is an example of a cost that usually behaves in this manner. *Fixed costs* are those that are usually related to a time period and remain unchanged when volume of activity changes. Examples of such costs are rents, rates and depreciation.

Accounting for material costs

The receipt, storage and issue of raw materials for production (direct materials) and that of oil, grease, cleaning materials, etc., for use in running a factory (indirect materials) require to be dealt with and recorded methodically if accurate information is to be available at any time regarding the amount of stock on hand and the amount of stock already committed to production.

The purchase of materials is initiated by a *purchase requisition*, which is a form requesting the purchasing department to obtain the required materials. Requisitions for materials normally carried in stock usually originate from the stores ledger clerk; requisitions for extraordinary items are prepared in the department making the request. Copies of the purchase requisition are sent to the accounting department for use in checking the supplier's invoice. The invoice acts as a basis for determining the cost of materials to be entered in the stock records which are kept by the accounting department. These records consist of *perpetual* (or *running accounts*) which record each item of material received, issued and on hand, both in quantity and value, and a *control account* for controlling these accounts. These records are kept in a *subsidiary ledger*, usually referred to as a stores ledger, which fulfils two main functions in material costing and control: (1) pricing the issue of materials, and (2) providing a check on quantities in stock.

Materials are issued against *material requisitions* which are prepared in the departments requiring the material. When delivery is made, the requisition is signed as an acknowledgement of the receipt of the material. It is passed to the accounting department where a cost is assigned to the material issued. The appropriate stores ledger account and the stores control account are credited and the appropriate job or process account is debited. Exhibit 1 below is a flowchart illustrating materials accounting.

The costing of materials issued requires mention at this stage. Pur-

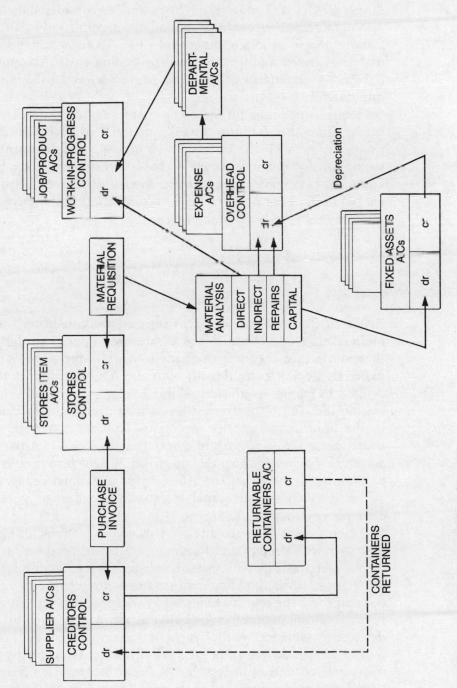

Exhibit 1   Materials accounting flow chart

chases effected at different points in time may be made at different prices. In Part 1, we discussed alternative methods of expressing cost flows (FIFO, LIFO and average cost), and we considered their effects on the values shown on the profit and loss account and balance sheet. Clearly, this is an important consideration as regards the costing of materials issued and the process of assigning costs. Accounting for the cost of materials will allow the firm to select a basis which will minimize distortions.

Finally, accounting for materials enables reasoned decisions to be made about the quantities of each material to be bought and the timing of such purchases. For this purpose, an assessment of the maximum and minimum stock level for each material has to be made and recorded in order to reduce the possibility of investing too much capital in stocks or not carrying sufficient stocks and thereby risking disruptions to the production process.

Accounting for overhead costs

Exhibit 1 illustrates the different treatment accorded to direct and indirect materials. When materials are used directly in the process of manufacture they are charged to work-in-progress. When the materials do not enter directly into the finished product they are debited to factory overhead. Exhibit 1 serves as a useful vehicle for tracing the control of overheads. Factory overhead is accumulated in the appropriate expense accounts—indirect materials, repairs, depreciation, etc.—which are transferred to separate departmental accounts. Each departmental supervisor is held responsible for the costs of his department. The efficiency of individual departments is achieved by comparing actual costs with a budget or standard as explained in Chapter 13.

Departments which are directly engaged in manufacturing activities, such as assembly and finishing, are called production departments. Departments which assist indirectly by rendering services—purchasing, stores, building maintenance—are referred to as service departments. The services rendered by a service department give rise to internal transactions between that department and the processing departments that receive the benefit of the services. The costs incurred by the service departments are periodically charged to the factory overhead accounts of the producing departments. From the production departments, overhead costs are allocated to products as indicated in Exhibit 1. The subject of overhead costing is dealt with later in this chapter.

Accounting for labour costs

Compared with accounting for material costs, accounting for labour costs is relatively simple. This is because labour, unlike materials, cannot be stored. It is recorded directly in the manufacturing process.

Exhibit 2 below illustrates the various functions associated with the process of accounting for labour costs. Thus, *financial labour costs* include a host of additional expenses borne by the employer on behalf of the employee. Income tax, insurance contribution, holiday pay, etc., are all included in the total payroll. As regards *cost distribution and analysis*, a wages analysis charges each job or other cost unit with the appropriate amount of labour cost. At the end of each week, the *wages analysis* should be totalled and the grand total should agree with the total wages shown as payable on the payroll.

The treatment of indirect labour costs is not illustrated in Exhibit 2. This should, of course, be similar to that accorded indirect materials discussed previously.

Accounting for cost of goods sold

Two financial statements of a manufacturing business—cost of goods sold and profit and loss account—are the subject of Questions 2, 3 and 4. Question 2 shows how the flow of costs are summarized by these statements. Question 3 illustrates how the statement of cost of goods sold is divided into five parts: direct materials section (consisting of opening stock, purchases and the final stock, direct labour section, factory overhead, work in progress stock (representing costs in process at the beginning and costs still in process at the end) and finished goods stock, beginning and ending. Question 4 involves the preparation of a statement of cost of goods sold and a profit and loss account. A profit and loss account comprises sales revenue from which is deducted cost of goods sold to give gross profit. As illustrated in Question 2 the deduction of non-factory expenses (e.g. administration and selling) from gross profit gives net profit.

Question 1
Using the columns provided, indicate whether the costs shown below are:

(a) Direct or indirect costs in relation to the product.
(b) Fixed or variable costs in relation to output.

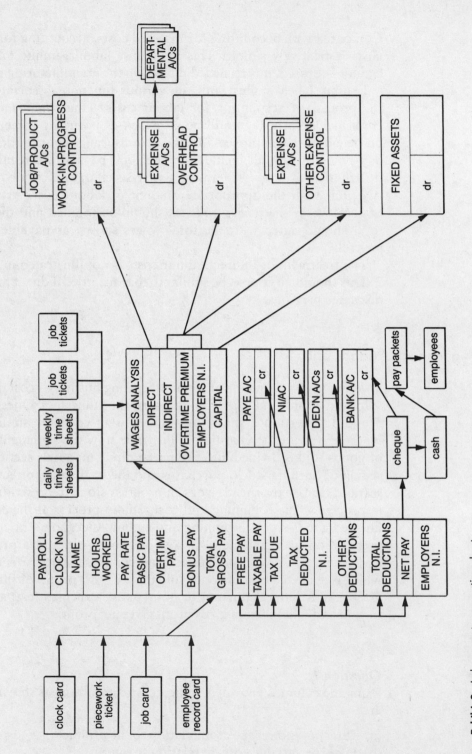

Exhibit 2 Labour cost accounting chart

	Direct / indirect costs	Fixed / variable costs
1 Factory heating	....	....
2 Advertising	....	....
3 Operator's wages	....	....
4 Depreciation of machinery	....	....
5 Machinery repairs	....	....
6 Personnel department	....	....
7 Consumable tools used in production	....	....
8 Raw materials used in production	....	....
9 Packing	....	....
10 Salesmen's salaries	....	....
11 Production manager's salary	....	....
12 Factory rent	....	....
13 Power	....	....
14 Machinery and equipment insurance	....	....
15 Carriage inwards	....	....
16 Storekeeper's salary	....	....

Question 2
Figure 9.2 below illustrates some fundamental relationships in basic costs.

Required
(1) You are required to fill in the spaces on the left-hand side by inserting the following items:

	£
Administration	800
Carriage inwards	25
Closing stock of finished goods	900
Closing stock of raw materials	625
Closing stock of work-in-progress	500
Direct wages	500
Gross profit	5,000
Manufacturing overhead	900
Opening stock of finished goods	800
Opening stock of raw materials	600
Opening stock of work-in-progress	400
Purchases	1,000
Selling expenses	500

(2) You are required to fill in the details omitted from the five oblong blocks on the right-hand side of Fig. 9.2.

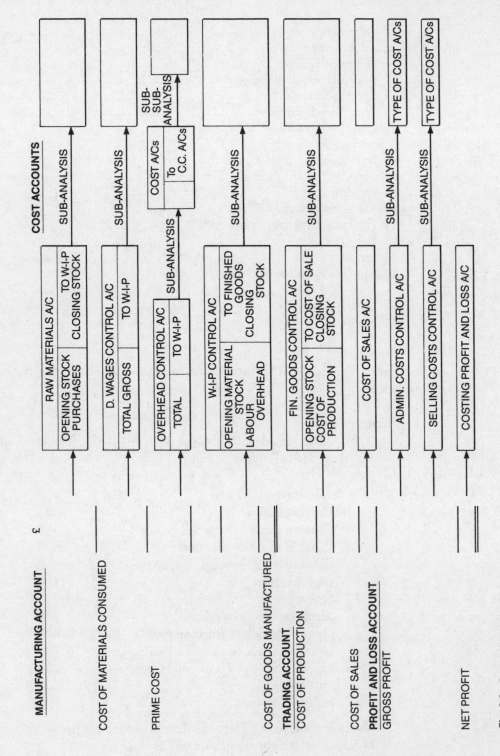

Fig. 9.2 Basic cost accounting

Question 3
The statements of cost of goods sold for the Imperial Manufacturing Company in respect of the years ended 31 December 19X1 and 19X2 are given below.

Required
Fill in the spaces.

Imperial Manufacturing Company
Statements of cost of goods sold for the years ended 31 December

	19X1 £	19X2 £
Direct materials		
Raw materials stock 1 January	10,000	....
Raw materials purchases	....	....
	50,000	55,000
Raw materials stock 31 December	12,000	15,000
	....	....
Direct labour	30,000	....
Factory overhead	....	25,000
Manufacturing costs incurred in 19X1 and 19X2	....	....
add: Work-in-progress stock 1 January	20,000	22,000
	....	....
less: Work-in-progress stock 31 December	....	24,000
Cost of goods manufactured	....	....
add: Finished goods stock 1 January	30,000	....
	....	....
less: Finished goods stock 31 December	25,000	28,000
Cost of goods sold	90,000	95,000

Question 4
The following balances, which are listed in alphabetical order, were taken from the accounting records of the Alpine Manufacturing Company for the year ended 31 December 19X1:

	£
Administrative salaries	20,000
Depreciation of office machinery	11,000
Depreciation of factory buildings	15,000
Direct labour	85,000
Factory heat, light and power	10,000
Factory indirect labour	30,000
Factory insurance	6,000
Factory supervision	20,000

Factory supplies used	15,000
Finished goods stock 1 January 19X1	95,000
Finished goods stock 31 December 19X1	100,000
Inspection	10,000
Purchases of raw materials	100,000
Raw materials stock 1 January 19X1	60,000
Raw materials stock 31 December 19X1	45,000
Sales	500,000
Sales salaries	12,000
Stationery, supplies and postages	1,000
Work-in-progress stock 1 January 19X1	20,000
Work-in-progress stock 31 December 19X1	25,000

Required

Prepare a statement of the cost of goods sold, and a profit and loss account for the year ended 31 December 19X1.

Predetermined overhead costing

Three procedures are involved in assigning factory overheads to products. First, all factory costs incurred in a period are distributed to production and service departments. Some costs may be allocated to departments, that is, charged directly; for example, the wages of personnel working in a department may be traceable directly to that department. In other cases, where overhead costs cannot be directly traceable to particular departments, they must be apportioned to departments on the principle of benefit received. Second, all overhead costs accumulated in the service departments are assigned to production departments on a basis which applies the benefit received criterion, e.g. floor space occupied, number of employees. Third, the overhead accumulated in production departments is absorbed by specific units of production on the basis of some factor that lends itself to direct measurement, such as labour hours, labour cost or machine hours. In computing overhead rates the objective is to use a measure that is closely related to the amount of overhead incurred by the individual products.

In this section we are concerned with the computation of predetermined overhead rates which have several advantages over incurred rates. First, the incurred rate is not available until after the end of the period. Second, incurred rates may fluctuate widely, thereby obscuring the cost relationships between products. Finally, cost control considerations necessitate the computation of bench-marks against which performance can be evaluated. The mechanics of computing predetermined overhead rates involves the use of budgeted rather than actual levels of costs and activity. Questions 5, 6, and 7 illustrate these procedures. Question 7 deals with the problem of choosing the level of activity for computing overhead rates. Practical capacity is the volume of production which would be attained if sales demand permitted the plant to operate continuously at some theoretical level of efficiency. Expected capacity is the volume of production required to meet the sales demand anticipated for the coming year. Normal capacity is the average volume of production needed to meet sales demand over a cycle of years long enough to even out cyclical fluctuations in sales volume.

Question 5

James Wilson Engineering Co. has three production departments and two service departments. Budgeted overhead expenses for the year 19X2 are as follows:

| | Production departments | | | |
	Drilling £	Milling £	Assembly £	Total £
Traceable (or allocated) over-heads				
Indirect materials	50,000	15,000	80,000	145,000
Indirect labour	40,000	20,000	100,000	160,000
Heat and light	10,000	8,000	15,000	33,000
Total traceable overheads	100,000	43,000	195,000	338,000

| | Service departments | | |
	Maintenance £	Canteen £	Total £
Traceable (or allocated) over-heads			
Indirect materials	60,000	85,000	145,000
Indirect labour	80,000	40,000	120,000
Heat and light	20,000	15,000	35,000
Total traceable overheads	160,000	140,000	300,000

	Total £
Non-traceable overheads	
Factory rent	100,000
Supervisory salaries	200,000
	300,000

Other data are as follows:

	Drilling	Milling	Assembly	Maint'nce	Canteen	Total
Square metres of floor space	50,000	40,000	70,000	20,000	20,000	200,000
Number of employees	110	70	150	40	30	400
Maintenance hours	3,000	2,000	5,000	—	—	10,000
Machine hours	60,000	40,000	100,000	—	—	200,000

Required

Apportion the non-traceable overheads to the production and service departments, and the service department overheads to the production departments using the bases which you consider to be most appropriate. By using the machine hour basis, calculate the departmental overhead rates by means of which overheads may be charged to product costs. The format shown by Fig. 9.3 may be helpful to you.

	Basis	Drilling £	Milling £	Assembly £	Maintenance £	Canteen £	Total £
Overhead costs							
Indirect material	....	....	....	....	....	....	....
Indirect labour	....	....	....	....	....	....	....
Heat and light	....	....	....	....	....	....	....
Factory rent	....	....	....	....	....	....	....
Supervisory salaries	....	....	....	....	....	....	....
	....	....	....	....	....	....	....
Apportionment of service							
Department							
Maintenance	....	....	....	....	....	—	—
Canteen	....	....	....	....	—	....	—
	....	....	....	—	—	....
Computation of overhead							
Rate							
Machine hours		....	....	....			
Machine hour rate		....	....	....			

Fig. 9.3

Question 6

Speciality Products Limited computed predetermined overhead rates for the year ended 31 December 19X1 for two of its departments, A and B, from the following estimates:

	Dept A £	Dept B £
Indirect materials	90,000	100,000
Indirect labour	200,000	30,000
Supervisory salaries	70,000	10,000
Employee benefit services	20,000	2,000
Depreciation—factory buildings	30,000	80,000
Depreciation—factory equipment	30,000	150,000
Repairs and maintenance	5,000	25,000
Power and light	3,000	8,000
Maintenance	2,000	10,000
Total	450,000	415,000

Estimates of direct labour costs, direct labour hours and machine hours for 19X1 were as follows:

	Dept A	Dept B
Direct labour costs	£200,000	£50,000
Direct labour hours	150,000 hrs	25,000 hrs
Machine hours	100,000 hrs	415,000 hrs

During January 19X1 the firm completed three orders. Only Departments A and B were involved in working on these orders. Details of costs and other data pertinent to these orders are given below:

		Job 101	Job 102	Job 103
Direct materials cost		£1,000	800	1,500
Direct labour costs	—Dept A	£2,000	2,500	3,000
	—Dept B	£ 500	300	600
Direct labour hours	—Dept A	1,600 hr	2,000 hr	2,800 hr
	—Dept B	1,000 hr	1,300 hr	1,500 hr
Machine hours	—Dept A	800 hr	600 hr	1,400 hr
	—Dept B	2,000 hr	2,500 hr	3,000 hr

Required

(1) Compute predetermined overhead rates for the two departments, based on (a) direct labour costs; (b) direct labour hours; (c) machine hours.

(2) Which method of absorbing overhead costs would you recommend for these two departments and why?

(3) Compute the cost of the three orders completed during January 19X1.

Question 7

The managing director, the manager of the machining department and the accountant of the Zebronx Co were in disagreement as to the most appropriate way of computing factory overhead rates.

The Managing Director: 'I believe in efficiency. I realize that we can't, of course, operate at a 100% level without interruption. Some interruptions are inevitable, and should be taken into account in computing a level of activity for the calculating of factor overhead rates. According to my estimates, these interruptions should reduce theoretical capacity by 10%. The more we produce, the lower our costs, and this allows us to price more competitively.'

The Machining Department Manager: 'I disagree with this viewpoint. We should be concerned with expected capacity, this is, what we expect to produce next year. For the machining department, for example, the expected poor trading conditions have led us to budget for an output of 75% of theoretical capacity. By using the expected activity level, the costs which we shall incur next year will be related to what we expect to produce.'

The Accountant: 'I think that you are both wrong. The crux of the matter is that part of factory overhead costs are fixed over a number of years. These overhead costs are incurred for the benefit of production over these years, and are not, therefore, related merely to next year's output. We need a longer run concept for computing factory overhead rates than next year's expected activity level. Normal capacity is such a concept. According to my estimation, normal capacity for the machining department is 80% of theoretical capacity.'

The following additional data are given:

Theoretical capacity	500,000 units per annum
Fixed factory overheads	£150,000
Direct labour hours per unit	0.2 hours
Variable factory overheads per unit	£0.3

Required

(1) Calculate the direct labour hour rate for applying factory overhead costs to the machining department based on the practical, expected and normal capacity levels for that department.
(2) Which 'capacity level' do you consider to be the most appropriate one to use for determining the factory overhead rate?

Under- or over-absorbed factory overheads

When predetermined factory overhead rates are used to determine product costs, it would be very unusual for the actual factory overheads incurred to agree exactly with the factory overheads absorbed into product costs. Assume that a firm computes a direct labour hour rate as follows:

$$\frac{\text{estimated overhead costs}}{\text{estimated direct labour hours}} = \frac{£40,000}{20,000} = £2.00 \text{ per direct labour hour}$$

During the accounting period, 18,000 actual labour hours were consumed and actual factory overheads incurred amounted to £38,000. The following journal entry would record actual factory overheads incurred:

Factory overhead control account	£38,000	
Creditors / cash account		£38,000

The following entry applies overhead costs to the work-in-progress stock:

Work-in-progress control account	£36,000	
Factory overhead control account		£36,000

In this example, the factory overheads incurred during the accounting period exceed the factory overheads applied to product costs. Consequently, factory overheads are *under-absorbed* by £2,000, and this sum will be debited to cost of goods sold as follows:

Cost of goods sold	£2,000	
Factory overhead control account		£2,000

Job order costing

A job order costing system is designed to account for product costs in a situation where each unit of product or batch of product is different from each other unit or batch. It has the following characteristics:

(1) Each job is assigned a number and a separate accounting document called a *job order cost sheet* is drawn up for each job.
(2) All direct job material and labour costs put into process are assigned to specific jobs and are recorded on the appropriate job order cost sheets.
(3) Overhead costs are assigned to each job on an appropriate basis.
(4) Work-in-progress inventory is the sum of the values recorded on the individual job order cost sheets.

Question 8

J. M. Daniels Company uses a job order cost system. On 1 January 19X1, the company had a work-in-progress stock balance of £44,000.

This account was made up of the following items:

Job No.	Direct materials £	Direct labour £	Factory overheads £
101	10,000	3,000	2,000
102	15,000	8,000	2,000
103	2,000	1,000	1,000

The following transactions were completed during the month:

(a) Materials were requisitioned for production:

Job No. 101	£12,000
Job No. 102	£6,000
Job No. 103	£14,000
Indirect materials	£8,000

(b) Paid wages totalling £84,000. This was distributed as follows:

	Hours	£
Job No. 101	20,000	41,000
Job No. 102	12,000	25,000
Job No. 103	4,000	8,000
Indirect labour		10,000

(c) Additional factory overheads incurred during January were £40,000.

(d) Applied factory overheads to jobs at the rate of £1.50 per direct labour hour.

(e) Completed jobs Nos 101 and 102 which were despatched to the customer.

Required

(1) Prepare job cost sheets for the three jobs, using the following format:

Job No. 101	Materials	Labour	Over-heads	Total	Status*		
	£	£	£	£	I	F	D
Balance January 1	....	....	....	....	....	....	....
Added during January	....	....	....	....	....	....	....
Total January 31	....	....	....	....	....	....	....

Repeat for Job Nos 102 and 103.

*Status: I —in progress at the end of the month,
            F —finished but not delivered at the end of the month,
            D —finished and delivered at the end of the month.

(2) Complete the factory overheads account for January 19X1.

(3) Explain the reasons for the balance disclosed on the factory overheads account at the end of January 19X1.

(4) What is the value of work-in-progress stock?

Question 9

The Brown Manufacturing Company uses a job order costing system. The trial balance at 30 November 19X1 is shown below:

	£	£
Plant and machinery	122,000	
Prepaid expenses	2,000	
Raw materials	5,000	
Work-in-progress	10,000	
Finished goods	20,000	
Debtors	15,000	
Cash	16,000	
Share capital		100,000
Retained earnings		20,000
Wages payable		10,000
Creditors		20,000
Accumulated depreciation		40,000
	190,000	190,000

The stock balances in the above trial balance have been derived from control accounts. These are supported in the subsidiary ledgers as follows:

Raw materials		Work-in-progress		Finished goods	
	£		£		£
Material X	2,000	Job No 100	7,000	Product A	10,000
Material Y	2,000	Job No 101	3,000	Product B	8,000
Material Z	1,000			Product C	2,000
	5,000		10,000		20,000

Cost-related transactions for December 19X1 are summarized below:

(1) Purchases of materials amounted to £25,000 as follows:

	£
Material X	10,000
Material Y	10,000
Material Z	5,000

(2) Materials requisitioned and placed in production amounted to £23,000, of which £3,000 were indirect materials. Direct materials were charged to jobs as follows:

Job	Amount £	Material	Amount £
102	10,000	X	5,000
103	8,000	Y	11,000
104	2,000	Z	4,000
	20,000		20,000

(3) Wages paid for the month amounted to £30,000 of which £8,000 were indirect. Direct wages were charged to jobs as follows:

Job	Amount £
102	6,000
103	9,000
104	7,000
	22,000

(4) £10,000 was incurred in respect of factory overheads, and this amount was additional to the costs incurred in respect of indirect materials and indirect labour.

(5) Depreciation on plant and machinery for the month amounted to £3,000.

(6) Factory overheads applied to jobs on the basis of direct labour costs were as follows:

Job	Overhead rate
102	100%
103	120%
104	90%

(7) Job Nos 100, 101, 102 and 103 were completed during the month and taken into finished goods stock, Job Nos 100 and 102 being taken into Product A and Job Nos 101 and 103 into Product B.

(8) Cost of goods sold during the month amounted to £66,000 and related to individual products as follows:

Product	Amount £
A	35,000
B	30,000
C	1,000
	66,000

Required

Complete the T accounts below:

(1) To record the opening balances, transactions and closing balances in (a) the control accounts, (b) the subsidiary ledgers and (c) the factory overheads account.

(2) Prepare a statement agreeing the balances shown in the control accounts with those appearing in the subsidiary ledgers.

(a) Control accounts

Raw materials account	Work-in-progress account	Finished goods account

(b) Subsidiary ledgers

Materials ledger	Job ledger	Finished goods ledger
Material X account	Job 100 account	Product A account
£ £	£ £	£ £
	Job 101 account	
	£ £	
Material Y account	Job 102 account	Product B account
£ £	£ £	£ £
	Job 103 account	
	£ £	
Material Z account	Job 104 account	Product C account
£ £	£ £	£ £

(c) Factory overheads account

£	£

Process costing

In job order cost accounting, work performed and costs incurred are identified with specific customers' orders. Where the firm manufactures identical units of product on a continuous basis, it is often impossible to relate specific costs to specific orders. In these circumstances, costs are not accumulated in terms of job orders but in terms of cost accounting periods by the department in which the products are made. Emphasis is not on total costs but on the average cost per unit produced. The unit cost is computed by dividing the number of units completed in the department into the corresponding department costs. These unit costs are applied to the number of units transferred through the manufacturing process and ultimately are identified with the units completed and sold. Before a product is completely manufactured, it may be transferred from one department to another in a series of processing operations. Each unit of product will carry the costs that have been assigned to it by the various departments in which it has been processed.

Process costing is widely employed for a variety of different products such as cement, sugar, flour where the units of the product are expressed in terms of a suitable weight or measure, for example, the standard unit production for cement is a tonne.

As regards the detailed recording of costs, process costing employs *production cost reports* instead of the job order cost sheets discussed in the previous section.

The production cost report

The production cost report shows the quantities of product, the total cost and the unit costs associated with a particular department (or departments) during a period. It summarizes data in a form which may best be visualized as follows:

UNITS to be accounted for: units in process at beginning of period + units started or transferred in during period	=	UNITS accounted for: units transferred to next department or to finished goods during period + units in process at end of period

COSTS to be accounted for: costs in process at beginning of period + costs charged to department during period	=	COSTS accounted for: costs transferred to next department or to finished goods during period + costs in process at end of period

Example 1

At the beginning of January 19X1, there were 1,000 units in Department A, complete as to material and 1/5 complete as to conversion costs. There were 200 units in process in Department B, half complete as to material and 1/5 complete as to conversion costs.

There were 6,000 units started in production in Department A and 6,400 units completed and transferred to Department B in January. There were 6,300 units completed and transferred to finished goods from Department B during the month.

	Total cost £	Transferred – in cost £	Material cost £	Conversion cost £
Stocks of work-in-progress on 1 January				
Dept A	1,150		1,000	150
Dept B	470	350	50	70
Costs incurred during the month				
Dept A	10,950		6,000	4,950
Dept B	25,530	11,200	3,200	11,130

On 31 January, there were 600 units in progress in Department A, complete as to material and 2/3 complete as to conversion costs. In Department B, there were 300 units in progress, 2/3 complete as to material and 1/3 complete as to conversion costs.

Required

Prepare production cost reports for January 19X1 for the two departments.

Suggested Solution

Preparing a Production Cost Report for Department A

Five steps provide a uniform approach to solving most process cost problems, as follows:

(1) *Measuring the physical flow of units*

A quantity schedule is prepared for each department showing the number of units of the product processed during the period. For Dept A, this schedule is as follows:

Work-in-progress on 1 January	1,000 units (all materials and
Units started in process during the month	1/5 conversion costs)
	6,000
Total units to be accounted for	7,000
Units transferred out (i.e., to Dept B)	6,400
Work-in-progress on 31 January	600 (all materials and
Total units accounted for	7,000 1/5 conversion costs)

Note

Conversion costs represent direct labour and factory overhead costs.

(2) *Calculating equivalent units of production*

The physical flow of items in (1) above is converted into units to which costs have been attached. In order to apportion costs when stocks of partially finished goods are involved, a common measure is required by which to express the sum total of production. Therefore, both work-in-progress and finished goods are expressed in terms of completed units known as *equivalent units of production*.

In this example, the weighted average method of stock costing is used. This method makes no distinction between opening stocks and those resulting from current production. Therefore, in computing equivalent units and their unit costs, units are treated as though they were all started and completed during the period, thereby assuming that there were no opening stocks.

Accordingly, the equivalent units of production are as follows:

	Equivalent units	Material costs equivalents	Conversion costs equivalents
Units transferred to Dept B	6,400	6,400	6,400
Closing stock of units in process	600	600	400 (2/3)
	7,000	7,000	6,800

(3) *Total costs accumulated during the period*

This schedule summarizes the total costs which are to be accounted for in respect of the production of the period.

	Total cost £	Material costs £	Conversion costs £
Opening work-in-progress	1,150	1,000	150
Costs added during the period	10,950	6,000	4,950
Total costs to be accounted for	12,100	7,000	5,100

(4) *Cost per equivalent whole unit*

To calculate the cost per equivalent whole unit, the total costs shown in (3) are divided by the equivalent units in (2) above, as follows:

	Total cost £	Equivalent units £	Unit cost £
Material costs	7,000	7,000	1.00
Conversion costs	5,100	6,800	0.75
	12,000		1.75

As we stated above, the weighted average method of stock costing is used, and the unit cost obtained by these calculations are applied to the units as shown in (5) below.

(5) *The apportionment of costs*

The total costs incurred are apportioned to the stocks transferred to Department B and to those remaining in Department A as follows:

	Equivalent	Unit cost £	Total costs £
Transferred to Department B	6,400	1.75	11,200
Closing stock in Department A			
Material costs	600	1.00	600
Conversion costs	400	0.75	300
			900
Total costs accounted for			12,100

These schedules and computations are incorporated in the production cost report for Department A as shown below.

Production cost report for the month
ending 31 January 19X1

Quantities	Department A Physical flow	Equivalent units Materials	Conversion costs
Work-in-progress, opening stock	1,000		
Units started (or transferred in)	6,000		
Total units to be accounted for	7,000		
Units transferred out	6,400	6,400	6,400
Work-in-progress, closing stock	600	600 (2/3)	400
	7,000	7,000	6,800

Costs	Total £	Materials £	Conversion costs £	Equivalent whole unit £
Work-in-progress, opening stock	1,150	1,000	150	
Current costs of period	10,950	6,000	4,950	
Total costs to be accounted for	12,100	7,000	5,100	
divide by equivalent units		7,000	6,800	
		£1.00	£0.75	£1.75

Apportionment of costs	Equivalent units £	Unit cost £	Total cost £
Costs transferred out	6,400	1.75	11,200
Work-in-progress, closing stock			
Transferred in costs	—	—	—
Materials	600	1.00	600
Conversion	400	0.75	300
Total in progress			900
Total costs accounted for			12,100

Question 10
Prepare a production cost report for Department B for the month ending 31 January 19X1 using the data given in the previous example.

Note
The five steps listed earlier should be taken when preparing this report. Transferred-in costs arise in Department B, and these are the costs which have been transferred out of Department A into Department B. These costs sometimes cause problems for students, but it should be evident that so far as Department B is concerned, units transferred from Department A may be viewed as if they were the raw materials of Department B, for the costs transferred from Department A to Department B are similar to the material costs incurred by Department A although called 'transferred-in costs'. Therefore, in computing the costs for Department B three kinds of costs are involved: transferred-in costs from Department A, raw material costs added in Department B and conversion costs incurred in Department B. In order to record these costs in the production cost record, it is necessary to add another column headed 'transferred-in costs' in the cost section of the report. Note, also, that the space inserted on the production cost report for Department A under the heading 'work-in-progress, closing stock' in the apportionment of costs section should be incorporated in your report for Department B.

The flow of costs in a process cost system

Figure 9.4 below shows the flow of costs through the ledger accounts which are used in a process cost system. Note that the costs of direct

Fig. 9.4 Ledger accounts and the flow in a process cost system

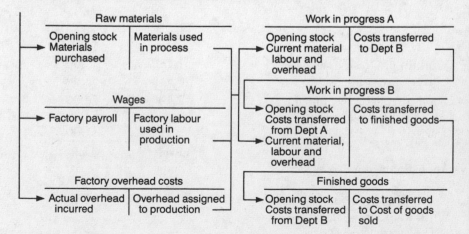

materials, direct labour and manufacturing overheads are debited to the process accounts of particular departments as they are incurred.

When goods are transferred from one department to another, their corresponding costs are credited to the process account of the first department, and debited to the process account of the department receiving the goods. When the goods are completed, their corresponding costs are transferred to the finished goods account. Finally, when they are sold, these costs are transferred to the cost of goods sold account.

Processing losses

It would be unrealistic to expect that all the materials put into process will end up in saleable product. Cost calculations must recognize that processing losses have to be accepted as part of the costs of manufacture. These processing losses fall into two broad categories:

(1) *Normal losses* where the amount of loss does not exceed some predetermined allowance. Normal losses are absorbed in process costs and are anticipated as unavoidable costs of manufacturing. Accordingly, normal losses increase the cost per unit of the commodity processed.

Example 2
Normal losses in Department A are approximately 5% of recorded manufactured units. The production record for January 19X1 was as follows:

	Units
Started in process	10,000
Spoilage	500
Units completed	9,500

During this month, recorded manufacturing costs were £19,000. Therefore, since losses are within the normal limit of 5% of recorded costs, this loss may be spread over the total units produced to yield the following unit cost:

$$\frac{\text{cost of production}}{\text{no. of units completed}} \quad \frac{£19,000}{9,500} = £2.00 \text{ per unit}$$

The accounting treatment of normal losses is to credit the process account with the amount of the loss. Should the spoiled units have any value which could be recovered by sale, this should be credited to the process account and debited to a normal loss account. The normal loss account will eventually be credited with the sums received from sales.

(2) *Abnormal losses* occur where the amount of loss goes beyond a limit which is regarded as acceptable. In these circumstances, the loss should not be considered as an expense of manufacture and, therefore, should not be absorbed into product costs. It should be written off to profit and loss account.

Example 3

Assume that the spoilage rate in Department A had been 1,000 units, and that the rate of normal loss remains at 5%. Clearly, the loss runs to 10% and is 5% above the normal loss level. The procedure is to absorb the normal rate of loss into the product costs, thereby computing the number of completed units as being 9,500 at a unit cost of £2.00. The quantity and the costs of the abnormal loss of 500 units is credited to the process account and debited to the abnormal loss account, and will ultimately be transferred to the profit and loss account.

Accounting for opening work-in-progress stocks

As we have already noted, when there are opening stocks in progress, the production of an accounting period will consist of units partially completed in the previous period and of units started in the current period. The costs of these different batches will vary from time to time—particularly under periods of inflation—and this will be reflected in the unit costs which are assigned to the output. Two methods commonly used in accounting for the costs of completing opening work-in-progress stocks are the weighted average method, which we have used in this chapter, and the FIFO method discussed in Part 1. In some countries, the LIFO method is popular.

The authors believe that the best method of accounting for the flow of stocks is by the use of standard costs which reflect current prices and current operating conditions. By using standard costs, the necessity of choosing between alternative accounting methods is avoided, and all units are transferred in (or out of) a process at a uniform cost. Standard costing will be discussed in Chapter 13.

Question 11

The Incredible Gadget Corporation manufactures a single product. Its operations are a continuing process carried on in two departments—the machining department and the assembly and finishing department. *Materials are added to the product in each department without increasing the number of units produced.*

In May 19X1, the records showed that 75,000 units were put in production in the machining department. Of these units, 60,000 were completed and transferred to the assembly and finishing department, and 15,000 were left in process with all materials applied but only one-third of the required labour and factory overhead costs. In the assembly and finishing department, 50,000 units were completed and transferred to the finished stock room during the month, 9,000 units were in process on 31 May, 1,000 units having been destroyed in production with no scrap value. All the required materials had been applied to the 9,000 units and two-thirds of the labour had been applied to the costs, but only one-half of the prescribed material and labour had been applied to the 1,000 units lost in process. There was no work-in-progress in either department at the beginning of the month of May. *The cost of units lost in production should be treated as additional overhead in the assembly and finishing department.*

Cost records showed the following charges during the month:

	Materials £	Labour £	Factory over-heads £
Machining department	120,000	87,100	39,000
Assembly and finishing depart-ment	41,650	101,700	56,810*

does not include the cost of spoiled units

Required
(a) Using the statement below compute the unit cost for the month.
(b) Prepare a schedule showing the details of the work-in-progress stock in each department at the end of the month. (AICPA)

Incredible Gadget Corporation
Computation of unit costs for the month ended 31 May 19X1

	No of actual units	No of equivalent units	Total costs £	Cost per unit £
Machining dept	....	....	....	....
Materials	....	....	....	....
Labour	....	....	....	....
Overheads	....	....	....	....
Transferred to assembly and finishing dept	....	....	....	....
Closing stock of work-in-progress	....	....	....	....
Assembly and finishing dept				
Materials:				
Cost of materials added	....	....	....	....
Cost of materials spoiled	....	....	....	....

Transferred to finished goods	....	....	....	....
Closing stock of material in process	....	....	....	....
Labour:				
Cost of labour	....	....	....	....
Cost of labour in spoiled units	....	....	....	....
Transferred to finished goods	....	....	....	....
Closing stock of labour in process	....	....	....	....
Overheads:				
Costs of overheads	....	....	....	....
Spoiled units:	....	....	....	....
Machining Dept costs	....			
Assembly and finishing dept costs	....	....	....	....
Materials	....	....	....	....
Labour	....	....	....	....
Transferred to finished goods	....		....	....
Closing stock of overheads in progress	....	....	....	....

Question 12

The Northern Refining Co. produces a product TS from a raw material TR. The product TS passes through three processes: crushing, refining and finishing. It is then filtered into drums.

During July 19X1, 1,500 tonnes of TR were processed at a cost of £10 a tonne. The output for the month for each process and the normal waste (calculated on the number of units entering the process concerned) were:

Process	Output in tonnes	Normal waste
Crushing	1,250	10%
Refining	1,000	20%
Finishing	900	10%

The following figures were extracted from the books of the company for July 19X1:

	Crushing £	Refining £	Finishing £
Direct materials added	1,100	1,780	900
Wages	2,200	980	2,190
Power	650	460	360
Sundry expenses	300	280	150
Sale of bags	350		

The product TS is filtered into drums without further processing at a cost of £1.00 per tonne. The cost of the drums, which are returnable and for which customers are charged specifically, is not included in the cost of manufacture.

Waste from the crushing process has no value, but waste produced in the refining and finishing processes is sold for £4.00 and £2.00 per tonne respectively.

The production for the month of July is sold at £40 per tonne and the selling and administration costs for the month amount to £5,700.

Required

Prepare accounts for the crushing, refining and finishing processes to show:

(1) The total cost of each process.
(2) The cost per tonne of the finished product in each process.
(3) The total cost of the product TS in drums.
(4) The cost per tonne of the product in drums.

Note

The suggested narration for the crushing process account is inserted in the accounts below.

| | | The Northern Refining Company Limited | | | Cost per tonne |
| | | Crushing process account | | | |
	Tonnes	£		Tonnes	£	£
Raw materials	....	....	Sale of bags	....	....	....
Direct materials added	....	....	Normal waste	....	....	....
Wages	....	....	Output trans-			
Power	....	....	ferred out	....	....	....
Sundry expenses	....	....	Abnormal waste	....	....	....

Question 13

M. A. Chemicals Limited process a range of products including a detergent 'Washo', which passed through three processes before completion and transfer to the finished goods warehouse. During April, data relating to this product were as shown:

	Process 1 £	2 £	3 £	Total £
Basic raw material (10,000 units)	6,000	—	—	6,000
Direct materials added in process	8,500	9,500	5,500	23,500
Direct wages	4,000	6,000	12,000	22,000
Direct expenses	1,200	930	1,340	3,470
Production overhead				16,500
(production overhead is absorbed				
as a percentage of direct wages)	Units	Units	Units	
Output	9,200	8,700	7,900	
Normal loss in process, of input	10%	5%	10%	
All loss has a scrap value, per unit of	£0.20	£0.50	£1.00	

There was no stock at start or at end of any process.

Required

Prepare the following accounts: (i) Process 1; (ii) Process 2; (iii) Process 3; (iv) Abnormal loss; (v) Abnormal gain. (ICMA)

Joint costs and by-product costs

Where two or more products are obtained from a common process, they are usually referred to as joint products if they are of significant value. A product which has a comparatively trivial value in relation to the principal product is referred to as a by-product. Generally, a by-product is merely incidental to the manufacture of the principal product.

Joint products

The objective of joint product cost accounting is to assign a portion of the total joint costs to each joint product in order that unit product costs may be calculated. However, the assignment of costs to joint products is largely arbitrary.

Example 4

Two products, X and Y, are jointly produced at a cost of £30,000. 5,000 kilograms of product X are completed and the sale price is

£4.00 per kilogram. 10,000 kilograms of product Y are completed and the sale price is £2.00 per kilogram.

Consider the effect on the gross profit margin of three methods of assigning costs:

(1) The relative weights of the output.
(2) The relative sales value of the output.
(3) The relative selling price per unit of the products.

Solution	Method 1		Method 2		Method 3	
	X	Y	X	Y	X	Y
	£	£	£	£	£	£
Revenue	20,000	20,000	20,000	20,000	20,000	20,000
Production costs	10,000	20,000	15,000	15,000	20,000	10,000
	10,000	—	5,000	5,000	—	10,000

Joint product costing is essential for the purpose of profit measurement, but it has very little relevance for decision-making as regards individual joint products. Consider the example given above. If the calculation of the profit margin for product Y established by method 1 had produced an overall loss, this loss would not have led to a decision to stop producing and selling product Y. For to stop producing product Y would also mean ceasing the production of product X. Therefore, the relevant accounting information for decision-making purposes is the total revenue and the total profit associated with *both* joint products.

Question 14

In the conversion of a tonne of raw material, Riverdale Manufacturing Company produces three products, A, B and C, in the following proportions:

Product	Weight in kilos
A	700
B	600
C	400
Waste of no value	300
	2,000

The costs of processing one tonne of material up to the point where the joint products A, B and C split off are:

	£
Direct material	3,250
Direct labour	1,704
Manufacturing overheads	1,934

Each product requires further processing before it is ready for sale. Further costs incurred for each tonne of raw material put into the primary processes are:

	Products		
	A	B	C
	£	£	£
Direct materials	600	1,090	1,000
Direct labour	420	780	710
Manufacturing overheads	233	227	618

There is no loss of weight after the split-off point. The market value of each product is:

Product	
A	£10 per kilo
B	£15 per kilo
C	£20 per kilo

Required

Using the method you consider to be the most suitable, draw up a statement showing the total costs and cost per kilo of producing each of the joint products. Explain why you have used the method you have chosen for ascertaining these costs. Where necessary, work to the nearest £.

By-products

Where a by-product is of small value, no formal accounting for this by-product is needed. The process account relating to the main product is credited with the value which could be recovered from the sale of the by-product.

Where a by-product has considerable value, it is necessary to apportion the total processing costs up to the split-off point from the main product. The process account of the main product is credited and the by-product account is debited with the processing costs applicable to the by-product. If further processing is necessary before the by-product is ready for sale, the additional costs are debited to the by-product account, which becomes, in effect, a new process account.

Question 15

William Goodnight manufactures three products, A, B and C, from a single basic raw material. The three products are split off from one another at the end of process 2. The following percentages of the three products are consistently obtained from a given quantity of material put into process 2:

Product	Percentage of the quantity of material put into process 2
	%
A	40
B	30
C	20
Waste of no value	10
	100

As a result of steam treatment, the output weight at the end of process 1 is normally 5% more than the input weight.

At the end of process 2, product A is in a finished form ready for delivery in bulk to buyers; product B has to pass through process 3 before completion at a further cost of £1 per 100 kilos; product C requires packaging at a cost equal to 25% of the selling price.

The selling prices of the finished products are as follows:

Product	
A	£3 per 100 kilos
B	£4 per 100 kilos
C	£0.25 per 100 kilos

Required
Illustrate, giving reasons, what arrangements you would make for the costing of the three products.

Recording costs and financial transactions

The importance of cost control accounts for controlling the detailed records in a cost accounting system was illustrated in Fig. 9.1 In this respect, the function of cost control accounts is similar to that of the control accounts in the financial accounting system. In this section, two principal systems for recording cost and financial transactions are examined:

(1) Separate cost accounting and financial accounting.
(2) Integrated cost and financial accounting.

Separate cost and financial accounting

This system requires that separate ledgers be maintained for cost accounting and financial accounting. In the cost ledger, a cost ledger control account (or general ledger control account) is necessary to render the cost ledger self-balancing. For example, the purchase of raw materials would be recorded by means of a credit to the cost ledger control account and a debit to the raw materials control account. If a transaction affects only the cost accounting system (for example, a transfer from the raw materials control account to the work-in-progress control account) no entry is necessary in the cost ledger control account.

The accounting implications of separate cost and financial accounting systems may be seen by working carefully through the following example. Thereafter, an attempt should be made to answer the two questions which follow.

Example 5

The following balances appear in the cost ledger of the Green Manufacturing Company at the beginning of the account period:

	£	£
Raw materials control account	7,000	
Work-in-progress control account	6,000	
Finished goods control account	9,000	
Cost ledger control account		22,000
	22,000	22,000

During this period, the following transactions occurred:

	£
Purchases of raw materials	12,000
Direct wages paid	20,000
Administration costs incurred	5,000
Selling and distribution costs incurred	8,000
Raw materials issued to production	10,000
Factory overhead incurred	10,000
Factory overhead absorbed by production	9,000
Goods sold in the period: at sales value	60,000
at cost	35,000
Transferred to finished goods	30,000

Required

Write up the accounts in the cost ledger and take out a trial balance at the end of the period.

Solution   Cost Ledger of Green Manufacturing Co.
Raw materials control account

	£		£
Balance b/d	7,000	Work-in-progress control	10,000
Cost ledger control	12,000	Balance c/d	9,000
	19,000		19,000
Balance b/d	9,000		

Work-in-progress control account

	£		£
Balance b/d	6,000	Finished goods control	30,000
Work-in-progress control	10,000	Balance c/d	15,000
Direct wages control	20,000		
Factory overhead control	9,000		
	45,000		45,000
Balance b/d	15,000		

Finished goods control account

	£		£
Balance b/d	9,000	Cost of sales	35,000
Work-in-progress control	30,000	Balance c/d	4,000
	39,000		39,000
Balance b/d	4,000		

Direct wages control account

	£		£
Cost ledger control	20,000	Work-in-progress control	20,000

Administration cost control account

	£		£
Cost ledger control	5,000	Cost of sales	5,000

Selling and distribution cost control account

	£		£
Cost ledger control	8,000	Cost of sales	8,000

Factory overhead control account

	£		£
Cost ledger control (overhead cost incurred)	10,000	Work-in-progress	9,000
		Costing profit and loss (unabsorbed overhead)	1,000
	10,000		10,000

Cost ledger control account

	£		£
Sales (profit and loss)	60,000	Balance b/d	22,000
Balance c/d	28,000	Raw materials control	12,000
		Direct wages control	20,000
		Administration cost control	5,000
		Selling and distribution cost control	8,000
		Factory overhead control	10,000
	88,000	Profit and loss	11,000
			88,000
		Balance b/d	28,000

Cost of sales account

	£		£
Finished goods control	35,000	Transfer to profit and loss	48,000
Administrative cost control	5,000		
Selling and distribution cost control	8,000		
	48,000		48,000

Costing profit and loss account

	£		£
Cost of sales	48,000	Sales (cost ledger control)	60,000
Unabsorbed factory overhead	1,000		
Net profit—transferred to cost ledger control	11,000		
	60,000		60,000

Closing trial balance

	£	£
Raw materials control	9,000	
Work-in-progress	15,000	
Finished goods control	4,000	
Cost ledger control		28,000
	28,000	28,000

Question 16

The following balances are extracted from a company's cost ledger as at 1 March.

	£	£
Raw materials control account	50,836	
Work-in-progress control account	12,745	
Finished stock control account	25,980	
Cost ledger control account		89,561
	89,561	89,561

Further transactions took place during the following quarter, as follows:

	£
Factory overhead—allocated to work in progress	11,786
Goods finished (at cost)	36,834
Raw materials purchased	22,422
Direct wages—allocated to work in progress	8,370
Raw materials issued to production	16,290
Cost of goods sold	41,389
Raw materials credited by suppliers	836
Customer's returns (at cost) of good finished stock	2,856
Stock audit—raw material losses	1,236
Work-in-progress rejected (with no scrap value)	1,764

You are required to:

(a) Write up the four accounts in the cost ledger.
(b) Schedule the remaining balances.
(ICMA)

Question 17

J. Limited operates a separate cost accounting and financial accounting system. The accountant has prepared final accounts as shown below and a reconciliation of cost and financial accounts statement has been produced. As cost accountant you are required to show how the following accounts would appear in the cost ledger:

(a) Raw materials control.
(b) Work-in-progress ledger control.
(c) Finished goods ledger control.
(d) Cost of sales.
(e) Profit and loss.

Manufacturing, trading and profit and loss account for the
year ended 31 October 19X4

	£		£
Raw materials:		Trading account:	
Opening stock	236,489	Cost of goods manufac-	
		tured	1,558,082
Purchases	972,102		
	1,208,591		
Returns	18,724		
	1,189,867		
Closing stock	248,526		
	941,341		

Direct wages:	£	
Paid	256,483	
Accrued	23,797	280,280
Production expenses		342,895
		1,564,516

Work-in-progress:	£		
Opening stock	126,423		
Closing stock	132,857	6,434	
		1,558,082	1,558,082

	£		£
Finished goods:		Sales	2,124,816
Opening stock	154,832	Returns	25,921
Goods manufac-			
tured	1,558,082		
	1,712,914		
Closing stock	148,321		
	1,564,593		
Gross profit c/d	534,302		
	2,098,895		2,098,895
		Gross profit b/d	534,302
Administration:			
Salaries	68,724	Interest received	1,246
Expenses	92,461		
Sales:			
Salaries	24,216		
Expenses	42,586		
Distribution:			
Wages	10,249		
Expenses	34,867		
Discount allowed	2,571		
Debenture interest	1,400		
Net profit c/d	258,474		
	535,548		535,548
Dividends	100,000	Net profit b/d	258,474
Corporation Tax	116,520		
Balance, at year end	41,954		
	258,474		258,474

Statement reconciling the profit of cost and financial accounts

	£	£
Profit per financial accounts		258,474
add:		
Discount allowed	2,571	
Debenture interest	1,400	3,971
Differences in stocks		
Raw material, opening	6,245	
Work-in-progress, closing	4,369	
Finished goods, opening	1,684	12,298
less:		274,743
Interest received	1,246	
Differences in stocks		
Raw materials, closing	6,914	
Work-in-progress, opening	4,123	
Finished goods, closing	1,536	13,819
		260,924

Production overhead has been absorbed in the cost accounts at 110% of direct wages. (ICMA)

Note
Before posting these accounts, it will help if the difference between the opening and closing stocks is computed as follows:

Opening stocks to give more profit = less cost (value)
Closing stocks to give more profit = more cost (value)

Opening stocks			Financial accounts £	Cost accounts £
Raw materials			236,489	
	difference	–	6,245	230,244
Work-in-progress			126,423	
	difference	+	1,123	130,546
Finished goods			154,832	
	difference	–	1,684	153,148

Closing stocks			Financial accounts £	Cost accounts £
Raw materials			248,526	
	difference	–	6,914	241,612
Work-in-progress			132,857	
	difference	+	4,369	137,226
Finished goods			148,321	
	difference	–	1,536	146,785

Integrated cost and financial accounting

The integration of cost and financial accounting systems enables one ledger only to be maintained for both cost and financial accounting. This has two advantages over the system of keeping separate cost and financial accounts:

(1) There is no necessity to reconcile the cost and financial records. When the two sets of records are recorded separately each will usually give a different profit figure which has to be reconciled with the other.
(2) There is no duplication of work, thereby reducing the clerical and administrative costs involved in maintaining two separate systems.

We have noted earlier in this section that the purpose of a cost ledger control account is to make the cost ledger self-balancing. There is no need to maintain a cost ledger control account in an integrated system which records both cost and financial accounting transactions.

Question 18

C. Ltd operates an integrated accounting system. You are required to:

(1) Open and write up the accounts for May 19X1.
(2) Prepare a profit and loss account for May 19X1.

The trial balance at 1 May 19X1 was as follows:

	£000s	£000s
Raw material stock	138	
Work-in-progress stock	34	
Finished goods stock	62	
Debtors	200	
Creditors		140
Expense creditors		58
Wages accrued		11
PAYE Tax		45
Bank	40	
Freehold buildings	360	
Plant and machinery, at cost	240	
Provision for depreciation, plant and machinery		60
Issued share capital		600
General reserve		120
Profit and loss account		40
	1,074	1,074

The following information is given of the transactions that took place in May 19X1:

	£000s
Sales	320
Purchase of raw materials	92
Raw materials returned to supplier	4
Production overhead incurred	88
Selling and distribution costs incurred	42
Administration costs incurred	37
Direct wages incurred	42
Raw materials issued:	
To production	80
To production maintenance department	10
Raw materials returned to store from production	2
Abnormal loss in production	5
Cost of finished goods sold	210
Payment received in respect of sales	330
Payments made for raw materials purchased	101
Discounts allowed	11

	£000s
Discounts received	3
Payments made to expense creditors	140
Direct wages paid	34
PAYE tax deducted from wages	16

You are informed that:

(1) Depreciation of plant and machinery is provided for at 10% per annum of cost.
(2) Production overhead is absorbed on the basis of 250% of direct wages incurred.
(3) Selling and distribution costs incurred in May 19X1 are charged against the profit of May 19X1.
(4) Work-in-progress was valued on 31 May 19X1 at £39,000.

It is not intended in this text to discuss the accounting implications of long-range planning in any detail. It is important to point out, however, that, if a firm is to achieve all its objectives both in the long-range and in the short-term, some attempt must be made to plan effectively in both these time periods. To this end, long-range planning should be based on a clear view of the firm's total objectives, and planning in the short-term should take a similar view.

In reality, long-range planning may be a complex process especially if several different objectives are sought, which require both quantitative and qualitative factors to be taken into account. However, the assumption of a multi-objective enterprise in this text would present some serious problems. First, by and large, the accounting process places its own emphasis on the profit objective. Second, many organizational objectives require information other than purely accounting information, and perhaps the integration of accounting and non-accounting information, that is, the integration of monetary with non-monetary measurements. For example, profit may be calculated simply from the monetary data lodged in the double-entry bookkeeping records. The aim of securing good industrial and employee relations would require non-monetary data to indicate that the firm has been successful in attaining this objective. The overall effect of good industrial and employee relationships would also manifest itself on profit levels; therefore, that element of profitability which relies on good industrial and employee relations could only be indicated by some reporting system in which monetary and non-monetary data is integrated.

In this chapter, it is assumed that the objective of the firm is to maximize the shareholders' wealth over time. The importance of this assumption is that it provides a justification for many financial techniques which are employed to assist the selection of decisions alternatives facing the firm. The most important of these decisions are the capital budgeting decisions, which usually involve substantial financial commitments and which have very great significance for profitability both in the long run and in the short term. This is because these decisions relate directly to the productive capacity of the enterprise, and its ability to maintain and increase profit levels.

Accordingly, this chapter is divided into the following sections:

The nature of capital investment decisions.
Methods of evaluation.
Calculating the cost of capital.
Evaluating risk.
Appendixes: Dividends as a basis for the valuation of shares.
Present value of £1.

The nature of capital investment decisions

Essentially, all capital investment decisions involve selecting the most profitable investment alternative for the funds available to the enterprise. Typical investment projects include the following:

(1) Projects involving the expansion of productive capacity, for example, additional buildings, plant, etc.
(2) Projects involving product or process improvements.
(3) Projects involving the replacement of assets such as buildings, plant, etc.

The central feature of capital investment decisions is the comparison of the forecasts of future cash flows which are expected from the investment with the forecasted cash outlays involved in financing the capital investment. The typical pattern of cash flows associated with a capital project is irregular, beginning usually with a substantial cash outlay which is followed by cash inflows over a period of time.

The main difficulties of making sound capital investment decisions stem from the uncertainty and the risk to which they are subjected, and the reliance which must be placed on the forecasts of future events and cash flows. Given that substantial sums are usually involved and that the 'time-profile' of the expected cash inflows may have a very irregular shape, it is easy to see why these decisions are not susceptible to easy solutions.

Example 1

A typical capital project involving the expansion of plant capacity may result in the following time-profile of net cash outflows and net cash inflows:

Year	Cash outflow (−) Cash inflow (+)
	£
0	− 300,000
1	+ 40,000
2	+ 50,000
3	+ 55,000
.	....
.	....

It does not follow that all the cash outflows will be incurred at the outset of the project. Indeed, many projects anticipate future cash outflows arising, for example, a multi-stage building project, a major trunk road programme or a large civil engineering programme.

Methods of evaluation

The essential problem when making capital investment decisions is always the allocation of scarce resources towards competing ends. Usually, several alternatives are available to an enterprise for attaining the desired objective, for example, a decision to expand plant capacity may well involve the comparison of different methods of achieving this end.

The evaluation of alternative investment projects involves ranking the several projects, and choosing the alternative which appears to be the best according to the criteria applied. The more commonly used methods of evaluation are as follows:

(1) The payback period.
(2) The accounting rate of return.
(3) Discounted cash flow.

The payback method

This method is commonly used to express the time required for the cash outlays to be recovered.

Example 2

Locmine Ltd is considering five alternative investment projects, A, B, C, D and E.

Table 1 below below indicates the initial outlays and the expected cash inflows throughout the years.

Table 1

	A	B	C	D	E
	£	£	£	£	£
Outlays Year 0	30,000	30,000	30,000	25,000	25,000
Outlays Year 1	—	—	10,000	—	—
Inflows Year 1	10,000	15,000	—	5,500	8,000
Inflows Year 2	10,000	15,000	11,000	5,500	8,000
Inflows Year 3	10,000	5,000	12,000	5,500	5,000
Inflows Year 4	10,000	—	15,000	5,500	5,000
Inflows Year 5	10,000	—	2,000	1,800	3,000
Scrap in Year 6	1,500	1,000	2,000	1,800	3,000
Payback in years	3	2	5	Never	3.8

With no other considerations than payback, the company would select project B since it has the shortest payback period.

As may be seen from this example, the essence of this method of investment appraisal is simply determining the length of time required to recoup the initial outlay. However, the payback method has several disadvantages, as follows:

(i) It ignores the time value of money.
(ii) It cannot distinguish between projects having the same payback period.
(iii) The scrap value rarely enters into consideration.
(iv) It does not consider the lifetime of the project.
(v) It gives no indication of the profitability of a project, which is management's basic economic objective.

It is sometimes claimed that the payback method is useful when a firm has a short-term liquidity problem. However, this is hardly a sufficient condition for the use of this method since the supply of long-term finance is more likely to be determined by the profitability of the enterprise. Some attempts to overcome the inadequacies of this method involve using discounted cash flows, and this point will be discussed later in this chapter. It is true to say, however, that the payback period is always a factor which management wishes to determine, and for this reason, the payback method is generally used in combination with other methods of investment appraisal.

The accounting rate of return

This method attempts to quantify the profit expected to be derived from the investment projects under consideration, in accordance with conventional accounting procedures, and expresses the profit forecast as a percentage of the capital expenditure involved. It assumes, therefore, that accounting procedures can be applied to isolate the profit associated with a project. However, unlike cash flow, profit is susceptible to problems in definition as is the capital expenditure used as an asset base for calculating the rate of return. For example, as regards the latter point, the asset base could be defined as the initial capital outlay or it could be defined as the 'average capital employed' after taking into account the depreciation written off over the life of the project.

A further difficulty is deciding what rate of return is acceptable. For reasons which will not be considered in this text, it is claimed that the accounting rate of return does not reflect the shareholders' required rate of return on investments.

Example 3

The account of Samatan Ltd has prepared the following profit forecasts for the five years to 19X9, based on the purchase of a new machine having a five-year life and costing £20,000. The sales revenues shown below are associated with the new product which will be manufactured with the new machine.

	19X5 £	19X6 £	19X7 £	19X8 £	19X9 £
Sales	8,000	10,000	12,000	12,000	10,000
less: Cost of production	4,000	4,500	5,000	5,000	4,500
Depreciation	4,000	4,000	4,000	4,000	4,000
	8,000	8,500	9,000	9,000	8,500
Profit	0	1,500	3,000	3,000	1,500
Capital employed	16,000	12,000	8,000	4,000	0

Average capital employed $\dfrac{20,000}{2} = \underline{10,000}$

Average profit $\dfrac{9,000}{5} = \underline{1,800}$

Accounting rate of return over the period $\dfrac{1,800}{10,000} \times 100 = \underline{\underline{18\%}}$

The acceptability of the rate of return of 18% would depend on the view which the directors of Samatan Ltd have of the required rate of return. In this respect, experience tends to show that the desired rate of return is a function of past performance, reference also being made to inter-firm comparisons to test whether the firm's own experience conforms with the industry or sectorial average.

In this example, the costs of production do not represent a constant proportion of sales revenue, indicating thereby that fixed costs have entered into the calculation of profit. This factor illustrates the problems which may arise when using the accounting rate of return for the evaluation of capital investment projects.

Question 1

Trilport, a company which manufactures and sells novelty souvenir items for holiday resorts, is considering a new product. It is expected that the machinery initially required will cost £100,000 and that the profit before depreciation will be as follows:

	£
1st year	11,000
2nd year	36,300
3rd year	65,800

It is also expected that the life of the machine will be three years and that the scrap value is likely to be £10,000. The company uses the straight-line method of depreciation.

Required
Calculate the accounting rate of return for this project.

Discounted cash flow methods

There are two variants of the discounted cash flow method (DCF):

The net present value (NPV) method.
The internal rate of return method (IRR).

Both methods are based on the proposition that investors will be persuaded to invest if the inducement by way of return on capital is sufficiently high.

The net present value

The acceptability of an investment project according to this method depends on the present value of future net cash flows from the project being equal to or greater than the investment outlay. This method requires a forecast of the profile of future net cash flows, which are then discounted by an appropriate discount rate. Usually, this discount rate is the rate of return which investors would expect from the type of investment represented by the activities of the company. If the net present value, that is, the excess of the discounted future net cash flows is greater than the expected cash outlay, the investment project is said to have a positive net present value.

The internal rate of return

This method requires that a forecast of future net cash flows be made, in the same way as for the net present value method, but instead of discounting these net cash flows by the rate of return expected by investors (known as the market rate of return), it is required to ascertain the exact discount rate which will discount the future net cash flows to the sum represented by the cash outlays. If the rate of return established in this way is greater than the cost of capital, that is, the market rate of return expected by investors, the project is acceptable.

These two variants of DCF may be expressed algebraically as follows:

NPV rule: accept a project if

$$A \leqslant \frac{a_1}{(1 + i)} + \frac{a_2}{(1 + i)^2} + \cdots + \frac{a_n}{(1 + i)^n}$$

IRR rule: accept a project if $r \geq i$, where

$$A = \frac{a_1}{(1+r)} + \frac{a_2}{(1+r)^2} + \ldots + \frac{a_n}{(1+r)^n}$$

in both cases where A is the cash outlay, a_1 is the net cash inflow of year 1, i is the cost of capital to be used in discounting under the NPV rule and r is the rate of return which discounts the net cash flows to a value equal to the investment outlays.

It may be noted that where there is only one initial outlay and one project for consideration on a simple accept/reject basis, both methods will lead to the same conclusion. The NPV method, however, is considered to be generally a better method to use.

Example 4

Urdos Ltd is considering the purchase of a new plant which would allow cash savings to be realized as shown in the schedule below. The cost of the new plant is £60,000 and it is expected to have a scrap value of £5,000 at the end of its working life of eight years. The finance director of the company has estimated the company's cost of capital to be 10%.

You are required to determine the acceptability of this project by using the NPV method. Additionally, you are required to calculate the internal rate of return associated with the project. For simplicity, it may be assumed that the forecasted cash savings are realized on the last day of the accounting year, as follows:

year 1 £10,000; year 2 £10,000; years 3–7 inclusive £13,850 per annum; year 8 £12,750.

Using discount tables giving the present value $V^n = 1/(1+i)^n$, the present value of these forecasted cash savings are as follows:

Year	Forecasted cash savings	Discounting coefficient	Net present value
	£		£
1	10,000	0.909	9,090
2	10,000	0.826	8,260
3	13,850	0.751	10,401
4	13,850	0.683	9,460
5	13,850	0.621	8,601
6	13,850	0.564	7,811
7	13,850	0.513	7,105
8	12,750	0.467	5,954
8	5,000	0.467	2,335
			69,017

Therefore, the NPV of the project is £69,017 − £60,000 = £9,017. Thus, the project is acceptable.

Question 2
Calculate the NPV of the project submitted to Samatan Ltd on the assumption that the company's cost of capital is 12%, and that all production costs were cash and were paid on the last day of each year. Assume also that all revenues were received on the last day of the year. Is this project worth accepting? A table of net present values is provided in Appendix 2.

Question 3
Calculate the NPV of the five projects considered by Locmine Ltd using the data given in that example and assuming that the cost of capital is 15%. Rank these projects in accordance with your conclusions. Assume cash flows were paid on the last day of each year.

Calculating the Internal Rate of Return

The calculation of IRR involves a process of trial and error, and requires the following stages to be completed:

  (i) Select a discount rate and reduce the net cash flow to their NPV.
 (ii) If the NPV is positive, select a higher discount rate and repeat the process.
(iii) If a negative NPV results, it is evident that the IRR lies in the range between the two discount rates employed. This provides the basis for a linear interpolation with which to calculate the exact rate of return.

Example 5
If a particular series of net cash flows, discounted at 14%, have a NPV of £120, and a NPV of − £40 when discounted at 18%, the discount rate which will reduce these net cash flows to zero is

$$14\% + \frac{120}{120 + 40} \times 4\% = 17\%$$

$$18\% - \frac{40}{120 + 40} \times 4\% = 17\%$$

It should be noted that, although the foregoing example uses a gap of 4% for the purpose of demonstration, in an actual situation the range should be as small as possible.

Example 6

The IRR relating to the investment project considered by Urdos Ltd may now be calculated:

Year	Forecasted cash savings (£)	Discounting coefficient at 12%	Present value (£)	Discounting coefficient at 15%	Present value (£)
1	10,000	0.893	8,930	0.870	8,700
2	10,000	0.797	7,970	0.756	7,560
3	13,850	0.712	9,861	0.658	9,113
4	13,850	0.636	8,808	0.572	7,922
5	13,850	0.567	7,853	0.497	6,883
6	13,850	0.507	7,021	0.432	5,983
7	13,850	0.452	6,260	0.376	5,207
8	12,750				
8	5,000	0.404	7,171	0.327	5,804
			63,874		57,172

$$\text{IRR} = 12\% + \left(\frac{3,874}{6,702} \times 3\% \right) = \underline{13.7\%}$$

Question 4

Calculate the IRR for the five projects considered by Locmine Ltd using the data given in that example.

The payback period revisited

The payback method may be used in conjunction with present values of expected cash flows.

Example 7

Use the data on Locmine Ltd in the earlier example, and calculate the payback period for project A using a discount rate of 15%.

	Year	Cash flows	Discounting coefficient at 15%	Present value
		£		£
	1	10,000	0.870	8,700
	2	10,000	0.756	7,560
	3	10,000	0.658	6,580
	4	10,000	0.572	5,720
	5	10,000	0.497	4,970
Scrap	5	15,000	0.497	745

Therefore, the outlay of £30,000 will be recouped after 4.3 years.

Question 5

Gorron Ltd are considering a project put forward by the marketing director for manufacturing a new form of storage cupboard for use with the company's existing range of kitchen utensils. The following data are available:

(1) Cost of additional plant £36,000. The company's policy of writing off assets over six years using the straight-line method is to be applied to this plant, and no scrap value is expected at the end of six years.

(2) Unit sales are expected to be as follows:

Year 1	400 units	Year 4	550 units
Year 2	500 units	Year 5	750 units
Year 3	550 units	Year 6	750 units

The selling price is expected to be £25 per unit.

(3) The unit cost of production is as follows:

	£
Direct material	2
Direct labour	2
Factory overheads	5
	9

The variable element of the factory overheads amounts to £1, and the fixed element is applied as 100% of the sum of direct material and direct labour costs. Depreciation is dealt with separately.

(4) For the purpose of making a decision regarding this project, the accountant has prepared Exhibit A for the board of directors.

Exhibit A

Gorron Ltd
Storage cupboard project profit forecast

	1	2	3	4	5	6
Sales—Units	400	500	550	550	750	750
	£	£	£	£	£	£
Value	10,000	12,500	13,750	13,750	18,750	18,750
less Material	800	1,000	1,100	1,100	1,500	1,500
Labour	800	1,000	1,100	1,100	1,500	1,500
Overheads	2,000	2,500	2,750	2,750	3,750	3,750
Depreciation	6,000	6,000	6,000	6,000	6,000	6,000
	9,600	10,500	10,950	10,950	12,750	12,750
Profit	400	2,000	2,800	2,800	6,000	6,000
	10,000	12,500	13,750	13,750	18,750	18,750

(5) The cost of capital for Gorron Ltd is estimated to be 15%.

Required

From the foregoing data, calculate:

(i) The payback period.
(ii) The NPV.
(iii) The IRR.
(iv) The accounting rate of return.
(v) The present value payback period.

Note

Assume in each case, with the exception of (i) above, that all cash flows occur at the end of the year. Ignore taxation.

Calculating the cost of capital

The use of the discounted flow method of investment appraisal requires knowledge of the company's cost of capital, which may be taken to be the desired minimum rate of return.

In computing the cost of capital, it is a familiar proposition that an individual shareholder will require the return of the capital sum which he is proposing to invest or has invested plus some additional return in the form of interest or dividend in the future, if he is to regard the investment of his capital as worth while.

This problem becomes more complex when applied to computing the cost of capital to a limited company involving groups of individuals who have subscribed for shares in return for the expectation of future dividends. In this situation, the extent of the reward expected by individual shareholders may be estimated by the relationship between the dividend accruing to shareholders and the share price.

Example 8

If a company has consistently paid a dividend of 45 pence per share, and is expected to continue to do so, and assuming that the share price (ex-dividend) stands at £3.00, then the expected yield established by the market is $45/300 \times 100 = 15\%$. If it is now assumed that shareholders become dissatisfied with this return, they would presumably want to sell their shares and the price would be driven down until it reflected the appropriate rate of return.

This example shows the manner in which the desired rate of return on investment, and hence the cost of capital would be determined under conditions of stable dividends and stable share prices.

Two further points should be made:

(1) It is assumed that the sale of shares is made by the marginal shareholder selling a marginal share of his holding. Hence, the

assumption always is that the share price is fixed on the margin. Accordingly, it is more appropriate to refer to the marginal rate of time preference of money as the rate used to described the yield.

(2) Most shareholders have expectations which extend beyond the steady state described in the example above. These expectations may best be expressed as relating to increased future dividends. Accordingly, the most appropriate rate of return is one which combines the yield and the prospect of dividend growth. Such a rate would be computed by combining the rate of return expressed by the next dividend with the observed growth rate in dividend.

Example 9

Assume that the data given in the previous example were modified to indicate that there was an expected growth of 10% in the dividend, then the appropriate rate of return on investment would be

$$\frac{45 \text{ p}}{£3.00} + 10\% = 15\% + 10\% = 25\%$$

Appendix 1 to this chapter provides a further explanation of this important point in the computation of the cost of capital.

Where a company has long-term borrowings in the form of fixed interest loans such as debentures, the interest payable must be taken into the calculation of the cost of capital. A slight complication arises in this respect because most taxation systems allow for the deduction of interest in arriving at taxable profit. This means that the rate of interest i is effectively reduced by the rate of tax. Accordingly, the cost of capital, where capital is raised in the form of irredeemable debentures rather than by the issue of shares, is calculated as follows:

$$i = \left(\frac{\text{interest payable}}{\text{market price of debentures}} \times 100 \right) \times (1 - \text{Corporation Tax rate})$$

Where the debentures are redeemable, it is necessary to relate the yield to the date of redemption.

Once the cost of both equity (ordinary shares) and loan capital has been determined, the two may be combined to produce the weighted average cost of capital (WACC). This is achieved by taking the market value of the ordinary shares and the market value of the loan capital as representing the total value of the company, and applying those market values as proportional weights to the cost of the components as calculated.

Example 10
The following data are given in respect of P.A.U. plc:

	Market value £	Cost of capital %	Total
Ordinary shares	80,000	18	14,400
Debentures	20,000	12	2,400
	100,000		16,800

Therefore,

$$\text{WACC} = \frac{16,800}{100,000} \times 100$$

$$= \underline{16.8\%}$$

Question 6
The balance sheet of Contrest plc reveals the following capital structure:

	£
Issued ordinary shares of £1 each fully paid	400,000
12% Irredeemable debentures	100,000

A dividend of 36 pence per share has been paid consistently in the past, and future dividends are expected to be maintained at this level. The current quoted price of the shares ex-dividend is £2.25, and that of the debentures is £80 (for each £100 holding).

Assuming the Corporation Tax is 50%, and ignoring any question regarding the legality of non-redeemable debentures, you are required to calculate the cost of capital to Contrest plc.

Evaluating risk

The central problem in the selection of capital investment projects is the risk associated with the uncertainty attaching to forecasts of future events and, in particular, to forecasts of future net cash flows. Probability analysis is one technique which may be applied to evaluating risk under conditions of uncertainty.

Probability analysis

In its most simple form, probability analysis involves estimating the probability of different cash flows occurring in relation to one project. This may be achieved by making three estimates of the future net cash flows associated with each investment project: an optimistic estimate, a pessimistic estimate and an estimate of the most likely outcome. By assigning probabilities to these predictions, it is possible to judge the risk of an unacceptable loss and the most likely present value of each project.

Example 11

Assume that there is a three out of 10 chance of an optimistic outcome being realized, a five out of 10 chance of the most likely outcome being realized and a two out of 10 chance of the pessimistic outcome occurring. Accordingly, the following probabilities may be attached to the cash flow forecasts associated with the three different types of outcome:

	Probability
Optimistic estimate	0.3
Likely estimate	0.5
Pessimistic estimate	0.2
	1.0

The cash flow forecasts associated with these outcomes are:

Cash flow forecast	Optimistic	Most likely	Pessimistic
	£	£	£
Year 1	1,200	1,000	800
Year 2	9,000	6,000	3,000
Year 3	14,000	10,000	5,000

Assuming that the investment outlay is £10,000, the analysis of the present value of the project under the risk conditions stated above is as follows:

£

Year 1	$(£1,200 \times 0.3) + (£1,000 \times 0.5) + (£800 \times 0.2) =$	1,020
Year 2	$(£9,000 \times 0.3) + (£6,000 \times 0.5) + (£3,000 \times 0.2) =$	6,300
Year 3	$(£14,000 \times 0.3) + (£10,000 \times 0.5) + (£5,000 \times 0.2) =$	10,200
	Expected returns	17,520

If it is now assumed that the appropriate discount rate, being the cost of capital to the company is 10%, the net present value of this project may be calculated as follows:

	Expected cash flow	Discounting coefficient	Present value
	£		£
Year 1	1,020	0.909	927.18
Year 2	6,300	0.826	5,203.80
Year 3	10,200	0.751	7,660.20
	Present value of expected returns		13,791.18
	Investment outlay		10,000.00
	NPV of project		3,791.18

Decision trees

Decision tree analysis may be used to illustrate the risk associated with multi-stage projects, where the outcome of subsequent stages is subject to a degree on success of prior stages. In other words, the value of subsequent stages is conditional upon the value of prior stages. An example of decision tree analysis applied to the budgeting process is given in the next chapter. Question 7 below shows how decision tree analysis may be used to evaluate two investment projects.

Question 7

The XYZ Company Limited is considering a major investment in a new productive process. The total cost of the investment has been estimated at £2,000,000 but if this were increased to £3,000,000, productive capacity could be substantially increased. Because of the nature of the process, once the basic plant has been established, to increase capacity at some future date is exceptionally costly. One of the problems facing management is that the demand for the product is very uncertain. However, the market research and finance departments have been able to produce the following first estimates:

Investment A (£3m)			Investment B (£2m)		
Demand probability		Annual net cash flow £m	Demand probability		Annual net cash flow £m
0.3	Years 1–4	1.0	0.4	Years 1–4	0.6
	5–10	0.7		5–10	0.5
0.5	Years 1–4	0.8	0.4	Years 1–4	0.6
	5–10	0.4		5–10	0.2
0.2	Years 1–10	0.1	0.2	Years 1–10	0.2
Cost of capital		10%	Cost of capital		10%

You are required to prepare a statement which clearly indicates the financial implications of each of the projects.

The format given below will help you with your answer.

	Years	Cash flow £m	Present value cash flow £m	Present value of expected value £m
0.3	1–4 5–10			
0.5	1–4 5–10			
0.2	1–10			
			less: Capital cost	3.00
			Expected NPV	
0.4	1–4 5–10			
0.4	1–4 5–10			
0.2	1–10			
			less: Capital cost	2.00
			Expected NPV	

£3m investment

£2m investment

Appendix 1: Dividends as a basis for the valuation of shares

Ignoring the question of risk, an accepted theory indicates that the value of a share is the present value of the sum of the dividends payable to the holder of that share.

Using the following symbols

V_0 = market value of share at present time
D_1 = dividend to be received at end of the first year
n = number of shares
k = marginal rate of time preference (discount rate)
g = rate of growth in dividend
$V_{1,2,3}$ = market value of share at end of year 1, 2, 3, etc.

the above proposition can be shown more clearly. The value of a share to the present holder is the next dividend plus the market value one year hence if his intention was to hold the share for only one year.

This is represented by the following formula,

$$V_0 = \frac{1}{n} \frac{D_1}{(1+k)} + \frac{1}{n} \frac{V_1}{(1+k)} \tag{1}$$

Similarly for the next shareholder who buys this share and who intends to hold it for one year.

$$V_1 = \frac{1}{n}\frac{D_2}{(1+k)} + \frac{1}{n}\frac{V_2}{(1+k)} \tag{2}$$

This process can be carried on indefinitely and it becomes apparent that the value of the share is the stream of dividends associated with it and as each successive dividend is further in the future the present value of each one is smaller and is discounted by a larger amount, thus:

$$V_0 = \frac{1}{n}\left(\frac{D_1}{1+k} + \frac{D_2}{(1+k)^2} + \frac{D_3}{(1+k)^3} + \dots + \frac{D_\infty}{(1+k)^\infty}\right) \tag{3}$$

which can be expressed

$$V_0 = \frac{1}{n}\sum_{t=1}^{\infty}\frac{D_t}{(1+k)^t} \tag{4}$$

As long as the dividend remains constant this can be simplified to

$$V_0 = \frac{1}{n}\frac{D_1}{k} \tag{5}$$

by the normal progressive reduction, the result of which is perpetuity.

When the unchanging dividend assumption is relaxed to consider growth the position may be shown thus:

The dividend D grows by a percentage g each year so that where D_0 was the last dividend $D_1 = D_0(1+g)$ and we can retrace the valuation procedure thus

$$V_0 = \frac{1}{n}D_0\left(\frac{1+g}{1+k} + \frac{(1+g)^2}{(1+k)^2} + \frac{(1+g)^3}{(1+k)^3} + \dots\right) \tag{6}$$

if both sides of Eq. 6 are multiplied by

$$\left(\frac{1+k}{1+g}\right) \text{ then } \left(\frac{1+k}{1+g}\right)V_0$$

$$= \frac{1}{n}D_0\left(1 + \frac{1+g}{1+k} + \frac{(1+g)^2}{(1+k)^2} + \dots\right) \tag{7}$$

and assuming $k > g$ (if it were not, the value $= \infty$) take Eq. 6 from Eq. 7; then the remaining equation is

$$\left(\frac{(1+k)-(1+g)}{1+g)}\right)V_0 = \frac{1}{n}D_0\left(1 - \frac{(1+g)^N}{(1+k)^N}\right) \tag{8}$$

and since $k > g$ and $N \to \infty$ this simplifies to

$$V_0 = \frac{1}{n} \frac{D_0 (1 + g)}{k - g} \tag{9}$$

As $D_0 (1 + g) = D_1$ this means that

$$V_0 = \frac{1}{n} \frac{D_1}{k - g} \tag{10}$$

and rearranging and now expressing D_1 and V_0 in terms of one share the following results:

$$k = \frac{D_1}{V_0} + g \tag{11}$$

which is the cost of equity shares expressed as a percentage return.

Appendix 2: Present value of £1

Future years	1%	2%	4%	6%	8%	10%	12%	14%	15%	16%	18%	20%	22%	24%	25%	26%	28%	30%	35%	40%	45%	50%
1	0.990	0.980	0.962	0.943	0.926	0.909	0.893	0.877	0.870	0.862	0.847	0.833	0.820	0.806	0.800	0.794	0.781	0.769	0.741	0.741	0.690	0.667
2	0.980	0.961	0.925	0.890	0.857	0.826	0.797	0.769	0.756	0.743	0.718	0.694	0.672	0.650	0.640	0.630	0.610	0.592	0.549	0.510	0.476	0.444
3	0.971	0.942	0.889	0.840	0.794	0.751	0.712	0.675	0.658	0.641	0.609	0.579	0.551	0.524	0.512	0.500	0.477	0.455	0.406	0.364	0.328	0.296
4	0.961	0.924	0.855	0.792	0.735	0.683	0.636	0.592	0.572	0.552	0.516	0.482	0.451	0.423	0.410	0.397	0.373	0.350	0.301	0.260	0.226	0.198
5	0.951	0.906	0.822	0.747	0.681	0.621	0.567	0.519	0.497	0.476	0.437	0.402	0.370	0.341	0.328	0.315	0.291	0.269	0.223	0.186	0.156	0.132
6	0.942	0.888	0.790	0.705	0.630	0.564	0.507	0.456	0.432	0.410	0.370	0.335	0.303	0.275	0.262	0.250	0.227	0.207	0.165	0.133	0.108	0.088
7	0.933	0.871	0.760	0.665	0.583	0.513	0.452	0.400	0.376	0.354	0.314	0.279	0.249	0.222	0.210	0.198	0.178	0.159	0.122	0.095	0.074	0.059
8	0.923	0.853	0.731	0.627	0.540	0.467	0.404	0.351	0.327	0.305	0.266	0.233	0.204	0.179	0.168	0.157	0.139	0.123	0.091	0.068	0.051	0.039
9	0.914	0.837	0.703	0.592	0.500	0.424	0.361	0.308	0.284	0.263	0.225	0.194	0.167	0.144	0.134	0.125	0.108	0.094	0.067	0.048	0.035	0.026
10	0.905	0.820	0.676	0.558	0.463	0.386	0.322	0.270	0.247	0.227	0.191	0.162	0.137	0.116	0.107	0.099	0.085	0.073	0.050	0.035	0.024	0.017
11	0.896	0.804	0.650	0.527	0.429	0.350	0.287	0.237	0.215	0.195	0.162	0.135	0.112	0.094	0.086	0.079	0.066	0.056	0.037	0.025	0.017	0.012
12	0.887	0.788	0.625	0.497	0.397	0.319	0.257	0.208	0.187	0.168	0.137	0.112	0.092	0.076	0.069	0.062	0.052	0.043	0.027	0.018	0.012	0.008
13	0.879	0.773	0.601	0.469	0.368	0.290	0.229	0.182	0.163	0.145	0.116	0.093	0.075	0.061	0.055	0.050	0.040	0.033	0.020	0.013	0.008	0.005
14	0.870	0.758	0.577	0.442	0.340	0.263	0.205	0.160	0.141	0.125	0.099	0.078	0.062	0.049	0.044	0.039	0.032	0.025	0.015	0.009	0.006	0.003
15	0.861	0.743	0.555	0.417	0.315	0.239	0.183	0.140	0.123	0.108	0.084	0.065	0.051	0.040	0.035	0.031	0.025	0.020	0.011	0.006	0.004	0.002
16	0.853	0.728	0.534	0.394	0.292	0.218	0.163	0.123	0.107	0.093	0.071	0.054	0.042	0.032	0.028	0.025	0.019	0.015	0.008	0.005	0.003	0.002
17	0.844	0.714	0.513	0.371	0.270	0.198	0.146	0.108	0.093	0.080	0.060	0.045	0.034	0.026	0.023	0.020	0.015	0.012	0.006	0.003	0.002	0.001
18	0.836	0.700	0.494	0.350	0.250	0.180	0.130	0.095	0.081	0.069	0.051	0.038	0.028	0.021	0.018	0.016	0.012	0.009	0.005	0.002	0.001	0.001
19	0.828	0.686	0.475	0.331	0.232	0.164	0.116	0.083	0.070	0.060	0.043	0.031	0.023	0.017	0.014	0.012	0.009	0.007	0.003	0.002	0.001	
20	0.820	0.673	0.456	0.312	0.215	0.149	0.104	0.073	0.061	0.051	0.037	0.026	0.019	0.014	0.012	0.010	0.007	0.005	0.002	0.001	0.001	
21	0.811	0.660	0.439	0.294	0.199	0.135	0.093	0.064	0.053	0.044	0.031	0.022	0.015	0.011	0.009	0.008	0.006	0.004	0.002	0.001	0.001	
22	0.803	0.647	0.422	0.278	0.184	0.123	0.083	0.056	0.046	0.038	0.026	0.018	0.013	0.009	0.007	0.006	0.004	0.003	0.001	0.001	0.001	
23	0.795	0.634	0.406	0.262	0.170	0.112	0.074	0.049	0.040	0.033	0.022	0.015	0.010	0.007	0.006	0.005	0.003	0.002	0.001			
24	0.788	0.622	0.390	0.247	0.158	0.102	0.066	0.043	0.035	0.028	0.019	0.013	0.008	0.006	0.005	0.004	0.003	0.002	0.001			
25	0.780	0.610	0.375	0.233	0.146	0.092	0.059	0.038	0.030	0.024	0.016	0.010	0.007	0.005	0.004	0.003	0.002	0.001	0.001			
26	0.772	0.598	0.361	0.220	0.135	0.084	0.053	0.033	0.026	0.021	0.014	0.009	0.006	0.004	0.003	0.002	0.002	0.001				
27	0.764	0.586	0.347	0.207	0.125	0.076	0.047	0.029	0.023	0.018	0.011	0.007	0.005	0.003	0.002	0.002	0.001	0.001				
28	0.757	0.574	0.333	0.196	0.116	0.069	0.042	0.026	0.020	0.016	0.010	0.006	0.004	0.002	0.002	0.002	0.001	0.001				
29	0.749	0.563	0.321	0.185	0.107	0.063	0.037	0.022	0.017	0.014	0.008	0.005	0.003	0.002	0.002	0.001	0.001	0.001				
30	0.742	0.552	0.308	0.174	0.099	0.057	0.033	0.020	0.015	0.012	0.007	0.004	0.003	0.002	0.001	0.001	0.001					
40	0.672	0.453	0.208	0.097	0.046	0.022	0.011	0.005	0.004	0.003	0.001	0.001										
50	0.608	0.372	0.141	0.054	0.021	0.009	0.003	0.001	0.001	0.001												

Budgetary planning focuses on the short term, normally one year, and is concerned with detailing the financial implications of those organizational goals which the firm intends to achieve in the short-term period ahead. Budgetary planning is related directly, therefore, to long-range planning since the rationale for short-term goals may be appreciated only in terms of the firm's long-term objectives and goals. The budgetary planning process shows how resources will be acquired and used by an organization to achieve its objectives. It enables an organization to evaluate the expected results of a given period's activities before they take place. If expected earnings are unsatisfactory, new plans may be drawn up which remedy the situation. This illustrates how the budgetary process enables the firm to control its future performance.

Several features of budgetary planning are particularly significant, as follows:

(a) The less stable the conditions which face an organization the more necessary and desirable is budgeting. Management must plan for changing business conditions in order that appropriate action may be taken to deal with changes that may occur. This is operationalized by introducing flexibility into the budgeting process.

(b) The starting point in budget preparation is the identification of the primary limiting factor affecting operations. Normally, this will be the volume of sales that can be made, but shortages of materials, labour or plant capacity may in some cases set the limits on activity.

(c) Budgets are based on forecasts. In the area of profit planning, sales forecasting is of critical importance.

(d) Profit planning requires an understanding of the characteristics of cost and their behaviour at different operating levels. The relationship between costs and revenues and, therefore, profits at different levels of activity may be expressed graphically or in report form. Both methods are illustrated in this chapter.

(e) Budgetary planning facilitates the co-ordination of the various activities of an organization into a harmonious working unit towards a common set of objectives. For example, production schedules can be developed in accordance with sales expectations, purchases of materials can be integrated with production and stock requirements and manpower requirements can be correlated with anticipated production and sales.

(f) Budgeting contributes to effective management control which requires the comparison of actual results with the budgeted objectives at regular and frequent intervals. The disclosure of variations enables management to focus attention on the areas that require immediate corrective action. Flexible budgets permit cost control because they are designed to change in accordance with the level of activity actually attained. A comparison of these with actual costs permits the cost performance of individual managers to be controlled.

This chapter considers the problems of budgeting for profitability. It begins with a discussion of the problems of setting profit goals and establishing sales forecasts. Next, the role of cost-volume-profit analysis for short-term profit planning is examined. The need to allow for uncertainty is discussed prior to the examination of the budgeting process itself. The financial implications of the budgeting process are twofold. First, they concern forecasts of profits and changes in assets and liabilities resulting from the budget. Second, they are critical to the financial management of the enterprise by revealing the pattern of cash surpluses or deficits associated with the budget plan. The chapter concludes with a discussion of the manner in which flexibility may be introduced into the budgeting process.

Establishing profit goals and sales forecasting

Cash flows and profit performance

In the last analysis, cash flows into and out of the business enterprise are the most fundamental events upon which accounting measurements are based, and are critical to the survival of the firm and its progress towards achieving its objectives. Cash flows are translated into profit numbers, and profit-making continues to provide the most important rationale for business organizations. Nevertheless, it is evident that business organizations have a social dimension and social responsibilities which cannot be ignored and which must be considered along with the profit targets.

One important social purpose of profit is its role in securing capital for the enterprise by offering the possibility of a return on the capital invested. This capital in turn provides the means whereby the firm may obtain those other resources which it requires to provide employment, goods and services and other social ouputs.

In the past, much attention was directed to the possibility of profit maximization as a desired business goal. In accounting, this problem generally has been discussed in terms of the 'adequacy' of profit, which may be expressed conveniently as a desired rate of return on capital employed (ROCE). This may be formulated in two different ways. First, as a return on the shareholders' equity in accordance with the following formula:

$$ROCE = \frac{\text{profit after tax}}{\text{shareholders' equity}} \times 100$$

Second, as a return on the total assets of the firm. Since assets are usually partly financed by debt capital and partly by equity capital, interest is normally added to net profit in this interpretation of ROCE as follows:

$$ROCE = \frac{\text{profit before interest and tax}}{\text{total assets}} \times 100$$

The need to analyse various aspects of financial performance is met by expanding these formulae to draw attention to the three factors which cause changes in the ROCE, namely:

(i) Increases or decreases in sales.
(ii) Increases or decreases in costs.
(iii) Increases or decreases in capital employed, expressed either as shareholders' equity or total assets.

Accordingly, the formula may be stated as follows:

$$ROCE = \frac{\text{sales}}{\text{shareholders' equity}} \times \frac{\text{profit after tax}}{\text{sales}}$$

or

$$ROCE = \frac{\text{sales}}{\text{total assets}} \times \frac{\text{profit before interest and tax}}{\text{sales}}$$

Question 1

At 31 December 19X0, the Hallam Company's condensed financial statements showed the following results:

	£ (000s)		£ (000s)
Total assets	2,000	Sales	1,200
Shareholders' equity	1,500	Cost of goods sold	700
Debentures	400	Gross trading profit	500
Current liabilities	100	Operating expenses	50
Total capital	2,000	Interest on debentures	40
		Profit before tax	410
		Tax (50%)	205
		Net profit	205

The company's accountant compared these results with those of the company's competitors. He concluded that the Hallam Company should be enjoying at least an annual return on equity capital of 15%.

Required
 (i) What rate of operating profit on total assets would the company have to earn in 19X1 to yield a 15% rate of return on equity capital?
(ii) Determine what the operating profit ratio (as a percentage of sales) would have to be in the year 19X1 to enable the company to attain the target rate of return, assuming that all other key factors remain constant.

Sales forecasting

The management problem may be seen as being a search for courses of action which will enable the organization to attain its objectives. In this respect, the function of the budget may be construed as providing data relevant to the choice which has to be made between alternative courses of action. Essentially, therefore, forecasting is addressed to the problem of providing data relevant to the analysis of future events which is a critical aspect of budget planning.

Sales forecasting is of particular importance to planning both in the long range and in the short term, since anticipated sales provide the basis for plans and action in all areas of a business enterprise. Thus, it is indispensable as a basis for establishing production schedules which in turn have a deterministic influence on levels of activity throughout a business organization. In effect, sales forecasting serves as an important tool of analysis for integrating and co-ordinating current operations.

A number of methods are used for forecasting sales. The simplest approach is to rely on estimates provided by sales personnel to build up a forecast of demand for the firm's goods. At the other extreme, market research surveys may be conducted and statistical techniques may be applied to the analysis of the data by means of such surveys. Large firms usually employ a variety of techniques in combination in the process of building up sales forecasts. Thus, such a firm might well rely on the following techniques for forecasting sales in the short term.

 (i) Estimate the level of the gross national product in the next year relying on various published data sources and making such adjustments to official government forecasts as are considered appropriate for the company's purposes.

(ii) Formulate a forecast of the economic conditions likely to affect the industry in which the firm operates.

(iii) Estimate the total sales potential of the industry or market in which the company operates, as well as the possible demand for each major product of the company, using various techniques such as time series analysis, statistical correlation techniques and computer simulation.

(iv) Utilize information provided by the company's salesmen to build up sales forecasts.

All these techniques would be used in conjunction to product forecasts which would be tested against one another in the process of formulating the final sales forecast.

Question 2

A company manufactures and sells three different products. For the purpose of preparing a sales forecast for the year 19X6, the sales director relies on the following table showing the performance of the three products in the four years to 19X4 and reflects the current rate of achievement in the year 19X5.

	Product A			Product B			Product C		
	Sales quantity	Sales price £	Sales revenue £	Sales quantity	Sales price £	Sales revenue £	Sales quantity	Sales price £	Sales revenue £
19X1	1,210,000	1.50000	1,815,000	500,000	10.0000	5,000,000	100,000	5.0000	500,000
19X2	1,331,000	1.65000	2,196,150	501,000	10.5000	5,260,500	90,000	5.5000	495,000
19X3	1,464,000	1.81500	2,657,342	499,500	11.0250	5,506,988	81,000	6.0500	490,050
19X4	1,610,000	1.99650	3,215,383	500,000	11.5763	5,788,150	72,900	6.6550	485,150
19X5	1,771,561	2.19615	3,890,614	500,200	12.1551	6,079,981	65,610	7.3205	480,298

Initially, the sales director wishes to ascertain the trends in the market performance of the three products in order to forecast sales in 19X6.

Required

Calculate the trends in the market performance of the three products, and assuming that these trends in performance indicated by the past five years will continue into 19X6, formulate sales forecasts for the three products for 19X6.

Question 3

A company sells three products in two counties. It relies on salesmen's forecasts for the purposes of budgeting sales, but has noted that the salesmen's original estimates generally have been 10% higher than actual sales. The following estimates for 19X5 have been prepared from the information supplied by salesmen.

County	Product A (units)	Product B (units)	Product C (units)
Yorkshire	50,600	80,000	101,200
Lancashire	79,200	257,000	92,400

According to market research agencies, business conditions are forecast to improve by 15% in Yorkshire and by 20% in Lancashire in the year 19X5. Unit sales of the three products in the current year (19X4) are running at the following annual rate:

County	Product A (units)	Product B (units)	Product C (units)
Yorkshire	40,000	50,000	80,000
Lancashire	60,000	150,000	70,000

Required

Analyse these estimates with a view to establishing a correlation, if any, between the two different sets of forecasts. Discuss your conclusions.

The role of cost–volume–profit analysis

Planning

In the short term, the firm's output capacity is fixed. The essential problem is, therefore, to make the best use of existing capacity. The principal variables in the analysis of the short term are costs, revenues and output volume. Profit is examined as the outcome of the relationship between these variables. This analysis requires an understanding of cost behaviour, and in particular how to distinguish between fixed and variable costs.

Question 4

The following graphs reflect the pattern of certain overhead costs in a manufacturing company in a given year. The vertical axes represent the total cost incurred, whilst the horizontal axes represent the volume of production or activity. The zero point for both cost and volume is at the intersection of the two axes.

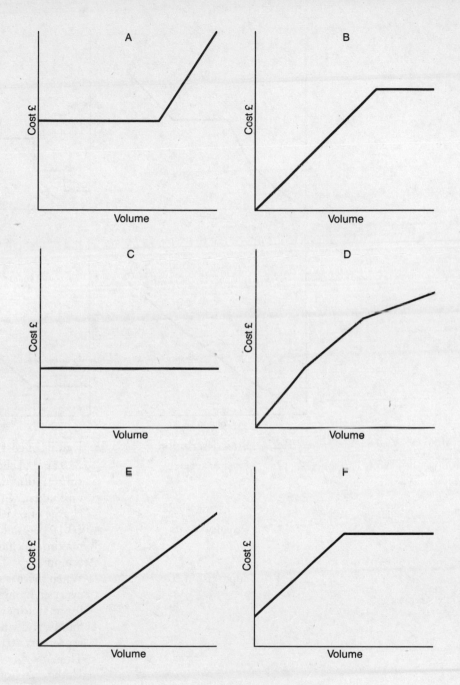

Required

(i) Identify which graph represents the overhead cost items shown below. (N.B. A graph may be used more than once.)

Ref.	Brief description	Details of cost behaviour
1	Depreciation of equipment	When charged on a straight-line basis.

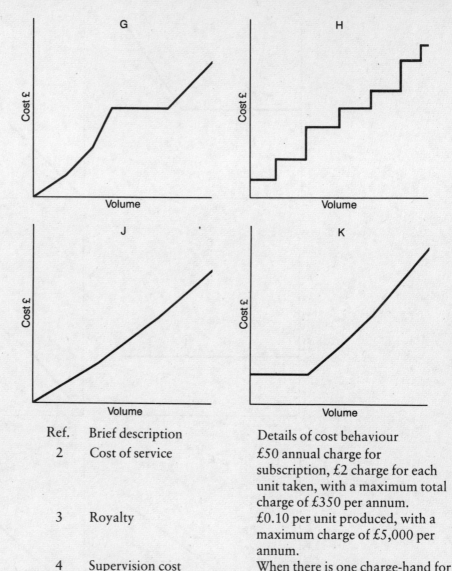

Ref.	Brief description	Details of cost behaviour
2	Cost of service	£50 annual charge for subscription, £2 charge for each unit taken, with a maximum total charge of £350 per annum.
3	Royalty	£0.10 per unit produced, with a maximum charge of £5,000 per annum.
4	Supervision cost	When there is one charge-hand for every eight men or less, and one foreman for every three charge-hands, and when each man represents 40 hours of production. Thus:

Under 320 hours	One charge-hand
321–640 hours	Two charge-hands
641–960 hours etc.	Three charge-hands plus one foreman.

Ref.	Brief description	Details of cost behaviour
5	Depreciation of equipment	When charged on a machine-hour rate
6	Cost of a service	Flat charge of £400 to cover the first 5,000 units:
		Per unit
		£0.10 for the next 3,000 units
		£0.12 for the next 3,000 units
		£0.14 for all subsequent units
7	Storage/Carriage service	Per tonne
		£15 for the first 20 tonnes
		£30 for the next 20 tonnes
		£45 for the next 20 tonnes
		No extra charge until the service reaches 100 tonnes: then £45 per tonne for all subsequent tonnage.
8	Outside finishing service	Per unit
		£0.75 for the first 2,000 units
		£0.55 for the next 2,000 units
		£0.35 for all subsequent units.

(ii) Give an example of an overhead cost item that could represent those graphs to which you do not refer in your answer in (i) above.

(iii) Draw one graph of a pattern of an overhead cost item not shown and give an example of an overhead cost item that it would represent.   (ICMA)

The contribution margin statement

A major reason for the separation of fixed from variable costs lies in the need to measure the contribution margin, which is the difference between sales revenue and variable costs. It represents the contribution towards fixed costs and profit associated with a given level of activity. It is a critical aspect of the analysis of cost—volume—profit relationships in the firm as a whole, as well as being useful in considering incremental production and incremental selling decisions. These latter decisions will be discussed in Chapter 12.

The contribution margin statement has a distinct advantage over conventional profit statements for profit planning purposes because of the differentiation which is made between fixed and variable costs. This differentiation is important because it draws attention to the impact on profit of different output levels.

Question 5

The accountant of the Sheeply Engineering Company, which is a single-product firm, drew up a conventional profit statement for the previous year showing the following results:

	£	%
Sales revenue	100,000	100
Cost of sales:		
Materials	15,000	15
Labour	20,000	20
Factory overheads	20,000	20
	55,000	55
Gross margin	45,000	45
Selling and administrative expenses	35,000	35
Net profit	10,000	10

In order to understand the implications of the cost–volume–profit relationships underlying these results for profit-planning purposes and for making the predictions implied in the profit planning process, the accountant separated all costs into fixed and variable elements and used this information to produce the following contribution margin statement:

	£	%
Sales revenue	100,000	100
Variable costs:		
Materials	15,000	15
Labour	20,000	20
Factor overheads	15,000	15
Selling and administrative expenses	10,000	10
	60,000	60
Contribution margin	40,000	40
Fixed costs:		
Factory overheads	5,000	
Selling and administrative expenses	25,000	
	30,000	40
Net profit	10,000	

Required

(i) Construct a contribution margin statement which illustrates the effects on net profit had sales revenue been (a) £80,000, (b) £120,000.

(ii) Use this contribution margin statement to discuss the advantages which the contribution margin approach has as an aid to profit planning.

The break-even chart

Cost–volume–profit analysis lends itself to graphic representation by means of the break-even chart which is illustrated in Fig. 11.1. The total revenue line goes through zero at zero volume and through any point that represents the unit selling price multiplied by any volume. The intersection of the total revenue and total cost lines indicates the break-even point at which the firm makes zero profits. All points lying below the break-even point indicate a loss, while points above the break-even level represent a profit.

Fig. 11.1

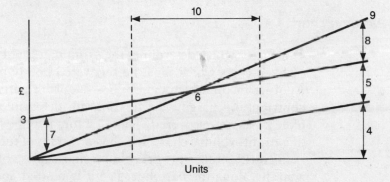

This means of constructing a break-even chart assumes linear relationships over a wide range of activity. With respect to costs, it implies that total fixed costs and variable costs per unit are constant over the entire range. With respect to revenue, it implies the same selling price per unit regardless of the sales volume. The range over which these assumptions are valid is called the *relevant range*.

Question 6
Identify the numbers shown in Fig. 11.1.

The break-even chart may be drawn to show more detail. The profit area may be divided into sections to show the desired dividends and after-dividend net profit; variable costs may be analysed as between materials, labour and factory overheads; and fixed costs may be analysed as between factory and administrative and selling expenses.

Question 7
The following data relate to a manufacturing company:

	£
Annual sales	700,000
Direct materials	100,000
Direct wages	150,000

	£
Variable factory overheads	70,000
Fixed factory overheads	130,000
Fixed administrative and selling expenses	40,000
Variable selling and distribution expenses	100,000

Required

On a single graph, display the cost–volume–profit relationships for total costs, and also for each category of costs. Identify the break-even point. (ICMA)

The profit–volume chart

One factor which determines the profit pattern of a firm is the amount of fixed costs which must be recovered before profits can be made. Another factor which determines the profit pattern is the size of the contribution margin, for this margin determines the *rate* at which fixed costs are recovered. These factors may be illustrated by means of a profit–volume chart, which is a variant of the break-even chart.

In constructing a profit–volume chart, sales volume is plotted horizontally along the base line. Profit is plotted above the base line as a positive figure; losses are plotted below the base line as negative amounts. The profit pattern is determined by connecting the profit (loss) at any two volumes. Figure 11.2 illustrates a profit–volume chart.

Fig. 11.2 Profit–volume chart

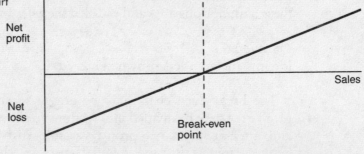

Question 8

Two firms, X and Y, have both reported results which show a return on sales of 5%, but they have different cost structures. Firm X depends mainly on manual labour and uses little machinery, and as a result has a cost structure in which variable costs are high and fixed costs are low. By contrast, firm Y is highly mechanized and uses less labour. Consequently, its fixed costs are relatively high, and its variable costs are relatively low. Their reported results are as follows:

	Firm X		Firm Y	
	£	%	£	%
Sales revenue	100,000	100	100,000	100
Variable costs	80,000	80	20,000	20
Contribution margin	20,000	20	80,000	80
Fixed costs	15,000	15	75,000	75
Net profit	5,000	5	5,000	5

Required

Assuming that each firm has a maximum potential sales revenue of £150,000, plot their profit patterns on the same profit–volume chart. Discuss the implications of these profit patterns for each firm.

Another useful function of the profit–volume chart is that it may be applied to the analysis of the profit pattern of the various products of a multi-product firm. It provides management with a very rapid pictorial interpretation of the contribution margin associated with different products.

Question 9

The following data relate to a manufacturing company producing a wide range of products which may be classified into three main groups:

Product group	Annual sales	Variable costs
	£	£
A	3,000,000	1,000,000
B	3,000,000	2,000,000
C	3,500,000	3,000,000

Fixed costs total £2,500,000.

Required

Plot on a graph the contribution margin slopes for the three product groups in alphabetical order to enable you to plot the average marginal profit slope for the total output. What information may be derived from the graph? What conclusions can it be used to illustrate? (ICMA)

Note

This kind of graph indicates the profit path of each product. It is constructed as follows:

(i) The profit path for all products is drawn.
(ii) The profit path of each product is plotted. It starts with the product with the highest contribution margin ratio. The line begins at the total fixed cost point and (in this example) is drawn

from the £3 million sales point. This line indicates the amount of fixed costs recovered by this product.

(iii) The profit path of the product with the second highest contribution margin is plotted from the £3 million sales point. Therefore, it will extend the line which represents the first product. However, since the contribution margin ratio applicable to the second product is lower, the slope of the line will be less steep.

(iv) The product with the lowest contribution margin ratio is plotted last. Its path should end at the point where the profit path for all products end.

Calculating the break-even point

One method of calculating the break-even point makes use of the contribution margin concept.

Example 1
On the basis that the unit sale price is £10, that the variable costs are £6 per unit and that fixed costs are £30,000 a year, calculate the break-even volume of sales.

Let x be the number of units required. The unit contribution margin is the difference between unit sale price and unit variable costs.

$$x = \frac{\text{fixed costs} + \text{net profit}}{\text{unit contribution margin}} = \frac{£30,000 + 0}{(£10 - 6)} = 7,500 \text{ units.}$$

Example 2
Using the same values calculate the break-even sales revenue.

In this case we make use of the contribution margin ratio to calculate the sales revenue required to cover fixed costs, as follows:

$$x = \frac{\text{fixed costs} + \text{net profit}}{\text{contribution margin ratio}} = \frac{£30,000 + 0}{40\%} = £75,000$$

Alternatively, the break-even revenue may be found from the following:

$$x = \frac{\text{fixed costs} + \text{net profit}}{1 - \dfrac{\text{total variable costs}}{\text{total sales revenue}}} = \frac{£30,000 + 0}{1 - \dfrac{£60,000}{£100,000}} = £75,000$$

The effects of changes

Another important application of cost–volume–profit analysis lies in its ability to assess how changes in the three important short-term profit variables—sales revenues, fixed costs and variable costs—interact with output volume changes to influence the profit level.

Question 10

The president of Beth Corporation anticipates a 10% wage increase to factory employees (variable labour) on January 1 of next year. No other cost changes are expected. Overhead will not change as a result of the wage increase. The management needs assistance to formulate a reasonable product strategy for next year.

A regression analysis indicates that volume is the primary factor affecting costs. Semi-variable costs have been separated into their fixed and variable segments. Opening and closing stocks never differ materially.

The following current year data have been assembled for the analysis:

	£
Current selling price per unit	80.00
Variable cost per unit:	
Direct materials	30.00
Direct labour	12.00
Factory overhead	6.00
Total variable cost per unit	48.00
Annual volume of sales	5,000 units
Fixed costs	£51,000

Required

(i) The increase in the selling price necessary to cover the 10% wage increase and still maintain the current contribution margin ratio.

(ii) The number of units to be sold to maintain the current net profit if the sales price remains at £80 and the 10% wage increase goes into effect.

(iii) The management believes that an additional £190,000 in machinery (to be depreciated at 10% annually) will increase present capacity (5,300 units) by 30%. If all units produced can be sold at the present price and the wage increase goes into effect, how would the estimated net profit, before capacity is increased, compare with the estimated net profit after capacity is increased? Prepare computations of estimated net profit before and after the expansion.

(AICPA)

Question 11

The Wellstyled Dress Manufacturing Company makes a particular type of dress. The selling price is £12 per dress and 3,000 dresses were produced and sold during the year.

Based on the production of 3,000 dresses per annum, the following are the estimated unit costs of manufacture:

	Cost per dress (£)
Materials	2.60
Labour	2.90
Variable overheads	1.70
Fixed overheads	.80
	8.00

Variable overheads vary directly with output, but fixed overheads do not change whatever the output level.

It is estimated that, if the selling price of this type of dress were increased or decreased on either side of £12 per dress, the number of dresses sold would vary as follows:

Selling price per dress (£)	Number of dresses sold per annum
14	2,000
13	2,600
12	3,000
11	4,000
10	5,000

Required

Determine the selling price which should be adopted in order that profits may be maximized.

Risk and profit planning

The analysis of uncertainty and risk discussed in the previous chapter may also be applied to the budgeting process. The uncertainty implied in the forecasts involved in the budgeting process is measured subjectively as the dispersion around the most likely outcome. The expected outcome may be computed, therefore, as the average of all possible outcomes. These possible outcomes are referred to as conditional values, because they represent values which are conditional upon a stated probability of occurrence.

The following data illustrate the manner in which an expected value may be computed from sales forecasts (denoted as 'events' hereunder), to which probabilities of occurrence have been attached.

Event	Probability	Conditional value	Expected value
1	0.05	27,000	1,350
2	0.30	29,000	8,700
3	0.35	30,000	10,500
4	0.15	31,000	4,650
5	0.10	33,000	3,300
6	0.05	35,000	1,750
		Expected value	30,250

The expected value represents the weighted average of the distribution of conditional values. It is calculated by attaching to the conditional values the 'weights' indicated by the probability of occurrence. The expected value implies that given a long enough period of time in which to test the assumptions underlying the probabilities attached to the different conditional values, the actual sales achieved would most probably equal the expected value.

Question 12

Commercial Products Corporation, an audit client, requested your assistance in determining the potential loss on a binding purchase contract which will be in effect at the end of the Corporation's fiscal year. The Corporation produces a chemical compound which deteriorates and must be discarded if it is not sold by the end of the month during which it is produced.

The total variable cost of the manufactured compound is £25 per unit and it is sold for £40 per unit. The compound can be purchased from a vertically integrated competitor at £40 per unit plus £5 freight per unit. It is estimated that failure to fill orders would result in the complete loss of eight out of 10 customers placing orders for the compound.

The Corporation has sold the compound for the past 30 months. Demand has been irregular and there is no sales trend. During this period sales per month have been:

Units sold per month	Number of months*
4,000	6
5,000	15
6,000	9

*Occurred in random sequence

Required
(i) For each of the following, prepare a schedule (with supporting computations in good form) of the:

(1) Probability of sales of 4,000, 5,000 or 6,000 units in any month.

(2) Contribution margin if sales of 4,000, 5,000 or 6,000 units are made in one month and 4,000, 5,000 or 6,000 units are

manufactured for sale in the same month. Assume all sales orders are filled. (Such a schedule is sometimes called a 'pay off table'.)

(3) Average monthly contribution margin the Corporation should expect over the long run if 5,000 units are manufactured every month and all sales orders are filled.

(ii) The cost of the primary ingredient used to manufacture the compound is £12 per unit of compound. It is estimated that there is a 60 per cent chance that the primary ingredient supplier's plant may be shut down by a strike for an indefinite period. A substitute ingredient is available at £18 per unit of compound but the Corporation must contract immediately to purchase the substitute or it will be unavailable when needed. A firm purchase contract for either the primary or the substitute ingredient must now be made with one of the suppliers for production next month. If an order were placed for the primary ingredient and a strike should occur, the Corporation would be released from the contract and management would purchase the compound from the competitor.

Assume that 5,000 units are to be manufactured and all sales orders are to be filled.

(1) Compute the monthly contribution margin from sales of 4,000, 5,000 and 6,000 units if the substitute ingredient is ordered.

(2) Prepare a schedule computing the average monthly contribution margin the Corporation should expect if the primary ingredient is ordered with the existing probability of a strike at the supplier's plant. Assume that the expected average monthly contribution margin from manufacturing will be £65,000 using the primary ingredient or £35,000 using the substitute and the expected average monthly loss from purchasing from the competitor will be £25,000.

(3) Should management order the primary or substitute ingredient during the anticipated strike period (under the assumptions stated in (ii(2)) above)? Why?

(4) Should management purchase the compound from the competitor to fill sales orders when the orders cannot be otherwise filled? Why?

(AICPA)

The budgeting process

The steps involved in preparing a budget are illustrated in Fig. 11.3 below. As may be seen, all the various steps in the budgeting process

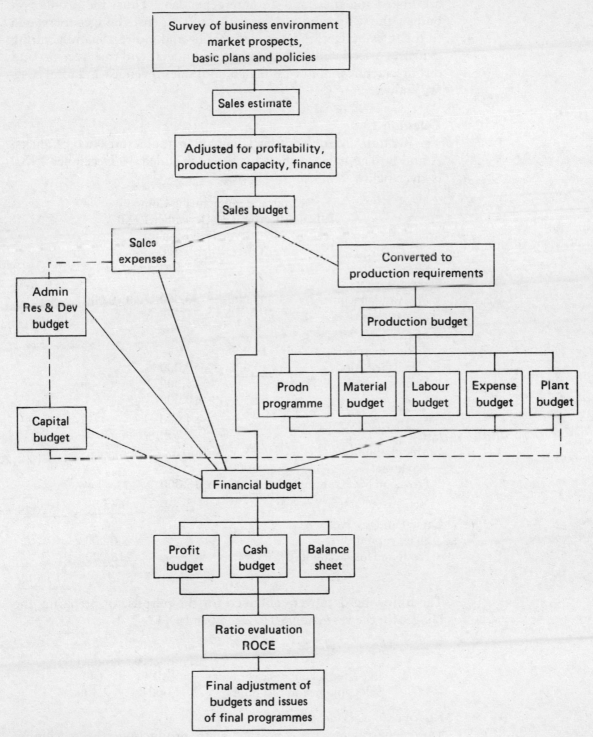

Fig. 11.3 Outline of budget procedure

are linked together, and are interdependent. Thus, the production budget, the selling and administrative and expenses budget are related to the sales budget; the material, labour and indirect manufacturing expenses are related to the production budget; and cash receipts and disbursement cannot be estimated until sales revenues and total costs are known.

Question 13

The Redmires Manufacturing Company manufactures two products, A and B. The balance sheet for the year ended 31 December 19X0 is given below:

The Redmires Manufacturing Company
Balance sheet as at 31 December 19X0

	Cost £	Provision for depreciation £	£	£
Fixed assets				
Plant and machinery	200,000	50,000	150,000	
Current assets				
Stocks				
Raw materials	19,000			
Finished goods	40,000	59,000		
Debtors		15,000		
Cash		10,000		
		84,000		
less:				
Current liabilities				
Creditors	8,000			
Provision for taxation	10,000	18,000		
Net current assets			66,000	216,000
Capital and reserves				
Share capital			200,000	
Profit and loss account			16,000	
				216,000

The following data were obtained for the purpose of preparing the budget for the year ending 31 December 19X1.

The sales forecast

	Product A	Product B
Expected selling price per unit	£30	£40
Sales volume forecast (units)	4,000	2,500

Factory Costs Forecast

Two departments are concerned with production: the machining department and the finishing department.

(a) *Direct Costs*

The following are cost estimates for the year ending 31 December 19X1:

	£
Materials:	
Material X	3.00 per unit
Material Y	1.00 per unit
Direct labour:	
Machining department	2.00 per unit
Finishing department	3.00 per unit

The direct material and direct labour content in each unit of the finished product is estimated as follows:

	Product A	Product B
Finished product (content of each unit)		
Material X	2 units	4 units
Material Y	1 unit	2 units
Direct labour: Machining dept	2 hours	1 hour
Finishing dept	1 hour	1 hour

(b) *Factory Overheads*

Factory overheads are applied on the basis of direct labour hours. At the expected output levels, the following costs are forecasted:

	Machining dept Fixed £	Machining dept Variable £	Finishing dept Fixed £	Finishing dept Variable £
Indirect labour	7,000	—	3,000	—
Indirect materials	—	3,000	—	9,000
Repairs	2,000	1,000	500	500
Rates	6,000	—	1,000	—
Depreciation	8,000	—	2,000	—
Heat and light	—	1,000	—	500
Power	1,000	1,000	500	500
	24,000	6,000	7,000	10,500

Stock Forecast

	Material X units	Material Y units
Raw materials:		
Desired closing stock	8,000	2,000
Opening stock	6,000	1,000

	Product A units	Product B units
Finished goods:		
Desired closing stock	1,100	500
Opening stock	100	1,000

Selling and Administrative Expenses Forecast

	£
Selling expenses:	
Salaries	10,000
Advertising	4,000
Administrative expenses:	
Office salaries	12,000
Sundry expenses	4,150

Cash Payments

The cost of raw materials purchases, direct labour, factory overheads, selling and administrative expenses will be met in full in cash. At 31 December 19X1, it is estimated that outstanding debtors and creditors will stand at £25,000 and £8,000 respectively. Tax owing at the beginning of the year will be paid during the year. Machinery purchases during the year estimated to cost £20,000 will be paid for.

Taxation

Profits are taxed at the rate of 50 pence in the £.

Required

(1) Complete the sales budget below:

Sales Budget
Year 19X1

	Units	Selling price £	Revenue £
Product A	....	....	....
Product B	....	....	....
Budgeted revenue			....

(2) Complete the production budget below:

Production Budget
Year 19X1

	Product A units	Product B units
Planned sales	....	....
Desired closing finished goods stock	....	....
Total production required	....	....
less: Opening finished goods stock	....	....
Budgeted production	....	....

(3) Complete the direct materials used budget below:

Direct materials used budget
Year 19X1

	Product A			Product B			Total
	Material Content (units)	Produc- tion	Usage	Material Content (units)	Produc- tion	Usage	Usage
Material X	....	....	....	....	....	....	....
Material Y	....	....	....	....	....	....	....

	Cost per unit £	Cost of materials used £
Material X	....	....
Material Y	....	....
Budgeted materials cost		============

(4) Complete the direct materials purchases budget below:

Direct materials purchases budget
Year 19X1

	Material X units	Material Y units
Desired closing stock	....	....
Units needed for production	....	....
Total required	....	....
less: Opening stock	....	....
Purchases required	....	....
Cost per unit	£	£ ....
Budgeted purchase cost	£ ============	============

(5) Complete the direct labour budget below:

Direct labour budget
Year 19X1

	Labour content in product	Units produced	Total labour hours	Rate per hour	Total labour cost
	hours	units	hours	£	£
Machining Dept					
Product A	....	....	....	....	....
Product B	....	....	....	....	....
Finishing Dept					
Product A	....	....	....	....	....
Product B	....	....	============	....	============
Budgeted labour hours and cost			============		============

(6) Complete the factory overhead costs budget below:

Factory overhead costs budget
Year 19X1

	Machining Dept at expected 12,000 direct labour hours		Finishing Dept at expected 7,000 direct labour hours	
	Fixed costs	Variable costs	Fixed costs	Variable costs
	£	£	£	£
Indirect labour	....	....	....	....
Indirect materials	....	....	....	....
Repairs	....	....	....	....
Rates	....	....	....	....
Depreciation	....	....	....	....
Heat and light	....	....	....	....
Power	....	....	....	....
Budgeted overhead costs	============	============	============	============
Rate per direct labour hour	============	============	============	============

(7) Complete the expected unit cost to manufacture schedule below:

Estimate unit cost to manufacture
Year 19X1

		Product A		Product B	
	Unit cost	Units in product	Cost	Units in product	Cost
	£		£		£
Material X	....	....	....	....	....
Material Y	....	....	....	....	....
Direct labour: Machining	....	....	....	....	....
Finishing	....	....	....	....	....
Factory overhead:					
Machining—Fixed	....	....	....	....	....
—Variable	....	....	....	....	....
Finishing —Fixed	....	....	....	....	....
—Variable	....	....	....	....	....
Estimated unit cost to manufacture			============		============

(8) Complete the closing stock budget below:

Closing stock budget
19X1

	Units £	Unit cost £	Total cost £	£
Direct materials				
X	....	....	....	....
Y	....	....	....	....
Finished products				
A	....	....	....	....
B	....	....	....	....
Budgeted closing stock				....

(9) Complete the cost of goods sold budget below:

Cost of goods sold budget
Year 19X1

	£
Direct materials used (3)	....
Direct labour (5)	....
Factory overheads (6)	....
add: Finished goods, opening stock	....
less: Finished goods, closing stock	....
Budgeted cost of goods sold	....

(10) Complete the selling and administrative expenses budget below:

Selling and administrative expenses budget
Year 19X1

	£	£
Selling expenses		
Salaries	....	
Advertising	....	....
Administrative expenses		
Office salaries	....	
Sundry	....	....
Budgeted selling and administrative expenses	....	....

(11) Complete the budgeted cash flow below:

Budgeted cash flow
Year 19X1

	£	£
Cash balance, opening		....
add: Receipts		....
Total cash available		....
less: Payments		
Purchases (4)	....	
Direct labour (5)	....	
Factory overheads (excluding depreciation) (6)	....	
Selling and administrative expenses (10)	....	
Tax	....	
Machinery purchases	....	....
Budgeted cash balance, closing		....

(12) Complete the budgeted profit statement below:

Budgeted profit statement
Year 19X1

	£
Sales (1)	....
Cost of goods sold (9)	....
Gross margin	....
Selling and administrative expenses (10)	....
Net profit before tax	....
Tax (50%)	....
Budgeted net profit after tax	....

(13) Complete the budgeted balance sheet below:

Budgeted balance sheet
31 December 19X1

			£	£
Fixed assets				
	Cost £	Provision for depreciation £		
Plant and machinery	....	....	....	
Current assets				
Stocks				
Raw materials	....			
Finished goods	....	....		
Debtors		....		
Cash		....		

contd. next page

contd.	£	£	£	£
less:				
Current liabilities				
Creditors	....			
Provision for taxation	....	....		
Net current assets			....	....
Capital and reserves				
Share capital				....
Profit and loss account			....	....
			....	

Budgeting for cash

The budget plans are critically important for financial management purposes, for they indicate the consequential cash effects of profit-planning decisions. Given the nature of business arrangements, such as the need to grant and to obtain credit and the need to undertake expenditure which will have a delayed effect on the cash position and give rise to cash flows in the future, financial management implies not only monitoring the cash-flow effects of planned events, but ensuring that sufficient finance is available to provide for the needs of the business. These needs evidently are related to the time profile of payments for goods and services, and capital expenditure, and are critically important for maintaining sufficient liquidity to meet the claims of creditors.

The importance of the cash budget, therefore, is not only to reflect the cash effects of the budget plans but to indicate the timing of surpluses and shortfalls, thereby providing for an efficient method of cash management.

Example 3

Consider the case of two persons, John Briggs and Geoffrey Knowles, who wish to start a business manufacturing a cheap alarm clock, and to form a partnership for this purpose. The date for commencing operations is 1 July 19X1. Their accountant has collected the following information for the purpose of estimating their initial capital requirements for the first six months of business:

(a) A suitable factory has been found which will cost £30,000 freehold but the present owners are prepared to offer it for £15,000 immediate cash payment and a mortgage on the balance with interest payable at the rate of 8% per annum on the last day of every month.

(b) Equipment and plant costing £18,000 must be acquired and paid for in July 19X1.

(c) Each alarm clock made will cost £4, costs consisting of £2.50 per clock for wages in the factory and £1.50 per clock for material. Selling price will be twice the prime cost, i.e., £8 each, and expected sales are as follows, in units:

July	August	September	October	November	December
Nil	1,500	1,800	1,800	2,000	2,000

Ten per cent of all sales will be for cash and the balance will be sold to customers for settlement in the month following delivery of the clocks.

(d) Materials, production overheads and administration overheads will be acquired from creditors who will expect to be paid in the month following that of the supply of the goods or services. Production overheads are likely to be incurred at the rate of £1,600 per month and administrative overheads at the rate of £1,400 per month.

(e) Sufficient materials will be purchased in July to (a) manufacture 1,500 alarm clocks; and (b) to maintain a level of raw material stock of £1,000. The stock of finished clocks will be maintained at 1,500 during the six months under review and the production level for any month is that of the month's sales.

(f) All other expenses are paid in the month in which they are incurred.

(g) Briggs and Knowles hope to be able to withdraw £2,000 each in December.

(h) An emergency cover of £2,000 is to be included in any estimation of working capital.

(i) The firm will be called Briggs Knowles and Co., and Briggs and Knowles are equal partners.

(j) Advertising to be paid for in July—£2,000, August and September—£1,000 per month, and £500 per month thereafter.

(k) Selling and distribution costs are as follows: to be paid in September £800, in October and November £900 per month, and in December £1,000. Nothing will be outstanding at the end of December.

The steps in the preparation of the cash budget are as follows:

Step 1: Prepare a schedule of cash payments which will be incurred in respect of day-to-day operations (Table 1).

Step 2: Prepare a schedule of cash receipts from sales (Table 2).

Step 3: Prepare a schedule of payments and receipts on a month-by-month basis showing the cumulative balance (Table 3).

Step 4: From Table 3, determine the largest estimated negative monthly balance. In this example, it is £21,750 falling at the end of August, and it represents the initial funding needed in respect of working capital (Table 3).

Step 5: Bring these various elements together in Table 4 to calculate the initial capital required.

Step 6: Prepare opening balance sheet for Briggs Knowles and Co.

Step 7: Prepare summarized cash budget for the months of July to December 19X1.

These steps are illustrated below:

STEP 1

Table 1
Schedule of Cash Payments for Operations

	Jul £	Aug £	Sep £	Oct £	Nov £	Dec £	
Factory wages	7,500 (1)	3,750 (2)	4,500	4,500	5,000	5,000	
Materials	—	5,500 (3)	2,250	2,700	2,700	3,000	3,000 O/S
Production overheads	—	1,600	1,600	1,600	1,600	1,600	1,600 O/S
Administration overheads	—	1,400	1,400	1,400	1,400	1,400	1,400 O/S
Advertising	2,000	1,000	1,000	500	500	500	
Interest	100	100	100	100	100	100	
Selling and distribution	—	—	800	900	900	1,000	
Drawings—B. and K.						4,000	
	9,600	13,350	11,650	11,700	12,200	16,600	

	£	£

(1) Wages for July are calculated:
units for stock	1,500
units for sale—August	1,500
	3,000 × 2.50 = 7,500

(2) Wages for August are calculated:
units for sale	1,500 × 2.50 = 3,750

and so on for the following months.

(3) Materials for August are calculated:

Bought and consumed in July

Produced for	1,500
Produced for sale—August	1,500

$$3,000 \times 1.50 = 4,500$$
$$+ \ 1,000 \ \text{stock}$$
$$\underline{5,500}$$

STEP 2

Table 2

Cash from Sales

	Jul £	Aug £	Sep £	Oct £	Nov £	Dec £	Receivable at 31 December
Cash sales	—	1,200	1,400	1,400	1,600	1,600	
Cash from debtors	—	—	10,800	12,960	12,960	14,400	14,400
		1,200	12,240	14,400	14,560	16,000	

STEP 3

Table 3

	Payments	Receipts	Balances Overspent	Balances In hand	Cumulative balance overspent
	£	£	£	£	£
July	9,600	—	9,600		9,600
August	13,350	1,200	12,150		21,750
September	11,650	12,240		590	21,060
October	11,700	14,400		2,700	18,360
November	12,200	14,560		2,360	16,000
December	16,600	16,000	600		16,600

STEP 4

From Table 3: determine the largest estimated negative monthly balance.

STEP 5

Table 4

Schedule of Assets

	£
Freehold factory	30,000
less mortgage to be shown as a liability	15,000
	15,000
Plant and equipment	18,000
	33,000
To this can be added the emergency cover for working capital	2,000
Working capital (see Step 4)	21,750
Capital to be introduced	56,750

Briggs £28,375; Knowles £28,375

STEP 6

Briggs Knowles and Co
Balance sheet as at 1 July 19X1

Capital accounts	£		£
Briggs	28,375	Cash	56,750
Knowles	28,375		
	56,750		56,750

STEP 7

Summarized cash account

	Jul £	Aug £	Sep £	Oct £	Nov £	Dec £
Wages	7,500	3,750	4,500	4,500	5,000	5,000
Materials	—	5,500	2,250	2,700	2,700	3,000
Production and administration overheads		3,000	3,000	3,000	3,000	3,000
Selling and distribution	—	—	800	900	900	1,000
Advertising	2,000	1,000	1,000	500	500	500
Factory	15,000	—	—	—	—	—
Plant and equipment	18,000	—	—	—	—	—
Interest	100	100	100	100	100	100
Drawings	—	—	—	—	—	4,000
	42,600	13,350	11,650	11,700	12,200	16,600
Balance c/fd	14,150	2,000	2,590	5,290	7,650	7,050
	56,750	15,350	14,240	16,990	19,850	23,650
Receipts						
Balance b/fd	—	14,150	2,000	2,590	5,290	7,650
Capital introduced	56,750					
Cash sales	—	1,200	1,440	1,440	1,600	1,600
Cash from debtors	—	—	10,800	12,960	12,960	14,400
	56,750	15,350	14,240	16,990	19,850	23,650

The procedure adopted in this example of Briggs Knowles and Co. can be utilized to calculate any future requirements not only on starting a business but also for calculation of cash required for expansion. The answer is always to be prepared to cover the highest 'overspent' or 'overdrawn' balance. It must be noted that the intervals for calculating each balance should be as small as possible, usually a month. It is not sufficient to add all expense payments and all cash receipts for six months, a year, or whatever the period under review may be to determine the final balance. This aggregates the results at the end of the review period and disguises the fact that revenues in earlier months may not cover all outgoing expenditure at that stage with the result that cash would run short. Equally, because of the cost of money it would not be sensible to overestimate the cash requirements which would result in liquid funds being idle for long periods of time.

Question 14

The following information has been gathered by the accounting department of the Newgear Engineering Company Ltd relating to the forecasts of activity for the next six months to December 31 19X8.

19X8	Sales £000s	Selling and distribution costs £000s	Raw materials £000s	Wages £000s	Production overhead £000s	Admin. overhead £000s
May	190	6.2	70	18	12	5
June	168	6.8	72	18.4	12.2	4.8
July	176	7	80	19.6	12.6	4.8
August	168	6.4	90	21	14	4.6
September	190	28	110	26	17.2	4.8
October	240	30	80	20.8	16.2	6
November	250	32	60	18	11.8	5.2
December	236	14	56	14	9.8	5

From the long-term capital budget it is known that a payment of £22,000 must be made in July 19X8 and a further £172,000 in December 19X8 for new equipment.

In addition, a dividend is expected to be paid in August 19X8 of £46,000 and £20,000 of the 5% Debentures are due for redemption on 30 September 19X8 @ 104.

Debtors are allowed two months' credit and creditors (for materials and overheads) grant one month's credit.

It is known that the balance in hand at the bank on 1 July 19X8 will be £192,000.

Required
Prepare a cash budget for the six months to December 19X8, showing the expected bank balance at the end of each month.

Question 15
XYZ Engineering Co. Ltd proposes to reorganize the warehouse layout. New facilities will be installed and extra labour engaged. The plan is intended to be put into operation during the four months to December 19X8, and has the following financial implications:

(1) Forecast balance sheet as at 31 August 19X8

		£000s		£000s
Issued share capital		1,400	Plant and machinery at cost	1,200
Reserves		200	*less* depreciation to date	528
Retained profit		280		672
		1,880	Investments	250
Trade creditors	170		Stock	230
Accrued charges			Debtors	600
Rent	16		Bank	326
Other	12	198		
		2,078		2,078

Note

Trade creditors represent the purchase of goods during August 19X8. Debtors represent the sales made in July and August, at the rate of £300,000 per month.

(2) The additional plant costing £400,000 will be delivered and paid for in September 19X8.

(3) Goods to be purchased per month:

September—£140,000,   October to December—£200,000.

(4) The company consistently obtains a gross margin of 40% of sales value which is expected to continue.

(5) Monthly figures for other costs are:

	September (£)	October to December per month (£)
Wages	32,000	48,000
Selling expenses	10,000	14,000
Establishment expenses	6,000	10,000

One quarter of the above costs would be outstanding at the end of the respective month and would be paid in the following month.

Rent for the warehouse is £8,000 per month, and is paid quarterly in arrears on 30 September and 31 December, etc.

Depreciation is to be provided at the rate of £14,000 per month on plant.

(6) Administration expenses monthly:

	September (£)	October to December per month (£)
Salaries	40,000	44,000
Office expense	4,000	6,000

Advertising will continue at £20,000 per month, but will rise to £60,000 for October and November.

(7) Forecast sales are:

	£
September and October	300,000 per month
November	320,000 per month
December	500,000 per month

(8) It is expected that existing credit terms will be continued.

(9) The parent company has agreed to advance on loan monthly such sums as may be necessary to keep the overdraft to an agreed limit of £200,000. No interest on overdraft or loan is to be considered in the problem.

Required

(a) Prepare a cash budget showing the monthly support by the parent company.

(b) Prepare a profit statement month by month for the period.

(c) Prepare a forecast balance sheet as at 31 December 19X8.

Providing flexibility in budgeting

In a previous section, it has been assumed that once the level of sales has been forecast, the budgeting problem consisted of determining the costs of production needed to support the expected level of sales. This approach, called fixed budgeting, consists of establishing a budget for a forecasted sales level and only for that level.

Flexible budgeting assumes that actual sales may in fact be greater or less than the forecasted sales. Accordingly, it takes account of the cost structure peculiar to the firm in estimating the total costs associated with different alternative levels of sales. The flexible budgeting approach has a number of advantages over fixed budgeting. First, costs are budgeted for a predicted range of sales rather than one level of sales. For this reason, it allows the firm to meet the problem of uncertainty by the preparation of operational plans for various sales and output levels. Second, it enables management to monitor performance more accurately by the availability of budgeted costs for different levels of activity. Hence, if the actual sales level should change during the year, information about actual performance is comparable with budgeted information related to that level of performance. Third, it facilitates the control of performance by establishing performance standards which take account of possible variations in total sales and output levels.

Question 16

James Smith was recently appointed accountant to the Household Appliance Company which used a fixed budget to measure its performance against objectives. The following data show the actual performance for the month compared with the budgeted figures:

Items of cost	Actual	Budgeted
Units produced	73,500	75,000
	£	£
Direct materials	37,020	39,000
Direct labour	5,950	6,000
Factory supplies	1,550	1,500
Indirect labour	710	726
Repairs and maintenance	2,300	2,250
Insurance	350	355
Rates	2,000	2,000
Depreciation	2,200	2,200
	52,080	54,031

Smith makes a study of the fixed and variable elements of the various cost factors, and produces the following information of the fixed elements in the budget:

	£
Indirect labour	126
Repairs and maintenance	750
Insurance	55
Rates	2,000
Depreciation	1,000
	3,931

Dissatisfied with the variance resulting from current practice, Smith decides to recommend the installation of a system based on flexible budgets. Using the information given above, write a report to the managing director explaining this new system. Use the formats below to assist your explanation:

(i) Compute the variable and fixed elements of costs as follows:

Output = 75,000 units	Budget total £	Fixed element £	Variable element £	Variable rate per unit of output £
Direct materials				
Direct labour				
Factory supplies				
Indirect labour				
Repairs, etc.				
Insurance				
Rates				
Depreciation				

(ii) Using the calculations derived from (i) above calculate the following:

Finished units	Actual cost of production (1) £	Total budget allowance (2) £	Original budget (3) £	Total variation (4) (1) − (3) £	Expense variation (5) (1) − (2) £	Volume variation (6) (2) − (3) £
Direct materials						
Direct labour						
Factory supplies						
Indirect labour						
Repairs, etc.						
Insurance						
Rates						
Depreciation						

This chapter is divided into four sections. The first section examines the data which is relevant for making tactical decisions and focuses in particular on the nature of relevant costs. The second section analyses the contribution margin approach as providing a method for evaluating alternative courses of action. Where there is a limiting factor, the contribution margin approach indicates which alternative course of action offers the highest contribution having regard to the limiting factor. The third section instances several classical examples of situations involving tactical decisions, as follows:

Make or buy.
Sell or process further.
Operate or close.

The fourth section considers the complexity introduced into the selection of the best alternative when more than one limiting factor operates. In this section, linear programming is discussed as a technique for finding feasible solutions to decision problems which contain two limiting factors. The analysis is limited to the case of two limiting factors only, since this text is intended only to be an introductory text.

In the two previous chapters, we examined the problem of planning for profitability in its two time periods, namely, planning in the long range and planning in the short term. Both chapters were concerned essentially with the productive capacity of the firm. Long-range planning was seen to involve considerations of growth in output and profit: short-term or budgetary planning was seen to require the best use of existing resources.

Although this chapter is concerned with short-term decisions, these decisions are different in nature to those considered in Chapter 11. Budgeting for profitability assumes that the profit plans laid down at the outset of the accounting period will provide the framework of activity for the entire period. In this chapter, we examine a variety of 'one-off' decisions, for example, 'should a special order be accepted at a price lower than the established selling price?'; 'should a loss-making department continue or should it be closed?'; 'should more of product A be produced than of product B?'. Obviously, such decisions have an effect on both time periods discussed in Chapters 10 and 11. Nevertheless, they are classified as short-term tactical decisions, and as their title indicates, they represent changes of a tactical nature to both long-range and short-term plans. In this sense, it is evident that a decision to produce more of one product than another may be seen as having long-range and short-term effects: by contrast, a decision to accept a special order effects only short-term profits on a once-and-for-all basis, though it does indicate a willingness to alter a pricing rationale which has its source in long-range and budgetary planning.

Relevant data for making tactical decisions

Decision-making is a matter of choosing between alternative courses of action. Different decisions call for different data. Therefore, data must be specially tailored to meet the decision needs of particular situations. In considering each decision problem, the overriding consideration is identifying the relevant benefits and relevant costs associated with the decision. Relevant data is that which is oriented towards the future, since decisions are concerned with future events. Past benefits and costs resulting from previous decisions cannot be considered as relevant to a current decision, except that in a limited way, past experiences train one to make better judgements in the future.

Relevant benefits and relevant costs have, in addition, a special meaning when applied to decision-making. Relevant benefits are those which serve to distinguish one alternative from another. Relevant benefits are those which are compared as a means of establishing the total difference between alternatives. Such costs are termed 'differential' or 'incremental' costs.

Crucial to the choice between different alternatives is the concept of differential cost known as the 'opportunity cost'. It is expressed by the sacrifice entailed in selecting the chosen alternative rather than the next best one. For example, where the choice is between investing company funds in plant and machinery *rather* than in securities, the opportunity cost associated with investing the funds in plant and machinery *rather* than in securities is the lost opportunity of deriving income from such securities. The opportunity cost is never recorded in the accounting process, for it is an ephemeral cost which appears only at the moment of time when a decision has to be evaluated in terms of a choice between two or more alternative courses of action. Some writers argue that the opportunity cost has no real value in decision-making other than to indicate that a search has taken place and the best use of a resource has been selected.

In this section, therefore, we examine the nature of the data which is relevant to decision-making and involves a choice between alternative uses of resources.

A number of different techniques are employed in the analysis of decision problems. Some of these techniques have their roots in accounting theories about the treatment of costs, particularly those relating to absorption costing and marginal costing, whilst others have their origins in the application of economic principles to decision situations; among these is the opportunity cost principle referred to above. It must be borne in mind that accounting systems from which data are drawn are constructed purely to determine profit, and consequently may be, and frequently are, unsuitable for decision-making purposes.

Question 1

Crestet Ltd, a manufacturing company making novelty car accessories, has been left with a stock of alloy figurines for car bonnets following their banning as dangerous by the police authorities. The stock amounts to 8,000 units and their manufacturing costs per unit were as follows:

	£
Materials	1.20
Labour	0.80
Fixed overheads	0.50
	2.50

Prior to being banned, the selling price was £3.00 per unit. The casts for these figurines cost £1,000 when originally acquired. The company has examined the situation and has concluded that the following alternative courses of action could be adopted:

(a) Sell the figurines as scrap metal for £6,500.
(b) Rework them by putting a base on them which would allow them to be sold as household ornaments at a price of £3.20 each. Such work would require £2 per unit of additional labour and a fixed overhead charge of £1 each would be entailed in terms of the company's absorption costing system. No further materials would be required.
(c) Melt them down and use the metal as a substitute in a strong-selling line where the metal currently used costs 50% more than the metal used in the figurines. This process would incur a materials loss of three-eighths of the original metal.

Required

You are asked to identify and, where appropriate, calculate:

(1) The decision which would result in the greatest benefit to Crestet Ltd.
(2) The opportunity cost of the metal.
(3) The relevant data.
(4) The sunk cost, i.e. which has already been incurred and will not be affected by subsequent decisions.

Question 2

George Jackson operates a small machine shop. He manufactures one standard product available from many other similar businesses and he also manufactures products to customer order. His accountant prepared the annual profit statement shown below:

	Customer sales £	Standard sales £	Total £
Sales	50,000	25,000	75,000
Material	10,000	8,000	18,000
Labour	20,000	9,000	29,000
Depreciation	6,300	3,600	9,900
Power	700	400	1,100
Rent	6,000	1,000	7,000
Heat and light	600	100	700
Other	400	900	1,300
Total expenses	44,000	23,000	67,000
Net profit	6,000	2,000	8,000

The depreciation charges are for machines used in the respective product lines. The power charge is apportioned on the estimate of power consumed. The rent is for the building space which has been leased for 10 years at £7,000 per year. The rent, and heat and light are apportioned to the product lines based on amount of floor space occupied. All other costs are current expenses identified with the product line causing them.

A valued custom-parts customer has asked Mr Jackson if he would manufacture 5,000 special units for him. Mr Jackson is working at capacity and would have to give up some other business in order to take this business. He cannot renege on orders already agreed to but he could reduce the output of his standard product by about one-half for one year while producing the specially requested custom part. The customer is willing to pay £7.00 for each part. The material cost will be about £2.00 per unit and the labour will be £3.60 per unit. Mr Jackson will have to spend £2,000 for a special device which will be discarded when the job is done.

Required

(1) Calculate the following costs related to the 5,000 unit custom order:

    (a) The incremental cost of the order.
    (b) The full cost of the order.
    (c) The opportunity cost of taking the order.
    (d) The sunk costs related to the order.

(2) Should Mr Jackson take the order? Explain your answer.

Question 3

The following costs and other data apply to two component parts used by Derbyshire Electronics Ltd:

	Part A4 £	Part B5 £
Direct material	0.40	8.00
Direct labour	1.00	4.70
Factory overheads	4.00	2.0
	£5.40	£14.70
Units needed per year	6,000	8,000
Machine hours per unit	4	2
Unit cost if purchased rather than made by the firm	£5.00	£15.00

In past years, Derbyshire Electronics has manufactured all its required components. However, in 19X5, only 30,000 hours of otherwise idle machine time can be devoted to manufacturing components. Accordingly, some of these components must be purchased from outside suppliers.

In producing component parts, factory overheads are applied at the rate of £1 per machine hour. Fixed capacity costs, which are not affected by any make-or-buy decisions, represent 60% of the applied factory overheads.

Required

(1) Assuming that the 30,000 hours of available machine time are to be utilized so that the company realizes the maximum potential cost savings, determine the relevant production costs that should be taken into account in assessing unit costs of production for the purpose of deciding which components to manufacture.
(2) Compute the number of units of the two components which the company should produce rather than buy if it allocates the available machine hours on the basis of the maximum cost savings per machine hour.

The contribution margin and limiting factors

In Chapter 11, we noted the importance of the contribution margin approach to cost–volume–profit analysis. In this chapter, we explore the usefulness of this approach in making short-term tactical decisions involving production or output alternatives.

Where there are no limiting factors constraining production, the product with the highest contribution margin per unit should be produced up to the point where demand is satisfied. In these situations, the most important constraint upon the firm is its ability to sell.

Example 1

Consider the data which relate to a firm manufacturing two products, X and Y, as follows:

	Product X	Product Y
	£	£
Selling price per unit	3	10
Variable costs per unit	2	8
Contribution margin per unit	1	2

Clearly, if a sales constraint exists the firm should produce as many units of Product Y as possible.

Where there is single limitation, for example, a constraint on production owing to restricted capacity, the firm should maximize the total contribution margin having regard to the limiting factor.

Example 2

Assume that the firm has a production constraint limiting output to 50,000 machine hours. Product X requires one machine hour and Product Y requires four machine hours. This limiting factor is expressed in terms of the contribution per machine hours, as follows:

	Product X	Product Y
Contribution margin per unit	£1	£2
Divided by the machine hours required per unit	1	4
Contribution margin per machine hour	£1	£0.50

Therefore, the firm should produce and sell Product X in preference to Product Y, given that the existing demand and cost structure remain the same, since it will be making the most profitable use of the existing and limited machine hour capacity.

Question 4

The Marcia Company has asked your assistance in determining an economical sales and production mix of their products for the coming year. The company manufactures a line of dolls and a doll-dress sewing kit. The company's sales department provides the following data:

Doll's name	Estimated demand for next year (units)	Established net price (£)
Laurie	50,000	5.20
Debbie	42,000	2.40
Sarah	35,000	8.50
Kathy	40,000	4.00
Sewing kit	325,000	3.00

To promote sales of the sewing kit, there is a 15% reduction in the established price for a kit purchased at the same time as a Marcia Company doll.

From the accounting records, you develop the following data:

(1) Production standards per unit

Item	Material (£)	Labour (£)
Laurie	1.40	0.80
Debbie	0.70	0.50
Sarah	2.69	1.40
Kathy	1.00	1.00
Sewing kit	0.60	0.40

(2) The labour rate of £2.00 per hour is expected to continue without change in the next year. The plant has an effective capacity of 130,000 labour hours on a single-shift basis. Present equipment can produce all of the products.

(3) Next year's total fixed costs will be £100,000. Variable costs will be equivalent to 50% of direct labour cost.

(4) The company has a small stock of its products that can be ignored.

Required

(1) Prepare a schedule to compute the contribution margin of a unit of each product. Use the format shown by the headings below:

Item	Sale price £	Variable costs				Contribution margin £
		Material £	Labour £	Overheads £	Total £	
....	....	....	....	....	....	....
....	....	....	....	....	....	....
....	....	....	....	....	....	....
....	....	....	....	....	....	....
....	....	....	....	....	....	....

(2) Prepare a schedule computing the contribution margin per unit of each product. Use the format shown by the following headings:

Item	Contribution margin per unit £	Labour cost per unit £	Contribution margin per £ of labour cost £
....	....	....	....
....	....	....	....
....	....	....	....
....	....	....	....
....	....	....	....
....	....	....	....

(3) Prepare a schedule computing the total labour hours required to produce the estimated sales units for next year. Indicate the item and the number of units that you would recommend be increased (or decreased) in production to attain the company's effective productive capacity. Use the format given below for your answer:

Item	Estimated unit sales	Labour hours per unit	Total labour hours
Laurie	....	....	....
Debbie	....	....	....
Sarah	....	....	....
Kathy	....	....	....
Sewing kit	....	....	....
Total hours required			....
Effective productive capacity			....
Hours required in excess of effective productive capacity			....

(4) Without regard to your answer in (3) above, assume that the estimated sales units for the next year would require 12,000 labour hours in excess of the company's effective productive capacity. Discuss the possible methods of providing the missing capacity. Include in your discussion all the factors which must be taken into consideration in evaluating the methods of providing the missing capacity.   (AICPA adapted)

The following question illustrates the contribution margin approach under the condition of a limiting factor, which in this instance is land.

Question 5

On a farm of 200 acres, the farmer plans to sow 100 acres of barley, 20 acres of kale, and to use 80 acres on which to graze milk cattle.

For the barley, seed will cost £2.50 per acre, and for fertilizers £3.50 per acre. It is expected that the yield will be 1.50 tonnes per acre, which will be sold at £25 per tonne.

The kale will cost £2 per acre for seed and £5 per acre for fertilizers. The kale produced will be fed to the cattle.

On the 80 acres, 40 milking cows will be kept, and in addition to the kale other feeding stuffs will cost £1,000 in all for the year. Each cow should produce one calf which will be sold at £10 each, together with an annual milk yield sold at £120. Cows will 'depreciate' at the rate of £10 per annum.

Other farm costs (which are unlikely to change, however the farm is worked) are, per annum:

	£
Farmworkers wages	1,800
Rent, rates, etc.	1,200
General charges	3,000

A suggestion is made that kale should be purchased instead of grown: if this is done it is estimated that kale will cost £12.50 per cow, per annum.

Required
Prepare figures to indicate to the farmer whether the kale should be purchased or grown. If the kale is purchased, show how the 20 acres could be used to best advantage.   (ICMA)

Examples of tactical decisions

The contribution margin is helpful in a number of decision situations where it is necessary to assess the net advantage to be gained from pursuing one course of action rather than another. These decisions typically include make or buy, sell or further process, continue or close down a particular activity, keep or replace an asset, buy or lease an asset. It is evident that in choosing one alternative course of action rather than another, the opportunity cost which is associated with that preference is the loss of the contribution margin associated with the next best choice. The examples and problems appearing so far in this chapter have referred to these typical situations in illustrating the nature of relevant costs and the importance of the contribution margin method. In this section, we shall be concerned with an analysis of tactical decisions themselves.

The make or buy decision

The 'make or buy' decision is one tactical decision commonly encountered in industry. The procedure for arriving at a decision is essentially one of comparing costs that will be incurred as a consequence of the alternative courses of action. Before illustrating the approach to such a comparison, it must be pointed out that occasionally the cost differential may not be the eventual deciding factor. Thus, it may well be that a component required for a major product of a company may be purchased from an external supplier at a cheaper price than the company is able to manufacture it for, but if the security of supply is in question, it is evident that the cost disadvantage would not prevent the company from undertaking its manufacture. In the example given below, it is assumed that no such factors apply.

Example 3

G. A. Illac Ltd manufactures a range of travel cases all of which require small locks. The company has always manufactured its own locks but to suit new forthcoming designs it proposes to review the policy and needs data to aid in making the decision. The accounts department consults its records and produces the following:

(1) Existing plant can manufacture the new locks and so no new investment is needed.
(2) As the plant is specialized it has virtually no scrap value.
(3) Unit costs for the new locks are estimated as follows—per hundred locks

	£
Material	38.50
Labour	25.00
Variable overhead	12.00
Fixed overhead	35.00
	110.50

Fixed overhead has been applied at the predetermined machine hour rate of £3.50 per hour in accordance with the absorption costing system presently in use.

(4) Foreseeable demand for the new range of cases, bags, etc., for which the locks are needed, has been estimated at 20,000 per annum.
(5) A quotation has been obtained from the Jumilee Lock Company Ltd at a price of £100 per 100 locks for a suitable design.
(6) On this basis the purchasing manager recommends the acceptance of the quotation. Can this be supported by the data?

Comment

This simple example raises the question whether an absorption costing system is appropriate for decision making. A knowledge of how such a system works is a prerequisite to understanding whether the form of data supplied is relevant. Since the information supplied indicates that the fixed overhead applied is an *allocation* of *already committed resources* then no future decision can effect this. The company is concerned to maximize future benefits either by increased contribution or, as in this case, reduced cash flows out. Note that the position would be different if the company had to purchase more plant in order to make the new locks as this would require a large outflow and it would be necessary to calculate some annual equivalent cash flow as a cost of manufacture or some other appropriate technique which will be demonstrated hereafter. It becomes clear in the case of G. A. Illac Ltd that the real basis for a decision is a comparison of incremental cash flows. Thus, cost of buying is compared against the variable costs of manufacture and this can be generalized by the following decision rule: buy if $D(M + L + V) > D(P)$ or, equally, make if $D(P) > D(M + L + V)$ where D is the unit demand for the relevant period, M is the materials per unit, L is the variable labour per unit, V is the variable overhead per unit and P is the purchase price per unit. In this case the relevant figures point to manufacture as

$$\text{purchase}\left(\frac{20,000}{100} \times £100\right)$$
$$> \text{manufacture}\left(\frac{20,000}{100} \times (38.50 + 25 + 12)\right)$$
$$= £20,000 > £15,100$$

Therefore cash savings from manufacture = £4,900 p.a.

This is pursued one stage further by considering the situation if G. A. Illac Ltd had needed to buy new plant costing £15,000 to start production. The procedure is similar to that already adopted but new data are needed before this can be assumed completely.

The new data needed will be:

(1) The expected commercial life of the lock in the new design form.
(2) The cost of capital for the company.
(3) The scrap value of plant at the end of its useful life.

Suppose now that the figures for these three points in the case of G. A. Illac Ltd were:

(1) 5 years expected life.
(2) Cost of capital—15%.
(3) Scrap value—nil.

The decision now depends on whether the present value of the cash savings, £4,900 p.a., is greater than the outlay.

So, using present value of an annuity for 5 years at 15%

$$£4,900 \times 9_{\overline{5}}\rceil^{15} = 4,900 \times 3.3522 = £16,426$$

which, being greater than £15,000, means that the component should be manufactured.

In similar cases to this latter one, the procedure can be summarized by:

(a) Determining the net cash advantage, C by the method described earlier.
(b) Apply the net present value rule in the following way:

$$\text{accept manufacture if } \sum_{t=1}^{n} \frac{C}{(1+k)^t} \geq I$$

where C is the cash advantage per annum, k is the discount rate—cost of capital, I is the initial capital outlay and n is the life of project

Question 6

The management of Scoopa Company has asked your assistance in arriving at a decision whether to continue manufacturing a part or to buy it from an outside supplier. The part, which is named Faktron, is a component used in some of the finished products of the company.
The following data are typical of the company's operations:

(1) The annual requirement for Faktrons is 5,000 units. The lowest quotation from a supplier was £8.00 per unit.
(2) Faktrons have been manufactured in the precision department. If Faktrons are purchased from an outside supplier, certain machinery will be sold and would realize its book value.
(3) Following are the total costs of the precision machinery department during the year under audit when 5,000 Faktrons were made:

	£
Materials	67,500
Direct labour	50,000
Indirect labour	20,000
Lighting and heating	5,500
Power	3,000
Depreciation	10,000
Property taxes and insurance	8,000
Payroll taxes and other benefits	9,800
Other	5,000
	178,800

(4) The following precision machinery department costs apply to the manufacture of Faktrons: material, £17,500; direct labour, £28,000; indirect labour, £6,000; power, £300; other, £500. The sale of the equipment used for Faktrons would reduce the following costs by the amounts indicated: depreciation, £2,000; property taxes and insurance, £1,000.

(5) The following additional precision machinery department costs would be incurred if Faktrons were purchased from an outside supplier: freight, £0.50 per unit; indirect labour, for receiving, materials handling, inspection, etc., £5,000. The cost of the purchased Faktrons would considered a precision machinery department cost.

Required

(1) Prepare a schedule showing a comparison of the total costs of the precision machinery department:
 (i) When Faktrons are made,
 (ii) When Faktrons are bought from an outside supplier.

(2) Discuss the considerations in addition to the cost factors that you would bring to the attention of management in assisting it to arrive at a decision whether to make or buy Faktrons. Include in your discussion the considerations that might be applied to the evaluation of the outside supplier.   (AICPA adapted)

Question 7

The buying department of Artix Ltd has been obtaining quotations for non-returnable crates which the company uses to export its main products.

For the number they require in anticipation of the next year of operations, the lowest figure obtained is £33,600.

They have drawn up a comparative statement of the difference between buying in and manufacturing the crates themselves, which is the present method used by the company. This statement, prepared from cost records, is set out below. In obtaining the figures, the buying department learnt that the company has spare plant capacity and the crates are being made in an otherwise idle section of the factory.

You are required to:

(a) Comment on the figures and recommendation.
(b) List any additional factors which you feel may influence the decision.

Artix Limited
Comparison of costs between buying and making packing crates

	Cost of manufacturing £	Cost of buying £
Cost of buying crates		33,600
Cost of materials	16,000	
Specialized labour	6,400	
General labour—allocated on hourly basis	4,800	
Supervisory labour—allocated	3,200	
Variable overhead	1,600	
Fixed overhead (including £3,000 depreciation for special purpose crate machinery which was purchased two years ago)	6,400	
	38,400	33,600
Advantages of buying crates over manufacturing:	£4,800	

Therefore it is recommended that the crates be bought.

Question 8
The 'sell or further process' decision

The accountant of the Sandygate Company is preparing information to determine whether the products which the company makes should be sold or further processed. The company produces three products, A, B and C, as a result of a series of processes.

Standard costs for the coming year are as follows:

	£
Direct materials	70,000
Direct wages	30,000
Variable overheads	45,000
Fixed overheads	60,000

Standard outputs and selling prices at this volume of production are:

	Tonnes	£ per tonne
A	1,000	150
B	500	100
C	600	50

The overhead absorption rate in respect of each process is the same.

Facilities are available for carrying out further processes of a similar nature, and its is found that all three products can be further processed and sold at higher prices. Any one product, any combination of two products, or all three products can be further processed and, by the addition of further materials and the application of further labour, the following results can be achieved.

	A	B	C
Weight processed, tonnes	1,000	500	600
Cost of added materials	£10,000	£3,000	£7,000
Cost of added labour	£4,000	£2,000	£2,000
Sales values of production	£170,000	£62,000	£45,000

Required

Prepare an analysis which could be used in deciding whether to sell or process further, and make recommendations on the basis of the figures presented in this analysis.

Question 9

Dropping a product line

The chairman of Eastern Company wants guidance on the advisability of eliminating product C, one of the company's several products, since it showed a loss during the past year. The loss on product C was determined as follows:

	£	Product C £
Sales		350,000
Cost of sales:		
Raw materials	80,000	
Labour		
Direct	150,000	
Indirect	18,000	
Fringe benefits (15% of labour)	25,200	
Royalties (1% of product C sales)	3,500	
Maintenance and repairs (fixed)	2,000	
Factory supplies	2,100	
Depreciation (straight-line)	7,100	
Electrical power (variable)	3,000	
Scrap and spoilage (variable)	600	
Total cost of sales		291,500
Gross profit		58,500
Selling, general and administrative expenses:		
Sales commissions	15,000	
Officers' salaries	10,500	
Other wages and salaries (fixed)	5,300	
Fringe benefits (15% of wages, salaries and commissions)	4,620	
Delivery expense (variable)	10,000	
Advertising expense	26,000	
Miscellaneous fixed expenses	10,630	
Total selling, general and administrative expenses		82,050
Operating loss		(23,550)

All costs classified as fixed costs have been apportioned to products, and no change is expected if product C is eliminated. Advertising is a direct cost traceable to product C.

Required
Revise the statement above to give the chairman of the company relevant information to enable him to decide whether or not to drop product C.   (AICPA adapted)

The contribution margin approach is also useful in pricing decisions since it focuses attention on the advantage associated with a possible increase in the level of sales resulting from a price alteration. The classical example of this situation is the acceptance of the special order, which is an order with an offer of a price lower than the established price. The acceptance of the special order depends on the contribution to net profit which would result from the additional sales involved.

Question 10

'Special order' pricing

E. Berg and Sons build custom-made pleasure boats which range in price from £10,000 to £250,000. For the past 30 years, Mr Berg Sr has determined the selling price of each boat by estimating the costs of material, labour, a prorated portion of overhead, and adding 20% to these estimated costs.

For example, a recent price quotation was determined as follows:

	£
Direct materials	5,000
Direct labour	8,000
Overhead	2,000
	15,000
Plus 20%	3,000
Selling price	18,000

The overhead figure was determined by estimating total overhead costs for the year and allocating them at 25% of direct labour.

If a customer rejected the price and business was slack, Mr Berg Sr would often be willing to reduce his markup to as little as 5% over estimated costs. Thus, average markup for the year is estimated at 15%.

Mr Ed Berg Jr has just completed a course on pricing and believes the firm could use some of the techniques discussed. The course emphasized the contribution margin approach to pricing and Mr Berg

Jr feels such an approach would be helpful in determining the selling prices of their custom-made pleasure boats.

Total overhead which includes selling and administrative expenses for the year has been estimated at £150,000 of which £90,000 is fixed and the remainder is variable in direct proportion to direct labour.

Required
(1) Assume the customer in the example rejected the £18,000 quotation and also rejected a £15,750 quotation (5% markup) during a slack period. The customer countered with a £15,000 offer.
  (a) What is the difference in net profit for the year between accepting or rejecting the customer's offer?
  (b) What is the minimum selling price Mr Berg Jr could have quoted without reducing or increasing net profit?
(2) What advantages does the contribution margin approach to pricing have over the approach used by Mr Berg Sr?
(3) What pitfalls are there, if any, to contribution margin pricing?

In addition to being relevant to a range of short-term tactical decisions, the contribution margin approach may also be used as a penetrating tool of analysis to examine the entire operations of a business firm.

Question 11

The analysis of the firm's activities

Ace Publishing Company is in the business of publishing and printing guide books and directories. The board of directors requires a cost study to determine whether the company is economically justified in continuing to print, as well as publish, its books and directories. The following information is obtained from the company's cost accounting records for the preceding fiscal year:

	Publishing £	Printing £	Shipping £	Total £
Salaries and wages	275,000	150,000	25,000	450,000
Telephone and telegraph	12,000	3,700	300	16,000
Materials and supplies	50,000	250,000	10,000	310,000
Occupancy costs	75,000	80,000	10,000	165,000
General and administrative	40,000	30,000	4,000	74,000
Depreciation	5,000	40,000	5,000	50,000
Total	457,000	553,700	54,300	1,065,000

Departments

Additional data

(a) A review of personnel requirements indicates that, if printing is discontinued, the publishing department will need one additional clerk at £4,000 per year to handle correspondence with the printer. Two layout men and a proofreader will be required at an aggregate annual cost of £17,000; other personnel in the printing department can be released. One mailing clerk, at £3,000, will be retained; others in the shipping department can be released. Employees whose employment was being terminated would immediately receive, on the average, three months' termination pay. The termination pay would be amortized over a five-year period.

(b) Long-distance telephone and telegraph charges are identified and distributed to the responsible departments. The remainder of the telephone bill, representing basic service at a cost of £4,000, was allocated in the ratio of ten to publishing, five to printing, and one to shipping. The discontinuance of printing is not expected to have a material effect on the basic service cost.

(c) Shipping supplies consist of cartons, envelopes and stamps. It is estimated that the cost of envelopes and stamps for mailing material to an outside printer would be £5,000 per year.

(d) If printing is discontinued, the company would retain its present building but would sublet a portion of the space at an annual rental of £50,000. Taxes, insurance, heat, light, and other occupancy costs would not be significantly affected.

(e) One cost clerk would not be required (£5,000 per year) if printing is discontinued. Other general and administrative personnel would be retained.

(f) Included in administrative expenses is interest expense on a 5% mortgage loan of £500,000.

(g) Printing and shipping-room machinery and equipment having a net book value of £300,000 can be sold without gain or loss. These funds in excess of termination pay would be invested in marketable securities earning 5%.

(h) The company has received a proposal for a five-year contract from an outside printer under which the volume of work done last year would be printed at a cost of £550,000 per year.

(i) Assume continued volume and prices at last year's level.

Required

A statement setting forth in comparative form the costs of operation of the printing and shipping departments under the present arrangement and under an arrangement in which inside printing is discontinued. Summarize the net saving or extra cost in case printing is discontinued.   (AICPA adapted)

Linear programming

So far in this chapter, we have examined the employment of resources where a *single* constraint or limiting factor applied. Linear programming is a mathematical technique which is relevant and useful where the employment of resources is subject to two or more constraints or limiting factors. Since this is an introductory text, the application of linear programming is limited to the illustration of two constraints only.

Example 4

Evron Ltd is a small manufacturing company that makes two types of heating boilers, one for the housing sector of the building industry and called the Evminor, and a larger one for commercial and industrial premises which is called the Ronmajor. Both are standard and with buoyant demand the company believes it can sell as many of each as it can produce at the present price. The contribution from these two products is: from the Evminor £40, from the Ronmajor £48. (Contribution is taken as selling price less the variable costs of manufacture.)

The production statistics reveal the following data concerning the time taken by the processes in each of the two manufacturing departments.

	Hours taken on each product	
Department	Evminor	Ronmajor
Casting and welding	3	6
Assembly and testing	4	2

Hours available each week—casting and welding dept, 120
assembly and testing, 64

It is now necessary to see what is required when faced with this sort of problem. Right away it can be assumed that the company wishes to use its resources so as to obtain the maximum benefit expressed as contribution. This can be stated as an objective thus: since the number produced of each of the products has to be considered in formulating a mathematical approach to the solution of how scarce resources should be used, they are variables which can be expressed as

Number of Evminors produced X
Number of Ronmajors produced Y

(In deciding which variables enter into a linear programming formulation two criteria must be observed: (a) the variables must, when quantified, yield a plan to be followed, and (b) they must be controllable.)

Evron Ltd's objective can now be expressed as 'maximize the total contribution from the sale of X Evminors with a contribution of £40 each and of Y Ronmajors with a contribution of £48 each'. More concisely, this is written: maximize £40X + £48Y.

As the resources are limited, the quantity of each that can be produced is restricted, and it is necessary to establish a form for the mathematical expression of this fact for each of the departments which contain the restrictions.

The casting and welding department has only 120 hours available per week so that the number of Evminors made × 3 hours plus the number of Ronmajors made × 6 hours cannot exceed 120 hours. Or, more concisely, $3X + 6Y \leqslant 120$, which now expresses this departmental constraint. Similarly for the assembly and testing department, the situation can be expressed, $4X + 2Y \leqslant 64$.

The whole expression can now be gathered together in this way in terms of weekly activity:

maximize $40X + 48Y = (B)$ benefit as described

subject to:

$3X + 6Y \leqslant 120$ (casting and welding)
$4X + 2Y \leqslant 64$ (assembly and testing)

and

$X \geqslant 0$ and $Y \geqslant 0$.

These latter two restrictions are necessary to prevent a solution occurring where X could be produced at a negative cost of Y and vice versa.

Having now set up the mathematical form which allows a solution to be advanced, it is convenient to see the problems expressed graphically. A graph is drawn with axes of X and Y Evminors and Ronmajors (see Fig. 12.1). On this graph are plotted the two departmental constraints which would show all combinations of Ss and Ys, the two limits of which are set by calculation of the number of Xs made if no Ys at all were made and the other limit would likewise be calculated from an assumption of no Xs made at all and all hours devoted to Ys.

For the casting and welding department this would be

$3X + 0Y = 120,$ $X = 40$
$0X + 6Y = 120,$ $Y = 20$

and for the assembly and testing department the figures are

$4X + 0Y = 64,$ $X = 16$
$0X + 2Y = 64,$ $Y = 32$

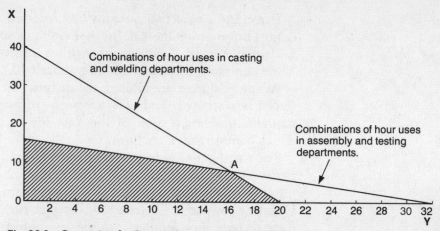

Fig. 12.1 Constraints for Evron Ltd expressed graphically

The shaded area is the feasible solution area as it is only in here that the requirements for each product can be met in terms of hours in *both* departments. At point A all resources are used in both departments. Furthermore, since the slope of a straight line is a constant the exchange rate between X and Y can be calculated in the following manner in the case of the casting and welding department

$$\frac{\text{The change in } X}{\text{The change in } Y} \qquad \frac{X_2 - X_1}{Y_2 - Y_1}$$

Taking any two points $(0 - 40)$ and $(20 - 0)$

$$\frac{0 - 40}{20 - 0} = -2$$

This represents the marginal rate of substitution of Evminors for Ronmajors. For every Ronmajor two Evminors have to be given up.

For the assembly and testing department the marginal rate of substitution (slope of line) is as follows.

Taking away two points as previously

$$\frac{0 - 16}{32 - 0} = \frac{-1}{2}$$

which means that for every Ronmajor put through the assembly and testing department one half Evminor has to be given up.

A solution can now be attempted by reading off from the graph the point of intersection of the two constraint lines.

With sufficient accuracy in graphing technique these would be found to be

$$X = 8 \quad \text{and} \quad Y = 16$$

so that the profit maximization function could be calculated:

$$[£(40 \times 8) = 320] + [£(48 \times 16) = 768] = \underline{£1,088}$$

Within the shaded area of Fig. 12.1, the feasible region, any combination can be achieved but patently some solutions would leave resources unused; so a few trial-and-error attempts based on the marginal rates of substitution should be undertaken to verify the accuracy of this solution as a producer of maximum profit. Similarly, progress to greater quantities than point A admits cannot be undertaken as either of the constraints would hold.

Finally, it must be clearly stated that when faced with a real problem of this type a graphical solution is hardly to be advised and is only included here because of the useful insights that it affords as a teaching method. More explicitly mathematical solutions are available. In the above case the total use of all scarce resources is indicated by the intersection of the two constraint lines so that they can be restated as equations rather than as inequalities:

Casting and welding department $3X + 6Y = 120$
Assembly and testing department $4X + 2Y = 64$

and this can be solved as a simultaneous equation to yield $X = 8$ and $Y = 16$.

Once the number of constraints is greater than two, additional features have to be included and more advanced methods of solving the relevant equation adopted. However, it is not proposed to pursue these here as they fall outside the scope of an introductory text.

Question 12

Clamart Company Ltd operates a car valet scheme. They accept bookings from clients who wish to have their cars thoroughly cleaned and offer two services, the normal and the super. The processes involved are split into two operations: first, external cleaning and second, internal cleaning. Because of the type of polishing and buffing machinery used, the operations are separate, and resources cannot be switched from one process to the other. The number of hours available in the interior cleaning section is 360 in any week and a normal service takes four hours in this section whilst a super service takes five hours. The number of hours available in the exterior cleaning section in any week amounts to 540. In this department a Normal service takes ten hours while a Super service take 6 hours.

After allowing for the variable cost element in each service, the contribution amounts to £2.00 for a Normal service and £3.00 for a Super service. Before accepting bookings, Clamart Company Ltd wishes to know how many of each type of service it should accept as there are known to be many potential clients waiting to use both of the services.

Required
(1) Set out a linear programme which clearly indicates the company's objectives and constraints.
(2) Graph the data set out in the above problem.
(3) Suggest a use of resources compatible with the company's objectives, based on:
   (a) Graphical methods.
   (b) Algebraic methods.

Question 13
Beekley, Inc., manufactures widgets, gadgets and trinkets and has asked for advice in determining the best production mix for its three products. Demand for the company's products is excellent and management finds that it is unable to meet potential sales with existing plant capacity.

Each product goes through three operations: milling, grinding and painting. The effective weekly departmental capacities in minutes are: milling, 10,000; grinding, 14,000; painting, 10,000.

The following data are available on the three products:

	Selling price per unit	Variable cost per unit	Per unit production time (in minutes)		
	£	£	Milling	Grinding	Painting
Widgets	5.25	4.45	4	8	4
Gadgets	5.00	3.90	10	4	2
Trinkets	4.50	3.30	4	8	2

Required
Determine the following in equation form:

(1) The objective function.
(2) The capacity constraint.
(3) The non-negativity requirements.

(ACIPA adapted)

The control of profitability relies emphatically on an information-monitoring system in which data relating to actual performance may be compared with data relating to planned performance, so that any significant variances may be spotted rapidly, investigated, and, if possible, corrected by management action. From an accounting point of view, the control of profitability really means monitoring the budget plan as an action plan and investigating the possible causes for any variances between planned and actual performance. In effect, the accountant is concerned with the following tasks:

(1) Monitoring that output is running at the planned level, that costs are no higher than anticipated, and that any significant variances in output and cost levels are noted, investigated and reported to management.
(2) Monitoring that the output is being sold at the planned level, that the planned revenue is no less than anticipated, and that any significant variances in sales volume and revenues are noted, investigated and reported to management.

This chapter therefore is addressed to an examination of the means whereby the accountant is able to perform the above tasks. The first part of the chapter is thus concerned with the control of costs, and the second is addressed to the control of revenue.

We discussed the problem of budgeting for profitability in Chapter 11, and noted the importance attached to forecasts of future revenue and future costs in the process of formulating the budget plan. Indeed, the realization of the budget plan implies that the forecasted revenues and forecasted costs will be reflected in the financial results themselves.

The control of profitability has several different aspects. It requires an organizational framework which is itself effective in securing the performance of tasks. It depends also on maintaining an efficient use of plant capacity and maintaining a level of technical and manufacturing efficiency. It relies heavily on external factors bearing directly on the capability of the firm to maintain output and sales. Clearly, these aspects raise very large issues and are mentioned here to preclude the possibility that readers may think that accounting control systems *by themselves* are sufficient to control profitability.

Control of costs

The reader will recall that the budgets are constructed on the basis of estimates of expenditure prepared by departments in relation to planned levels of output or activity. These estimates are usually based on predetermined costs—called standard costs—which relate to the detailed activities involved in production. It will be recalled that the cost accounting framework examined in Chapter 9 was designed to attach costs to units of production. Hence, standard costs are intended to impose standards of performance on the manner in which units of output are produced.

The control of costs is addressed, therefore, to the problem of cost efficiency in relation to planned levels of output. This efficiency is established in the first instance in the manner in which standard costs are determined. Any bias introduced at this stage may well accumulate into a significant level of budget slack, which will reflect the relative financial inefficiency implied in the use of organizational resources under these conditions. On the other hand, too much counter-biasing to prevent slack when standard costs are determined may well have harmful effects on attitudes throughout the organization by suggesting standards of performance which are known to be unattainable. Bias may be unintentional when it is caused through forecasting errors: it is intentional when those responsible for providing information for setting performance standards seek to build into this information some spare or surplus capacity. Hence, the determination of standard costs and budgeted costs has both quantitative and behavioural implications of considerable importance for cost efficiency. In this book we are concerned mainly with the quantitative aspects, which really means getting the numbers right.

Given that unit costs of production under the conventional absorption costing method consist of both direct and overhead costs, it follows that the unit costs of production will vary according to different output levels. This is because overhead costs contain a significant proportion of fixed costs which, expressed as fixed overhead costs per unit of output, will fluctuate as the output level itself varies. Hence, monitoring cost efficiency under conditions of fluctuating output levels calls for a system of flexible budgeting which will express both standard and budgeted costs in terms of different output levels.

This chapter is divided into the following topics: the nature of standard costs; the special difficulties created by overhead costs, which were mentioned above; and flexible budgeting.

Standard costing

Standard costs are predetermined costs based on what costs are expected to be in the accounting period to which the budget relates. Basically, a system of standard costing is one which records and accumulates costs in the form of standard costs as well as actual costs. Its objectives are twofold. First, to establish standard costs as measures against which to evaluate performance and to assume that these costs are being attained for such purposes as profit measurement, pricing, etc. Second, to highlight variances between actual costs and standard costs only as *exceptions*, thereby permitting management and accountants to focus their attention on the behaviour of costs *only* when actual costs diverge from standard costs. This leads to a better control of costs and hence profitability through the identification of variances, and to the supply of more informative profit statements illustrating the profit impact of variances by showing excessive costs as waste and cost savings as gains. Figure 13.1 illustrates the flow of costs under a standard cost accounting system.

Standard costs are applied to the three major categories of production costs: materials, labour and factory overheads. The *standard costs of raw materials* per unit consists of two elements — quantity and price. The standard quantity is generally developed by engineers and reflects the most economical use of materials consistent with product design and quality. An allowance for spoilage in the manufacturing process should express what amounts only to normal and unavoidable waste. Likewise, the *standard cost of labour* per unit of output consists of two elements—the standard time, expressed in standard hours or proportion of the standard hour required per unit of output, and the standard hourly wage rate. Finally, the standard overhead cost is derived from an estimate of the overhead costs which should be incurred at a particular volume of activity.

At the heart of a standard costing system is the *standard cost sheet*, which reflects the predetermined or estimated costs of what one unit of the product would cost if it were produced efficiently. It includes detailed estimates of material quantities and prices, labour quantities and rates, and factory overheads expressed also as quantities and rates. These details provide a benchmark for assessing the efficiency with which the product is being produced in terms of actual quantities and costs.

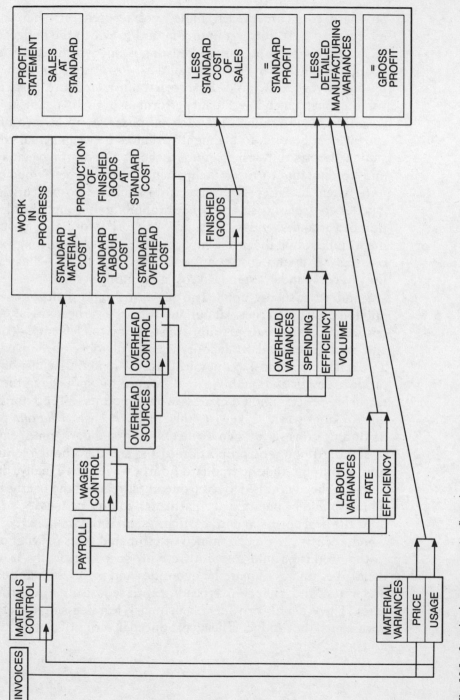

Fig. 13.1 Standard cost accounting flow chart

Question 1

The Middleton Company produces a single product in lots of 1,000. To manufacture each unit of this product 10 kg of material X and 10 kg of material Y are the standard quantities required. The standard labour cost per unit is as follows:

Department 1: 1 hour at £2.20   Department 2: 1 hour at £2.60

The manufacturing overhead cost budget for the year showed the following data:

Plant operating capacity	60%	80%	100%
Budgeted factory overheads	£48,000	£57,600	£64,000

The plant-operating capacity for the coming year is expected to be 60%. The maximum output capacity of the plant is 24,000 units per annum.

The price of materials purchased varies according to the size of contracts placed during the year as indicated in the following schedule:

Material X		Material Y	
Quantity contracted for:	Price per kg	Quantity contracted for:	Price per kg
Less than 100,000 kilos	£1.20	Less than 250,000 kilos	£2.00
100,000–250,000 kilos	1.00	250,000–350,000 kilos	1.80
250,000–350,000 kilos	0.80	350,000–450,000 kilos	1.60
Over 350,000 kilos	0.60	Over 450,000 kilos	1.50

Required

From the information given above, prepare a standard cost sheet for 1,000 units of output. Use parallel columns showing the comparative standard costs for each of the three capacity levels.

The analysis of variances

Direct materials and direct labour variances

The direct materials variance consists of two elements—a price variance and a usage variance, and may be calculated as follows:

Price Variance

(actual quantity × actual price) − (actual quantity × standard price)

Usage Variance

(actual quantity × standard price) − (standard quantity × standard price)

Hence, the direct materials variance is:

Price variance + usage variance.

The direct labour variance also consists of two elements—a wage rate variance and an efficiency variance, and may be calculated as follows:

Wage Rate Variance

(actual hours × actual rate) − (actual hours × standard rate)

Efficiency Variance

(actual hours × standard rate) − (standard hours

× standard rate)

Hence, the direct labour variance is:

wage rate variance + efficiency variance

A variance is described as favourable where the formula leads to a negative number, that is, where the standard set is greater than the actual results. A variance is described as unfavourable where the formula leads to a positive number, that is, when the actual result is greater than the standard. Thus, the direct materials price variance would be favourable where the actual price is less than the standard price. By contrast, it would be unfavourable where the actual price is greater than the standard price.

It is evident that in the case of the direct materials variance, the price and the usage variance may be self-cancelling to a degree. Hence the importance of analysing these component variations when examining the direct materials variance. The same applies in the analysis of the direct labour variance.

The following example illustrates the manner in which these variances may be calculated.

Example 1

The Williamson Manufacturing Company produces one product—widgets. The standard cost sheet for a widget shows the following data:

Standard cost per unit

Direct materials:
    2 kg of material A at £0.90 per kg
Direct wages:
    0.50 hours at £2.00 per hour.

During January, the following data were collected:

Units produced	500
Material A used in production	1,100 kg
Material A purchased	1,200 kg
Price paid	£1.00 per kg
Direct labour hours worked	260
Actual wage rate per direct labour hour	£2.05 per hour.

Required

Calculate the direct material and the direct labour variances.

Suggested Solution

(1) <u>Direct materials variance</u>

	£
Material price variance	
Actual quantity purchased × actual purchase price	
(1,200 kg × £1.00)	1,200
less: Actual quantity purchased × standard purchase price	
(1,200 kg × £0.90)	<u>1,080</u>
Variance owing to price (actual price greater than standard)	<u><u>120 U</u></u>
Alternative calculation:	
Actual price paid per kg	£1.00
less: Standard price per kg	<u>0.90</u>
Variance per kg (unfavourable)	£0.10
× actual quantity purchased	<u>1,200</u>
Material price variance	£ <u><u>120 U</u></u>

	£
Material usage variance	
Actual quantity used × standard purchase price	
(1,100 kg × £0.90)	£990
less: Standard quantity in actual production × standard price	
(550 widgets × 2 kg) × £0.90	<u>900</u>
Variance owing to usage (actual usage greater than standard)	£ <u><u>90 U</u></u>
Alternative calculations:	
Actual quantity used in production	1,100 kg
less: Standard quantity in actual production	<u>1,000 kg</u>
Variance in quantity used	100 kg
× standard price per kg	£0.90
Material usage variance	<u><u>£90 U</u></u>

Direct material variance	
Price variance + usage variance =	
(£120 U + £90 U) =	<u><u>£210 U</u></u>

(2) <u>Direct labour variance</u>

	£
Wage rate variance	
Actual hours worked × actual rate	£533
(260 hours × £2.05)	
less: Actual hours worked × standard rate	
(260 hours × £2.00)	<u>520</u>
Wage rate variance (actual rate in excess of standard)	<u><u>£13 U</u></u>

Alternative calculation:

	Actual wage	£2.05
less:	Standard wage rate	2.00
	Variance in wage rate	0.05
	× actual hours worked	260
	Wage rate variance	£13 U

Labour efficiency variance £

	Actual hours worked × standard rate	
	(260 hours × £2.00)	520
less:	Standard hours based on actual production	
	× standard rate	
	(500 widgets × 0.5 hours) × £2.00	500
	Labour efficiency variance (actual rate in excess of standard)	£20 U

Alternative calculation:

	Actual hours worked	260
less:	Standard hours in production	250
	Variance in hours	10
	× Standard wage rate	£2.00
	Labour efficiency variance	£20 U

Direct labour variance

Wage rate variance + Labour efficiency variance
£13 U + £20 U = £33 U

Question 2

Using the prime cost data given below for March, you are required to calculate the following variances:

(i) Materials cost: material price; material usage.
(ii) Wages cost: wages rate; labour efficiency.

Standard prime cost data for one unit of product Z are as follows:

	Ref.	Kg	Price per kg £
Materials:	DM1	6	1.50
	DM2	10	0.60

	Grade	Hours	Rate per hour £
Wages	A	8	1.00
	B	5	0.80

The following actual data for the month of March concerning the prime cost of Product Z are given:

Material purchased and consumed:

Ref.	Kg	Price per kg £
DM1	62,400	1.40
DM2	103,000	0.55

There was no stock of raw material at either the beginning or the end of the month.

Wages grade	Hours	Paid Rate per hour £
A	79,800	1.10
B	50,500	0.75

Units produced: 10,200   (ICMA)

The accounting disposition of variances

Standard costs should be integrated with the financial accounting records in order to facilitate the preparation of meaningful management reports. This integration is effected by means of the double-entry principle, which permits the interlocking of the standard costing system with the financial accounting system. Stocks of raw materials, work-in-progress and finished goods are recorded at the standard cost. Figure 13.1 (page 358) illustrates the flow of standard costs, and the manner in which this flow is related to the transformation of stocks from raw materials to finished goods. At the same time, the costs of acquiring the resources actually used are recorded in the financial accounting system, and the integration of the two systems leads to differences between standard costs and actual costs emerging as variances. The variances not only have to be investigated but must be incorporated rationally in the integrated accounting system. In effect, they are recorded in separate variance accounts, which provide the required control information for management purposes. An unfavourable variance is shown as a debit in the appropriate variance account, and a favourable variance is recorded as a credit in the appropriate variance account. The treatment of direct materials and direct labour costs would be as follows:

(1) Direct materials cost

(a) *Purchase of materials*

Debit materials account with materials at standard cost.

Credit creditors account at actual cost.

Debit or credit the difference between standard cost and actual cost to the materials price variance account. Thus, an unfavourable variance would be debited and a favourable variance would be credited to the materials price variance account.

Example 2

Ten units of material Y were purchased for £20. The standard cost was £18. The credit to the creditors account is £20 analysed as consisting of £18 at standard cost and £2 unfavourable price variance.

Creditors account			
			£
		Materials account	18
		Price variance account	2

Materials account			
	£		
Creditors account	18		

Price variance account			
	£		
Creditors account	2		

As may be seen, debiting the acquisition of stocks to the materials account at standard cost immediately reveals the existence of a price variance, should there be a difference between standard price and actual price. When large stocks are held, the attention of management is drawn to the dimension of the variance much sooner than would be the case if the price variance were only known at the time of issue of stock to production.

(b) *The issue of material*

Debit work-in-progress account with the material issued at the standard quantity at standard price.

Credit the materials account with the actual material issued at the standard price.

Debit or credit the difference between the standard quantity and the actual quantity at standard price to the materials usage variance account.

Example 3

Five units of material Y were issued to Job 101. The standard quantity for this job was four units and the standard price was £1.8 per unit. The work-in-progress account for 101 is debited with £7.2 (four units at £1.8), the materials account is credited with £9 (five units at £1.8), and the difference of £1.8 is debited as an unfavourable usage variance to the materials usage variance account.

Materials account		
		£
	Work-in-progress account	
	—Job 101	7.2
	Materials usage	
	variance account	1.8

Work-in-progress account—Job 101	
	£
Materials account	7.2

Materials usage variance account	
	£
Materials account	1.8

(2) Direct labour cost

Debit wages account with actual wages paid.

Credit cash account with actual wages paid.

Debit work-in-progress account with the standard costs of labour.

Credit the wages account with the standard cost of labour.

Debit or credit the appropriate variance accounts with the difference between the standard wage and the actual wage cost incurred, as follows:

Debit or credit the wage rate variance account.
Credit or debit the wages account.
Debit or credit the labour efficiency variance account.
Credit or debit the wages account.

(3) Completion of job

Debit the finished goods account with the standard cost of production.

Credit work-in-progress account with the standard cost of finished goods.

Question 3
Using the data given in Question 2, show the entries you would make in the following accounts: creditors, materials, wages, work-in-progress, materials price variance, materials usage variance, wage rate variance, labour efficiency variance.

Question 4
Wellington Manufacturing Co. Ltd makes two products, X and Y, and has established the following standards for materials and direct labour in respect of each product:

	Product X kg	Product Y kg	Price per kg £
Direct materials—A	40	80	0.6
Direct material —B	60	20	0.8

	Hours	Hours	Rate per hour £
Direct wages —Cutting	2	4	2.0
—Assembling	10	5	1.6

The actual costs incurred during the previous month were as follows:

	Product X kg used	Product Y kg used	Price per kg £
Direct material—A	41,000	115,000	0.65
Direct material—B	63,000	29,000	0.75

	Hours	Hours	Rate per hour £
Direct wages—Cutting	1,950	5,950	1.9
—Assembling	9,850	7,400	1.7

The actual number of units produced were: Product X   1,010 units
Product Y   1,550 units

Required
Calculate the following variances and show their accounting disposition:

Direct materials price variance.
Direct materials usage variance.
Wage rate variance.
Labour efficiency variance.

Control of factory overheads

Factory overhead costs are of two types—variable factory overheads and fixed factory overheads. Cost standards for the variable factory overheads are set in the same way as those for direct materials and direct labour, and the variances employed in the control of variable factory overheads consist of a spending variance and an efficiency variance. Given that fixed overhead costs are fixed for a range of output, the fixed factory overhead variance is of little significance at the operating level. The fixed factory overhead variance consists of a spending variance, which is the difference between actual expenditure and budgeted expenditure, and a volume variance, which relates to the under or over-absorption of overheads. The responsibility for the fixed overhead spending variance lies usually at top management level, while the fixed overhead volume variance is usually related to the effectiveness of the sales function rather than to that of the production function. The constituent variances of the total overhead variances are illustrated in Fig. 13.2 below.

In Chapter 9, we discussed the problem of choosing a suitable basis for absorbing overhead costs into product costs. It was noted that the number of units produced, the number of direct labour hours worked or the number of machine hours spent on a unit of the product may be appropriate to particular circumstances. Clearly, where the units of product are not homogeneous, it is impracticable to use the volume of output as a basis for absorbing overhead costs. This problem is overcome by the use of standard hours. A standard hour measures the amount of work which should be performed in one hour. It should be stressed that a standard hour is a *unit of work*, not time, which enables the output of different types of products to be referred to a common denominator for the purpose of measuring output.

In effect, the standard hour provides means of converting production into standard hours and imposing performance standards in terms of the number of standard hours allowed for a given output. This is achieved by multiplying the number of units to be completed by the standard time allowed for each unit.

Example 4

The Office Furniture Department of Pressed Steel Manufacturing Co, produces chairs, desks and office tables. The following table shows the total work content of each type of product of a particular month measured in standard hours:

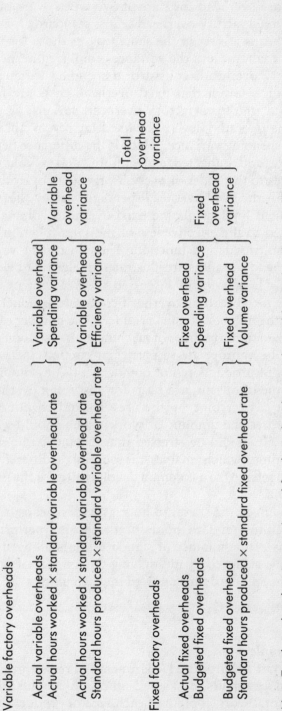

Variable factory overheads

Actual variable overheads
Actual hours worked × standard variable overhead rate } Variable overhead Spending variance

Actual hours worked × standard variable overhead rate
Standard hours produced × standard variable overhead rate } Variable overhead Efficiency variance

Variable overhead variance

Fixed factory overheads

Actual fixed overheads
Budgeted fixed overheads } Fixed overhead Spending variance

Budgeted fixed overhead
Standard hours produced × standard fixed overhead rate } Fixed overhead Volume variance

Fixed overhead variance

Total overhead variance

Note: Total overhead variance = (actual fixed overhead + actual variable overhead) − (standard hours produced × variable overhead rate + fixed overhead rate).

Fig. 13.2 Factory overhead variance

Product	Standard hours per unit	Quantity produced	Output in standard hours
Chairs	10	300	3,000
Desks	25	200	5,000
Office tables	20	100	2,000
			10,000

These data illustrate that the department manager is allowed 10,000 standard hours for the production which he attained. Whether the department actually required more or less than 10,000 standard hours to reach this output is a measure of its productive efficiency. Assume that only 9,500 standard hours were required to produce this output, and that the departmental variable overhead rate is £1.00 per standard direct labour hour (or machine hour as appropriate), the resulting favourable variable overhead efficiency variance will be £500 (500 standard hours × £1.00).

Example 5
The following data applied to the machining department of Better Products Ltd:

	Flexible budgets			Budget formula
Standard direct labour hours (SDLH)	4,000	5,000	6,000	
Variable factory overhead:	£	£	£	£
Indirect material	4,000	5,000	6,000	1.00 per SDLH
Inspection	1,600	2,000	2,400	0.40
Cutting tools	400	500	600	0.10
	6,000	7,500	9,000	1.50 per SDLH
Fixed factory overhead:				
Supervision	2,500	2,500	2,500	2,500 per month
Depreciation	1,500	1,500	1,500	1,500
Insurance	1,000	1,000	1,000	1,000
	5,000	5,000	5,000	5,000 per month

Normal activity level = 5,000 standard hours
= 2,500 units of product.

The data applicable to the previous month's operations are as follows:

Actual output for the month		2,300 units
Actual direct labour hours worked		4,700
Variable overhead costs:	£	£
Indirect material	4,700	
Inspection	1,750	
Cutting tools	430	6,880
Fixed overhead costs:		
Supervision	2,600	
Depreciation	1,450	
Insurance	1,050	5,100

Required
Calculate the overhead variances for the previous month's operations.

Suggested Solution
(1) Standard direct labour hours in normal activity level

$$\frac{5,000 \text{ standard hours}}{2,500 \text{ units of output}} = 2 \text{ standard hours}$$

Therefore, standard direct labour hours in actual output

2,300 units × 2 hours = 4,600 standard hours

(2) Variable factory overhead variance:

	£
(a) *Spending variance:*	
Actual variable overheads	6,880
less: Actual hours worked × standard variable overhead rate	
4,700 hours × £1.50 (£7,500 ÷ 5,000)	7,050
Spending variance	170 F

	£
(b) *Efficiency variance:*	
Actual hours worked × standard variable overhead rate	7,050
less: Standard hours in actual output × standard variable overhead rate	
4,600 × £1.50 (£7,500 ÷ 5,000)	6,900
Efficiency variance	150 U

(c) *Variable factory overhead variance:*
Spending variance + efficiency variance
£170 F + £150 U   20 F

(3) Fixed factory overhead variance:

	£
(a) *Spending variance:*	
Actual fixed overheads incurred	5,100
Budgeted fixed overheads	5,000
Spending variance	100 U

	£
(b) *Volume variance:*	
Budgeted fixed overheads	5,000
less: Standard hours in actual output × standard fixed overhead rate	
4,600 hours × £1.00 (£5,000 ÷ 5,000)	4,600
Volume variance	400 U

(c) *Fixed factory overhead variance:*
Spending variance + volume variance
£100 U   +   £400 U   500 U

Question 5

Using the data given in the foregoing example, calculate the variable factory overhead variance for the individual cost items relating to the machining department of Better Products Ltd. Use the information derived from your computations to complete the following performance report:

Variable cost	Costs incurred	Budget allowance at standard time	Total variance	Spending variance	Efficiency variance
	£	£	£	£	£
Indirect material	4,700				
Inspection	1,750				
Cutting tools	430				
	6,880	6,900	20 F	170 F	150 U

Question 6

The Bronson Company manufactures a fuel additive which has a stable selling price of £40 per drum. Since losing a government contract, the company has been producing and selling 80,000 drums per month, 50% of normal capacity. Management expects to increase production to 140,000 drums in the coming fiscal year.

In connection with your examination of the financial statements of the Bronson Company for the year ended 30 September 19X0, you have been asked to review some computations made by Bronson's cost accountant. Your working papers disclose the following about the company's operations:

(1) Standard costs per drum of product manufactured:

Materials:
8 kg of miracle mix	£16
1 empty drum	1
	£17
Direct labour—1 hour	5
Factory overhead	6

(2) Costs and expenses during September 19X0:

Miracle mix:
500,000 kg purchased at cost of £950,000;
650,000 kg used
Empty drums:
94,000 purchased at cost of £94,000;
80,000 used
Direct labour:
82,000 hours worked at cost of £414,100

Factory overhead:	£
Depreciation of building and machinery (fixed)	210,000
Supervision and indirect labour (semi-variable)	460,000
Other factory overhead (variable)	98,000
	768,000

(3) Other factory overhead was the only actual overhead which varied from the overhead budget for the September level of production; actual other factory overhead was £98,000 and the budgeted amount was £90,000.

(4) At normal capacity of 160,000 drums per month, supervision and indirect labour costs are expected to be £570,000. All cost functions are linear.

(5) None of the September 19X0 cost variance is expected to occur proportionally in future months. For the next fiscal year, the cost standards department expects the same standard usage of materials and direct labour hours. The average prices expected are: £2.10 per kilo of miracle mix, £1 per empty drum and £5.70 per direct labour hour. The current flexible budget of factory overhead costs is considered applicable to future periods without revision.

Required

(a) Prepare a schedule computing the following variances for September 19X0:
  (1) Materials price variance.
  (2) Materials usage variance.
  (3) Labour rate variance.
  (4) Labour usage (efficiency) variance.
  (5) Variable overhead spending variance.
  (6) Variable overhead efficiency variance.
  (7) Volume variance.

(b) Prepare a schedule of the actual manufacturing cost per drum of product expected at production of 140,000 drums per month— using the following cost categories: materials, direct labour, fixed factory overhead, and variable factory overhead.

(AICPA adapted)

Question 7

Ross Shirts, Inc., manufactures short-sleeved and long-sleeved men's shirts for large stores. Ross produces a single-quality shirt in lots to each customer's order and attaches the store's own label to each. The standard costs for a dozen long-sleeved shirts are:

		£
Direct materials	24 metres @ £0.55	13.20
Direct labour	3 hours @ £2.45	7.35
Manufacturing overhead	3 hours @ £2.00	6.00
Standard cost per dozen		26.55

During October 19X9, Ross worked on three orders for long-sleeved shirts. Job cost records for the month disclose the following:

Lot	Units in lot	Material used	Hours worked
30	1,000 dozen	24,100 metres	2,980
31	1,700 dozen	40,440 metres	5,130
32	1,200 dozen	28,825 metres	2,890

The following information is also available:

(1) Ross purchased 95,000 metres of material during the month at a cost of £53,200. The materials price variance is recorded when goods are purchased and all stocks are carried at standard cost.

(2) Direct labour incurred amounted to £27,500 during October. According to payroll records, production employees were paid £2.50 per hour.

(3) Overhead is applied on the basis of direct labour hours. Manufacturing overhead totalling £22,850 was incurred during October, of which £9,700 was fixed and £13,150 variable.

(4) A total of £288,000 was budgeted for overhead for the year 19X9 based on estimated production at the plant's normal capacity of 48,000 dozen shirts per year. Overhead is 40% fixed and 60% variable at this level of production.

(5) There was no work in progress at 1 October. During October lots 30 and 31 were completed and all material was issued for lot 32 and it was 80% completed as to labour.

Required

(1) Prepare a schedule computing the standard cost for October 19X9 of lots 30, 31 and 32.

(2) Prepare a schedule computing the materials price variances for October 19X9 and indicate whether the variance is favourable or unfavourable.

(3) Prepare schedules computing (and indicating whether the variances are favourable or unfavourable) for each lot produced during October 19X9 the:
(a) Materials usage variance in metres.
(b) Labour efficiency variance in hours.
(c) Labour rate variance in £.

(4) Prepare a schedule computing the:
  (a) Variable overhead spending variance.
  (b) Variable overhead efficiency variance.
  (c) Fixed overhead spending variance.
  (d) Volume variance.
  (e) Total overhead variance.   (AICPA adapted)

Control of revenues

Budgets are based on estimates of likely revenues and likely expenses and reflect the financial implications of production and sales at the anticipated level. The tradition of accounting is very much focused on the control of costs. As we saw earlier in this chapter, the accountant is able to set up standards of performance for different output levels in terms of budgeted expenditure, and these standards are themselves based upon the concept of the standard cost, which is a predetermined unit cost of production.

Not all costs are, of course, subject to control. Thus, it is possible to control such costs which relate directly to inefficient production in a factory. However, wage rates and the market price of raw materials as well as a whole range of services, such as electricity, gas, etc., are not subject to the firm's control. Nevertheless, the accountant is able to identify uncontrollable variances and to make due allowance for the possibility of cost increases.

The position is rather different as regards the control of revenue. This depends very much on the market, which is the major source of uncontrollable variances. As a result, stress is placed on trying to obtain an initially reliable forecast of sales at a given price. The role of the accountant is one of trying to analyse the sales performance as a function of the organization. This is achieved by variance analysis applied to sales. There are three main variances:

(1) *The sales price variance:*

  (actual contribution per unit − standard contribution per unit)
  × number of units sold

(2) *The sales volume variance:*

  (actual units sold − budgeted units) × standard contribution per unit

(3) *The sales mix variance:*

  (actual units sold − actual total sales in budgeted mix proportions)
  × (standard contribution per unit of each product)

Question 8
The Hallam Steel Co., is engaged in the manufacture of three products, X, Y and Z. The data which relate to January 19X0 are as follows:

Budgeted sales: Product X 2,000 units at £12 (standard contribution margin £6)

Product Y 2,000 units at £8 (standard contribution margin £4)

Product Z 2,000 units at £5 (standard contribution margin £1)

Actual sales: Product X 1,500 units for £15,000
Product Y 2,500 units for £17,500
Product Z 3,500 units for £21,000

Required
Calculate the following variances:

(1) The sales price variance.
(2) The sales volume variance.
(3) The sales mix variance.

Use the format given below for your answer.

	(a)	(b)	(c)	(d)	(e)	(f)	(g)	(h)
Product	Actual contribution £	Actual quantity Units	Standard contribution margin £	Value £	Actual quantity in standard proportions Units	Standard contribution £	Value £	Budgeted margin £
X								
Y								
Z								

Sale price variance
Sales
Sales mix variance

PART 3
Case Problems and Analysis ─────────

Introduction

The purpose of Parts 1 and 2 was to outline the practices associated with financial and management accounting, and to relate these practices to a set of basic objectives which may be regarded as constituting the elements of a theoretical framework of accounting.

In a very fundamental sense, this text may be identified with the view that the essence of accounting is to be found in the provision of information which is directly relevant and useful to the management of organizations and all the functions which form an integral part of the management of economic and social resources. Although the proprietorship concept of the firm has been adopted for the purposes of examining financial accounting practices, shareholders and investors are really concerned with the manner in which the measurement of the firm's resources affects the value of their investments. Indeed, financial and management accounting are not two separate aspects of the accounting function, but are integral elements of the function of providing information for decision-making about the allocation of resources to organizations and the use of resources within organizations.

Decision-making may be considered as being the last stage in the process of solving a problem. The manner in which a problem is perceived and understood, and the success which will attend the decision which attempts to solve that problem depends significantly on the quality and the relevance of available information. Herein lies the central importance of the accounting function.

Accordingly, this part has the following purposes:

(1) To place accounting in a problem-solving context in two senses:
    (a) Problem-solving as regards the generation of information.
    (b) Problem-solving in applying accounting information to the process of decision-making.
(2) To give insights into difficulties and complexities involved in decision-making and to analyse the usefulness of accounting information in that context.
(3) To provide a broad and realistic basis by which to understand the interdependence of financial and management accounting.
(4) To extend the range and experience of the knowledge contained in Parts 1 and 2 to a collection of problems of increasing complexity.

This part consists of eleven case problems and one case study, all of which raise several issues of importance for accounting theory and practice. To assist the reader to identify these issues, each case problem contains a preamble stating the issues involved. The questions on the case problems are graded in terms of their increasing complexity. By contrast, the case study requires the reader to analyse the issues involved, and the questions which are posed are not intended to be exhaustive. The case problems and the case study are as follows:

Case Problem 1   T. Albert
Case Problem 2   M. Primel
Case Problem 3   Mesland Supplies Limited
Case Problem 4   Thiron Manufacturing Company Limited
Case Problem 5   Inland Tours Limited
Case Problem 6   Latham Engineering Company Limited
Case Problem 7   Olivet Hardware Company Limited
Case Problem 8   Bartle plc
Case Problem 9   The Westbourne Company Limited
Case Problem 10   Jones Limited and Evans Limited
Case Study   Crimicar Components Limited

Case Problem 1: T. Albert

This problem is concerned with the following issues:

(1) The design of a financial accounting system and its operation.
(2) Recording financial accounting data.
(3) The control of financial assets and liabilities.
(4) Checking the accuracy of financial accounting operations.
(5) Extracting information from the financial accounting system.
(6) Analysing the financial results of a business.
(7) Discussing the relevance of financial accounting information to investors and managers of a business.

T. Albert commenced trading on 1 January 19X7 retailing clothes. His initial capital was a deposit of £15,000 in his account with the Westland Bank Limited. He rented shop premises and employed a full-time shop assistant. Albert devoted the whole of his time to managing the business. Transactions for January 19X7 were as follows:

No.	Date	Description
1	1st	Six months rent in advance paid by cheque £625.
2	1st	Collected £2,500 worth of clothes from The Unac Wholesale Company Ltd on one month's credit.

No.	Date	Description
3	1st	Withdrew £40 from the bank for a cash float.
4	2nd	Cash sales £45.
5	2nd	Annual Insurance paid in advance by cheque £24.
6	2nd	Received display equipment from Evron Fittings Ltd valued at £500 payable at the end of February 19X7.
7	3rd	Cash sales £112.
8	3rd	Took delivery of clothing invoiced at £1,600 from Tracas Fabrics Ltd.
9	4th	Wages paid by case £28.
10	5th	Cash sales £82.
11	5th	Banked £200.
12	8th	Returned Unac Wholsale Company defective goods which were invoiced at £120.
13	8th	Returned £12 in cash to customer whose trousers had split on first wearing.
14	9th	Received order for the supply of sports clothing to the value of £210 from the Newgate Education Authority and despatched the order.
15	9th	Cash sales £56.
16	10th	Paid cheque for purchase of £2,140 worth of goods direct from manufacturer's warehouse.
17	11th	Wages paid by cash £28.
18	12th	Cash sales £114.
19	14th	Paid electricity by cheque £18.
20	14th	Paid advertising by cheque £39.
21	14th	Cash sales £74.
22	15th	Supplied protective clothing to Bilden Construction Co. Ltd £350.
23	16th	Cash sales £28.
24	16th	Banked £200.
25	17th	Withdrew for personal use £50 from bank.
26	18th	Rates for 1 January to March 19X7 paid by cheque £240.
27	19th	Cash sales £208.
28	19th	Wages paid by cash £28.
29	21st	Received cheque for £150 on account from Bilden Construction Co. Ltd.
30	21st	Cash sales £38.
31	22nd	Cleaning expenses cash £13.
32	22nd	Cash sales £142.
33	23rd	Postage stamps purchased by cash £5.
34	24th	Banked £150.

No.	Date	Description
35	24th	Cash sales £16.
36	25th	Wages paid by cash £28.
37	25th	Cash sales £23.
38	26th	Paid on account to Unac Wholesale Company Ltd by cheque £1,500.
39	26th	Cash sales £51.
40	28th	Paid for tea, milk etc., £10 cash.
41	28th	Cash sales £15.
42	29th	Cash sales £49.
43	29th	Paid Tracas Fabrics Ltd by cheque £1,600
44	30th	Withdrew £60 from till for own use.
45	30th	Cash sales £37.
46	30th	Wages paid by cash £28.
47	31st	Cash sales £95.

Required
(1) Design a financial accounting system which would be suitable to the type of business conducted by T. Albert, and write a report to him advising him on the manner in which he ought to operate this system. Specify the books of accounts which he should purchase and the manner in which they should be entered.
(2) Assume that T. Albert has purchased the books of accounts which you have recommended, demonstrate the operation of the financial accounting system you have designed by entering all the transactions for January 19X7 in these books.
(3) Explain how the financial accounting system you have designed may be used for the purpose of financial control, and in particular, for the control of the following financial assets and liabilities:
(a) Cash.
(b) Debtors.
(c) Stock.
(d) Creditors.
(4) Explain how it is possible to check the accuracy with which the financial accounting system has been operated, and discuss any limitations associated with the control procedure you have in mind.
(5) Discuss the manner in which the financial accounting system may be used to provide T. Albert with the following information:
(a) The efficiency with which his business is being conducted.
(b) The profit which he is earning.
(c) The changes in the value of his business through time.
Illustrate your answer to this question by preparing a profit and loss account and a balance sheet for the month of January 19X7.

In this connection, you are advised that stock on hand at 31 January 19X7 is valued at cost at £5,080, and that an additional sum of £14 should be provided for electricity consumed during January 19X7. Ignore depreciation.

(6) Analyse the financial results for January 19X7 and comment upon these results.
(7) Discuss critically the relevance and the usefulness of the financial information contained in the profit statement and the balance sheet for January 19X7 to the decisions facing T. Albert both as the owner of the business and its manager.

Case Problem 2: M. Primel

This problem is concerned with the following issues:

(1) The purpose of profit determination.
(2) Problems arising in the process of measuring profits.
(3) Cash flow and accruals accounting.
(4) Depreciation and profit determination.
(5) Depreciation and the replacement of fixed assets.
(6) Stock valuation and profit determination.
(7) The case for and against cash-flow accounting and accruals accounting.
(8) Objectives of financial management and the role of accounting information.
(9) Economic and accounting concept of income.

M. Primel commenced business as a timber merchant two years ago. He had bought sawing equipment for £5,000 and a truck with lifting gear for £4,000 on the first day of business. He now began to realize that due to heavy use the sawing equipment would have to be replaced at the end of the third year and the truck at the end of the fourth year of use. On examining his bank statement, it became evident to him that he would have difficulty in financing the replacement of these assets. Primel's nephew James was studying accounting with a view to eventually qualify as an accountant. Primel took the opportunity of discussing his worries with his nephew at a family party.

'I can't understand it,' he said, 'I've been making profits and I've only taken out the profit I thought I was earning.'

'Can I come round tomorrow to see your profit and loss account?' suggested James.

'I haven't got any,' replied Primel. 'I know how much cash I make each month and simply take it out. I pay all my expenses on the nail and always get paid in cash for the timber I supply. As a result, I don't need to keep accounting records and to prepare profit and loss accounts to know what I am earning. Everything I want to know is in my bank statement.'

'What about the unsold timber which you have in the yard?' asked James.

'Oh, I take account of that at what I paid for it,' replied Primel.

'Listen, Uncle,' said James, 'unless you begin to keep your financial records on a proper basis, you will run into serious trouble. It is important that you should know exactly what is your profit before you decide how much you can afford to take out of the business. Besides, the income tax authorities will want a set of accounts from you. I'll write to you tomorrow and explain how you should calculate your profit and in particular how you should allow for depreciation and deal with closing stock.'

'I would be very grateful if you would,' replied Primel.

Required

(1) Write a letter to Primel suggesting how he should calculate his profit. Illustrate your explanation by a simple calculation and make up the figures which you require for this purpose. Explain in your letter how such a profit and loss account would assist Primel.

(2) Analyse the problems implied in providing for the depreciation of fixed assets. Consider, in particular, the problem of planning for the replacement of assets and providing the necessary funds for their replacement. Illustrate your answer by reference to the facts in this case.

(3) Examine the importance of stock valuation to the process of profit determination. In what sense is this issue of importance to Primel's problem?

(4) Consider the case for and against both cash-flow and accruals accounting. In this context, refer to the controversy between proponents of cash-flow accounting and defenders of accruals accounting. Discuss the view that cash-flow accounting is particularly relevant to financial management decisions, whereas accruals accounting is really concerned with profit determination. tion.

(5) Examine the limitations of accounting concepts of profit for the purposes of decision-making.

Case Problem 3: Mesland Supplies Limited

This problem is concerned with the following issues:

(1) Converting partial financial accounting systems to complete financial accounting data.
(2) Processing and recording financial accounting data.
(3) Accruals accounting and the treatment of accrued expenses.
(4) Adjustments for closing stock, depreciation, bad and doubtful debts.
(5) Treatment of discounts allowed and received.
(6) The cash book and the petty cash book.
(7) Preparation of financial statements—trial balance, profit and loss account and balance sheet.
(8) Control of debtors and creditors.
(9) Accounting conventions.
(10) Analysis of profitability.

Mesland Supplies Limited was established to operate a general supplies stores at a large camping site on the South Wales coast. A wide variety of goods are sold, ranging from foodstuffs to small items of boating and caravan equipment. Trading is generally conducted on a cash basis, but credit terms are allowed to some permanent site residents and to some site owners.

The company's accounting year runs to 31 December, but its trading activity is concentrated over the summer holiday period. The company's directors and sole shareholders Mike and Brenda Turner were unable to keep proper records during the boom season which occurred in 19X6, when an unusually long period of good weather brought many holidaymakers to the region. During the whole of this period, both Mike and Brenda were so busy that they were compelled to concentrate on serving customers and running the store. When the season closed at the end of September, they went on holiday to the Canary Islands, and on their return assembled as much information as possible with a view to preparing their annual accounts to 31 December 19X6.

The company's balance sheet as at 1 January 19X6 was as follows:

Mesland Supplies Limited
Balance sheet at 1 January 19X6

	Authorized £	Issued and fully paid £
Fixed assets		
Fittings as written down value		1,000
Motor van at written down value		800
		1,800
Current assets		
Stock at cost	7,254	
Debtors and prepayments	3,920	
Balance at bank	960	
Cash	40	
	12,174	
less Sundry trade creditors	3,016	9,158
		10,958
Capital and reserves		
Ordinary shares at £1 each	20,000	10,000
Profit and loss account		958
		10,958

A petty cash book had been kept in rough and it is summarized below:

	£		£
Balance at 1 January 19X6	40	Wages and salaries	3,048
Cash sales	32,838	Paid into bank	31,074
Receipts from debtors	4,918	Van petrol, oil and repairs	336
		Advertising	168
		Directors' salaries	2,702
		Sundry expenses	238
		Payment to creditors	208
		Balance at 31 December 19X6	22
	37,796		37,796

The bank statement had been reconciled with the cheque book stubs and pay-in counterfoils, and as a result the following cash summary had been drawn up:

	£		£
Balance at 1 January 19X6	960	Payments to trade creditors	33,188
Receipts from debtors	2,012	Purchase of motor van on 30	
Cash banked	31,074	September 19X6	2,000
Sale of motor van on		Purchase of shop fittings on	
30 September 19X6	600	31 March 19X6	1,200
Balance at 31 December		Rent, nine months to 30	
19X6	4,546	September 19X6	450
		Rates, eighteen months to 31	
		March 19X7	720
		Sundry expenses	892
		Vehicle tax, year to 31	
		December 19X6	40
		Van insurance, twelve	
		months to 30 September	
		19X7	80
		Advertising	622
	39,192		39,192

Further investigations brought to light the following information:

(1) At 31 December 19X6, inventory was worth £9,302, trade debtors were £4,040 and trade creditors were £3,086. There were also unpaid accounts of £82 for sundry expenses and £58 for advertising.

(2) There was an unpaid account of £74 for sundry expenses outstanding at 31 December 19X5.

(3) The insurance on the old van for the year ended 30 September 19X6 (which had been paid on 24 September 19X5) was £72.

(4) Depreciation is to be provided on shop fittings at 10% and on the motor van at 20% on closing balances.

(5) A provision for doubtful debts should be raised (at the end of the year) of 5% of trade debtors. During the year, bad debts amounting to £42 have been written off and are not included in the total of trade debtors at 31 December 19X6.

(6) During 19X6, discounts allowed amounted to £156 and discounts received to £792.

Required
(1) Examine the problems involved in converting the partial financial accounting system to a complete financial accounting system based on double-entry principle.

(2) Write a report to the directors of the company setting out recommendations regarding the type of financial accounting system which would be adequate for the company's needs and within the capability of its directors to operate. Make specific recommendations which would enable them to operate such a system without difficulty. Illustrate your recommendations by an appropriate chart of accounts.

(3) Process and record all the accounting data given above in the company's financial accounting system. For this purpose, establish all the accounts which will be required.

(4) Extract a trial balance as at 31 January 19X6 as a check upon the accuracy of manner in which data has been processed and recorded. Comment upon the usefulness of the trial balance as a control mechanism for accurate data processing, and examine any weaknesses which may be inherent in this control mechanism.

(5) Make such adjustments to the trial balance as are necessary to take account of accrued expenses. Illustrate the manner in which accrued expenses may be incorporated into the accounting system by means of the journal.

(6) Examine the theoretical problems implied in the accounting treatment of the undermentioned items:

> Closing stock.
> Depreciation.
> Bad debts.
> Doubtful debts.

Show how these accounts would appear on 31 December 19X6 when they have been completed as at that date on the basis of the information you are given.

(7) Discuss the means by which stricter control could be imposed on petty cash.

(8) Discuss the usefulness of a columnar cash book as a means of providing an integrated view of cash flows through the company. Refer also to the manner in which discounts would be treated, and illustrate your answer by processing the information given. You are recommended to use appropriate accounting stationery.

(9) Using the extended trial balance method, prepare a profit and loss account for the year ended 31 December 19X6 and balance sheet as at that date.

(10) Discuss the problems implied in the control of debtors and creditors, and illustrate your answer by completing appropriate control accounts.

(11) Name the accounting conventions which you have found to be most significant for the manner in which you have dealt with the questions given above, and examine the manner in which you have been influenced in the treatment of accounting data.

(12) Discuss critically the role of accounting conventions on the generation of financial accounting information.

(13) Use the limited information available to you to analyse the profitability of Mesland Supplies Limited during the year ended 31 December 19X6.

Case Problem 4: Thiron Manufacturing Company Limited

This problem is concerned with the following issues:

(1) Profit determination and the recognition of revenue.
(2) Accounting conventions.
(3) Cash versus accruals accounting.
(4) Product costing.
(5) Asset valuation.
(6) Analysis of profitability.
(7) Elements of the theory of finance.

The Thiron Manufacturing Company Limited was established on 1 January 19X7 for the purpose of making harpsichords. Miles Watson, the managing director had had 20 years' experience in the manufacture of pianos and harpsichords and was an acknowledged technical expert in this field. He had invested his life's savings of £15,000 in the company, and his decision to launch the company reflected his desire for complete independence. Nevertheless, his commitment to the company represented a considerable financial gamble, and he paid close attention to the management of its financial affairs and ensured that a careful record of all transactions was kept.

The company's activities during the year ended 31 December 19X7 were as follows:

(1) Four harpsichords had been built and sold for a total sum of £8,000. Watson calculated their cost of manufacture as follows:

	£
Materials	2,000
Labour	2,800
Overhead costs	800

(2) Two harpsichords were 50% completed at 31 December 19X7. Heavenly Music Limited had agreed to buy these two harpsichords for a total of £4,500 and had made a down payment

amounting to 20% of the agreed sale price. Watson estimated their costs of manufacture to 31 December 19X7 as follows:

	£
Materials	900
Labour	800
Overhead costs	100

(3) Two harpsichords had been rebuilt and sold for a total of £3,000. Watson paid £1,800 for them at an auction and had spent a further £400 on rebuilding them. The sale of these two harpsichords was made under a hire purchase agreement under which Thiron Manufacturing Company received £1,000 on delivery and two payments over the next two years plus interest of 15% on the outstanding balance.

At the end of the company's first financial year, Miles Watson was anxious that the company's net profit to 31 December 19X7 should be represented in the most accurate manner. There appeared to him to be several alternative bases by which the transactions for the year could be interpreted. It was clear to him that in simple terms, the net profit for the year should be calculated by deducting expenses from revenues. As far as cash sales were concerned he saw no difficulty. But how should the harpsichords which were 50% completed be treated? Should the value of the work done up to 31 December 19X7 be included in the profit of that year, or should it be carried forward to the next year when the work would be completed and the harpsichords sold? As regards the harpsichords sold under the hire purchase agreement, should profit be taken to 19X7 and spread over the years in which a proportion of the revenue is received?

Required

(1) Prepare a profit and loss account for the year ended 31 December 19X7 on a basis which would reflect conventional accounting principles.

(2) Examine the problems implied in the timing of the recognition of revenues and illustrate your answer by the facts in the case of Thiron Manufacturing Co.

(3) Discuss the significant accounting conventions which would be relevant to profit determination in this case, and discuss their limitations in this context.

(4) Discuss the nature of the financial accounting information which would be most relevant to the needs of Miles Watson. State the hypotheses on which you base your interpretation of his information needs.

(5) Prepare a cash flow statement for the year ended 31 December 19X7 and contrast the information which you derive from such

a statement with the profit and loss account which you have already prepared.

(6) Discuss the advantages and disadvantages of cash flow and accruals accounting.

(7) Examine the basis on which cost of the company's products is established, and explain the objectives of product costing. Do you consider that these objectives have been met by the manner in which harpsichords have been costed?

(8) Consider the problems implied in the valuation of harpsichords uncompleted at 31 December 19X7.

(9) On the basis of the information available, comment upon the profitability of the Thiron Manufacturing Company Limited.

(10) Evaluate the investment made by Miles Watson in the Thiron Manufacturing Company using such a discount rate as you consider to be relevant to the company, and assuming that the rate of interest on completely risk-free investments is 5% p.a.

(11) Discuss the alternative bases on which Miles Watson would wish to value the company solely as an investor. Make such assumptions as you wish to illustrate your argument.

Case Problem 5: Inland Tours Limited

This problem is concerned with the following issues:

(1) Preparing a cash budget.
(2) Cash budgeting and financial planning.
(3) Capital budgeting.
(4) Analysis of solvency and creditworthiness.
(5) Depreciation of fixed assets.
(6) Financing the replacement of fixed assets.

George Ingram had been a canal boat enthusiast for many years. He had spent all his spare time and cash on his converted barge. When his aunt died and left him £25,000, he immediately considered the possibility of turning his hobby into a business. He had long thought of owning several boats and hiring them out during the holiday season, and now it seemed that his dream could become a reality.

Ingram's first step was to establish that it would cost £30,000 to acquire three fully-equipped boats which would be suitable for his purpose, and he approached his bank for a loan to make up the difference. The bank manager said he was willing to help, but as a prior condition requested a forecast of his cash needs, for he believed that Ingram would require rather more than £5,000 to establish his business. The bank manager advised Ingram to employ an accountant to prepare a cash forecast in support of his application for a bank loan.

This suggestion was promptly acted upon, and subsequently Ingram had a meeting with Ronald Stockton, a partner in a firm of chartered accountants. Following this meeting, Stockton drew up a list of questions for Ingram to answer. He suggested that a limited company be the best form of organizational structure to adopt, and both agreed that Inland Tours Limited would be a suitable name for the proposed company.

The list of questions which Stockton sent to Ingram was as follows:

(1) How many boats do you believe you need to start the business?
(2) What would be the total purchase price of these boats?
(3) Will you rent or purchase office accommodation?
(4) What would be the fixed costs associated with operating the boats?
(5) What would be the variable costs associated with operating the boats?
(6) What do you estimate to be a reasonable forecast of your revenues for the first six months of business?
(7) What trade terms would you negotiate with your customers and suppliers?
(8) Do you expect to employ staff to assist you?
(9) When would you expect to commence business in order to take advantage of this year's holiday season?

Ingram devoted a fortnight to find out the information which Stockton requested. His reply to the questions listed above was as follows:

(1) Three boats would be needed and they would have a life of 10 years.
(2) Bridgewaters Marine Builders Ltd would supply three boats at £10,000 each, fitted to specification. They would require payment on delivery of the boats.
(3) Offices could be rented at an annual rent of £1,000 payable in one sum in advance.
(4) Licensing, insuring and repairs would amount approximately to £200 per month.
(5) Fuel and mooring costs borne by the company would amount to approximately £20 a month. Customers would pay fuel and mooring charges incurred during the hiring period.
(6) During the holding season from April to September, each of the boats could be hired out at an average of £100 per week. However, this level of revenue could be achieved only if an agency were employed, and this would mean paying a commisions to

the agency of 10% on all bookings through the agency. It is expected that the agency would account for 50% of bookings. (Assume 4 weeks for each calendar month.)

(7) Customers would pay the full hire charge on taking possession of the boat. Bookings made through the agency would be remitted generally one month in arrears. All suppliers would require payment on invoice until the creditworthiness of the company was established.

(8) No staff would be employed. Living expenses of £100 per week would be needed.

(9) To take advantage of this year's holiday season, the company should be in a position to commence operation on 1 April 19X8.

Ingram attached the following note to his reply to Stockton:

'Additionally, I will bring my van into the business at a valuation of £3,500, as we shall need it for everyday use. I expect that running costs will be about £10 per week, and that the van will last for 5 years.'

On receiving Ingram's letter, Stockton instructed one of his articled clerks to prepare a cash budget for the six months starting 1 April 19X8. He suggested that a safety margin of £1,000 should be introduced into the calculation of Ingram's cash needs.

Required

(1) Prepare a cash budget for the six months to 30 September 19X8 on the basis of the information given above.

(2) Comment on the usefulness of cash budgeting to financial planning and financial management. Illustrate your answer by reference to the circumstances revealed in the cash budget you have prepared.

(3) Assuming zero inflation over the life of the boats, use the information you are given to apply a capital budgeting analysis to the proposed acquisition of the three boats. For this purpose, you may assume that the cost of capital is 10% over the whole period.

(4) Consider the position of the bank as a creditor of the company under the following circumstances:
(a) Loan of £5,000 to be repaid in 12 months at 10% interest.
(b) Loan of £5,000 to be repaid in 3 years at 10% interest.
(c) Loan of £5,000 do be repaid in 5 years at 10% interest.
Discuss the factors which you, as a bank manager, would consider to be critically important when contemplating granting a loan to Inland Tours Ltd. Develop such information as would be needed to consider the loan under the circumstances stipulated above.

(5) Suggest methods of dealing with the depreciation of the boats which would be most appropriate to circumstances of Inland Tours Limited. In your answer you should refer to all the various alternative methods of depreciation of which you are aware, and consider their relative merits.

(6) Assuming that the company will wish to provide for the replacement of the boats at the end of ten years, and that this period will be entirely free of both general and specific inflation, suggest alternative methods of planning for the replacement of the three boats. Make such assumptions regarding the internal rate of return and the cost of capital as you wish to develop your argument.

Case Problem 6: Lathan Engineering Company Limited

This problem is concerned with the following issues:

(1) Preparation of company accounts.
(2) Financial statements and users' needs.
(3) The disclosure of information to users of financial statements.
(4) The information needs of shareholders.
(5) The accounting approach to profit determination and valuation.
(6) Extending the scope of information disclosure.
(7) The adequacy of financial information for the evaluation of company performance.
(8) Non-financial measurements and company performance.
(9) Accounting standards and information disclosure.

Jennifer Wainwright had been employed as a trainee accountant for the last eighteen months by the Lathan engineering Company Limited. During that time, she had usually been engaged on routine accounting matters such as the preparation of the weekly payroll and the analysis of suppliers' invoices.

As she was also preparing for a professional accounting qualification, she had encountered rather more advanced matters in the course of her studies, and wished to have the opportunity of being given more demanding work. She expressed this wish to Gordon Holroyd, the chief accountant, and he appeared sympathetic to her request for work which would not only be more challenging but would also assist her in her studies. Holroyd recalled his own feelings when he too was obliged, as a junior trainee, to tick entries in debtors and creditors ledgers as well as such mundane but necessary tasks as making tea for his seniors. After discussing her progress with her, he said:

'There will be opportunities very soon to move to more responsible work, as Norman and Victor are being transferred to our Consett factory. I think that you could take over Norman's work, but in the meantime, I'd like you to do something for me. In fact, you can regard it as a test to show me how well you are getting on with your studies.'

He then went to his filing cabinet and presented a file to Jennifer.

'What's this?' she asked.

'It's the first draft of our trial balance for the year to 30 June 19X0,' replied Holroyd, 'and what I want you to do is to prepare the profit and loss account and balance sheet. As you can see, we've already prepared the trading account of the profit and loss account as far as calculating the gross profit, so that you can really start from there.'

'I think I can do that for you,' answered Jennifer, 'but I am not entirely sure that I know all the disclosure requirements of the Companies Acts.'

'That doesn't matter now,' Holroyd assured her, 'What I want you to do is to prepare the accounts in a form which you think would be helpful to a shareholder, and would show him how the company has done this year. Can you do that?'

'Well, yes,' replied Jennifer, 'but is all the information there?'

'There are some notes of adjustments which should be made in the file, but if you'd like to know anything else which you think would be useful to a shareholder, just make a note of it in the file.'

'I'll start right away,' said Jennifer enthusiastically, 'and I'll come and see you tomorrow if that's all right with you.'

'Fine,' said Holroyd, 'but can you make it about 2.30 in the afternoon as I'm tied up all morning?'

When Jennifer Wainwright returned to her desk and opened the file, she found the following trial balance at 30 June 19X0 for the Lathan Engineering Company Ltd.

	£	£
Ordinary share capital		180,000
Preference share capital		200,000
Investments at cost (a) quoted	64,000	
(b) unquoted	151,000	
Freehold land and buildings at cost	163,650	
Plant and machinery at cost	197,000	
Share premium account		20,000
9% Debentures (secured on property)		80,000
Provision for depreciation to 30 June 19X9		
Freehold land and buildings		15,200
Plant and machinery		67,600
General reserve		30,000

Continued	£	£
Bank overdraft		26,170
Creditors		37,650
Balance on trading account		104,600
Audit fee	650	
Debtors	61,440	
Retained earnings		45,130
Income from quoted investments		3,120
Income from unquoted investments		8,440
Administration expenses	12,410	
Legal expenses	680	
Bank interest	2,210	
Establishment expenses	8,460	
Directors' emoluments	13,050	
Debenture interest	7,200	
Preference dividend	7,000	
Ordinary dividend—interim	9,000	
Stock at 30 June 19X0	120,160	
	817,910	817,910

In addition, she found the following notes in the file:

(1) The authorized share capital is:

   200,000   7% preference shares of £1 each.
   240,000   ordinary shares of £1 each.

(2) All the issued ordinary shares are fully paid.
(3) Depreciation to be provided for 19X0 as follows:

   Property   2% on cost.
   Plant, etc   10% on cost.

(4) Sales turnover was £410,760.
(5) Provide for the preference dividend due.
(6) A final dividend of 10% on the ordinary shares as proposed.
(7) Ignore taxation.

Required
(1) Prepare the profit and loss account for the year ended 30 June 19X0 and a balance sheet as at that date in accordance with the requirements of the Companies Act 1985.
(2) Comment on the salient features of the financial statements you have prepared in so far as they provide meaningful information for users' needs. For the purpose of your answer, make such hypotheses concerning the identity and the information needs of users of financial statement as you consider to be necessary for the purposes of your answer.

(3) Discuss the disclosure requirements contained in the Companies Act from the viewpoint of both the directors of the company and its shareholders.

(4) Identify the main information objectives of shareholders and assess the extent to which these objectives are satisfied by the financial accounts you have prepared.

(5) Comment critically on the accounting approach to profit determination and valuation.

(6) List the additional items of financial information which you consider to be essential to shareholders to enable them to evaluate their investment in the company and to make decisions concerning their shareholdings. Argue the case for and against the disclosure of such additional financial information.

(7) Comment on the adequacy of financial information as providing a means of communicating the most significant features of a company's performance, not only to shareholders but to such other groups of users of financial statements as you have earlier considered.

(8) What type of non-financial information would you consider to be necessary to allow external users of company information to make value judgements about the company's use of social resources and the company's contribution to the social output.

(9) Review the work of the Accounting Standards Committee, by identifying the key problems on which attention has been focused and discussing the contribution which the committee has made towards the solution of the information disclosure problems which you have already perceived.

Case Problem 7: Olivet Hardware Company Limited

This problem is concerned with the following issues:

(1) Statements of sources and application of funds.
(2) Analysis of financial performance and financial status.
(3) Financial structure and leverage.
(4) Market ratios.
(5) Growth, retained earnings and shareholders interests.

When the board of directors of the Olivet Hardware Company Limited received their company's profit and loss account for the year ended 31 December 19X8 and the balance sheet as at that date, their attention at their meeting on the 16 February 19X9 focused immediately on the disparity between the fall in the level of the cash at the bank and the improved net profit result. The chairman's son,

Frank Olivet, who had just been appointed to the board of directors after graduating from university with an honours degree in business studies in July 19X8, pressed his father for an explanation. The latter commented as follows:

'Well, we've bought new equipment so that we can make some of those items which we are all agreed are becoming too costly to buy from our suppliers.'

'But I thought that the loan from the bank of £25,000 was to cover that expenditure,' said Frank.

'Not entirely, Frank,' replied his father, 'we had other commitments as well.'

'Look,' said Frank, 'there are several factors which account for the change in the cash balance. Is there any chance of showing them all in one separate statement?'

'Well, I'll certainly ask the auditors if it is possible to do that, and I'll let you all know what they say at our next meeting. Now can we move to the next item on the agenda?' said the chairman.

The balance sheets of the Olivet Hardware Company Limited as at 31 December 18X7 and 19X8 are given below, together with some additional information relating to the financial results of the year ended 31 December 19X8.

The net profit for the year ended 31 December 19X8 was arrived at after charging a loss of £800 on the sale of plant which cost £8,000 and which had been written down to £1,000 in the books of the company.

Required

(1) Prepare a statement which would help the board of directors to understand the changes in working capital and the balance at the bank which have occurred in the year 19X8.

(2) Examine the information given above and write a report to the board of directors drawing attention to those features of the company's performance and financial status which you deem important. Explain the reasons why you consider them to be important. Illustrate your answer by means of such ratio analyses as you consider to be relevant.

(3) Comment on the company's financial structure on 31 December 19X8. What do the changes in the financial structure which have occurred since 1 January 19X8 imply for shareholders?

(4) Assume that the Olivet Hardware Company Limited is a public company whose shares are quoted on the Stock Exchange. What further significant ratios could be examined?

(5) Examine the company's profitability, its rate of expansion and the level of retained earnings in terms of what they imply for

	19X7			19X8		
		Depreciation			Depreciation	
	Cost	provision		Cost	provision	
	£	£	£	£	£	£
Fixed Assets						
Freehold property	20,000	7,500	12,500	20,000	8,000	12,000
Plant and machinery	50,000	30,000	20,000	104,600	34,600	70,000
	70,000	37,500	32,500	124,600	42,600	82,000
Trade investment at cost			10,000			10,000
			42,500			92,000
Current Assets						
Stock	11,000			17,000		
Debtors	9,000			15,000		
Cash at bank	4,000	24,000			32,000	
Creditors: amounts falling due within one year						
Trade creditors	7,000			11,000		
Bank overdraft	—			13,000		
		7,000			24,000	
Net current assets			17,000			8,000
			59,500			100,000
Creditors: amounts falling due after more than one year						
Loan			—			25,000
			59,500			75,000
Capital and Reserves						
Authorized and issued						
30,000 Ordinary shares of £1 each			30,000			30,000
Retained earnings						
Profit and loss account b/f	20,000			29,500		
Net profit for the year	9,500	29,500		15,500	45,000	
			£59,500			£75,000

the value of shareholders' interests. Make such assumptions as you require for the purpose of your argument.

Case Problem 8: Bartle plc

Bartle plc was incorporated on 1 May 19X1 with an issued capital of £1,200,000 in £1 ordinary shares and with £400,000 in 15% debentures. On that date, the company purchased fixed assets, cost £1,000,000, and stock at a cost of £400,000.

The annual accounts of the company, prepared on the historic cost convention were:

Profit and loss account for the year ended 30 April 19X2

	£	£
Sales		1,960,000
Opening stock	400,000	
Purchases	1,320,000	
	1,720,000	
Closing stock	660,000	
Cost of sales		1,060,000
Gross profit		900,000
Interest	60,000	
Depreciation	200,000	
Other expense	120,000	
		380,000
Profit before tax		520,000
Taxation		140,000
Profit after tax		380,000
Proposed dividend		120,000
		260,000

Balance sheet as at 30 April 19X2

	Cost	Deprecia-tion	
	£	£	£
Fixed assets	1,000,000	200,000	80,000
Current assets			
Stock		660,000	
Debtors		490,000	
Cash		500,000	
		1,650,000	
Creditors: amounts falling due within one year			
Creditors	330,000		
Taxation	140,000		
Proposed dividend	120,000		
		590,000	
Net current assets			1,060,000
Creditors: amounts falling due after more than one year			1,860,000
15% Debentures			400,000
			1,460,000
Capital and reserves			
Share capital			1,200,000
Profit and loss account			260,000
			1,460,000

Stock in hand at the end of the year may be assumed to have been purchased evenly throughout the last six months of the year.

Sales purchases and other expenses occurred evenly through the year. Debenture interest was paid when the General Price Index stood at 124.

The following indices are relevant:

	General price Index	Specific price indices Fixed assets	Stock
1.5.19X1	100	100	100
30.4.19X2	124	130	120

You may assume that the monthly change in all indices was constant throughout the financial year, and that the stock index is relevant for the calculation of the Monetary Working Capital Adjustment under SSAP 16 (Current Cost Accounting).

Required
(1) Prepare a profit and loss account for the year ended 30 April 19X2 and a balance sheet as at that date using the method of accounting recommended in SSAP 16.
(2) Identify, and explain the capital maintenance concepts upon which the method is founded.
(3) Discuss the purpose of the 'gearing' adjustment.
(4) Do the CCA results come closer to cash flow accounting than those produced using the historic cost convention?

Case Problem 9: The Westbourne Company Limited

This problem is concerned with the following issues:

(1) Break-even analysis.
(2) Profit planning.
(3) Contribution margin analysis.
(4) Absorption versus variable costing.
(5) Behavioural aspects of performance.
(6) Participation in management.

For two successive year, the Westbourne Company had not made a profit. In an effort to reverse this situation, the chairman decided to introduce a profit-sharing scheme with effect from 1 January 19X7 to motivate employees to work harder and more efficiently thereby reducing costs and restoring the company to profitability.

The relevant data for the year ended 31 December 19X6 were as follows:

Sale price per unit of product	£6
Sales volume in units	2,000,000
Total fixed manufacturing costs	£4,000,000
Total fixed administrative and selling costs	£800,000
Variable manufacturing costs per unit	£2.4
Variable administrative and selling costs per unit	£1.2
Normal capacity in units	3,000,000

There was no opening stock of unsold products at 1 January 19X7.

The profit-sharing scheme called for the establishment of a profit pool from which distribution would be made to employees in accordance with a predetermined formula. It was decided that this pool would amount to 30% of net profit before taxation, and would be deductible for tax purposes.

As an added measure to his strategy for restoring profitability, the chairman of the company sought to increase the volume of production and sales. He believed that such an increase would provide an extra incentive to his company's employees, since it would increase the dimension of the profit pool. Accordingly, he launched an intensive sales campaign requiring an increase in advertising expenditure of £300,000. He also initiated a programme for removing bottlenecks in the chain of production with the result that there was a smoother flow of production through the factory. As a result, the company was able to produce at its normal capacity level of 3,000,000 units, of which the sales force succeeded in selling 2,500,000 units.

When the chairman of the company was presented with details of the financial results for the year ended 31 December 19X7, he could hardly contain his jubilation. 'Our profit-sharing scheme has had excellent results. We are now a successful company,' he said. The financial results for 19X7 were as follows:

	£	£
Sales (2,500,000 units)		15,000,000
Manufacturing cost of sales:		
Variable costs (3,000,000 × £2.4)	7,200,000	
Fixed costs	4,000,000	
Cost of units produced	11,200,000	
less: Closing stock (500,000 £4.4)	2,200,000	9,000,000
		6,000,000

Gross profit
Administrative and selling costs:

Variable costs	3,000,000	
Fixed costs	1,100,000	
		4,100,000
Net profit before taxation and profit-sharing		1,900,000
less: Profit-sharing pool—30%		570,000
Net profit before taxation		1,330,000
less: Taxation at 50%		665,000
Net profit available for distribution		665,000

Required

(1) Calculate the profit for the year ended 31 December 19X6 and establish the break-even level of sales in value and volume terms.

(2) Discuss the strategy employed by the chairman of the company to restore the company to profitability. Has the chairman reason to be jubilant?

(3) Prepare a contribution margin statement for the years 19X6 and 19X7 based on variable costing principles. Comment upon the significance of the contribution margin in the analysis of profitability and its implications for profit planning.

(4) Discuss critically the conventional accounting approach to the analysis of output planning and profitability based on break-even analysis. Do you consider break-even analysis to be a useful management tool?

(5) Discuss the variable costing controversy in the light of providing cost information which is directly relevant to profit planning.

(6) When the chairman suggested the introduction of the profit-sharing scheme to the board of directors, he said: 'The only way to get employees to see the problem of profitability our way is to allow them to participate in the increased profits. They are simply not interested in anything else'. Discuss this statement in the light of theories of management with which you are familiar. Do you agree with the chairman's view?

(7) 'Profit-sharing arrangements only constitute the tip of a radical movement of reform in the management of business enterprises.' Comment on this view and illustrate your answer by reference to developments in participation in decision-making.

Case Problem 10: Jones Limited and Evans Limited

This problem is concerned with the following issues:

(1) Interfirm comparison.
(2) Comparability and financial reporting.

(3) Accounting standards.
(4) Judgement and objectivity in financial reporting.
(5) Treatment of research and development expenditure.

Jones Limited and Evans Limited are two companies which are engaged in the same trade. Their results for the year ended 31 December 19X7 are identical in every detail as may be seen from their profit and loss account and balance sheets below:

Jones Limited &
Evans Limited
Profit and loss account
for the year ended
31 December 19X7

	£
Sales	50,000
Cost of sales	30,000
Gross profit	20,000
Administrative and selling costs	10,000
Net profit before taxation	10,000
Taxation	5,000
Net profit after Taxation	5,000

Jones Limited &
Evans Limited
Balance sheet as at
31 December 19X7

		£
Fixed assets		
Factory building at cost		8,000
Plant and machinery:		
At cost	12,000	
Accumulated depreciation	7,000	
		5,000
		13,000
Current assets		
Stock	13,000	
Debtors	9,000	
Cash	1,000	
	23,000	
less: Creditors	11,000	
Net working capital		12,000
		25,000
Represented by:		
Share capital issued and fully paid		15,000
Retained earnings		10,000
		25,000

Analysed, these results produced the following identical ratios:

Net profit on sales $\dfrac{10,000}{50,000} = 20\%$

Asset turnover $\dfrac{50,000}{25,000} = 2\%$

Return on capital employed $\dfrac{10,000}{25,000} = 40\%$

Further information in respect of the year ended 31 December 19X7 is as follows:

(1) *Research and development*

Both companies spent £6,000 on research and development during the year. Jones Limited decided to carry forward half the cost of research and development on the grounds that the benefit from this expenditure would be felt in later years. The balance of £3,000 was written off against the cost of current sales. Evans Limited wrote off the entire sum of £6,000 against cost of sales in 19X7.

(2) *Factory buildings*

The factory building owned by Jones Limited was purchased in 19X5 and its current replacement cost is £20,000. The factory building owned by Evans Limited was purchased in 19X4 and its current replacement cost is £10,000.

(3) *Depreciation*

Jones Limited estimates the life of plant and machinery as 12 years and has charged £1,000 in the current year to the cost of sales in respect of depreciation. Evans Limited estimates the life of plant and machinery as 8 years and has charged £1,500 in the current year to the cost of sales in respect of depreciation.

(4) *Valuation of slow-moving stock*

Items which have been in stock for more than 12 months are written down by Jones Limited to half their original cost. At 31 December 19X7, stock which had originally cost £4,000 was written down to £2,000. By contrast, Evans Limited writes off all the items which have not moved for over a year, and as a result has charged £4,000 to the cost of sales in 19X7.

(5) *Provision for bad debts*

Evans Limited has been more realistic than Jones Limited in providing for bad debts. The difficult economic climate had made some of Evans' debtors insolvent in the subsequent year, thereby confirming the company's judgement of the value of debtors at 31 December 18X7. As a result, all losses had been provided for in 19X7. By contrast, Jones Limited had taken a far more optimistic view of the value of debtors at 31 December 19X7 than the economic climate warranted and included a debt of £1,000 which had been owing to the company for some time from a customer who was already in financial difficulties by 31 December 19X7.

Required

(1) In the light of the further information available, adjust the financial statements of both companies and bring them on the same basis.

(2) Compare the original ratios derived from the unadjusted financial statements with similar ratios derived from the adjusted financial statements and discuss the differences.

(3) Consider the lessons which may be drawn from this case concerning the problem of comparing the results of different companies.

(4) Discuss the proposition: 'since true comparability could never be established, for all companies are essentially different in some or many respects, the standardization of accounting practices will merely prevent companies from selecting means of interpreting results which are particularly suitable to their own circumstances'.

(5) 'Admittedly, no two companies are identical, but the uniformity in the treatment of data consequent upon the standardization of accounting practices will eliminate the element of judgement which can so easily inhibit objectivity in accounting.' Discuss this view.

(6) Discuss the relative merits of the alternative methods of treating research and development expenditure adopted by the two companies.

Case Problem 11: Crimicar Components Limited

Crimicar Components Limited was established in 19X0 for the purpose of manufacturing extractor fans. During the first five years of operation, the company had experienced a gradual increase in sales volume, and the current annual growth in sales of 5% is expected to continue into the foreseeable future. The plant is now producing at full capacity. The company had four directors as follows:

Bob Russell   —Managing Director
Peter Mayo   —Works Director
Jim Peters   —Sales Director
Bill Leatherbarrow—Financial Director and Accountant.

At a working luncheon arranged to allow for a wide-ranging discussion of the firm's future, the four directors expressed the following views:

Bob Russell *(Managing Director)*
'It seems to me that we are faced with two alternatives for next year. First, we could continue to operate at full capacity and with our existing facilities we could maintain an output of one million fans selling at £10 per unit. Secondly, we could try to increase production and sales by 5% to keep abreast of the rate of expansion in demand for our product. This alternative would have the result of increasing costs for we would have to institute weekend working to produce the higher level of output. However, a policy of steady

growth is preferable to one of maintaining a static position, and it is this policy that I suggest we adopt.'

Peter Mayo *(Works Director)*

'I think that you are being too cautious, Bob. We have several competitors who have a substantial share of the market. If the market for extractor fans increases by 5% next year, the planned increase in output that you envisage would merely maintain our present share of the total market. I believe that we should aim to obtain as large a share of the total market as possible. Therefore, we should consider a third alternative to the two which Bob has mentioned, and consider an increase in production by 10% through a modest expansion of plant capacity. This would bring the production volume up to 1,100,000 units. According to market research, we shall need to decrease our selling price to £9.50 in order to sell all the output we have at this level of operation. However, I think it would be worth it. If there are pickings to be made in the market, I think that we should make them. What do you think Jim?'

Jim Peters *(Sales Manager)*

'I agree with that sentiment, but I would favour a more radical alternative. I think that it is time that we began to think of seizing the competitive leadership in the market with regard to both price and volume. I suggest that we embark on an extensive modernization programme which will enable us to pursue a more expansionist policy. We could aim to increase volume by 20% which would bring production up to 1,200,000 units. According to market research, we would have to reduce our selling price to £9 a unit to sell the increased output.'

Bob Russell *(Managing Director)*

'One thing which concerns me is the behaviour of our competitors. For example, if they also intend to expand in order to produce and sell more at lower prices, what will be the financial effects of the alternatives suggested by Jim and Bob if the expected increase in sales is only half of that predicted?'

Bill Leatherbarrow *(Financial Director and Accountant)*

'I intend to prepare a report which will answer this question. I shall prepare summaries of the effects of all the four alternatives mentioned, indicating sales, contribution margins net operating profit and break-even sales and volume percentages. Furthermore, I will indicate which plan would seem to be the best both for next year and the long-term outlook, and for the other factors which ought to be considered. If I circulated the report and summaries, could we meet next week to discuss them?'

It was agreed that the course of action suggested by Bill Leatherbarrow should be followed. He immediately returned to his office and began to collect the information that he needed. He eventually came to the following conclusions:

(1) If next year's production was maintained at the current year's level, variable costs would remain at £5 per unit. Fixed costs would remain unchanged at £3,000,000.
(2) The alternative favoured by Bob Russell would increase both variable and fixed costs as a result of weekend working. Variable costs would rise to £5.50 per unit and fixed costs would increase to £3,025,000.
(3) The alternative proposed by Peter Mayo would decrease the selling price to £9.50. The ratio of variable costs to sales would continue to be 50%, and fixed costs would rise to £3,250,000.
(4) The alternative suggested by Jim Peters would result in a decrease in the ratio of variable costs to sales to 48%. This would be the result of increased production efficiency, a reduction in direct labour, and a small saving resulting from larger purchases of materials. Fixed costs would increase by £500,000.

Required
(1) Prepare Bill Leatherbarrow's report and illustrate the points you wish to make by such calculations, diagrams etc., as you feel will enable the board of directors to perceive immediately the issues involved.
(2) Examine the means open to Bill Leatherbarrow to take account of the risk involved in the several alternatives suggested at the board meeting. Illustrate your explanation and assume such data as will draw out the implication of the degree of risk which affects the several alternatives.
(3) Discuss the procedures for sales forecasting which you would recommend in this case.
(4) Consider the short-term and long-term implications of Bob Russell's recommended strategy.
(5) Discuss the capital budgeting implications of the problem facing the company.
(6) Comment upon the price elasticity of demand for the company's product, and discuss the formulation of a pricing policy which would help the company to achieve the objectives on which the recommended strategy is founded.
(7) Examine the company's cost structure and relate your conclusions to your view of the best strategy open to the firm to deal with the short-term and the long-term problem of output planning.

Index

Index